This volume is a significant step towards giving voice and recognition to Robert Mangaliso Sobukwe's towering contribution to this country's public life, history, and memory. Through his writings, testimonies and correspondence, his humanity, intelligence, and eloquence shine through ... *Darkest before Dawn* is a tremendous contribution to our history, politics and public memory.
— Bongani Ngqulunga, Professor, Department of Politics, University of Johannesburg and author of *The Man Who Founded the ANC: A Biography of Pixley ka Isaka Seme*

Sobukwe remains, *par excellence,* the personification of a particular form of freedom – decolonised freedom – that may yet lead post-apartheid South Africa from its present darkness into a new democratic dawn.
— Thula Simpson, Associate Professor, Department of Historical and Heritage Studies, University of Pretoria and author of *History of South Africa: From 1902 to the Present*

Sobukwe's writings are as much a testimony to the South Africa he lived as they are a prophecy to the South Africa to come if we continue on the current trajectory. We should not make the mistake of his contemporaries and ignore his message. A well-curated collection and a welcome insight into one of the most brilliant political minds of the twentieth century.
— Zukiswa Wanner, author of *Vignettes of a People in an Apartheid State* and *Love Marry Kill*

DARKEST BEFORE DAWN

Writings, Testimonies and Correspondence from the Life of Robert Mangaliso Sobukwe

Edited with a biographical account and conclusion by
Derek Hook and Leswin Laubscher

WITS UNIVERSITY PRESS

Published in South Africa by:
Wits University Press
1 Jan Smuts Avenue
Johannesburg 2001

www.witspress.co.za

Cover photograph by Ralph Ndawo, Robert Mangaliso Sobukwe in Mofolo, Soweto 1973

First published 2024

http://dx.doi.org.10.18772/22024108561

978-1-77614-856-1 (Paperback)
978-1-77614-857-8 (Hardback)
978-1-77614-858-5 (Web PDF)
978-1-77614-859-2 (EPUB)

Project manager: Alison Paulin
Copyeditor: Russell Martin
Proofreader: Inga Norenius
Indexer: Margaret Ramsay
Cover design: Hybrid Creative
Typeset in 11 point Crimson

This book is dedicated to the Sobukwe family.

Contents

List of Illustrations

Preface: Hearing Sobukwe

Of all the remarkable photographs that Peter Magubane took of Robert Mangaliso Sobukwe, perhaps the image that best encapsulates the first leader of the Pan Africanist Congress is one that at first glance might be overlooked. It is a photograph taken early on 21 March 1960, one of the first in a sequence that Magubane captured on that fateful day, which would culminate in the tragedy of the Sharpeville Massacre. The image has a transporting quality: one can imagine the chilliness of an autumnal Soweto morning, the scent of the leaves of the eucalyptus tree in the background, the scratchy surface of the gravel road beneath the feet of the men in the picture. It involves us. We, as viewers, are positioned alongside – slightly behind – a man who, like us, is witness to the scene. And while we are situated as onlookers, we are also – like him – invited to join the others, to step into the tableau before us, and take up a place in the history-making events that are about to unfold.

There is a spectrum of emotions on display in Sobukwe's comrades. Some are smiling, buoyed by the camaraderie of the moment; others are serious, cognisant perhaps of the magnitude of events about to take place; one appears hesitant, as if thinking twice about what their proposed course of action will commit him to; another seems to be awaiting clarification in response to a question he has just directed to Sobukwe; yet another is caught mid-stride, as if he can't wait to start the campaign, to begin the walk to Orlando police station. Yet despite these varying responses, all of these men are connected to one another and grounded by Sobukwe's presence; they are drawing confidence and courage from the political vision and the leadership that he so clearly embodies. Within a few minutes they will set off, heading towards the police station, where they will offer themselves up for arrest as

1. Robert Mangaliso Sobukwe (with his back to the camera) addressing comrades in Orlando, on the morning of 21 March 1960. (Photo by Peter Magubane, © Peter Magubane / David Gollan)

part of the Pan Africanist Congress anti-pass campaign, taking thus a step which will change not only their lives, but eventually also the course of a nation. Sobukwe famously spoke of 'a tree rooted in African soil', welcoming his audience, in the spirit of an Africanist communality, to 'Come sit under its shade and become ... leaves of the same branch and branches of the same tree' (this vol., part 1, n. 57). While the tree in the background of this photograph offers less by way of nurturance and comfort, it nonetheless bears witness to Sobukwe's offer of participation in, and commitment to, the project of a Pan-Africanist future.

What is so counter-intuitive about this photograph of Sobukwe – particularly if we regard it as a portrait – is that he does not even face us; his back is to the camera. What kind of encapsulating image has its subject facing away from the lens? Then it dawns on us: this is the most appropriate portrait for a man like Sobukwe for whom selflessness and sacrifice were the essential components of leadership. Disregarding the limelight of the camera, concerned far more with how this group of his fellow Pan Africanist Congress (PAC) members – and thousands more across the country – will carry out the task at hand, Sobukwe is captured in time, addressing his countrymen. The image serves as the visual counterpart to the epigraph inscribed on Sobukwe's tombstone: 'True leadership demands complete subjugation of self, absolute honesty, integrity and uprightness of character and fearlessness, and above all, a consuming love of one's people.'[1] The exact nature of Sobukwe's comments to these men remains, of course, unknown to us, yet it is in this gesture of conveying an essential message both to these men and, by extension, to the people more generally, that we found the consolidating theme for this book. Whether Sobukwe is offering a note of reassurance or is simply sharing the conviction that they are on the cusp of a great historical change, of taking back the land (*Izwe Lethu!*), of setting in motion the chain reaction of events that will eventually see the end of white minority rule in South Africa – whatever it may be – this message, this 'letter' to the people, is what has motivated the collection of texts that make up this volume.

Our aim in this respect has been to gather both the official 'letters' to the people – Sobukwe's speeches, his assorted PAC and political writings, his court testimonies – and less formal and more intimate 'letters' – comments made in his interview with Gail Gerhart, and select remarks from his written correspondence with Benjamin Pogrund, Nell Marquard, Bessie Head and others during his time in Kimberley after being released from Robben Island. This book is a continuation of a project started several years ago, of which another text, *Lie on Your Wounds: The Prison Correspondence of Robert Mangaliso Sobukwe,* was the first instalment. The aim there was to 'hear' Sobukwe through his letters, to come as close to a 'materialisation' of his speaking voice as could be realised on the page, and thereby allow for a range of his anecdotes, stories, jokes and opinions, along with a sampling of his diverse literary, cultural and social interests and preferences, to come to the fore, even, remarkably enough, in the restricted medium of censored prison letters. Such letters, writes Grahame Hayes (2021, 73), 'are the closest thing we are going to get to an "autobiography" of Robert Sobukwe'. It makes much sense, and it is our desire consequently, that the reader will read *Lie on Your Wounds* alongside this text.

An important caveat needs to be made at the outset. In case one assumes or is tempted by a certain arrogance to propose that, between these two books, we now have the arc of a life, we have to state forcefully: this book does not

1 We are here in agreement with Kwandiwe Kondlo's reflection on the 'political spirituality' of Sobukwe's leadership; see Kondlo 2019.

attempt to be a scholarly biography of Sobukwe. We do not provide a comprehensive chronology of life events, experiences, achievements, frustrations and challenges, genealogy, character development, context or analysis – at least not in the integrated and storied way a biography attempts. For such an exposure to Sobukwe, the reader is referred to Benjamin Pogrund (2015) and Thami ka Plaatjie (2019), whose books (respectively, *Robert Sobukwe: How Can Man Die Better* and *Sobukwe: The Making of a Pan Africanist Leader*) expressly aim to provide such background.[2] Additionally, documentary films by Kevin Harris (*Robert Sobukwe: A Tribute to Integrity*, 1996) and Mickey Madoda Dube (*Sobukwe: A Great Soul*, 2012) also proceed in a biographical manner to present Sobukwe's life and times to the viewer.

This being said, we do provide biographical material in what follows, along with contextual remarks, as well as comments about challenges, frustrations and psychological motivations. Of course, such biographical contextualisations and observations, even if reasonably inobtrusive or minimal, are never 'pure', never 'objective'. Even if one tempers the aims of such a biographical undertaking by offering, for example, the recognition that one can never adequately represent the life of another, by stressing that all one has attempted is to re-present the 'essence' of such a life, even this more modest presumption seems to us implausible. There is always a mediation, a filtering effect through which the story is rendered. The re-presentation of a life is always limited by our own motivations, relationships and ideologies. The subject always escapes. The 'real' Sobukwe, that is to say, the 'essential' Sobukwe, remains an unattainable desire. The best we can do is tell a story.

Our telling of the Sobukwe story, while motivated by the elusive goal of 'hearing' him speak, by the agenda of giving voice to the different 'letters' by means of which he addressed himself to others, is structured around an absence. Indeed, there is a certain strangeness to this intent to listen to Sobukwe's voice given that there are no existing recordings of him, just as there are no moving images to give us a corporeal sense of his movement, his mannerisms, his material presence. So much is left to the imagination and to our own projections that there is the constant risk that we make of him what we want him to be. This, of course, is not only an oral and material

2 To which we could also add Elias Ntloedibe's *Here Is a Tree: Political Biography of Robert Mangaliso Sobukwe* (1995) and Motsoko Pheko's *The Land Is Ours: The Political Legacy of Mangaliso Sobukwe* (1994).

statement, but also an ideological and appropriative one. And yet, such cautions notwithstanding, we wanted to hear Sobukwe, just as we want an audience to hear, and to hear *beyond* – perhaps *in contrast to* – their expectations of who Sobukwe was and what he might stand for.

One of the limitations of focusing on Sobukwe's prison correspondence – despite the richness of this material, its capacity to surprise us – is that it represents only one modality of Sobukwe's voice; it necessarily avoids the direct expression of Sobukwe's political beliefs. It is for this reason that we wanted this volume to incorporate Sobukwe's political writings, speeches and statements – inclusive of previously unpublished court testimonies, which have not typically been considered a part of his essential texts – so as to counterbalance the ostensibly 'apolitical nature' of his correspondence. (Then again, with Sobukwe, one senses that there is very little that is ever fully divorced from his political sensibilities; even the gardening he so loved gave expression, one suspects, to his Pan-Africanist dedication to the land – again, the refrain *Izwe Lethu!*) And yet Sobukwe's writings, speeches and testimonies, as bracing, articulate and undoubtedly pertinent as they still are, are best approached via an account of the life of the man himself. Consequently we have opted to begin this book with a narrative commentary entitled 'The Sun Here Is Scorching', which describes Sobukwe's years of 'internal exile' in Kimberley after his release from Robben Island. The approach adopted here, like that in *Lie on Your Wounds*, treats letters from that period as primary evidence – as the rudimentary building blocks – on the basis of which this story can be told. Admittedly, there is far less surviving correspondence from this period (certainly as compared with the Robben Island years). This dearth of material was compounded by a further consideration, namely, the wish to honour the Sobukwe family's request for a degree of privacy in respect of the contents of Sobukwe's post-Robben Island letters.[3] Nonetheless, a sampling of the letters from this period enables us to piece together a series of crucial moments from Sobukwe's life and to relate them in a unique way. Whereas Sobukwe's personal eloquence and warmth are apparent in letters to his friends – which are, by turns, jocular, teasing, intimate, moving, even occasionally sombre, heart-rending – his political, ethical and intellectual

3 This material is archived in the Robert Sobukwe Papers, Historical Papers Research Archive, University of the Witwatersrand, Johannesburg, http://historicalpapers-atom.wits.ac.za/correspondence-with-robert-sobukwe-and-concerning-him.

eloquence is most strikingly evident in the political texts. The book's second section is thus devoted to Sobukwe's speeches, articles and testimonies, starting with his rousing 'Address on Behalf of the Graduating Class at Fort Hare College' (1949). This is followed by a series of his articles for *The Africanist* and by texts explicitly written for the PAC ('Forward to 1958!', 'The Nature of the Struggle Today', 'Future of the Africanist Movement', the 'Opening Address' of the inaugural convention of the PAC, his memorable 'State of the Nation' speech, and the draft article 'One Central Government in Africa'). We include the co-authored PAC manifesto, sometimes attributed to Peter Raboroko, sometimes to Sobukwe and A.P. Mda, and at other times – perhaps most appropriately – to the PAC itself, even though it bears the undeniable imprint of Sobukwe's authorship and style. We then move to two carefully edited transcripts of Sobukwe's court testimonies in April and September 1960. Even here, in a setting so narrowly constrained by legal protocol and circumscribed manners of response, Sobukwe's conviction and commitment, verbal acuity and intellect shine through – as do the grace and gravity of his humanity.

Instructive and at times compelling, these historical documents nonetheless bring challenges of their own. Decontextualised, uprooted from the time and place of their writing, there is a risk that they are presented as merely historical, that they are viewed more as letters speaking to a past situation than as missives directed to the current circumstances of our present socio-historical conjuncture. These are documents of decolonisation, as vibrant and necessary today as they were when first written. Hence the provision of footnotes that illuminate various facets of the political, institutional and historical circumstances of the texts, and highlight how Sobukwe, and the broader aspirations of the Africanist vision he was willing to sacrifice his life for, remain urgent still today. We offer the same treatment for Sobukwe's fascinating and lengthy (1970) interview with Gail Gerhart, included in the book's third section on interviews, which contains also a warm and informative interview with Sobukwe's PAC comrade Joe Thloloe, conducted by Derek Hook.

We are left then with two different registers: the political and the personal voices of Robert Mangaliso Sobukwe. At times, these differing (yet occasionally intersecting) voices seem like those of two different persons altogether. To read these 'two Sobukwes' in tandem, to juxtapose Sobukwe's personal and political vernaculars, can be challenging, even at times seemingly dissonant. This overlapping of registers is not typically how he has been approached by scholars and historians of southern Africa and the apartheid and post-apartheid eras,[4] even though this is, arguably, exactly how we should read him if we are to disabuse ourselves of the assumption that we 'know' Sobukwe. It is likewise necessary if we are to grasp those facets of his thinking and leadership that remain the most steadfast and inspiring aspects of his legacy.

In closing, we offer an essay, 'The Afterlife of Robert Mangaliso Sobukwe', which, switching from the biographical approach of the book's first section and the documentary approach of its second, observes that Sobukwe's name has begun to appear with increasing frequency in South Africa today, and asks: why this renewed enthusiasm for a man whose political and intellectual legacy has remained dormant for the better part of the last four decades? This is not a line of questioning concerned exclusively with Sobukwe himself. It is an inquiry also into the particular social and political circumstances of the contemporary post-apartheid era; it is a questioning, furthermore, of the emerging – or re-emerging – conditions of political desire that have occasioned this revitalisation of Sobukwe's memory. There are, of course, many portrayals of Sobukwe, many varying uses made of his legacy, and to survey a cross-section of these depictions and utilisations of Sobukwe, as we do, does not mean that they all cohere or that they all need to be agreed upon. What does seem apparent is that the name Sobukwe often serves as the representative of a cluster of ideas and aspirations that have, all too often, been excluded from serious consideration in the post-apartheid public sphere. With this in mind, we suggest that one over-arching way of thinking about Sobukwe's legacy today would be as a personification of freedom.

References

Daitz, Emma. 2022. 'Towards a Future Without White People: Robert Sobukwe and the Category of the African'. *South African Review of Sociology* 55: 112–130.

Dube, Mickey Madoda. 2012. *Sobukwe: A Great Soul*. Shadow Films.

Harris, Kevin. 1996. *Sobukwe: A Tribute to Integrity*. Kevin Harris Productions, SABC, https://www.youtube.com/watch?v=VoPT5x_q9MY.

Hayes, Grahame. 2021. 'On Remembering Robert Mangaliso Sobukwe'. *Transformation* 106: 68–86.

Hook, Derek, ed. 2019. *Lie on Your Wounds: The Prison Correspondence of Robert Mangaliso Sobukwe*. Johannesburg: Wits University Press.

4 For a recent example of such a reading of Sobukwe – that is, one which combines his personal and political vernaculars – see Daitz 2022.

Kondlo, Kwandiwe. 2019. 'The "Political" Spirituality of Sobukwe's Leadership'. In *Robert Mangaliso Sobukwe: New Reflections*, edited by Benjamin Pogrund, 124–138. Johannesburg: Jonathan Ball.

Ntloedibe, Elias L. 1995. *Here Is a Tree: Political Biography of Robert Mangaliso Sobukwe.* Mogoditshane: Century-Turn Publishers.

Pheko, Motsoko. 1994. *The Land Is Ours: The Political Legacy of Mangaliso Sobukwe.* New York: Tokoloho.

Plaatjie, Thami ka. 2019. *Sobukwe: The Making of a Pan Africanist Leader*, vol. 1. Johannesburg: KMM Review Publishing.

Pogrund, Benjamin. 2015. *Robert Sobukwe: How Can Man Die Better.* Johannesburg: Jonathan Ball.

Acknowledgements

First and foremost, we wish to acknowledge, with deep appreciation, the support of the Sobukwe family in the preparation of this manuscript, and for their kind permission to reproduce sections of Robert Mangaliso Sobukwe's letters.

We are indebted to many people who have helped us during the life of this multi-faceted and challenging project. Gabriele Mohale and Elizabeth Marima at the Historical Papers Research Archive, University of the Witwatersrand, Johannesburg, were wonderfully supportive and helpful – and patient – throughout the production process. A very special word of thanks also to Patricia Rademeyer, whose skills in image sourcing and the daunting world of publishing rights and copyright permissions proved indispensable. Roshan Cader, our editor at Wits University Press, was likewise wonderful, and in more ways than can be listed here. This book would not exist in its current form without the input and guidance of these two consummate professionals. Thanks also to Russell Martin, Kirsten Perkins and Veronica Klipp, each of whom imbued the book with something special.

We owe thanks to colleagues at the South African journal *Psychology in Society* (*PINS*), particularly former editor Grahame Hayes and current editor Ronelle Carolissen. The 50th issue of this journal was dedicated to the work and legacy of Robert Mangaliso Sobukwe, and an earlier version of Gail Gerhart's interview with Sobukwe was included in that issue. Thanks to Will Worger for assistance in drawing our attention to unpublished materials – court transcripts – on Sobukwe. Sincere thanks also to the Estate of Bessie Head for permission to reprint sections of the letters she sent to

Robert Mangaliso Sobukwe. A special note of thanks to Joe Thloloe for kindly granting permission to reproduce his interview with Derek Hook.

A most sincere thank you to Benjamin Pogrund, whose writings on Sobukwe and whose lifelong relationship with the Sobukwe family proved inspirational throughout. Benjamin was always willing to take the time to offer input, reflections, corrections and insights on the manuscript, and we remain deeply appreciative of his encouragement and support.

At Duquesne University, Elizabeth Fein, chair of the Psychology Department, Kris Blair, dean of the McAnulty College and Graduate School of Liberal Arts, and Provost David Daucey, all provided assistance (in the form of subvention for publishing costs), which enabled us to reproduce previously published images or text. Thank you also to Marilyn Henline for enabling pretty much every research and administrative task related to this project. The project was supported by a Loogman Grant from the Center for Africa Studies at Duquesne University (special thanks in this respect to Gerald Boodoo).

We are indebted to the institutional support of the University of Pretoria (where Derek Hook is an extraordinary professor of psychology) and the University of the Western Cape (where Leswin Laubscher is an extraordinary professor of psychology).

Derek Hook thanks the following people whom he interviewed as part of the preliminary research for this book: Saths Cooper, Gail Gerhart, the Rev. Dumisani Methula, Johnson Mlambo, Morley Nkosi, Thami ka Plaatjie, Mogobe Bernard Ramose, Dini Sobukwe, and Malaika wa Azania. Terblanche Delport and Ndumiso Dladla at Unisa were great colleagues to work with (especially in setting up a research seminar on the topic 'Sobukwe Today' at the University of Pretoria), as was Grahame Hayes, who, as editor of the journal *Psychology in Society*, made possible – and, along with Derek, co-edited – a special issue on Sobukwe (see http://www.pins .org.za/issue.php?num=50).

Thanks to Joe Anderson and Alexandra Chomenko for invaluable research assistance; and Ethan Csont, Cristina Culler, Anna Kreienberg, Michael Maryniak, Michael Ryzner-Basiewicz and Prathma Sharma for transcription work.

Permissions

We gratefully acknowledge these publishers, institutions, estates and individuals for generously granting permission to republish sections of the following:

Letters

The Sobukwe family
Nell Marquard
Benjamin Pogrund

Interviews

Gail Gerhart and *Psychology in Society*: 'Gail Gerhart interviews Robert Mangaliso Sobukwe (1970)', *Psychology in Society* 50 (2016): 53–85 (used in chapter 11)

Joe Thloloe: Telephonic interview with Joe Thloloe conducted by Derek Hook, 25 June 2014 (used in chapter 12)

Article

Taylor & Francis: Derek Hook, 'A Threatening Personification of Freedom or: Sobukwe and Repression' in *Safundi: The Journal of South African and American Studies* 17 no. 2, 1–24 (sections used in the Conclusion).

Part I: Introduction

'The Sun Here Is Scorching': Robert Mangaliso Sobukwe, Kimberley, 1969–1978

In April 1969, Robert Mangaliso Sobukwe was finally released from Robben Island, where he had been kept under conditions of near-complete solitary confinement for six years. Nine years earlier, on 21 March 1960, Sobukwe had led the Pan Africanist Congress (PAC) in what he called a 'Positive Action' campaign, protesting against the draconian pass laws that regulated the movement, and thereby the lives, of all black South Africans. This mass action was met with a violent response on the part of the South African police. In Sharpeville, south of Johannesburg, officers opened fire on a crowd of protesters, killing approximately 80 and injuring as many as 297 people.[1] This event – the Sharpeville Massacre – drew widespread and international attention to the injustices of South Africa's system of apartheid and it led to a three-year jail sentence for Sobukwe for inciting people to protest against the laws of the country.

Not content that by May 1963 Sobukwe would have served the three years of his mandated sentence, the National Party government intervened

1 Historical research by Professors Nancy Clark and William Worger at Louisiana State University and the University of California, Los Angeles, has overturned the long-standing official statistics of the dead and injured for the Sharpeville Massacre. While the original police figure set the number of those killed at 69, this could be as high as 80; the original number of injured (178) has likewise been revised and stands now at an estimated 297.

2. A jubilant Zondeni Veronica Sobukwe upon receiving news of her husband's release from Robben Island, 1969. (Robert Sobukwe Trust / WikiMedia Commons)

by invoking a provision of the General Law Amendment Act. The resultant 'Sobukwe Clause' enabled Parliament to prolong the detention of any political prisoner on a year-by-year basis without bringing them to trial. It was on this questionable yet legal basis that Sobukwe was moved to Robben Island and kept apart from other prisoners – technically, he was no longer a prisoner as he had served his sentence. He remained there for a further six years. A short report published in the *Rand Daily Mail* provides a description of Sobukwe's living conditions on the Island:

> He lives apart from the other prisoners, in a bedroom study, which has another small room next to it and an ablution block. In some

3. Zondeni Veronica Sobukwe with the young twins, Dalindyebo and Dedanizizwe, early 1960. (APN32517, Drum Social Histories / BAHA /Africa Media Online)

> respects, he is treated rather like a high-ranking enemy officer during wartime. He has a radio and a record player, is allowed books and newspapers and occasional visits from his wife. Nonetheless he is a prisoner, living under conditions which combine something of the ingredients of both house arrest and exile, the strain of which would have cracked the sanity of many a lesser man. (Holiday 1968)

Sobukwe's release from Robben Island should have been a joyous occasion – and in many ways it no doubt was – yet it also plunged his family into a period of upheaval and crisis. The release came about as a result of Sobukwe's deteriorating mental condition. In April 1969 Sobukwe wrote to the minister of justice – a deeply uncharacteristic gesture for Sobukwe, who had always refused to negotiate with the apartheid authorities – making a series of startling allegations about how a series of devices employed by the security police was influencing parts of his body.[2] This communication set off alarm bells

2 While this letter has not survived, a subsequent letter dated 22 May 1969 (Wits Historical Papers Dept, Sobukwe Papers, Ba7.41), after Sobukwe was released, sets out these allegations in very stark terms.

for the minister and senior officials in the apartheid government, concerned as they were with how any claims of deteriorating health or torture in respect of Sobukwe might be received internationally. Psychiatric evaluations conducted on the Island prior to Sobukwe's release revealed that he was in many respects still himself – his personality structure, affective responses, and perception of reality all seemed largely intact. And yet the appearance of the delusionary belief – understandable given the prolonged period of isolation and surveillance – suggested that a more severe breakdown might follow. The government thus moved as quickly as possible to release Sobukwe, anxious lest they be accused of causing a delusional break in a man who had long since served his mandated period of incarceration. At midnight on 24 April, Minister of Justice P.C. Pelser announced that Sobukwe was to be released. Sobukwe received a letter informing him that he would not be detained beyond 30 June.

Sobukwe was, in a very significant sense, never a free man after his 1960 arrest. The apartheid government unleashed an onslaught of bureaucratic cruelties upon Sobukwe after his release from Robben Island. Here, as in so many other instances where authorities had made apparent 'allowances' in respect of Sobukwe – the provision of separate living quarters on the Island, permitting rare family visits, and so on – political calculation was the real determining factor, second only, one suspects, to the unspoken aim of ensuring further insidious means of punishment. Sobukwe was subject, until the end of his life, to banning orders[3] and the conditions of house arrest. He was forced to live in Galeshewe township in the geographically remote town of Kimberley, far removed from any friends, family, community or political comrades. Apartheid officials insisted he take on a low-ranking job that would have made him complicit in the apartheid policies that he went to jail protesting against (Sobukwe, needless to say, refused); they repeatedly refused to allow him to leave the country to take up offers of employment

3 Banning was a repressive and extra-judicial measure used by the South African apartheid regime against its political opponents. The Suppression of Communism Act of 1950 provided the legislative authority for banning orders; this Act defined nearly all opposition to apartheid as 'communism'. Individuals so branded could be restricted from attending any gatherings, moving outside a specific designated area, communicating with any other person or specific persons, entering certain places, receiving any visitors, continuing a profession, or engaging in any kind of disseminated writing.

he had received from the United States; and they obstructed his attempts to access the medical treatments that he needed, which would undoubtedly have extended his life.

The narrative that follows, an account of Sobukwe's years in Kimberley following his release from Robben Island, sets out to continue the historical record as relayed in *Lie on Your Wounds: The Prison Correspondence of Robert Mangaliso Sobukwe* (Hook 2019). *Lie on Your Wounds* focused on the period between March 1960 and May 1969; the following account takes up the story from June 1969 until Sobukwe's death in February 1978. The approach adopted here, like that in *Lie on Your Wounds,* treats letters from that period as primary evidence – as, indeed, the means through which the story might be told – even though there is far less surviving correspondence from these years. This dearth of material is compounded by a further consideration, namely, the wish to honour the Sobukwe family's request for a degree of privacy in respect of the contents of Sobukwe's post-Robben Island letters.[4] Nonetheless, a sampling of the letters from this period enables us to piece together a series of crucial moments from Sobukwe's life and to relate them in a unique way.

1969: 'In this period of drought'

On 14 May 1969, the *Rand Daily Mail* journalist Benjamin Pogrund received a telegram from his friend Sobukwe: 'Address is six Naledi Street Galashawe [*sic*] Kimberley Stop Would like meeting soon. Bob' (Ba7.38). Pogrund's response (Ba7.39), written the following day, reciprocates the desire to meet, even as it expresses Pogrund's need to balance happiness at the news of his friend's release with a sense of the challenges brought about by these new circumstances. Apparent also is Pogrund's dawning awareness of the restrictions imposed by Sobukwe's house arrest: 'Welcome, welcome. It's not quite home, but it's a big step anyway! I was so pleased to get your telegram [...] I want to see you too, and want to travel to Kimberley just as soon as possible.

4 This material is archived among the Robert Sobukwe Papers, Historical Papers Research Archive, University of the Witwatersrand, Johannesburg (http://historicalpapers-atom.wits.ac.za/correspondence-with-robert-sobukwe-and-concerning-him). We have, in the case of all cited letters, included the appropriate file numbers.

I thought of flying down today, just for the day, but then decided that your house arrest order probably applied to public holidays.'

The conditions of the banning orders placed on Sobukwe were severe.[5] It is in light of this, no doubt, that Pogrund gives voice to the exasperated state of not knowing quite how to address Sobukwe's release – a difficulty not unique to Pogrund, but one that family and friends of activists had to deal with frequently. It is not only a political, but also an affective conundrum, and one that affects the activist himself or herself, returning as they do to a changed world and relationships:

> What do I do? Do I welcome you back to freedom? That would be silly! But what I can do is to wish you well out of what you were in!
>
> I hope that we will soon be speaking on the fone and then seeing each other.

What is also apparent in Pogrund's letter is consternation at Sobukwe's physical and mental state following an earlier letter of 16 April (Bc44) that Sobukwe had sent to his wife, Zondeni Veronica,[6] noting 'a rather serious matter, affecting my health'. Pogrund now remarks, 'I was darned worried [...] we were all terrified on your account, fearing the worst!'

A letter by Sobukwe, written on 19 May after having received Pogrund's, expresses both happiness and yet also a sense of foreboding about the challenges ahead: 'Your welcome and welcoming letter arrived this morning and Veronica and I read with joy. She arrived on Thursday afternoon [...] and is

5 Sobukwe's banning orders prohibited him from leaving the municipal district of Kimberley. Between 6 pm and 6 am he had to remain inside the Naledi Street house, and he was not permitted visits other than by a doctor or a very limited number of close family members. He was not permitted to write – or in any way prepare – anything for publication, or to assist others in publishing any material. He was banned from providing educational instruction, with the obvious exception of his own children. No communication was allowed with any other banned person, or with any members of outlawed organisations (such as the African National Congress [ANC] and the PAC). He could not enter the premises of any university, school or related institution.

6 Sobukwe met Zondeni Veronica Mate while studying at Fort Hare. Originally from KwaZulu-Natal, Veronica was completing her training as a nurse at Victoria Hospital in Alice when protests at the hospital, which the local Fort Hare students encouraged and supported, led to their meeting and striking up a serious relationship. They married about six years later, on 6 June 1954, and settled in Soweto, Johannesburg.

returning to Joh'burg tonight. She hopes to see you on Wednesday.' Sobukwe then pivots:

> I am, of course, very anxious to meet you. There is so much we have to say to each other: and also I need your advice on a number of matters.
>
> My banning order confines me to my house between 6 p.m. and 6 a.m. every day, Saturdays and Public Holidays *INCLUDED*. So we can have a full day any day you choose to come. You will, of course, not be allowed into the location, but we can meet anywhere in town – in fact, anywhere in the Kimberley district. (Ba7.40)

Sobukwe informs Pogrund that he received his telegram of congratulations with great delight, along with those from his Cape Town friends and regular correspondents Nell Marquard and Eulalie Stott. He then turns directly to the salient issue: 'I was not hysterical when I wrote the letter[7] [...] I had cause to write the letter. And I am still of the same mind.'

Having offered this qualification – which worked perhaps less as an assurance than as a cause for further anxiety on Pogrund's part – Sobukwe moves on to a series of pragmatic issues: finding employment, furnishing the house, Veronica's final term of employment in Johannesburg, and so on. Sobukwe perhaps hoped to bury the real point of concern among the typical requests and comments that characterised his usual correspondence with Pogrund (such as remarks on Pogrund's own ongoing legal struggles, discussion of pressing topics of the day, and the content of 'the Joh'burg Dailies').

Three days later, however, in a letter dated 22 May (Ba7.41), Sobukwe addressed the minister of justice, P.C. Pelser, setting out in great detail the allegations he had already made the previous month that suggested distortions in his thinking, brought about (one might assume) by prolonged periods of solitary confinement on the Island. Sobukwe, in short, appears to have suffered from the temporary delusionary belief – understandable given the extremity of the social isolation and surveillance he had been subjected

7 Of 16 April.

to – that parts of his body were being controlled by gadgets devised by the security police.[8] It is important that we address this issue head-on, especially in an era when perceived mental health issues so often lead to stigmatisation. To undergo a period of delusional belief should in no way invalidate the courage, the intellect or the moral standing of the person who has such an experience. Just as physical torture results in bodily wounds, and in types of physical incapacity which can be treated, so psychological torture results in mental wounds, in instances of psychical incapacity which likewise can heal and need not be permanent. All of this is important to bear in mind in Sobukwe's case.

Anyone subjected to conditions of extreme isolation, surveillance and control is likely to experience symptoms of induced paranoia (particularly so, one might add, if the paranoia is based on an accurate premise, such as the idea that the most powerful people in one's country *do* in fact wish one ill).[9] Indeed, forced to live in conditions where virtually every facet of your existence is controlled; where you have been deprived of human contact and forced into years of solitary confinement; where your most basic functions are monitored by guards who, for the most part, regard you with contempt – these are such deeply alienating circumstances, a state some have referred to as one of social death, that an *absence* of psychological distress may be the aberration.[10]

---

8 We know a good deal more today than we did in Sobukwe's time about the devastating effects of both social deprivation and solitary confinement. In a literature review overviewing studies on the effects of solitary confinement, Kimberley Brownlee (2012), for example, noted the following effects: acute psychological and physical deterioration, despondency and depression, the feeling that one's self is disintegrating, various cognitive effects (forgetting of memories, difficulties in concentrating), hallucinations, panic attacks and, in some cases, lapsing into a semi-catatonic state or instances of self-mutilation. A rather banal way of putting it is not that one 'becomes' mad by some biological or constitutional dynamic as much as one is 'made' mad: a 'normal' human reaction to persistent trauma is a traumatised one.

9 Grahame Hayes (2021, 73) remarks that Sobukwe's symptoms would have been consistent with long periods of incarceration and solitary confinement, noting also: 'It is remarkable that he did not manifest these effects earlier. Today Sobukwe would probably have been legitimately diagnosed as suffering from PTSD (post-traumatic stress disorder)!'

10 Delusional beliefs are not, despite the commonplace assumption, necessarily indicative of a psychosis, particularly when they are short-lived and clearly occasioned by traumatic circumstances. We should bear in mind here that a delusion is often a transitory phenomenon (a loved one dies, for example, and one has a sense they speak to you), a temporary means of making sense of what is unbearably traumatic and cannot be processed

Two letters late in May are calm in tone, even as they indicate that Sobukwe is still recovering from his ordeal. In a note on 23 May (Ba7.42), Sobukwe remarks:

> I have not yet been able to phone you as I am not yet familiar with the terrain – the position of public telephones, etc. In fact I still know a limited part of town. My legs are not strong enough yet to cover the distances I should like to cover [...]
>
> Veronica has been offered a post at the local Isolation hospital. I wired her yesterday, as they wanted her to start on the 1st June.

It would have been disorienting, to say the least, for Sobukwe to have been relocated in such an abrupt fashion, moved from Robben Island to a non-prison existence in a very different part of the country, deposited alone in a modest and unequipped house in a town where he knew no one. This house, with its corrugated iron roof, tiny patch of lawn, face-brick walls and wire fence, would serve as his home for the next eight years.

On the 30th, Sobukwe commented on his wife's trip to Johannesburg and on his own anticipation of her return:

> I am always relieved when I hear you have met Veronica, and this time is no exception. I found, when I met my mother-in-law and sister-in-law last week or so that 'Benjie' was a name frequently mentioned and I was amazed to learn they hadn't met you [...]
>
> Veronica sent me a telegram saying she'll be coming over this week-end. I've been trying to clean up in order to make a 'favourable impression'. Incidentally, she smiles more often now and to me has never looked lovelier!

Despite the reassuring qualities of this letter, there is still a reminder that Sobukwe is undergoing a period of readjustment: 'P.S. I've been out

in any other way. This same postulate holds that delusions of this sort should be seen not as necessarily psychopathological but as attempts at recovery. Such delusions are often the first step in a reparative process in which the person reintroduces a modicum of meaning and order into their world, and settles upon an actionable plan, typically one in which they are afforded a degree of agency rather than being reduced to a persecuted object.

of circulation a long time and I am not familiar with the operation of your telephone service [...] As soon as I am able I'll phone you, be sure' (Ba7.47).

Despite the calmness of these letters, it is understandable that Pogrund was worried by what he imagined his friend was going through. In a letter of 1 June to Charlotte Taylor,[11] an American well-wisher and donor, Pogrund describes the situation in forthright terms:

> Bob has been released from Robben Island, but has been consigned, under house arrest and a stack of other restrictive orders, to Kimberley. I haven't yet been able to get down to see him, because of the trial,[12] but will be going within the next week or so. But the information I have received, from his wife and brother-in-law, is alarming in the extreme, because it is clear that he finally began to break under his continued imprisonment in isolation, and is now suffering from paranoid delusions. I saw a psychiatrist about it this afternoon and am taking urgent steps to ensure that he receives treatment. I am satisfied at this stage that the authorities released him as soon as they realised what they [had] done to him. I might say that, shortly before his release, I received information that all was not well with him and I had inquiries made. The Minister concerned gave his personal assurance that Bob was fine!
>
> I would ask you please to treat what I have written above as highly confidential. If you write to Bob, will you also please not refer to his being ill? The issue is extremely delicate at the moment, particularly

11 Charlotte L. Taylor of New York was a parishioner of Robert S. Bilheimer, a Presbyterian minister and co-founder of the World Council of Churches (WCC). Pogrund had met Bilheimer in the preparatory run-up to the Cottesloe Consultation of 1960, a gathering called by the WCC for delegates from its affiliated churches in South Africa to discuss the role of the church in the wake of Sharpeville. Aware of Sobukwe's situation, Bilheimer had secured an offer of occasional funding from Mrs Taylor to help with various expenses associated with the Sobukwe family.

12 In 1965, Benjamin Pogrund wrote a series of articles for the *Rand Daily Mail* exposing the terrible conditions and abuses in South African prisons. Pogrund, and his editor, Laurence Gandar, were put on trial for this exposé, and a number of Pogrund's informants were prosecuted. The trial ran from November 1968 to July 1969 in the Supreme Court in Johannesburg.

> as there will have to be negotiations with the Government to ensure that Bob is allowed to move to Johannesburg to receive treatment. He remains utterly lucid, but these paranoid ideas (which revolve around his belief that a 'machine' has been and is being used on him) must be tackled without delay.

Pogrund's observation that Sobukwe remained fundamentally lucid in other parts of his thinking had prognostic value. That this delusion hadn't affected all of Sobukwe's thought processes was an indication that the distortion in thinking would not be permanent. Pogrund, resourceful as always, was pro-active in responding to a difficult situation:

> Bob's release, so-called, has brought with it even greater financial burdens. The Government is supposed to be assisting him until he finds a job, but this assistance is not very substantial [...] The children, as far as I know, will continue to go to school in Lesotho, which means the outlay of quite a lot of money. But overshadowing all this at present is the fact that he is going to require medical treatment, which will be prolonged and expensive, even though the psychiatrist I saw is willing to assist by keeping his fees to a minimum. But within the next few weeks it will be necessary for the psychiatrist probably to fly to Kimberley and spend at least a day there with Bob – and this is going to cost a lot.
>
> Whenever I write to you about money, I stress that you have done enough and I ask instead whether it is possible to approach any other people you may know for help. If anything is available it can be sent to me, in the first place for payment of the likely medical fees, and in the second place, if enough is available, to assist Bob to settle down again to as normal an existence as possible. (Ba7.49)

While Pogrund was directing financial requests to well-placed donors and making arrangements for a psychiatrist to visit Sobukwe in Kimberley, Sobukwe himself received a sternly worded letter from the office of the minister of justice (Ba7.50).

Sir,

With reference to your letter dated the 22nd May, 1969[13] I have been directed by the Honourable the Minister of Justice to advise you that he has noted its contents.

The Honourable Minister has directed me to assure you that no physical influences of any nature are being brought to bear upon you. Your complaints in this respect are completely unfounded and any further accusations of this sort cannot be entertained.

With reference to your statement that the report of the psychiatrists was not made available to you the Minister has directed me to advise you that they merely confirmed what you state in your letter to be the case namely that you are not a psychotic case. They found also that

1. your personality is intact;
2. your volition is intact;
3. your emotional responses are appropriate; and
4. your behaviour does not reflect a break with reality.

Yours faithfully,
PRIVATE SECRETARY

Sobukwe would not have contested the medical pronouncements contained in the letter even though its authoritative and dismissive tone was obviously objectionable. It would appear, however, that he was still struggling with intrusive thoughts, a situation not helped by the fact that he was still alone and, furthermore, in an unfamiliar environment. It is evident, in a letter dated 5 June (Ba7.52), that Pogrund too was under immense pressure. Not only was he eager to get to Kimberley as soon as possible to get a first-hand sense of Sobukwe's condition, he was also awaiting the judgment in his own trial, and trying to figure out how best to negotiate the various restrictions of Sobukwe's banning order.

13 This letter would have been extremely worrying to the minister and senior government officials, concerned as they were with how any claims of deteriorating health or torture regarding Sobukwe might be received internationally. The uncharacteristic speed with which the government moved to release Sobukwe, the psychiatric assurance that he was 'fine' notwithstanding, betrayed their self-interest and their anxiety that they would be accused of causing a psychological breakdown in a man who had long since served his mandated term of imprisonment.

Dearest Bob

It looks as though the trial will be over tomorrow [...] I plan to fly to Kimberley on Wednesday morning and will probably stay at the Savoy Hotel in the centre of the town. I shall also hire a car, if such a thing is possible in Kimberley, so that I can get around [...]

I hope that the police will allow me to visit you at home to check on your furniture needs. But I think it is essential, for both your protection and for me, that any such permission be given in writing. Once you get my telegram, to say when I am coming, can you fix this up? And will you contact me, either at Kimberley airport or at the hotel?

I am so excited about seeing you again. It's been a long, long time.

[...]

Fondest wishes

4. Sobukwe, looking dapper and happy, poses with his children on 12 June 1969, soon after his release. (Photo by Benjamin Pogrund, with kind permission)

5. Benjamin Pogrund with the Sobukwe children (Dinilesizwe, Miliswa, and the twins, Dalindyebo and Dedanizizwe) on 12 June 1969, soon after Robert's release from Robben Island. (Photo by Benjamin Pogrund, with kind permission)

Fortunately, we have a record of Pogrund's impressions of the trip. On 16 June he wrote to his ally Helen Suzman (Ba7.54),[14] bringing her up to speed on the situation and requesting her assistance in finding Sobukwe employment.

My dear Helen,

[...]

I was glad to have the chance of seeing you at the start of the week, and to be able to talk to you about Bob's situation [...]

He and I spent the best part of three days together, and it was good to see him. On the whole he is in good shape – except for the

14 Helen Suzman (1917–2009) was a human rights activist and, for thirteen years, the sole representative of the Progressive Party in South Africa's Parliament between 1961 and 1974. She made regular visits to Robben Island to inquire into the well-being of the political prisoners there.

> references to the machine, which he describes with utter lucidity. The trouble is, what with bugging mechanisms and suchlike, I could not lightly dismiss his allegations. I checked the terms of his banning orders, and it seems that there is no difficulty about medical practitioners visiting him. I checked this point with the local Security man and he confirmed it; I also spoke to the local (municipal) Bantu Administration man, and he says he will issue permits to allow doctors from Johannesburg to visit Bob. I shall be arranging for a physician and a psychiatrist to go down [...]
>
> In regard to employment, Bob plans to enter into attorney's articles with a local African attorney. The police know about this and seem to be happy about it. The question of receiving financial aid during the period of articles is, however, a tricky point, and Bob has now written to the magistrate to obtain clarification. Failing this avenue, he would be interested in any job of reasonable status and pay with De Beers.[15] He does not like the idea of a job with the Kimberley Bantu Administration people, and I agree fully with this.

It is interesting to note how Pogrund here acknowledges that Sobukwe's allegations about surveillance ('bugging mechanisms') cannot simply be dismissed. As he would write years later in his biography, *Robert Sobukwe: How Can Man Die Better* (Pogrund 1997, 315), telling of his experiences of visiting Kimberley: 'He [Sobukwe] was under constant surveillance. The Security Police often drive past his home and office, just keeping an eye on him ... where they left off, informers were busy. He accepted that a number of people in Galeshewe had been suborned into spying on him.' Robert's son Dini Sobukwe likewise remarked that 'For almost a year in Kimberley, when he lived there, there was a Special Branch car parked in front of the house. Right in front of the house. All night long it would be there'. Continuing, Dini remarked: 'When we got to that house in Kimberley [...] we were pretty certain the house was bugged, 100 per cent sure' (pers. comm., 29 May 2014).

To claim, in the letter, that Sobukwe 'does not like' the idea of a job in Bantu Administration was, as Pogrund well knew, an understatement. Given Sobukwe's Pan-Africanist views and his unceasing commitment to opposing

15 The diamond mining company, which had a substantial presence in Kimberley, to which Sobukwe was restricted.

apartheid, a job in 'Bantu Administration' would have been anathema to him. Crucial as seeking alternative opportunities for employment was, it was part of a two-pronged strategy. Pogrund was, at the same time, approaching universities in the United States, exploring the possibility of an academic appointment for Sobukwe. To Marvin Wachman,[16] the president of Lincoln University, Pogrund directed the following request on 16 June:

> Dear Dr Wachman,
>
> As you might perhaps know, Robert Sobukwe was released from Robben Island Prison last month, and he is now under house arrest in Kimberley. He is not allowed to leave the municipal area and is banned from attending meetings or social gatherings.
>
> I have just returned from spending three days with him, and am writing to you on his behalf in regard to possible future opportunities for him in the academic sphere. He holds the degrees of B.A. (Fort Hare), B.A. Hons. (Rand) (in Bantu Languages), and B.Econ. (London). He lectured in Bantu Languages at Witwatersrand University (in Zulu and Xhosa) from 1954 to 1960. He has, of course, been in jail since then.
>
> I wonder whether there is any possibility of an academic appointment for him at Lincoln? And if not, I wonder whether I may ask for your advice as to which other American universities I could usefully write to?
>
> If I recall correctly, Lincoln conferred an Honorary Ph.D. on him some years ago.[17] In case you should wish to write to him about it (he has never received any official notification about it), his address is: Mr. Robert M. Sobukwe, 6 Naledi Street, Galeshewe Village, Kimberley, Cape, South Africa. (Ba7.56)

Having arranged for Sobukwe to be visited by a Kimberley-based physician (Dr R.L. Amoils) and for a Johannesburg psychiatrist (Dr David Wynberg)

16 Dr Marvin Wachman was a professor of American history who served as the president of Lincoln University and later also Temple University in Philadelphia. Lincoln, which was founded in Pennsylvania in 1854, was the first degree-granting black university in the United States. It has a long and illustrious academic history, counting some of the most influential figures in American and international life among its alumni (Langston Hughes, Nnamdi Azikiwe, Kwame Nkrumah, Paul Robeson, Thurgood Marshall, and Saara Kuugongelwa, prime minister of Namibia, being but a few examples).

17 In 1965.

to fly down to Kimberley for a consultation with Sobukwe, Pogrund allows himself, in his 18 June letter, a brief moment to reflect on being able to reconnect with his old friend:

> At long last you have foned me! Thank you for your call yesterday. I was so happy to hear from you and to hear you sounding so well. Will you fone me at least once a week – and if anything ever crops up, whenever you want to?
>
> Those were a happy three days together last week. Time passed all too quickly. But I promise to come down again as soon as possible. It did not seem as though five years had passed since we last saw each other. I was sorry, though, about the irritations caused by our being in a racial environment. One day, perhaps ... Although you have rather more optimistic views about this than I have! (Ba7.59)

By 23 June, Veronica had arrived in Kimberley and the final arrangements for Dr Wynberg's psychiatric consultation with Sobukwe had been confirmed. Nonetheless, it had been, as Pogrund wrote on the 22nd (Ba7.62), 'a nasty week, politically, hasn't it? The Lenkoe inquest,[18] with the shutter coming down hard, and the BOSS Bill[19] ... Did you see also that small report about Helen asking a question about the Kgoathe death[20] in jail and the Minister solemnly asking that the question stand over, with the Nats[21] laughing away

18 James Lenkoe, an anti-apartheid activist, was detained by the police on 5 March 1969 under the Terrorism Act; five days later he died in a prison in Pretoria. The official cause of death was hanging by suicide. However, a second post-mortem conducted at the request of the Lenkoe family found signs of electric shock on Lenkoe's toe, a bruise below the ear, marks on the neck and shoulders, and signs of haemorrhaging at the base of the skull.

19 On 16 June 1969 the Security Services Special Account Bill was passed into law, thereby securing secret funding for the Bureau for State Security (subsequently nicknamed BOSS by the press). Modelled after MI5, the Bureau was tasked with monitoring domestic security and intelligence. It reported directly to the prime minister, B.J. Vorster. It was feared and loathed for its ruthless operations against anti-apartheid activists. According to Pogrund (1997, 315), the creation of the agency marked the high point of police power.

20 Nicodemus Kgoathe, an anti-apartheid activist, died in police custody on 4 February 1969. He was detained on 11 November 1968 in the Silverton police station in Pretoria under the Terrorism Act. The government inquest into Kgoathe's death concluded that he died from broncho-pneumonia. Observation of his body by the district surgeon and his eldest son, Ben, revealed bruising on his eyes, arms, back and thighs, along with an enlarged liver.

21 Members of the National Party.

because they knew this meant it would not be raised again until next year with Parliament ending? I found it chilling.'

After a period of relative silence, Sobukwe, on 5 July (Ba7.63), put pen to paper and updated Pogrund on recent developments. While Sobukwe is sanguine in his description, it nonetheless affords us a glimpse into the daily frustrations and difficulties of his situation. After thanking Pogrund for the expenses incurred so as to make sure that he received the best medical care possible, Sobukwe describes his difficulties in respect of employment. The City Council had confirmed his possible employment – a clerical post in the municipality's Bantu Administration Department – and Sobukwe had promptly refused the offer. Becoming a cog in the 'Bantu Administration' machine was clearly not a possibility for Sobukwe. It would have gone against every fibre of his political being to accept such a job; it would have made him complicit in the very system that he had dedicated his life to fighting against, apartheid itself.

Sobukwe's response to the lack of employment was to continue his legal studies, to enrol at the University of South Africa[22] so that he could apply for his articles and start at H.Z.M. Nzimande's[23] legal office as a means of gaining practical experience in the field. This would itself involve further complications – Sobukwe was awaiting a response from the Department of Justice, from which he had requested permission to work in the legal profession. Perhaps feeling that the picture he was painting was a little bleak, Sobukwe went on to assure Pogrund that better things lay ahead, and that the house was increasingly looking and feeling like home. He pleaded with Pogrund not to worry about him, signalling that he was not worried about the future, and that the various challenges ahead would, in due course, be ironed out. His closing note was more sombre in tone: the radio had just announced the death of Thomas Mboya.[24] This, Sobukwe said, was a tragedy, as was the

22 The University of South Africa (Unisa), the distance-learning university located in Pretoria.

23 H.Z.M. Nzimande was a lawyer and, by all accounts, an old friend of Sobukwe's. He was also described by Sobukwe as 'the only African attorney in the whole of the Northern Cape'.

24 Thomas Joseph Odhiambo Mboya was one of the founding fathers of the Republic of Kenya and a leading member of Kenya's independence party, the Kenya African National Union (KANU). A young Mboya was central in securing support for Kenyan students to study at North American universities; Barack Obama Sr was one of the beneficiaries of this programme. Mboya was shot and killed on 5 July 1969 in a political assassination.

fact that it was often the most talented minds that were the most vulnerable to blind hatred.

Pogrund updated Sobukwe on 6 July (Ba7.64), sending him 'Counsel's Opinions regarding banning orders' and asking his friend if he could 'look at them in relation to your own bannings'. There is a brief reference to the psychiatrist's visit ('I was glad to have first-hand news of you from Dr Wynberg [...] He was certainly, and rightly, most impressed in meeting you') before Pogrund ends on a wishful note: 'I would prefer to see you and Veronica living in Johannesburg. To this end, I intend approaching officialdom in Pretoria to see what can be done.'

On 27 August, Pogrund wrote to Nana Mahomo,[25] a former PAC comrade of Sobukwe's, at the time resident in Geneva, requesting copies of Mahomo's MA dissertation on the PAC, and encouraging him to get in touch with Sobukwe:

> I was in Kimberley earlier this week and spent two days with Bob, my second visit to see him since his release. He is fairly well, although still adjusting to relative normality. It will take a while. He has turned down a job offered to him in the town's Bantu Affairs Department, and is hoping to undertake his legal articles to qualify as an attorney. We spoke fondly and warmly about you [...] He would be delighted to hear from you. If you want to write, his address is: 6 Naledi Street, Galeshewe Village, Kimberley, Cape. Just keep it non-political! He is inactive politically, and it will remain so. (Ba7.71)

Of interest here is Pogrund's qualification 'It will take a while', which suggests that he felt Sobukwe's recovery was still ongoing. By September, however, Sobukwe appears to have been fully immersed in his legal work in H.Z.M. Nzimande's office. In a letter of 2 September to Pogrund (Ba7.72), Sobukwe

25 Nelson 'Nana' Mahomo had been a member of the Transvaal ANC Youth League, but sided with the Africanists within the party and subsequently left the ANC to join the PAC. He was elected PAC secretary for culture in 1959 and was a member of the organisation's National Executive Committee. Mahomo was delegated to leave South Africa before the anti-pass campaign in 1960 and went on to act as one of the PAC's chief representatives abroad. There, he earned a master's degree from the Massachusetts Institute of Technology (MIT), and proceeded to produce several highly acclaimed documentary films.

speaks affectionately of Pogrund's baby daughter[26] ('It was a pleasure to have you down here [...] It was an even greater pleasure to hear Jenny's voice') and provides a brief sketch of his work conditions: 'Please excuse me if I forget to write. I am very busy in this office, I assure you. We have immense problems of organization. The office is still small but the demand is great and our resources are stretched to the limit. In addition we are serving very poor people and we have difficulty getting out money.'

While Pogrund took a rather dim view of Nzimande, who he felt was exploiting Sobukwe, using his fame as a way of drawing in clients while endlessly delaying the process of registering Sobukwe's articles, there is nonetheless an intimation, in the above comment, that Sobukwe may have found it rewarding to be, as he puts it, 'serving [the] very poor'.[27] Although Sobukwe's legal work may have provided a focus and proved a stabilising influence, he was not yet, certainly in Pogrund's view, out of the woods.

Sobukwe's (7 October) communication with Pogrund (Ba7.75) is notably upbeat, informing Pogrund of their conditions and discussing prospective purchases necessary for their new home: 'You will no doubt have heard from Dr. Wynberg that we have laid a carpet in the Lounge. Now the sun here is terribly hot: it is scorching. Our curtains in the Lounge have been burnt white where they meet [...] There is also the question of a stove and wardrobes for the room. We are concentrating on essentials at the moment and are not even thinking of replenishing our wardrobes.' Sobukwe adds that 'both my mother and my brother are spending a month with us', and that they will 'be joined on the 10th October by my mother-in-law and Dr. Ribeiro[28] and his wife'.

26 Jennifer, Benjamin Pogrund's daughter, was born in July 1961. She would become a filmmaker – in 1991–1992 she produced and directed a documentary on Nelson Mandela entitled *The Last Mile* – and also worked in the Department of International Relations and Cooperation in Pretoria.

27 Nzimande, Pogrund (1997, 339–341) writes, 'dragged his feet about having Sobukwe's articles of clerkship registered with the Cape Law Society' so as to benefit himself. Sobukwe's period of service could not technically begin until the articles were registered and 'the longer the delay the longer Sobukwe would be tied to Nzimande's office'. After Nzimande eventually registered Sobukwe's articles, in March 1971, he suggested that he and Sobukwe go into partnership together. 'But Sobukwe was sickened by the high fees he saw Nzimande levy on clients – black people, and often extremely poor. Sobukwe writhed at the prices they were paying, especially knowing that many of the people had been drawn to Nzimande's office because of him.'

28 Dr Fabian Ribeiro was the husband of Veronica Sobukwe's sister Florence. Ribeiro ran a general medical practice in Mamelodi township, Pretoria, and collected photographic

The upshot of this, he wittily informs Pogrund, is 'additional expenditure on food but also the purchase of some STATUS-SIGNIFYING items'. A busy time was on the horizon.

Sobukwe prepares Pogrund for disappointment, gently breaking the news (which Pogrund will have anticipated) that it is unlikely he will be able to attend his friend's forthcoming wedding to the artist Anne Sassoon: 'permission to attend my brother's confirmation service has been refused, what hope then that it will be granted for a marriage of "LIBERALS" – white at that!' That is to say: if apartheid officials had denied Sobukwe the opportunity to see his brother Ernest confirmed as an Anglican bishop – as reputable and Christian an event as one could imagine – they are unlikely to allow him to attend the nuptials of two white liberals who were fundamentally opposed to the apartheid regime. The letter also contains several other important pieces of information. Veronica, Sobukwe tells Pogrund, has gone to Durban to see her sister, stopping off at Johannesburg, and he, Sobukwe, has been kept busy at work, 'sweeping the floors and dusting the tables, suing and pleading on behalf of recalcitrant clients'. He ends with 'blessings on you and your bride! In this period of drought I can express my good wishes no more suitably than by applying the Tswana greeting! PULA! MAY THE RAINS POUR!'

Sobukwe was of course right to assume that he would not be granted permission to travel to Johannesburg for Pogrund's wedding on 26 October. On the 22nd Pogrund received the following telegram (Ba7.78), welcoming Anne to the family: 'PERMISSION REFUSED STOP WELCOME TO ANNE STOP JOINING GLORIOUS BROTHERS. SHALOM BOB'. The reference to 'Glorious Brothers', that is, Sobukwe and Pogrund, comes from Howard Fast's novel of the same name – something the two had previously discussed – about the 167 BC Maccabean revolt.

The letters from the latter months of 1969 suggest that despite ongoing challenges, Sobukwe was active, eager to engage, less tormented than was the case after his arrival in Kimberley. He resumed contact with his long-standing

evidence of police brutality, taking pictures of victims who came to him for medical treatment. Ribeiro was imprisoned for several months in 1980 on the charge of treason but, owing to the legal efforts of George Bizos, was released. On 1 December 1986, both Fabian and Florence Ribeiro were assassinated by the apartheid regime at their home in Mamelodi. Riberio was awarded the Order of the Baobab in 2004 for dedicating his life to the oppressed and for his contribution to the struggle for democracy.

6. Robert Mangaliso and Zondeni Veronica Sobukwe together at home, Galeshewe, Kimberley. (Photo by Peter Magubane, © Peter Magubane / David Gollan)

correspondent Nell Marquard[29] on 11 November (Bd2.17), thanking her for the 'Greek simplicity and brevity of your telegram on the occasion of my release'. He informed her that Veronica had resigned from the hospital and that 'The elder children [...] have just returned from school', adding both a reminder and a point of caution: 'I can receive letters from anybody, anywhere – except from banned persons. And, of course, the censorship continues. So we stick in our letters to the mundane and innocuous.'

One hears, in his note to Pogrund of 19 November (Ba7.77), the familiar cadence of Sobukwe's letter-writing style during the Robben Island years: the

29 Nellie Joan Marquard, born Van der Merwe, was a liberal intellectual, a member of both the Black Sash and the Liberal Party. She taught English literature at the University of Stellenbosch for many years and was involved in many forms of public service. She was married to the writer, publisher and prominent liberal Leo Marquard. On her death, her friend Moira Henderson (1981, 11) wrote of her: 'Her knowledge and wisdom and her gift of interpreting the historical significance of current trends and policies were qualities which were of immense value to the [Black] Sash. But more than that, she was a shining example of gentleness and courage, of humility and forcefulness, of courtesy and conviction.'

7. While Sobukwe's story is about his political life and the courage he exemplified as leader of the PAC, it is also inextricably about the relationship he shared with his wife, Veronica. (Photo by Peter Magubane, © Peter Magubane / David Gollan)

warm tone, the move between practical and more discursive topics, the gentle teasing: 'What an advantage it is to be a big shot! Here we are, with no hope of having telephones installed for at least three years and yours is installed in a matter of days! Behold the power of Jewish capitalism!'

In one of those remarks that indexes a lengthier in-person discussion that must, of necessity, remain undeveloped in writing, Sobukwe asks Pogrund to 'pardon me for failing to send my comments on the Nyerere[30] thing as promised'. If this remark were not enough to signal that Sobukwe's political sensibilities were as strong as ever, he adds: 'We have been hard at work in our slum quarters.' It sounds as if Sobukwe is entering a building

30 Julius Kambarage Nyerere was a Tanzanian anti-colonial activist, politician and political theorist. He served as prime minister and president of independent Tanganyika (from 1961) and thereafter as president of Tanzania until 1985. He was committed to African Nationalism and African socialism, promoting a political philosophy known as Ujamaa (a Swahili word referring to the community or nation as extended family).

phase. 'The office requires a great deal of re-organization, both physically and mentally,' he says, adding, a few lines later: 'We have been trying to make a garden here. So far it is more of an archaeological excavation [...] Now and again we come across an interesting formation and our hearts beat fast – Diamonds! we think. But we have unearthed no hidden treasures, so far.'

Regarding the LLB law course that the two men had discussed, Sobukwe is 'in two minds. I should very much like to do it – and "collect" another degree. But I also want to start earning as soon as possible.' While Sobukwe's reference to his children is brief ('The children – Miliswa and Dini – are fine'), it cannot but remind us that this will be the first end-of-year holiday that, for many years, the Sobukwe family would spend together in relatively 'normal' conditions.

1970: 'We are now strangers'

On 16 January Sobukwe wrote to Nell Marquard (Bd2.18), thanking her for the books she had sent him and providing a brief update on his current situation:

> I arrived here in May and stayed alone in an uncurtained room until my wife joined me on the 23rd June; the children had returned from school a week earlier.
>
> Veronica started work on the 1st July at the local hospital and resigned on the 31st, she's been home ever since.
>
> I met a friend here, who is the only African Attorney in the whole of the Northern Cape and he expressed willingness to have me serve articles under him. I've been in his office since the beginning of July. But my articles aren't registered yet. In other words not only am I not earning a living, but I haven't started on the course I hoped would ultimately make me financially independent.

Sobukwe's frustration with both Nzimande and his own lack of financial resources is clear enough. He remarks also on the difficulties of adjusting to life in Kimberley: 'For a time I knew nobody and people were scared to be seen talking to me. But I've made thousands of friends already and having been born and bred in the Karoo, I am quite at home here in every way. [...] We are now strangers at Graaff-Reinet and Joh'burg and Umtata. Where do we qualify to reside?'

The optimism implicit in Sobukwe's reference to the Karoo, to being 'quite at home in every way', is offset by his plangent remarks on the Sobukwe family nonetheless remaining strangers. The question Sobukwe asks ('Where do we qualify to reside?') would echo across the months and years to come, expressing not only the family's geographical displacement or their predicament of being held in a state of suspended animation but also their status as internal exiles within the country.

Regarding the circumstances of Pogrund's visits, Sobukwe tells his correspondent that 'We meet in the car he hires, drive around and have our lunch in the bushes' for the reason – and here follows one of Sobukwe's biblical allusions – 'that there is no room in the Inns'. Humorously, he notes that he is now known as 'the bishop's brother' for the reason that his sibling Ernest had been confirmed as a bishop in the Anglican Church, offering further that Ernest 'received letters addressed to "Bishop Robert Sobukwe" and is amused by it'.[31] 'How', he finishes, 'do you think, would I look in those medieval robes?' The levity continues. After asking Nell to pass along his best wishes to her husband Leo,[32] Sobukwe suggests that 'if he [Leo] can get me a job as Reader of books that do not fall within the penumbra of the Suppression of Communism act – in other words, Xhosa books – I shall be happy to accept'.

On 4 March 1970, Sobukwe received an offer from Marvin P. Miracle, the chairman of the African Studies Program at the University of Wisconsin, to travel to the United States, teach a summer course and begin work on a PhD. The professor opens his letter (Ba8.4) in expansive style:

31 Ernest Sobukwe was Robert's elder brother. Having qualified as a teacher, Ernest went on to train as a clergyman and was eventually confirmed as a bishop in the Anglican Church. During Robert's incarceration on Robben Island, Ernest was one of the very few visitors he was permitted to see.

32 Leo Marquard was a prominent figure in South African liberalism. He founded the National Union of South African Students (NUSAS) in 1924 and was instrumental in establishing the South African Institute of Race Relations, a liberal think tank, in 1929. He was also a leading figure in the Liberal Party, which he helped found in 1953. He was the author of *The Black Man's Burden* (1943), published under the pseudonym John Burger, and *People and Policies of South Africa* (1950). He worked as head of Oxford University Press in Cape Town during the 1950s and 1960s.

Dear Mr. Sobukwe:

[...] There have been favorable developments in our budgetary situation and I am delighted to be in a position to offer you immediate financial support, if you see your way clear to come to this University for work on a Ph.D.

We have the means to pay you at a rate of $500 per month from now until the end of 1970–71 academic year [...] During the next three months your duties would be solely assisting us prepare for a summer institute in Afro-American and African studies [...] During July and August we would want you to teach one of the courses offered at this Institute and would pay you at a rate of $1,220 per month. From September 1970 to June 1971 you would have no duties of any kind and would receive a fellowship from this African Studies Program for $340 per month [...]

We have worked out arrangements for your fare to this country and will be in touch about that shortly.

[...]

Let me say that the members of our African Studies Program are delighted that there is a possibility you will be coming to this University. We very much hope you will be able to accept this offer.

Not only does this letter give us a sense of Sobukwe's status in the eyes of colleagues in the scholarly domain of African Studies, but it also provides a poignant glimpse of a career, and a different life for the Sobukwe family, that could have been. Clearly excited by the news, Sobukwe writes about it in a letter to Pogrund five days later, on 9 March (Ba8.2): 'Wisconsin are offering me a fellowship for $1500 dollars per month [...] The Passport isn't through yet but it would appear I'm certainly going. Keep all this under your hat, until I give you the green light.'

Sobukwe's expansive mood is continued in a letter, written the following day, addressed to Anne Pogrund (Ba8.5). 'It was a real pleasure to meet you,' Sobukwe starts, confessing that 'I had coached myself to smile appropriately [...] when I met you, in order not to disappoint Benjie [...] It was a relief and pleasure to find that I did not need to dissimulate!' The excitement about America is evident: 'I have written to the States and the prospects are bright. But it is all still *sub rosa*!'

In a short note of 17 March to Pogrund (Ba8.6), Sobukwe remarks on a visit from the British journalist and author Anthony Sampson.[33] 'I met Anthony Sampson of the *Observer* this morning. He is pressing that I go to London! I might, mind you!'[34]

The following month, a further offer from the United States made its way to Sobukwe, this time via Pogrund's postbox. It was, no doubt, the result both of Sobukwe's growing international status and of Pogrund's enquiries, on Sobukwe's behalf, to a variety of US institutions. Frank Untermyer[35] of Roosevelt University reached out to Pogrund (Ba8.7), suggesting that 'Mr. Sobukwe [...] teach at Roosevelt University, and only two courses one term (Fall) and three the other (Spring) term. This would leave adequate time for Mr. Sobukwe to work on a Ph.D. in Linguistics at either Northwestern University, or the University of Chicago. The salary will remain, of course, as I originally described it, and we will also pay the transportation costs for Mr. Sobukwe and his family.'

Two weeks later, on 24 April, Untermyer wrote directly to Sobukwe (Ba8.8), clearly having received news that Sobukwe preferred the offer made to him by the University of Wisconsin:

> While, of course, we are all disappointed that you may not be with us at Roosevelt University, our primary purpose was to get you to the United States, so that you could commence your doctoral studies. That has been accomplished, and I am happy that you will be working at so eminent an institution as the University of Wisconsin. Wisconsin has, as I am sure you are aware, a distinguished Department of African Linguistics [...]

33 Anthony Sampson, a British writer and journalist, was the pioneering editor of South Africa's *Drum* magazine in the early 1950s. He later worked for the London *Observer* and authored 23 books, including the best-selling *Anatomy of Britain* (1962) and *Nelson Mandela: The Authorized Biography* (1999).

34 Sampson (1999, 118) subsequently reflected on this meeting himself: 'When I visited Sobukwe in 1970, while he was under house arrest in Kimberley, I found him tolerant and perceptive about South Africa, but also paranoid, convinced that his body had been bugged by the police.'

35 Frank Untermyer was a professor of political science and African studies at Roosevelt University from 1946 to 1982. He also taught at Ghanaian and Tanzanian universities in the 1960s. He helped found Roosevelt University in Chicago in 1945 and actively recruited African American and African students.

> I do have a suggestion whereby you could teach, if you choose to do so, at Roosevelt University, while pursuing your graduate work at Wisconsin. You may be aware that Madison is quite close to Chicago [...] If you would care to do so, you could put aside one day in each week in order to teach two courses at Roosevelt University [...] For each of these courses, Roosevelt University would pay a stipend of $1,000. Each course would be for one term, which runs from September, 1970 through January, 1971, and therefore we would pay $2,000 during that period. If you chose to continue the arrangement from February, 1971, through June, 1971, you would receive an additional $2,000, or a total, for the year, of $4,000.[36]

Heartening as this is – Untermyer was clearly willing to go the extra mile to get Sobukwe to Roosevelt – he had clearly underestimated the obduracy of South Africa's Ministry of Justice. The contrast between Untermyer's optimism and the stonewalling of apartheid authorities faced by the Sobukwe family could not have been greater. On 23 May 1970, Sobukwe directed a formal request to the Secretary of the Department of the Interior in Pretoria (Ab7), signalling his intent to leave the country: 'In the circumstances I beg to apply for an Exit Permit and would appreciate it greatly if I could be granted such exit permit as soon as possible to enable me to join the Graduate School at Wisconsin on the 22nd June, 1970.' While the offers from US universities would surely have introduced a measure of hope into the Sobukwe household, Sobukwe himself would have been under no illusions as to how likely they were to be granted permission to leave. Being blocked access to leave would, nevertheless, have been a difficult pill to swallow.

It was Veronica who, on 15 June, delivered the news to Pogrund in a letter at once affectionate ('My dear Benjie') yet tinged with despair (Ba8.10).

---

36 In the Robert Sobukwe papers, this letter is accompanied by a short, handwritten note addressed to Benjamin Pogrund:
Dear Mr. Pogrund, I have the nicest letter from Mr. Sobukwe, informing me that he would have preferred to come to Roosevelt University, but that he has already accepted a fellowship from Wisconsin. I have done my best, in this letter, to reconcile these two positions. I hope we can work something out.
With kindest and best wishes, and (as always) my gratitude,
Sincerely,
Frank Untermyer

Lamenting that she had not been able to meet Pogrund and his partner Anne ('I have not been quite well these days'), she then lays out the situation: Sobukwe had applied for a passport to leave the country and had heard back on 13 May that the minister of the interior had refused the request. Sobukwe had then requested an exit permit, noting to the relevant officials that he had already booked a seat for 18 June.[37] One gets a sense of how quickly things would have needed to happen if this plan was to succeed: Sobukwe was required to register at the Graduate School of Wisconsin on 22 June following an 18 June departure from South Africa, even as his passport request was still being processed in May.

In early June Sobukwe received the forms for an exit permit along with a covering letter requesting that he provide documentary evidence that he had been granted permanent residence in the United States. If this was not too steep a requirement, then the related request certainly was: Sobukwe needed to show in writing that the minister of justice was no longer restricting him to Kimberley. Sobukwe duly submitted such requests – unlikely as it was that he would have any success – but had not received a response at the time of Veronica's writing. Veronica continues: 'I have myself applied for an exit permit and have been told to forward a document stating that the U.S.A. are prepared to grant me permanent residence. I wish you could help me there.'

While Veronica's letter never speaks directly of unhappiness, it seems evident that what had already been a tumultuous year for her – relocation to Kimberley, financial troubles, relinquishing one job only to find herself in an unsatisfactory replacement position – had now been punctuated both by broken hopes and by the unending animosity of a state system intent on

37 If this sequence of events seems odd, it helps to bear in mind that requesting an exit permit was a last resort for those who had had their passport application refused. It was a drastic measure because once one had been issued an exit permit and crossed the border, one automatically relinquished one's citizenship. By law it had to be given to anyone who applied. This explains the apparent inconsistency behind Sobukwe's being granted it in the first place. The way the state got around this situation was to grant the exit permit – at least in theory – only to effectively invalidate it by insisting, by means of the Suppression of Communism Act, that Sobukwe not be allowed to leave Kimberley. According to Pogrund, it was only in very rare cases that requests for exit permits were ever denied. This provides further evidence – the 'Sobukwe clause' being another case in point – that the apartheid state greatly feared Sobukwe's influence, both nationally and internationally, and was willing to go to extraordinary lengths to silence him and restrict his movements.

relegating her family to the limbo of perpetual uncertainty and existential rootlessness.

Later that same month, a letter from the Ministry of Justice (Ba8.11) confirmed what the Sobukwe family suspected might happen:

> Ministry of Justice, Pretoria
> To Robert Sobukwe
> 24 June 1970
>
> Sir,
>
> With reference to your letter dated the 8th June, 1970 addressed to the Secretary of Justice, and by direction of the Honourable the Minister of Justice I wish to inform you that your application for the relaxation of the notices in force against you under the Suppression of Communism Act, 1950, to enable you to leave the country, has been refused.
>
> Yours faithfully,
> PRIVATE SECRETARY

The bluntness of this refusal, along with its patent absurdity – Sobukwe had always been opposed both to communism and to the making of political alliances with anyone with direct communist affiliations – would have only made it all the more maddening.

Although one wouldn't know it from Sobukwe's correspondence, he met in August with Gail Gerhart,[38] a young Columbia University graduate conducting her doctoral research on, to cite the title of her subsequent book, *Black Power in South Africa*. Gerhart and Sobukwe drove around Kimberley and she interviewed him, asking him a series of questions on the history of the PAC, the ANC, the Youth League and various aspects of Africanism. Fearful of the consequences for both of them should such an interview be recorded, Gerhart waited until after the spoken exchange and then spoke what she remembered of the interview into a tape recorder. The interview is instructive in many respects, and despite the limitations of its not being an actual verbatim transcript, Sobukwe's personality nonetheless shines through. Among the

38 Gerhart's interview with Sobukwe is included in this volume as chapter 11. The notes are in the Sobukwe Papers, file Cc1.

personal reflections Gerhart sketched after the two days of interviewing, she included the following remarks:

> *August 8 and 9, 1970*
> Sobukwe is a rather ordinary-looking man, about 5′ 10″, slightly stooped in his walk, energetic and jaunty. He chain-smoked through both our conversations. He has a warm laugh, a ready smile, a pleasant voice and eyes that light up – very small eyes with no lashes or brows. His speech is completely fluent; he rarely searches for words. Like A.P. Mda, he has a wide command of English idiom (Nana and P.K. 'didn't hit it off'). He used the word 'academic' several times to describe his own approach to analyzing problems. Has he perhaps picked up some things from his studies in prison that he now applies to things with hindsight? There was no point asking in the interview when it seemed likely that something was being given an ex post facto interpretation.
>
> Talking about the *tsotsis*,[39] he made a revealing statement to the effect that he never ever had doubted his own ability to convince any African of the rightness of his point of view. All he needed was a chance to talk to a person, e.g. any *tsotsi*. In effect he was saying he had such complete confidence in his own principles that he felt they were self-evident to anyone who would stop to give them consideration. This came up in the context of how he might have fared in the U.S. had his application for an exit permit been successful. He was saying that, in effect, he was confident of being able to win anyone's respect. He noted that the police in Kimberley 'respected him' and that he was 'respectful toward them'.
>
> He never expressed the sentiment 'my life's work may be finished, but I've done what I could', nor did he say anything to the effect that the struggle still goes on and I'm part of it still. He made no summary statements about his own life as it stands at this point.
>
> The second day we were parked near a path off the main road and two teenage boys passed, carrying sticks, wearing blankets, their

39 This colloquial term means 'gangster,' 'hoodlum' or 'thug'. It can also be used to refer to someone with 'street smarts', someone who does not necessarily have a permanent job and gets by through loafing or by 'street wits'. Parents may even refer (endearingly) to a 'naughty' or 'cunning' child as 'a little *tsotsi*'.

8. Sobukwe's childhood home, uMasizakhe, Graaff-Reinet. (Photo by Derek Hook)

> faces painted white. He didn't know what tribe[40] they were, but he said he remembered going through the same initiation process, with his face painted white. He remarked they had been in this condition for some time because their hair had already grown out from being shaved.
>
> The novel he is writing is not at all political. It draws characters from his childhood in Graaff-Reinet. The people in it are partly urban, not really still tribal; they are confused about their lives. The book has no moral. If it has any point, it is summarized by a saying in Xhosa that you must 'sleep on your wounds'. If you are hurting, never let anyone see it.

Much of this rings true, particularly perhaps the sense of Sobukwe's intellectual ('academic') prowess, his deep sense of solidarity with all African people, his belief in his political convictions, and the importance of mutual respect in relations with others. There is a surprise: the mention of the novel he is said to be writing. The love of 'the characters from his childhood in Graaff-Reinet' of course does not come as a surprise. What perhaps is revealing is that Sobukwe

40 In 1970 this term was not yet pejorative. Gerhart refers here to specific initiation rites observed in different ways by various African ethnic groups.

9. The Sobukwe family's church: the Methodist church, uMasizakhe. (Photo by Derek Hook)

10. The Valley of Desolation, just outside Graaff-Reinet. Sobukwe had an abiding love for Graaff-Reinet and the surrounding landscape of the Eastern Cape. (Photo by Derek Hook)

both lets Gerhart know that his exit permit has been denied and then speaks of 'sleeping on one's wounds', not allowing others to see your pain – one can only suspect that this proverbial remark pertained to Sobukwe himself at the time of the interview. Revealing also is the short note she appends in respect of Veronica's response to the situation: 'Veronica (his wife) has taken the denial of the exit permit very hard. She has even been sick, which he thinks is psychological. She was so excited about the chance of going that she knew the average temperature in Wisconsin was something like 50 degrees. Sobukwe said he never expected to get the permit.'

On 29 September, after a line had seemingly been drawn under plans to leave South Africa for the United States, Sobukwe wrote a short letter to Pogrund (Ba8.13) speaking in obviously coded terms about 'our microfilm', 'the mysterious transcript', the 'address of Accused #1', and 'a Mr. S involved in an appeal'. If the intent was to confuse or mislead anyone who was intercepting Sobukwe's correspondence with Pogrund, one can only assume this truncated style of communication was successful. Admittedly, Sobukwe's letter does contain references to court dates ('ON 25/4/1960 CASE RESUMES') and the court recording system ('BELT 59'), which somewhat gives the game away, even though it is not immediately clear who 'Mr. S' is or what particular case is being discussed. Fifty-two years after this exchange, in mid-2022, Pogrund was kind enough to shed light on this rather cryptic reference:

> The contents [of the letter] refer to what is usually overlooked: that despite the 'No bail, no defence, no fine' PAC slogan, Sobukwe and others did appeal (unsuccessfully) to the Supreme Court against the Johannesburg magistrate's jailing of them after Sharpeville. Magistrates' judgments were transcribed only if an appeal was lodged to enable the Supreme Court judges and defence lawyers to read the trial record. I knew this from my days reporting the magistrates' courts and I knew blue 'belts' – they were called – for recording. So, this letter deals with the transcript which had Sobukwe as accused No. 1 addressing the magistrate. The Mr. S in the letter is him.[41]

Sobukwe's ongoing situation of house arrest was the subject of parliamentary debate in early September 1970. Pogrund was carefully monitoring the

41 The case in question is R. versus Robert Mangaliso Sobukwe and Others (L.173/60), which began on 4 April 1960. An edited version of the transcript is included in this volume as chapter 9.

situation. In a letter to his friend Jill Wentzel[42] in which he requests further information (Ba8.14), Pogrund briefly outlines the debate:

> On 10 September 1970, in the House of Assembly, Helen Suzman asked the Minister of Justice, PC Pelser, how long he intended keeping Bob Sobukwe under restriction. Pelser replied Bob could not be allowed to go free altogether as long as he persisted in his attitudes.
>
> I am very keen to get the text of what Pelser said, either a photocopy of the page or even a scrawled note of the couple of sentences he probably uttered.

Wentzel responded, in due course, with a transcript of the relevant debate (Ba8.14):

> Assembly Debates
> 10 September 1970
>
> THE MINISTER. As regards Sobukwe. I want to say that we have restricted him in Kimberley. He was granted a house in Kimberley and allowance of R100 per month until such time as he could earn his own keep again. We realized that we could not put him in a place where he did not want to be and then simply leave him there without some means of gaining a livelihood or an income. After he had received the allowance of R100 for three months, he was offered employment at R60 a month. He turned up his nose at that and was not prepared to accept the position at R60 a month. It was not, as the hon. member said, the Hertzog Party[43] which forced me to do this, but it was because he did not want to accept this employment that I reduced his allowance by R60 a month. For three months this was the position, and then an offer of R1.200 a year was made to him. That he declined as well, and then we decided to take away his allowance completely. Subsequent to that he registered with an attorney, and

42 Jill Wentzel, like her husband, the attorney Ernie Wentzel, had been a founding member of the Liberal Party. She was also involved with the South African Institute of Race Relations, and the Black Sash, a women's organisation for social justice.

43 The Herstigte Nasionale Party (HNP), founded by the ultra-conservative Dr Albert Hertzog, son of General J.B.M. Hertzog, after he was ousted from the National Party in 1969.

my information is that financially the attorney was not in a position to pay him. Very recently he applied for assistance once again, and we immediately made two offers to him. There was one position with a salary of R1,200 a year, and a fortnight later another position with a salary of R1,380 a year was offered to him.

MRS. H. SUZMAN. What sort of job was that?

THE MINISTER. This position is in the Department of the hon. the Minister of Bantu Administration and Development. The hon. member also wanted to know from me whether we were going to detain him like that for ever. I cannot give the hon. member a reply to that, except that I can tell her that we cannot release him or lift the restriction on him as long as there is no change of heart on his part. That is certain. And that is a reply which I gave the hon. member over the years when he was still being detained on Robben Island. As long as Sobukwe persists in holding the convictions he does, we simply cannot allow him to be free altogether.

MRS. H. SUZMAN. How are you going to decide?

THE MINISTER. I am sorry, but I cannot give the hon. member a reply. However, we are in contact with him.

Suzman's questions expose what was so blatantly false and iniquitous about Pelser's (and the National Party's) position in respect of Sobukwe. The job offered to Sobukwe, which Pelser frames disingenuously as a good faith gesture, one which Sobukwe 'turned up his nose at', is, as becomes apparent, in the Department of Bantu Administration. To accept such a job would have made Sobukwe an agent of the administrative system of apartheid; it was, as such, something he would reject with every fibre of his being. Suzman's follow-up elicits not only echoes of the charge she had repeatedly made over the years in Parliament ('You can't surely punish him in perpetuity? That was not the sentence imposed on him by the courts') but also Pelser's inability to provide any reasonable criteria by means of which a decision on Sobukwe's freedom could be made (Ba8.14).

On 12 November, in a letter reminiscent of their correspondence during the Robben Island years, Sobukwe asks Pogrund for a series of books that he needs to enable him to continue his legal studies (Ba8.16). This, presumably, was a good sign for Pogrund, signalling that Sobukwe was able to move forward with his studies and that the delusions that had plagued the previous year were now a thing of the past.

Four weeks later, on 9 December, in a characteristically warm letter to Nell Marquard (Bd2.22), Sobukwe invokes the poet Tennyson before describing his Kimberley circumstances:

> We're well here, 'where all things always seem the same' as in the Lotus Land of Tennyson: the same problems, the same solutions, the same news, the same faces and the same pettiness and smallness.
>
> [...] The summers are scorchingly hot and the winters very severe, though snow is a rarity. Water is scarce and the soil is very clayey and poor.
>
> The house is spacious but the owner used old iron on the roof and we are already reduced to placing buckets and towels and baths at vulnerable spots, on rainy days. I have complained to the Municipal Council about the window latches that don't hold; the roof that leaks and dirty walls on the outside.

There is reference to a series of prospective mutual acquaintances, a brief mention of the political circumstances in Lesotho, prior to a merry Christmas sign-off:

> Do you happen to know Theodore Kloppenburg [*sic*],[44] a Hollander who lived in Durban and was banned in 1963? I received a letter from his wife in Nijmegen, Holland to the effect that he died in June some time.
>
> Benjie has been here to see me and so has Professor Wellington.[45] We had some stimulating discussions. The Professor is a Prog,[46] and their expert on South West Africa.

---

44 Theodore Johannes Kloppenberg had been involved in various anti-apartheid organisations and activities in Durban in the early 1960s with people like Eleanor Kasrils and Phyllis Naidoo. He was banned in April 1967 under the Suppression of Communism Act and left for the Netherlands after his banning expired in 1968.

45 Professor J.H. Wellington was the retired head of the Geography Department at the University of the Witwatersrand, who had become friendly with Sobukwe during the time both were employed by the university.

46 A colloquial term of reference for the Progressive Party, a liberal party founded in 1959 of which Helen Suzman was the sole representative in Parliament until 1974.

> [...]
>
> How is Leo these days? And are you thinking of visiting Lesotho again? They have quite an ass there running the country with the aid of certain Cock Roach who is head of both the Police and the Army – a kind of latter-day *SANDERS OF THE RIVER*![47]

1971: 'Kimberley is still the same'

On 24 February, Sobukwe resumed his correspondence with Mrs Marquard (Bd3.1), thanking her for the magazines (among them the *New Yorker, The Listener* and *The Guardian*), the books, and the Christmas gift she had sent him. 'I am almost ashamed to write,' he remarks: 'I have been owing you a reply for so long that if you were not you, you would have washed your hands of the ingrate by now!' Sobukwe continues in this vein, although he adds a note of levity, a reminder that his sense of irreverence remained undiminished:

> [...] not even a note to acknowledge your gifts of love: just a huge monastic silence!
>
> I loved both books. The Greeks always fascinated me – the classical lot, that is; not the cafe-owners we have around here.

There is some good news: the Law Society had confirmed that they had no objection to Sobukwe serving his articles, provided the prohibition in his banning order regarding court attendance would be relaxed. His hope of taking Roman Law the following year is, he cautions, contingent on his passing Latin, which he will have to 'start from scratch'. What a pity, he laments, jokingly, that 'you're so honest, I could have had you come up to Kimberley and write the exam for me. Of course there is the difficulty of the Reference Book which one has to produce before entering the exam room.' Jocular and friendly as this remark is, Sobukwe's allusion to the 'Reference Book' nonetheless serves to remind his correspondent about the restrictive conditions that he continues to live under.

---

47 An award-winning British film of 1935; the character Sanders was a district commissioner in colonial Nigeria. In 1970 Chief Leabua Johnson seized power in Lesotho, backed by the paramilitary Police Mobile Unit.

Meanwhile, attempts to bring the Sobukwe family to the United States were ongoing. William R. Cotter,[48] president of the Africa-America Institute in New York, an organisation providing financial assistance to African scholars in the States, wrote to Marvin Miracle, chairman of the African Studies Program at the University of Wisconsin, on 13 April (Ba9.3):

> It is my understanding that it is possible, as a result of a court action in South Africa that Dr. Sobukwe and his family will be allowed to leave South Africa in the next months.
>
> If this occurs, I want to confirm to you once more AAI's offer to pay up to $2,000 to defray the air transportation costs for Dr. Sobukwe and such other members of his family as can be covered by that amount of money.

The erroneous titular reference to 'Dr. Sobukwe' is instructive, an indication of how Sobukwe was viewed by colleagues in the United States: as both a leading political figure and a scholarly intellectual. Of course, Sobukwe's nickname had long since been 'Prof' among PAC comrades and friends precisely because of his intellectual talents. In his letter of 14 April to Pogrund (Ba9.4), Sobukwe remarks: 'It was a pleasure to have you and Anne around for the weekend, though it worries me to know that every time you come over we have to concern ourselves at some time or other with such mundane things as school fees and like matters bound up with filthy lucre – instead of engaging throughout in academic discussion as befits a research scholar of Wisconsin and a budding associate professor at Harvard.' While Sobukwe's tone is playful here, he seems also to be allowing himself to muse about the future, to consider the roles that he and his friend might go on to occupy. This is followed by a comment on the Easter holiday: 'A pleasure also was it to hear your voice over the phone, an indication that you did not die over the Easter weekend like that other Jew two thousand centuries [*sic*] ago. It appears that he was quite an agitator – not at all a long-bearded Zionist pacifist.'

48 William R. Cotter was a lawyer who worked as an assistant attorney general in northern Nigeria, White House fellow in the Johnson Administration, and president of the Africa-America Institute in the 1970s. He later became president of Colby College, a liberal arts college in Maine.

It is tempting, given the crisis of faith Sobukwe underwent on Robben Island, to read this as a hint that there was still something unresolved in his Christianity (Christians, after all, don't typically refer to Jesus as 'that ... Jew'). Then again, given Dini Sobukwe's description of the Christian habits of the family (in an interview with Derek Hook, 29 May 2014), that seems unlikely: 'Every night we prayed ... We'd always start with a hymn, maybe just one verse. And then he'd pray. And those were fascinating prayers.' However we choose to read Sobukwe's comments on Jesus, we have in his subsequent comment – 'he was quite an agitator – not at all a [...] pacifist' – a further indication that his political fire had not been doused.

Both Dini and Miliswa Sobukwe wrote to Pogrund from Lesotho over the coming weeks – perhaps at the urging of their father – with Dini remarking on 29 April (Ba9.7): 'Now that Tata is back home, I read a lot of English books [...] for example [...] one by Charles Dickens (*Hard Times*) ... which I think is very interesting'. In Miliswa's letter of 3 May (Ba9.8) she expresses what we might consider a broader family wish: 'I am always praying [to] God that we would be successful in our plan to U.S.A.'

Pogrund's correspondence with Sobukwe on 8 June (Ba9.12) expands upon a series of political thoughts he had expressed in a phone call with his friend earlier that day. While we have no transcript of Sobukwe's contribution to this discussion, Pogrund's comments are worth recounting at length because they allow us to (imaginatively) reconstruct what Sobukwe's own – no doubt quite distinct – position would have been in their debate on nationalism and African nationalism.

> As I was saying to you on the fone earlier today, what is nationalism? And more particularly, African nationalism? A book I have been reading, by Hans Kohn, starts off by defining nationalism as 'a state of mind, in which the supreme loyalty of the individual is felt to be due the nation-state'.[49] He goes on to talk about deep attachment 'to one's native soil, to local traditions and to established territorial authority'.
>
> The definition, clearly, is adequate enough when it applies to established nation-states, and equally clearly, is derived from a study of European history (and European in the geographical sense) from

49 Pogrund is probably referring to *African Nationalism in the Twentieth Century* (1961) by Hans Kohn and Wallace Sokolsky.

about the 18th Century onwards. I suppose it could even encompass Jewish Nationalism, for the whole striving of this nationalism was for the creation of a nation-state, even though for a considerable period of years such a state did not exist in actuality.

But what of African nationalism ... Which not merely covers people who exist within a particular nation-state (i.e. the African Nationalism say of Kaunda's party,[50] or Nyerere's,[51] etc) and whose striving occurs within the framework of their political nation-state; it covers, too, the strivings of the same people in regard to the continent of Africa as a whole. And it encompasses too the philosophic coming together of people both in the African continent and those who claim an historical link because of their forebears (e.g., Du Bois[52] and the early Pan-Africanist conferences which have [gave?] modern African Nationalism its start).

Then too, I have been looking at a very poor book by Prof. Ned Munger[53] on African and Afrikaner Nationalism. Poor as the book is he does trigger off some thinking because when he talks about African Nationalism in South Africa, he talks about *all* African striving, right from the start of modern-day political activity towards the end of the last century. He talks thus, later on, of African Nationalism

50 Kenneth David Kaunda was a key figure in the Zambian struggle for national liberation and the first president of Zambia from 1964 to 1991.

51 Julius Nyerere, president of Tanganyika and, later, Tanzania.

52 W.E.B. Du Bois was an American sociologist, historian and activist committed to civil rights, socialism and Pan-Africanism. He attended the Pan-African Conference in London in 1900, and helped organise the first Pan-African Congress in Paris in 1919, which was followed by subsequent congresses during the 1920s and 1930s. At the end of the Second World War, a Fifth Pan-African Congress was held in 1945 in Manchester, where Du Bois was appointed president of the meeting. For the first time the Congress was attended by delegates from Africa or Africans working or studying in the UK. Du Bois was the author of *The Souls of Black Folk* (1903) and *Black Reconstruction in America* (1935). He popularised the term 'the color line', coined by Frederick Douglass, which refers to racial segregation in the United States after the abolition of slavery. In *The Souls of Black Folk* he writes, 'the problem of the twentieth century is the problem of the color line'. He was a founder of the National Association for the Advancement of Colored People (NAACP) in 1909 and served as the editor of the organisation's journal, *The Crisis*.

53 Edwin S. Munger's *Afrikaner and African Nationalism: South African Parallels and Parameters* (1967). Munger, an American professor, rejected violence and international pressures to isolate South Africa, which he saw as counterproductive in effecting change; instead, he believed in 'bridge-building'.

as influenced by the communists, or of being influenced by US ideas of democracy, or by Nkrumah's African Socialism.[54]

OK, you might say, African Nationalism in SA is the broad sweep of ideas confined to local Africans only (and that statement in itself raises problems: Africans – Black-skinned people only??). But taking the point for the moment, what then of the different tribal groups? Particularly through the Bantustans, consciousness of one's own group, a shared land and cultural and historical tradition (which, clearly, must be some of the essential elements) is steadily coming to the forefront. So we have Xhosa nationalism, Zulu nationalism, etc. So where do these stand in relation to an African nationalism?

Have I irritated your mind enough to make you sit down and write me a long reply? I hope so.

I did not have the courage to mention this on the fone, but after blasting off at *The Star* last week about the description of you as the ANC leader, I was mortified to find that the *Mail*[55] perpetrated the same error, the next morning. The matter was vigorously taken up! Anyway, as you will probably have seen, both papers published corrections the next day.

Pogrund appears here to be questioning the viability not only of a truly Pan-Africanist standpoint ('what [...] of the different tribal groups?') but of a truly inclusive form of African Nationalism ('we have Xhosa nationalism, Zulu nationalism, etc.'). For Sobukwe, by contrast, Pan-Africanism is the overarching political agenda which eclipses both vying state-based African Nationalisms and, most certainly, any appeals to ethnic divisions ('different tribal groups') fostered by apartheid's Bantustan logic. Pogrund's remark that he may have 'irritated [Sobukwe's] mind' indicates that the two men maintained opposing viewpoints in respect of these questions.

Part of the chemistry of their relationship seems to have been their willingness to debate and to use the other's political standpoint – Pogrund the

54 Kwame Nkrumah was the first prime minister and president of Ghana, a founder of the Organisation of African Unity, and a recipient of the Lenin Peace Price in 1962. In a text entitled 'African Socialism Revisited', Nkrumah (1967) defined a distinctly African socialism that 'introduces a new social synthesis in which modern technology is reconciled with human values, in which the advanced technical society is realised without the staggering social malefactions and deep schisms of capitalist industrial society'.

55 *Rand Daily Mail.*

liberal, Sobukwe's more radical Pan-Africanist viewpoint – as a foil. While we do not know how fiery this exchange of political views was – the fact that it happened is, incidentally, a clear indication that Sobukwe had no intention of adhering to the letter of the law of his banning orders – we know that Pogrund stopped short in their telephone conversation of broaching a topic that would surely have angered Sobukwe. Given how vigorously the PAC differentiated itself from the more liberal Charterist views of the ANC,[56] Sobukwe would have objected to being described as the leader of the ANC, despite his own ANC Youth League history.

Sobukwe's note to Pogrund on the following day (9 June) is somewhat terse (Ba9.13). He opens by saying that he is glad to hear Pogrund is recovering from a recent operation, but from then on, he is direct and to the point. While Sobukwe was ready to debate many issues with his old friend, what he states so forthrightly in this letter is decidedly not open for further discussion:

> I have written to the Consulate giving them all the particulars I think they may require.
>
> The position is that I should like Veronica and the children to settle in the U.S.A. whatever my fate might be. If they can't return to South Africa, they can settle anywhere in Africa should they later desire to leave the States. And, of course, they'll return to South Africa one day when the Nats are dead and forgotten.
>
> I know what your feelings are on the matter, but I won't be happy until my family leave this country. Veronica is dead set on going and so are the children.

This declaration of intent not only forestalls the possibility of any further procrastinating discussion, it is bold also in another way. It is a statement made with the assurance of what the future will, in retrospect, surely verify: the Sobukwes will return to South Africa, the National Party will die. Finding fortitude in this way, by crossing the future and past tenses, that is, by means of an appeal to what, years from now, will be recognised and affirmed in what was struggled for, was also a characteristic of Sobukwe's political

56 Charterist here refers to the Freedom Charter adopted at Kliptown in 1955 as a policy document for the ANC, the racially inclusive opening line of which states: 'South Africa belongs to all who live in it, black and white'.

speeches. It was a means of fortifying an intent even under the most difficult of circumstances.

Sobukwe wrote to Nell Marquard the same day (Bd3.2) – fired up perhaps by having proclaimed his decision in such stark terms to Pogrund – offering her a personal reassurance alongside a measure of Stoic resolve:

> You know about the application before Court. Don't be anxious on my account. I am indifferent to the outcome. If I go, I go! If I don't, I don't and that's all there is to it. But I am determined that Veronica and the children should leave if that is at all possible.
>
> We've worked hard on the garden and it'll be a pity to leave it now.

The topic of gardening features in the earliest of Sobukwe's correspondence with Marquard. While clearly a safe topic (bearing in mind the varying forms of censorship that their exchanges were subject to) and a shared interest, a lingua franca of sorts, it was resonant for other reasons also. It is something he enjoyed a great deal, as Dini Sobukwe affirmed in an interview in 2014 ('he loved gardening ... it really was his passion ... [in] the yard, every single day after work he'd go and do that') and yet it also connected back to his political beliefs, involving as it did, of course, the African land.[57] Bearing this in mind, one appreciates how this reference to the expression of regret and sadness at having to leave the garden underscores the finality of Sobukwe's decision. In the letters quoted above, Sobukwe places the needs of his family above his own. Given that he has only just recently survived an ordeal of solitary confinement, such an insistence that his family depart even if he was unable to follow would have taken considerable resolve.

On 14 June, Sobukwe wrote to Raymond Tucker,[58] a lawyer who was providing assistance in respect of the Sobukwe family's attempt to leave the

57 The closing lines of Sobukwe's (1959) speech at the inaugural convention of the Pan Africanist Congress (this vol., ch. 6) extend this theme, using the image of a garden as a basis for the shared commonality and solidarity of Pan-Africanism: 'Here is a tree rooted in African soil, nourished with waters from the rivers of Afrika. Come and sit under its shade and become, with us, the leaves of the same branch and the branches of the same tree.'

58 Raymond Tucker, a Johannesburg attorney, defied the apartheid regime by providing legal defence in political trials.

country (Ba9.14). The letter, boldly titled APPLICATION TO LEAVE THE REPUBLIC OF SOUTH AFRICA, proceeds as follows:

> I acknowledge with thanks your letter of the 7th June, 1971 and the forms and documents therewith enclosed.
>
> [...]
>
> I am grateful for the documents and congratulate you on their meticulous preparation which, undoubtedly, enabled Counsel to present such a good case.
>
> We're both of us aware, I believe, that the Government may adopt some other measure to prevent my leaving the country. Please don't be anxious on my behalf. I can take it!
>
> However, my wife is sick and tired of this country and both of us would be glad to have our children grow up in a freer country.
>
> As my wife has been offered a post at the General Hospital at Wisconsin I should be pleased to know if she and the children could leave without me towards the end of July, should our government be reluctant to be separated from me [...]

Sobukwe was, alas, not wrong to suspect that the apartheid government would be 'reluctant' to see him leave.

By 22 July, Frank Untermyer had caught wind of the fact that Veronica Sobukwe might possibly take up a nursing job in the United States, and he wrote offering support (Ba9.17): 'I understand that there is a possibility that Mrs. Sobukwe may take up residence in Madison, Wisconsin, and also work there as a trained nurse. If there is any way I can provide assistance in preparing for that trip, I would be happy to do so. Of course, I shall look forward to meeting with your family after they arrive in this country.' With messages of this sort, one might have believed that the Sobukwe family's departure was imminent.

A month after his previous note to Marquard, Sobukwe wrote again on 26 July (Ba3.3), stressing once more what by now had surely become the family's abiding focus:

> Veronica is still set on leaving the country and we are arranging to obtain visas for her and the children even if I have to remain.

> Things seem to be moving fast these days and our rulers are at sixes and sevens – absolutely lost and confounded – the poor dears.
>
> Kimberley is still the same: cold and dusty in winter; hot and dusty in summer; intellectually arid throughout the year. The poverty remains stinking; the drinking colossal and the crime rate, contrary to all the researches of social scientists – singularly low, except for drunkenness, petty thefts and debts.

Despite the myriad challenges of living in Galeshewe and the various social ills arising from the poverty of this region – alcoholism being, for Sobukwe, seemingly foremost among them – the PAC leader remained intent on refuting racist stereotypes, stressing that crime there remained 'singularly low'. The condescending remark aimed at the apartheid authorities ('poor dears')[59] is a lovely example of Sobukwe's talent for utilising the vernacular of his audience in such a way that they would perfectly understand what he was getting at.

As he had done throughout the period of Sobukwe's imprisonment, Pogrund was again helping to organise funding and international assistance for the family. Untermyer wrote to him on 10 August (Ba9.18) to confirm that Veronica Sobukwe would soon be receiving a formal offer of employment from a Madison hospital, and offering to assist – with the help of the South African-born Daniel Kunene, acting director of the African Studies Program at Wisconsin, and a Presbyterian mission organisation in New York – with airfares. Tellingly, Untermyer says that 'we are all looking forward to the arrival of Mrs. Sobukwe and her children'. On 21 September, William Cotter confirmed in writing (Ba9.22) that the Africa-America Institute was 'prepared to pay up to $2,000 for the transportation from South Africa to Madison, Wisconsin for Mrs. Robert Sobukwe and her four children', a second indication that the plan at the time was to get Sobukwe's family out of the country, and as soon as possible, even if he himself was unable to join them.

---

59 This colloquial term implies a doddery, confused, ineffectual person, typically in old age. That the term combines – oddly enough – both affection and dismissiveness makes Sobukwe's remark all the more effectively condescending.

We see, in Sobukwe's letter of 12 October to Pogrund (Ba9.19), a return to his more expansive style. 'Things are quiet on the western front,' says Sobukwe, adding that 'The Minister of the Interior is keeping mum on Veronica's application for a renewal of her exit permit'. He continues:

> News from home is that my brother has been discharged from hospital. The arm was amputated close to the shoulder. Gangrene was setting in I am told.
>
> The details are still not emerging clearly. It appears that the ticket examiner assaulted my brother's friend – a young teacher who left college at the end of last year. He kicked him and trampled on him and killed him. My brother states that he intervened 'peacefully and reasonably'– which I don't believe. At any rate he was pushed through the passage door by the aforesaid ticket examiner at about 8 p.m. and lay next to the track until 8 a.m. the following morning when Railway police from Graaff-Reinet picked him up after receiving a report from the passengers on the train when the train stopped at Graaff-Reinet.
>
> My sister-in-law writes to say that they went with him after his discharge from hospital to lay a charge at Graaff-Reinet against the ticket examiner referred to above.

It is hard to ascertain how much contact Sobukwe had with Charles (the second of his two older brothers). Judging from his written correspondence dating back to 1963, it would seem that they were not frequently in touch. Nonetheless, this event – not merely an account of a killing, but of Charles himself being assaulted and lying unattended overnight for twelve hours – would have come as a terrible shock. What gives one pause here is not merely the horrendous details of the event, but how Sobukwe relates what happened, that is, with full awareness that such instances of apartheid's brutality were commonplace occurrences. Such was the frequency of assaults committed by the police and other agents of the state against black men and women that when they occurred – traumatic as they no doubt were – they did not necessarily come as a surprise. One is left with the sense that the charge laid against the ticket examiner would have come to nothing. Sobukwe signs off with a suitably cutting remark: 'I see that Vorster[60] is still playing up to the gallery as usual. It is a pity there is no Afrikaans equivalent of the *Sunday Times* to persuade the man to retire gracefully. I don't think even the Nationalist Party deserves so cruel a fate as to be burdened with such an incompetent comedian as a leader.'

On 11 November, fresh from a visit to Kimberley, Pogrund wrote to William Cotter providing an update on the Sobukwe family's petition to leave the country (Ba9.24):

> Bob Sobukwe's appeal was heard on Tuesday[61] and I returned last night from a quick visit to Kimberley, so I am now able to write in reply to your letter of September 21.
>
> The appeal apparently received a good hearing and there are some hopes of success on a majority decision of the five-judge Appeal Court. Judgment is likely within the next two to three weeks. If Bob wins he will want to leave very soon thereafter – provided, of course, that the Government does not take any further administrative action to hold him here. The idea is for Bob to travel alone, with his wife and children following at a later stage. Their application for exit permits are still snarled up in the red tape of government.
>
> [...]
>
> Bob is well, and will cheerfully accept whatever happens. We discussed the point raised in your letter about the ability of his wife to cope. We both appreciate your concern, but believe it will be all right.
>
> There has been a lot of trouble here.

Even though the communication cuts off on an ominous note – the second half of the letter has not survived – Pogrund sounds upbeat that there might be a realistic chance of the Sobukwe family's appeal prevailing. This underscores again the extent to which the Sobukwes were living on tenterhooks, in a state of suspension, waiting for their fate to be decided. Pogrund's remark that 'Bob is well' is reassuring. Similarly, his assessment that Sobukwe 'will

60 B.J. Vorster was the strong-arm minister of justice in Prime Minister Hendrik Verwoerd's cabinet, a position that was combined with that of minister of police and prisons in 1966. After Verwoerd's assassination in 1966, Vorster was chosen by the National Party to become prime minister.

61 9 November.

[...] accept whatever happens' is suggestive that the bedrock of resolve that had sustained Sobukwe during the Robben Island years was once again apparent.

1972: 'What's this country coming to?'

Less than a week into the new year, Sobukwe received a letter from the young novelist Bessie Head, who had written to him from Botswana (Ba10.1).[62] While Bessie starts somewhat tentatively, her confidence and her willingness to declare her affinity for Sobukwe soon become apparent:

Bessie Head
P.O. Box 15
SEROWE, Botswana
6th January, 1972

Dear Mr. Sobukwe,

I do not know whether you will remember me as much as I like and remember you. We had met briefly in 1960 just a few days before

62 Bessie Amelia Emery Head was born in Pietermaritzburg in 1937 to a white mother and a father who at the time was classified as 'non-white'. Her mother suffered mental health issues, and Bessie was placed first with a white and then subsequently a mixed-race ('coloured') foster family. The identity of her birth mother was hidden from her until her adolescence, and the discovery proved devastating to her. Having completed a two-year training certificate in teaching, Bessie took up a job as a teacher in a mixed-race school in Durban. In 1958, she resigned and relocated to Cape Town where she secured a position at the weekly *Golden City Post*, writing courtroom stories. The following year, she moved to Johannesburg to write and work for *Drum* magazine's sister publication, *Home Post*, where she met literary figures such as Dennis Brutus, Lewis Nkosi and Can Themba. Exposure to the ideas of black nationalism and Pan-Africanism – particular through the works of George Padmore and the leadership of Robert Mangaliso Sobukwe – proved important, and she went on to join the PAC. After the Sharpeville Massacre, she provided support to imprisoned PAC members and their families and was subsequently arrested herself. Although the charges against her were subsequently dropped, she succumbed to severe depression and attempted suicide. After a period of hospitalisation, she returned to Cape Town. In July 1961 she met Harold Head, and within six weeks the couple were married. After the breakdown of the marriage, Bessie successfully applied for a teaching job in Botswana (then the Bechuanaland Protectorate). She left South Africa in March 1964, never to return.

> the pass campaign. I was introduced to you by Matthew Nkoana[63] and that day you had been reading something about land reform in China and discussed it with me. A day or so later you bought me the Johannesburg *Star.* Then the next time I met you was the morning at Orlando police station where someone had tried to run away to Swaziland (I forget his name) and everything was turning upside down. Indeed, at that time I was not functioning so well, if I ever really do. I am extremely prone to having emotional stress and a very turbulent destiny. It hardly remains on even keel. So the best I might have done at that time was stutter very badly so I think you might not remember me.

Not only is this description historically informative – it locates Bessie Head at Orlando police station on the morning of Sharpeville, when 'everything was turning upside down' – it is also psychologically perceptive. Her brief sketch of Sobukwe's personality is apt. Sobukwe was, after all, the kind of man who would take the time to discuss matters of 'land reform in China' with a young colleague. Bessie goes on to explain what prompted the letter:

> A certain Miss Shala visited her brother at Swaneng Hill School.[64] My house is very near the high school and I sell vegetables to Mr. Shala. He told her to visit me and during the conversation she said that you were her next door neighbour. I was so happy to hear this that I asked her to take this letter and a paperback copy of my first novel,[65] which I enclose. You might not agree with some of the things I said about semi-literate politicians in Botswana. I found in many ways that I was not basically a politician, though circumstances

63 Matthew Nkoana, a former newspaper seller and political columnist, was part of the Africanist group within the ANC and a subsequent member of the PAC. He, like Sobukwe, was arrested in March 1960 for his involvement in the anti-pass campaign. Nkoana assumed a more prominent role when he became spokesperson for rank-and-file PAC members who stood trial apart from the organisation's leadership. After serving part of his sentence and being released, Nkoana became the chairman for the Witwatersrand region in the underground PAC. Given the threat of further arrest, Nkoana left South Africa in 1962, and went on to represent the PAC in Bechuanaland and Cairo.

64 Swaneng Hill School in Serowe, where Bessie Head settled, was founded by a South African exile, Patrick van Rensburg, who became a friend of Bessie's.

65 *When Rain Clouds Gather* (1968).

> in South Africa makes one some kind of political thinker and my first book was really to free myself of a sort of prison and to look more deeply at Africa's destiny which I hope will also be the destiny of mankind – a wealth of humanity and a richness of culture, without the dark taints of class arrogance and power-mongering.

While Bessie is cautious, noting areas of potential disagreement, she nonetheless establishes common ground through her stated commitment to Africa's destiny, surely something Sobukwe would have identified with immediately. Then comes her description of what did not appeal to her about the PAC:

> There is something else I wanted to say. I was not, in the final analysis attracted to the P.A.C. so much as I was attracted to your personality. I met too many horrible types of voracious people in that political party and disliked them. Yet there comes a time when a man states certain things very clearly with possibly unending truthfulness and that is meaningful. Not the funny performances of the Potlako[66] crew. And then, there are so many subtlties [*sic*], so many ways of capturing people's hearts and changing them that the widest and most generous heart is needed in one's dealings with mankind in general. I assumed you were my blood brother in that sense, and that like Darwin you were or had spotted life's incredible capacity to *evolve*. Nothing ever remains the same, especially emotional growth.

What is so striking about the distinction she draws here – between the 'horrible types' of the PAC and the 'unending truthfulness' clearly associated with Sobukwe himself – is that it explains how she was willing to join the PAC largely on the basis of the moral example of Sobukwe himself.

66 Potlako Kitchener Leballo was leader of the Africanist grouping within the ANC, and took a major role in the formation of the PAC in 1959. In an interview with Gail Gerhart (1968), Leballo provided insight into personal leadership differences between Sobukwe and himself: 'We called upon him [Sobukwe] to come from Standerton and I felt that myself, as a great organizer, I was not able to lead, I was too violent and ruthless, so I felt that a man who is a bit cool, like Sobukwe, highly educated and an intellectual, he would be able to come and assist us.' See also this vol., ch. 3, n. 1.

What she expresses in her letter is not only the immediacy of the connection she felt to Sobukwe, but also a sense of his personal sincerity and charisma. It was this, one might speculate, precisely this humanity – this largeness of spirit – that made Sobukwe so dangerous to the apartheid regime.

By the time of this letter Head had suffered a great deal, in both the personal and political spheres of her life. Not only had she been arrested for her involvement with the PAC – an event which precipitated a major depressive incident and a subsequent suicide attempt – but she had also experienced the onset of schizophrenia. Her reference to being 'extremely prone to [...] emotional stress and a turbulent destiny' was thus more than mere whimsy. She signs off in humorous fashion, with a comment that, interestingly enough, is not unlike the discreet disparagements that Sobukwe himself used to include in letters of the period, with a witty put-down directed to any apartheid official who may have opened the letter:

> I guess your mail is censored but sometimes possibly the censor could be in need of some education in philosophical matters and many other things so if you could write to me, and I to you, we might improve the mental outlook of your censor.
>
> Affectionately,
> Bessie

One suspects that despite his appreciation for both Head's letter and the gift of her novel, Sobukwe might have found her approach rather direct. Her personal disclosures perhaps lacked the degree of reserve and formality that he deemed proper, at least in the early stages of a relationship.

Sobukwe wrote to Pogrund on 9 February (Ba10.2). Pogrund had been subjected to a police raid earlier that month. Officials had seized a sizable portion of the documentary material that he had amassed on the topic of black politics in South Africa – the focus of his prospective doctoral research. Among these papers were notes Pogrund had taken while conducting previous interviews (including one with the newspaper photographer Robert Botha), which had for a short time been in police possession. Pogrund had then – ridiculously enough – been charged with theft for having such papers, even though the notes in question were his own. Hence Sobukwe's teasing admonishments:

> Hello Thief!
>
> There's an excuse for a Bantu to indulge in theft because he can at least argue that he acted under the pressure of necessity; but for a White man, and a White man of your standing, at that, there is just no excuse. 'Disgraceful' is the word that came to mind immediately I read the report in the paper. Honestly you are building up a reputation for yourself that is becoming extremely embarrassing to us of the family in defying the law (as the Prosecutor correctly observed) and stealing your own property. Why the blazes should you steal what you own? Why couldn't you just take it? It was yours, after all!

Sobukwe's affection for Pogrund really shines through here. This mock put-down, so playfully delivered, would have provided much comfort to Pogrund, delivered as it was from a man who had experienced the full brunt of the various harassments and (often patently absurd) accusations that the apartheid state could muster.

Sobukwe's correspondence with Nell Marquard had been somewhat intermittent since his release from Robben Island, no doubt owing to the challenging conditions of adjusting to Kimberley and the efforts and frustrations associated with his attempts to secure an exit passage from the country for his family. Perhaps because of somewhat more stable circumstances, 1972 saw a return to a more regular exchange of letters between Sobukwe and his liberal friend from Cape Town. Sobukwe often seems at his most conversational, free-ranging and relaxed in these letters, probably because he was less burdened with the legal and financial issues that had been so much a feature of his 1971 letters. It is worth bearing in mind that Sobukwe had not, at this point, met Marquard in person. Theirs was a friendship cultivated on the basis of written correspondence, a relationship, furthermore, free of obligation. Sobukwe suggests as much in his letter of 2 March (Bd3.4):

> One of the greatest privileges of friendship is that one can keep quiet and still communicate. Friends talk less to each other than to acquaintances. Their silence is communicative.
>
> [...] It's one of the lessons I have learnt recently. I remember reading an article in the *Reader's Digest* about a pastor in a small village to

> whom it was reported that the son of one of his congregants had been drowned. The woman, who tells the story says he did not philosophise or play the professional comforter. He came in, greeted them and wept. And she says she was comforted more by his tears than by his words. Because he loved; he felt.

This short account of empathy has an added, unstated significance. It was clear by now that the apartheid authorities were not going to allow Sobukwe to leave the country, and the desperate hope that the family had invested in this wish must, by then, have been painfully extinguished.

In the same letter, Sobukwe offers news about his mother, who had recently visited Galeshewe. Having failed his Latin examination, Sobukwe now needed to delay taking his Roman Law examination for a further year. Then follows a humorous reflection on his legal work with Nzimande:

> Ours is mostly a criminal practice and one soon learns to realize that the paying clients are the dagga and diamond smugglers and, consequently, to work hard for their release!
>
> [...]
>
> I can't specify the book I should like, Nell. But, I would like something by James Baldwin[67] or anyone of the Black writers in America.

Nzimande had finally registered Sobukwe's articles in March of the previous year, and so Sobukwe's description of the legal practice as 'ours' gives a sense of his growing authority in this realm. It would be fascinating to know what Sobukwe made of Baldwin and other similar African American authors of the period, but, as is affirmed by a subsequent letter, Marquard's attempts to send him such books were to prove unsuccessful.

On 20 April, Sobukwe responded to Bessie Head (Ba10.5), excusing the delay on his having misplaced her letter:

> My dear Bessie,
>
> It was a delight hearing from you [...]

67 James Baldwin was an African American writer who first came to public attention with his novel *Go Tell It on the Mountain* (1953).

In fact, I remember you very well. We met before the campaign as you say. But I had known you through your articles long before Matthew[68] introduced you to me. You were very intellectual and sceptical the day we met – quite suspicious, as many of our intellectuals were of the Africanism we propounded which, I admit, did have some racialist undertones then.

I enjoyed your book immensely and hope you will keep on writing more. I have refused to accept that I can be a 'refugee' anywhere on the continent. How can I, when the whole of it is mine.

It is interesting that Sobukwe recalls Head as 'sceptical [and] suspicious', a very different description from that offered by Bessie herself. After a few thoughts on the unforgiving gardening conditions in Kimberley ('a very dry place [...] We miss the fertile soil of Mofolo[69] and the plentiful rains and water'), Sobukwe reminisces about his time in prison:

Strange as it may seem I kept wondering, while in jail, what could have happened to you. I did not believe that you could last in (was it *Post* or *Drum* or both now?).

We got to know one another very well in jail and were pleasantly surprised by the experiences quite a number of the fellows had acquired through the years. We learnt a lot from each other.

Matthew filled up in jail and became quite handsome! But he remained a journalist, collecting material for a book or some character sketches. I don't know whether he ever wrote that book.

I do not hear anything from and about any of them. But I wish them all well and only hope they further their studies.

Oh yes, my post is censored and I consequently confine myself to the mundane.

It will be a pleasure to hear from you once more.

Affectionately,
Robert

68 Nkoana. See n. 63.

69 In Soweto.

Whereas Sobukwe's letter to Head remained largely formal, Head's response, a mere nine days later (on 29 April) was anything but (Ba10.6). Contact having been made, Bessie treats Sobukwe like a confidant and does not hesitate to vent her frustrations. While it is unnecessary to dwell on all the gossip that Bessie goes on to provide, the picture she paints of Matthew Nkoana – a figure often neglected by historians of the period – and his wife Maria, not to mention the conflict between Nkoana and Leballo, adds much of interest both to the history of the PAC and to the annals of political exile as experienced by anti-apartheid activists in the 1960s.

> Dear brother,
>
> Of course I was mad as hell that you took such a long time to reply! First of all, I have a lot of gossip. I saw Matthew when he came out of jail [...] [he] put on weight, and I agree with you that he looked quite handsome. Then many years later I met his wife in Francistown as we were all refugees together. Maria is such a complicated personality, first of all as a woman, intensely charming, vividly original but underneath that was the most awful pushiness and ambition [...] She insisted that Matthew was going to be the Prime Minister of South Africa one day and that you had always taken a junior role to Matthew. Actually the truth was that the woman had such a brilliant mind, she usually ran Matthew and if he got to be Prime Minister one day, why she would automatically run the government of South Africa [...] Then some time later when she had gone to join Matthew in London she sent me a pamphlet he had written, roundly condemning Potlako and some other fellows who had ousted him from P.A.C. (what there is of it in exile). The storm took place in Tanzania. They asked Nyerere to preside over the quarrel and Potlako and co. officially got Matthew shoved out. Then in retaliation Matthew produced a pamphlet, a short book in which he called Potlako a stunning idiot and a lot of other names which add up to dolt, loony bin, squanderer of money. Matthew got quite hysterical about all the vile names he called Potlako. Then he proceeded to outline his activities in London. They read like a James Hadley Chase novel. Matthew had a bed-sitter in London. He was in and out of cars tracking down South African spies. It seemed to be his major occupation because someone was always ringing him up to tell him of the arrival of a new

> spy in London; 'We talked for a while, then I knew he was a spy,' said the story time and again.

Bessie's flair for storytelling is clearly on display in this rather breathless account. She then switches gears, becoming more sombre and introspective. She relates how she had been transferred to Cape Town after being released from hospital but found herself unable to resume work as she 'could not pull out of the nervous breakdown'. Her short-lived marriage to Harold Head is mentioned, before she continues:

> As for myself, a long winding story leads from the morning I last said goodbye to you at Orlando police station. Not very long after that I tried to commit suicide. It was caused by many things. *Post*[70] transferred me to Cape Town after I came out of hospital and two months later I resigned because I could not work and could not pull out of the nervous breakdown. Then I was married for about a year to a hopeless sort of man and walked out of the house one day. I came to Botswana with my small boy[71] and I have lived here for about eight years. I left on an exit permit. You are quite right to say that it is madness to be a refugee in Africa. The situation is rather hilarious here in Botswana. They go on something terrible about having refugees as though we are not Africans like they are and this is not our land. The real strangers here are the white man and one day the white man will realise this – that when you are a stranger in another man's land you ought to be awfully polite and decent to the owner of the land. Here we have a situation where the owners are dispossessed. It often happens like that, brother, even in family relationships – the more dominant brother chucks the meeker brother out of his own house.

After a few remarks on the relations between the Batswana, the British and 'the Boer' or Afrikaner ('The Botswana [...] are very fond of the story of the three chiefs[72] who went to London to ask the Queen for protection from the

70 *Golden City Post.*

71 Howard Rex Head, born 1962.

72 In 1895 three Batswana chiefs, Bathoen, Khama and Sebele, travelled to London to plead with the British government not to hand over the British Protectorate of Bechuanaland to Cecil Rhodes's predatory company.

Boer [...] It turned out to be a super bargain because today they have a government of their own and the white man is awfully polite and decent here'), she turns to the topic of her most recent novel:

> I am enclosing this letter in my second book: MARU. It is a Setswana title I actually took from the Sesotho word meaning lightning and the name of one of the characters in the book. I wanted a Setswana word to correspond with STORM but I could not get the exact word and in the end settled for *MARU*.[73] You will notice that the dust jacket is designed in the shape of a lightning bolt and indeed the book is a tremendous success in London. It drew some of the best reviews I've had so far, much more than for my first book. It is actually a treatise on racialism as a poison in the human heart whether people are white or black and I chose the Bushman or Masarwa tribe here in Botswana for my jumping off point to hit at this thing in mankind that there must be a high or a low and the low are mercilessly ill-treated. Those who think they are high never think that they may be the most despicable people on earth. The bushmen are terribly despised here and you might have heard about this. So I made a Bushman girl marry one of their chiefs and threatened the whole of Botswana with death if they go on ill-treating the Bushman.
>
> I am suffering terribly as I go to the post office these days because a few weeks ago I posted off the typescript of my third book: A QUESTION OF POWER,[74] and I am waiting to hear from my British publishers about whether it is printable or not. The central characters of the book are Buddha and Jesus and the whole mess of the universe is blamed on Jesus. I am suffering terribly because I fear it may be rejected. It gives me a horrible sensation to open my post office box and find the rejection letter there.

Despite her foregoing remarks on African 'owners of the land' being 'dispossessed' by the white man – comments which would clearly have found their mark in a letter to Sobukwe – Head appears to have hit a wrong note here.

73 *Maru* was published in 1971.

74 Published in 1973 in Heinemann's African Writers Series.

Even though Sobukwe appreciated literary fiction, the story of conflict (or 'racialism') between native peoples of Botswana may have given him pause. And even if this was not particularly an issue, Head's apparent disdain for Christianity probably sat badly with a man who, despite his own apparent crisis of faith on Robben Island, came from a family deeply committed to Methodist Christian values: 'I don't know of any mystical father in the sky who would do what but he does. People are bloody sad to pray to a God they can't see. I like mankind to be God then we won't have that terrible situation we have in South Africa, that's why in my third book I set to work to totally demolish both Buddha and Jesus but I did it much better than Karl Marx.'

There is no record of any further letter from Sobukwe to Head. One suspects that what may have developed into a relationship of shared interests – a mutual love for Africa, or for literature – may have run aground with this letter.

In a letter of 9 May (Bd3.5), Sobukwe lets Nell Marquard know that he has not received the books she had sent: 'I have not yet received Baldwin's books and judging by past experience I am not likely to receive them. The Big Boss has probably decided that I am not mature enough to read those books. Result? They just got lost; they fail to reach their destination. I am told, however, that Baldwin's books are obtainable from the local C.N.A..[75] I'll try and get them. It's just a pity that whoever has the books you sent is not likely to be improved by them.'

One senses a turning point in the letters of this period. Sobukwe is noticeably less reticent to lambast apartheid's petty officials, perhaps feeling that having been denied the prospect of exiting the country, he had nothing to lose in openly stating his views. In the same letter he shares some frank views about Kenneth Kaunda:

> Kaunda's trouble is the trouble of all liberals, Nell. By definition, I think, a liberal cannot be consistent. It is only the communists and the Fascists who can because they bend the facts to fit their ideologies. The liberal, open to new and convincing ideas all the time, must of necessity embrace a superior and more convincing argument.
>
> It is worse when one is in government. But, mind you, detention without trial cannot be excused. If he is a humanist as he claims he

75 The South African news agent and bookstore chain.

> is, then Kaunda must have these men tried. Unfortunately he is trying to be a strong man, probably influenced by some members of the party, and is, in the process, destroying his image and making a fool of himself. Every time he tries this 'kragdadigheid'[76] of his he blunders.

While one might have expected Sobukwe to skirt the issue completely, or defend Kaunda against his detractors – Kaunda being, after all, an inspirational historical figure for Sobukwe and all those committed to the liberation of the African continent – he is willing to call attention to Kaunda's failings. We should be cautious here, however: Kaunda is not subjected to a wholehearted rejection. Even though Sobukwe's critical comments are forthright ('trying to be a strong man', 'making a fool of himself'), Kaunda remains – even if only tentatively – 'a humanist' and, significantly, an *Africanist* humanist, and this for Sobukwe remains a more foundational ethical basis than liberalism. Political liberalism, forever receptive to different perspectives, to new intellectual fads, leads all too easily – particularly under the pressures of governance – to vacillations of judgement. Sobukwe continues, improvising on a refrain, 'What's this country coming to?', that is repeated several times in the course of the letter:

> Things are getting more interesting by the day, both locally and overseas. 'The ungodly', we were told, 'shall neither slumber nor sleep.' But it would appear that the 'godly' too are subject to incurable insomnia.
>
> The tribal universities are, like the Bantustans, turning out other than our lords and masters had intended them. And I think the unkindest cut of all is that Turfloop,[77] the tribal college par excellence, should be, as a certain unsuccessful candidate for the now defunct Native Representative seats said of Fort Hare, 'die broeines van kom[m]unisme',[78] with sit-ups and sit-ins and sit-outs. What's this country coming to?

76 An Afrikaans term, meaning 'uncompromising, heavy-handed forcefulness', which was often applied to the apartheid regime.

77 Turfloop was the name of the town where the University of the North (later merged into the University of Limpopo) was established and was applied colloquially to the university itself.

78 Afrikaans for 'the breeding nest of communism'. On the Native representatives, see this vol., ch. 3, n. 5.

> And the other day, at the Revenue office here, a 'Messenger boy' complained that the 'missus' was attending to the White queue and ignoring them. A White man told him to shut up or else ... 'Ag nee baas'[79] said he, 'Jy praat nou ou tye se goed. Ons word nie meer ge——.'[80] What are things coming to?

Sobukwe's choice of words here is rather decorous. He alludes to, yet doesn't quite come out with, the vulgar phrase 'Ons word nie meer gemoer/gebliksem nie': that is, politely stated, 'We are no longer going to be beaten up.' Whether his avoidance of the crude term is a function of whom he is writing to or simply the result of his own sense of politeness and formality is hard to say, although both considerations seem to play their part here.

Regarding the broader thrust of Sobukwe's narrative, it is tempting to read his comments as prefiguring, if not the defiant political stance of the emerging Black Consciousness Movement, then the explosion of anti-apartheid political resistance that erupted in Soweto in 1976. While there may be something to be said for such a reading, we should bear in mind that the PAC's status campaign of 1958 had already, more than a decade earlier, taken aim both at such infantilising terms of reference and the pervasive apartheid logic according to which 'non-whites' should always give way to whites.

Two of Sobukwe's closing remarks deserve further comment:

> A friend of mine Jeff May, told me he was going to Cape Town and I asked him to call on you. But I don't think I need to warn you Nell that these are not my 'political' friends. They are my social friends with whom I discuss literature and the cinema and, perhaps, Timol and Maisels.[81]

79 Oh no, boss.

80 You are talking about things from the past. We are no longer to be [fucked up].

81 Ahmed Timol, an anti-apartheid activist and leader of the underground Communist Party, was arrested on 22 October 1971 in Johannesburg, tortured in police custody, and died five days later. Police claimed he died after jumping out of a window on the top floor of John Vorster Square in Johannesburg. The lawyer Israel A. Maisels, who led the defence of the 156 defendants in the Treason Trial of 1956–1961, represented the Timol family at the inquest into his death. In 2017, a judicial review of the Timol case found that he was murdered in police custody.

How are you and Leo getting on? As soon as my ban is lifted I'll drive down to Cape Town and spend a fortnight with you and let Blaar Coetzee[82] and his gang try and tell me I may not!

Sobukwe's assurance to Nell that Jeff May was 'not [one of his] "political" friends' poses, at least to the curious reader, the question whether Sobukwe was in fact still meeting with such friends. If one were to limit one's reading of Sobukwe's 1972 archived correspondence to the Marquard letters, it would be easy to get the impression that he was largely steering clear of political involvement and limiting his political activities – and communications – to what could be safely conveyed in letters. As it turns out, there was a definite flipside to this 'safe' correspondence.

That year Sobukwe met with Steve Biko. We know this because Biko himself offered this information when giving evidence in the 1976 SASO–BPC (South African Students Organisation–Black People's Convention) trial. Under cross-examination by the state prosecutor, Advocate Attwell, Biko offered the following (Arnold 1979, 179–180):

BIKO. I have met Mr. Sobukwe …
ATTWELL. In what connection?
BIKO. Because I wanted to meet him.
ATTWELL. When was this, Mr. Biko?
BIKO. It was in 1972.
ATTWELL. Was there anything specific you wanted to know from him?
BIKO. Well, no. I was on a tour of the country for Black Community purposes … because we were in Kimberley of course we took the opportunity of seeing Mr. Sobukwe.
ATTWELL. When in 1972 would this have been?
BIKO. This was about September, late August – September.

82 Blaar Coetzee served as minister of community development and public works under B.J. Vorster. As such, he controlled access to public facilities and residential spaces for the different 'races' in the country. Ironically, upon his retirement from politics in 1972, he was appointed ambassador to Rome, but was recalled a mere six months later because he deigned to criticise the government for not allowing 'coloureds' to attend events at the newly opened Nico Malan Theatre in Cape Town.

This brief snippet of testimony is telling because it affirms what we subsequently know to be the case: Sobukwe was meeting with an increasing number of activists and political leaders at the time.[83] Commenting on this period, Pogrund (1997, 350) remarks that 'BC [Black Consciousness] leaders regularly visited [Sobukwe], in defiance of his bans, slipping in and out of Kimberley under the noses of the Security Police as part of their consultations with leaders of different organizations'. Pogrund cites Saths Cooper (elected secretary of the BPC in 1972), who observed that 'He [Sobukwe] was consulted. His opinions were solicited and in effect his encouragement and blessings were received ... He was seen as one of the progenitors, one of the key thinkers, in the run-up to the development of Black Consciousness.' While the government's refusal to allow the Sobukwes to leave the country – which would have brought to an end his family's 'internal exile' – would obviously have been a bitter pill to swallow, this state of dejection was perhaps somewhat offset through his veneration by a younger generation of activists, who saw him not only as a veteran of the struggle, but as a progenitor of one of the most vital chapters in its history: that of Black Consciousness.

In commenting on his father's interest in black politics during his time in Kimberley, Dini Sobukwe remarked in an interview (with Derek Hook, 29 May 2014):

> Black Consciousness gave hope again because after 1960 things got terribly scary and people were just lying low ... and a lot had gone into exile as well ... Black Consciousness was able to get things at least moving and people inspired ... A lot of the discussions [Sobukwe had with visitors] were really about things like that. He was terribly, very, very excited about that ... there were still colleagues they talked to about the PAC ... They weren't of course supposed to talk or even meet ... One journalist asked him whether, it was a provocative question, whether he was still a member of the PAC. He said 'I never resigned'.

83 Consider, for example, Mogobe Bernard Ramose's description of visiting Sobukwe – along with a group of other Black Consciousness activists – in Kimberley during the 1970s: 'One of the things that struck me', Ramose recalled, 'was just his calmness. A very calm gentleman ... But it didn't mean that beneath the calmness there was no revolutionary fire' (Ramose and Hook 2016, 88).

11. Peter Magubane captured many memorable images of Sobukwe, including this double portrait, in which he and Sobukwe are clearly enjoying each other's company. (Photo by Peter Magubane, © Peter Magubane / David Gollan)

Several weeks after his missive to Nell Marquard, Sobukwe followed up with a further letter on 13 July (Bd3.6) in which he returned to many of the same topics. His exchanges with Marquard were clearly of value to him – she features prominently as a correspondent in the letters that have survived from this period – particularly because they afforded him the opportunity to think through and clarify his positions on a variety of important issues. He reports briefly on current events before offering a series of clarifications regarding his earlier letter: 'So much has happened during the past few weeks: the Storm-troopers in action at St George's Cathedral[84] and at the Wits and the Murray tribe gathering under the biggest vine in the world.'[85]

Even though references to current political events sometimes seem rather scant in his letters to Marquard, these short notes are evidence that Sobukwe had his finger on the pulse of anti-apartheid initiatives across the political

84 A protest by students from the University of Cape Town was held outside St George's Cathedral on 2 June 1972 and broken up by police, who baton-charged the students.

85 Nell Marquard was descended from the Murray family, who held a family gathering at Graaff-Reinet at Reinet House, where what is now the oldest vine in the country was planted by a forebear.

spectrum. The protests Sobukwe refers to here are of a particularly unique sort in that they not only involved large-scale protests by white students, but also that police brutality against those students was on full public display. Early in the year, black students at Fort Hare and the University of Zululand joined protesting students at Turfloop (now the University of Limpopo), incensed at the expulsion of a prominent student activist, Onkgopotse Tiro.[86] These protests spilled over to white campuses, where students also took up the issue of racially based quotas at universities. Peaceful protests at Wits University and by University of Cape Town students on the steps of St George's Cathedral were violently broken up by police. One might speculate that these events marked a kind of turning point, an anticipation of the wider non-racial anti-apartheid struggle that would start to coalesce in the later 1970s and early 1980s.

Sobukwe continues, forever attentive to literary details, expressing the need to correct an earlier biblical reference: 'Incidentally, about the quotation from the Scriptures, it was a deliberate misquotation. A friend of mine, in the days of our wine, used to say that the oppressor could not afford to sleep lest the oppressed wake up while he was asleep. Hence the adaptation to the "ungodly shall neither slumber nor sleep".' In respect of the biblical quote, Sobukwe is improvising on Psalm 121, which reads in part as follows: 'Indeed, he who watches over Israel will neither slumber nor sleep [...] The sun will not harm you by day, nor the moon by night [...] The LORD will watch over your coming and going both now and forevermore.' With this neat reversal of the biblical proverb (it is the godly who keep watch in the original, as opposed to the ungodly), Sobukwe finds a novel way of describing the anxious underside of apartheid racism, the unspoken fears of the oppressor that they will one day be replaced. Put differently, for every criminal on the run there is always the niggling anxiety whether this will be the day they are caught. Sobukwe was

86 Onkgopotse Tiro was an influential student activist at the University of the North and proponent of the nascent Black Consciousness Movement. After leaving South Africa in 1974, a mere two years after being expelled from the university, he was assassinated in Botswana, after opening a parcel bomb sent by the Bureau for State Security. What was particularly cruel and callous was that the parcel was stamped as coming from the International University Exchange Fund (where the South African spy Craig Williamson was based), and Tiro must have opened it eagerly, having just applied to continue his studies through the University of South Africa. Suspicions that the apartheid government must have been responsible were confirmed in 1981, when it was revealed as the work of BOSS.

always adept at using literary references – and, in the most inclusive sense, utilising Xhosa proverbs, quotes from contemporary fiction, philosophical or religious aphorisms, and citations from Shakespeare – to convey his thoughts in a distinctive and memorable way.

Then comes the topic that Sobukwe was clearly keen to expand upon: the role – and, more significantly, the failings – of liberals in politics:

> In my previous letter I perhaps did not express myself well regarding the political instability of the liberal. The point I was trying to make – made earlier by no other than Hitler – is that the intellectual is the most unreliable person because he is open to conviction. The Communist and the Fascist argue, like Jehovah's witnesses, within a prescribed framework, they do not permit argument to range outside this framework.
>
> The intellectual – which Liberals generally are – delights in exploring new fields and is ready to admit the cogency of an argument. He is thus able to say 'In the circumstances, given that premise, the argument is unchallengeable'. Now in politics Nell, the *Vulgus*[87] wants clean cut answers, a yea or a nay. And if Alan Paton,[88] in all sincerity, is to be heard to say that there might be some good in apartheid – which there probably might be – to the oppressed he has ranged himself on the side of the oppressor. The Communist and the Fascist will give a resounding No and Yes respectively to Apartheid – no qualifications. But the Liberal must be intellectually honest and must above all not be dogmatic, we believe. We call it independence of mind. But it can be very dangerous in politics.
>
> I'll anticipate your retort and agree that the Liberal himself has some basic tenets of faith against which he measures all ideologies and policies. But then these are ideals. If he can be persuaded that things are moving in that direction and that he must not be in a hurry, the steam is taken out of him. For by definition, he is incapable of indignation. He abhors violence and in seeking to avoid it, finds it his duty and task to persuade the indignant to 'cool it'. That, as

87 Latin for 'the people'.

88 The author and liberal Alan Paton. This comment is of a piece with a report of an interview with Paton in the *New York Times* of 2 November 1974 where he said that while apartheid was immoral, the idea of the development of the Bantustans was a good thing.

> you know, is already the advice the Liberals are giving to students. All peacemakers find it easier to persuade the weak to bear his burden than to persuade the strong and aggressive to refrain from their aggression. It is easier to persuade Poland to yield to Hitler's demands than to persuade Hitler to desist from making such demands.

Sobukwe seems far more content with these further articulations of his views on liberalism than he was with his remarks of 9 May. One turn of phrase that deserves further comment here is Sobukwe's qualification, at first glance somewhat incongruous, that – at least in terms of Alan Paton's world view – 'there might be some good in apartheid'. Sobukwe's stance here is to point to what would appear to be 'good' in apartheid, from the perspective of the oppressor, namely those apparent 'benefits' typically associated with the white 'civilising' colonial project, i.e. Western culture, education, religion, ostensibly democratic governance structures and so on. Quite clearly, such apparent 'goods' are anything but beneficial from the perspective of a colonised people. Moreover, one may argue that the 'good' of apartheid for the oppressed might well be in the awakening of a revolutionary spirit, and for the recognition of dignity and respect in a Pan-Africanist pride and revival.[89]

He then returns to the topic of Kaunda, in respect of which his remarks are likewise clarifying, before going on to make a rather audacious claim:

> As for Kaunda, he is a kind-hearted, good and honest man. But he does not understand power politics. He reacts to a national situation as though he were faced with an individual. That is why he so often acts out of character. His attitude seems to be: 'you think because I am a humanist I am a fool. I'll show you'. And he blunders, politically. In fact I am convinced now that Africa – the whole of it – will never have a really 'good' government until I assume the Presidency of a United States of Africa. It isn't that I am power-hungry. In fact I don't care for the position. I would be happier as a farmer or a teacher. But I can no longer resist the demand of events and history that I should

89 In this respect one might refer to Frantz Fanon's *Black Skin, White Masks* (2008 [1967]). Fanon, extemporising on Hegel, asserts that a new humanist dawn would arise from an 'authentic upheaval' of the masses, forged in 'the seriousness, the suffering, the patience, and the labor of the negative'.

> assume the leadership of the continent! So speaks a megalomaniac: in all sincerity.
>
> I have written a lot already but have not touched on all the points I should have liked to touch.
>
> But I would like to end by saying that the lot of the Liberal, whatever his colour or class is most unenviable. By his group or class he is regarded as a renegade, a traitor to the best interests of the group or class. By the oppressed he is viewed with suspicion as the expert salesman of the policies of the oppressor. He needs to be absolutely convinced of the justice of his cause, to persevere.

This requires little by way of further elaboration. Sobukwe is, in fact, crystal clear, combining a well-placed jab at Alan Paton with a stark warning regarding the 'slowly, slowly' appeasement strategies of those white liberals who are afraid of anything too radical, too disruptive, too aggressive. We find among these lines perhaps Sobukwe's most memorable pronouncement on liberals: 'By his group [...] he is regarded as a renegade, a traitor. By the oppressed he is viewed [...] as the salesman of the policies of the oppressor.' What this pithy analysis makes evident is that Sobukwe is definitively not a liberal, even though he nevertheless demonstrates considerable insight into the challenges confronting those of his friends (including Marquard herself) who would identify as such.

What, though, to make of Sobukwe's thoughts on his assuming the presidency of a United States of Africa? At first glance it seems difficult to determine if this is said in a somewhat flippant and idealistic or, alternatively, in a serious manner. There is a sense in which we could say that Sobukwe is speaking at both levels simultaneously, his meaning being contingent on how his readers engage with both him and his Pan-Africanist vision. Interestingly, the reference to assuming such a position is repeated in a letter to Pogrund on 15 January 1973 (Ba10.9), where Sobukwe mentions, somewhat casually, that foreign visitors meeting with him would have 'the honour [...] of talking to the future President of the United States of Africa'. While one might read this as self-deprecatory, the very fact of its repetition suggests that the comment is more than mere whimsy.

What seems sure is that this remark is not driven by mere hubris. Sobukwe's sincere conviction is that he does have the adequate temperament and leadership skills to handle 'power politics' at the highest level.

He is likewise assured that he would not succumb to the capriciousness of the liberal whose values are always contingent on what, intellectually, seems the most satisfying argument. One is reminded of Gerhart's written comments, after her interview with Sobukwe in 1970 (this vol., ch. 11): 'he had [...] complete confidence in his own principles [...] he was confident of being able to win anyone's respect'. In other words, Sobukwe's confidence in his leadership and his Pan-Africanist political vision, like the depth of his commitment to such values, was simply not in question. And so, while from our current historical standpoint, the goal of such an office (a presidency of a United States of Africa) might seem so remote as to be positively utopian, this need not have been the case for Sobukwe in an era that was witnessing what Harold Macmillan called the wind of change blowing through Africa, which is to say, the liberation and newly independent status being won by numerous African states.[90] Unachievable as such a goal may sound, one would have to say that if there were ever a visionary Pan-Africanist leader who could inspire belief in such an ideal, it would have been Sobukwe himself.[91] Added to this is the fact that Sobukwe, as we shall increasingly see, was not pursuing incremental political change, a politics of alliances, or even a politics of the possible; what revolutionary agenda, we might ask, ever pursued a merely realistic as opposed to a utopian goal?[92]

On 21 September, Sobukwe wrote to Pogrund (Ba10.7) informing him that payment was being demanded from him, 'of the sum of R1102.91 being taxed costs in the matter of R.M. SOBUKWE versus THE MINSTER OF

---

90 It helps to add a few historical points by way of contextualising Sobukwe's decolonial aspirations. Consider Quinn Slobodian's (2023) remarks on apartheid South Africa: 'In the 1970s, apartheid South Africa was in the midst of a [...] crisis. Since the 1950s, new flags had risen one by one across the African continent. Where once flew union jacks and the blue-white-and-red of the French tricolore now waved the Maasai shield of Kenya, the crane of Uganda and the black star of Ghana. When Portugal finally quit Africa [...] Angola put a machete on its flag, and Mozambique chose [...] the AK-47. Rhodesia became Zimbabwe in 1980, making South Africa's white minority rule an even more striking aberration.'

91 Pogrund's (1997, 348) comments on Sobukwe's dedication to his political vision deserve to be cited here. During his time in Kimberley, Sobukwe 'remained thoroughly committed to every one of his Africanist ideals. He believed as deeply as ever in his own relevance and that circumstances would inevitably draw him into the politics of power. This was a theme he constantly voiced to me, always in the most matter-of-fact way, as something which was so obvious that it did not bear elaboration or discussion.'

92 For an instructive description of how Sobukwe's political project differed fundamentally from a politics of negotiated pragmatism, that is, from politics 'as the art of the possible', and represents instead *a* logic of the impossible, see Delport (2016).

JUSTICE, the amount to be paid within 14 days of writing'. If one needed any further proof of the pettiness of the apartheid authorities or of the unending nature of the harassment to which they subjected Sobukwe, it was this. Sobukwe puts this amount in context, before adding a note of stoic resolve:

> I am tempted to tell them to go ahead with their action [...] I earn R50.00 a month and my expenditure amounts to R120.00 a month. I am, consequently, perpetually in debt. In fact, I am an insolvent. Let them go ahead then.
>
> [...]
>
> Looking forward to seeing you in the flesh instead of pictures posing as a representative of the establishment bearded and suited.
>
> Love to Anne and the kids.
>
> Bob
> OR RATHER
> Mangaliso ka-Sobukwe

This is an uncharacteristic way of signing off for Sobukwe or, rather, it combines his usual sign-off to Pogrund ('Bob') with an alternative mode of identification, namely the non-anglicised, African, isiXhosa name 'Mangaliso' with the proud prefix 'ka', meaning 'son of' Sobukwe – a reiteration of the legacy of his African ancestry.

On 26 September, there is another letter to Nell Marquard (Bd3.7). Sobukwe responds to a question from his Cape correspondent, and expresses admiration for the satirical tradition of *Punch* magazine:

> No you did not send me a copy of Leo's book on federation[93] and I certainly would love to have it. The only intellectual contact I have these days is through books. And federation is quite an issue these days. But the U.P.[94] we will have to count out, I think. They are incorrigible.
>
> I enjoyed the issue of 'Punch going Communist' very much. It is so rare to read a newspaper where the government and cabinet

93 Leo Marquard, *A Federation of Southern Africa* (1971).

94 The United Party, the official opposition in Parliament.

> ministers are treated as fallible human beings, not particularly intelligent at that.
>
> [...]
>
> I am doing South African Bantu and Native Law this year as one of my subjects and am reading a lot on Theophilus Shepstone[95] of whom my lecturers have a very high opinion. And the reason is obvious. He is the father of apartheid.

Sobukwe seems to be both polite and somewhat guarded here inasmuch as he would, presumably, have viewed a federalist approach to South Africa with more than a degree of suspicion, particularly if it amounted to little more than a revised form of a Bantustan vision of separate development. Even if regions or states within a federation could avoid organisation along the lines of majority ethnic groupings, for example by a solely geographical standard, the consequence would still be that certain regions would have disproportionate access to resources, and white dominance and privilege would be maintained, thereby failing to address fundamental and historical inequities of the national black majority. The comment on Shepstone is historically astute. It offers a different presumptive starting point and forebear than is typically the case when it comes to tracing the origin of apartheid's legislative logic of segregation (there is a tendency to focus on the role of Hendrik Verwoerd and the formal institutionalisation of apartheid policies in 1948). It helps to bear in mind here that it was Sobukwe's exposure to the policies of so-called Native Administration that played such a crucial part in igniting his political consciousness and his lifelong fight against white supremacy.

On 8 November Sobukwe prepared a short note to Pogrund (Ba10.8): 'There's nothing new to report, except that it is quite comforting to know that it is the Broederbond who are running the country. It helps to explain the

95 For all the easy attribution of apartheid to the Nationalist government, Sobukwe's astute insight here is that the ground for apartheid was prepared much earlier, notably by Sir Theophilus Shepstone, Secretary for Native Affairs in the British colony of Natal in the mid-1800s. Shepstone negotiated treaties to acquire vast tracts of land for the Crown, but he did so in a deliberate way both to ensure a steady 'native' workforce and to concentrate indigenous peoples in manageable, bordered geographies. The apartheid creation of Bantustans, or 'homelands' for different African ethnic groups, could thus be easily erected on Shepstone's 'foundations'.

crass stupidity and cretinous performance of the country's Prime Minister.[96] I found it quite depressing to think that a man who belonged to the legal profession could really be so stupid. Now I understand. Poor fellow. He's like the "front leaders" of later ANC days.'

Sobukwe has John Vorster in mind here, a figure whose extreme right-wing views are highlighted in the reference to 'the Broederbond'. Somewhat surprising is the comparison Sobukwe offers between Vorster and the 'front leaders' of 'later ANC days'. One assumes that with this comment he seeks to stress that certain 'figurehead leaders' are not always those capable of true leadership. For Sobukwe, representing the organisation publicly as spokespersons, but without being a member of the organisation as such, implied a certain committed distance from the organisation's beliefs and aims, as well as, more importantly, from the needs and demands of the people themselves. One has sympathy for a banned organisation wishing to maintain some presence, and means to convey its messages and goals, but the 'front leaders' (who were also not elected by members) almost inevitably engage in strategic politics, in 'the art of the possible', to the disadvantage of people's needs and demands. This was not Sobukwe's committed and ethically steadfast way, because such coalitions would inevitably divert the course of the struggle, diluting it, taking it out of the hands of those most oppressed by apartheid – African men and women.

1973: '[It is] rather petulant and fractious of late'

Sobukwe's letter to Pogrund of 15 January 1973 captures him in fine form (Ba10.9). There is affectionate irreverence in relation to religious holidays, a dig at the idea of New Year's celebrations, and a joke disparaging the Bantustan system:

> We've just finished celebrating the Christian's New Year, the Jews and Muslims having done their thing earlier.

---

96 B.J. Vorster. The Broederbond (Band of Brothers) was a secret society of leading Afrikaners who exerted an influence on South African society and government from behind the scenes in order to advance the Afrikaner nationalist cause, and to secure the appointment of Broeders in senior positions in government and the state.

> I am understandably quite unhappy about the present position and have been thinking seriously of having a Black New Year – a traditional New Year, so to speak. If it is necessary, that is, to celebrate New Year's day at all. After all each day is much like the one before, with nothing to tell, except our watches and self made calendars, that we have passed into another year.
>
> Why you guys should take Christmas off, though, I don't know. You have so many holidays of your own that it is really unfair on your poor Christian colleagues who have to work during your holidays. I think the Genootschap[97] for Afrikaans culture must be approached about this unfair treatment of Christians and preferential treatment of Jews and Muslims.
>
> Somebody, an ordinary Bantu lad, has just suggested that Bantustans are properly so named because that is where it is intended the Bantu should 'staan'[98] and make no progress whatsoever. Amusing how these Bantu can think isn't it.
>
> They are of course getting out of hand. Like the one who told a garage owner who threatened to assault him (they were quarrelling over the repairs affected on the Bantu's car) 'Don't show me your class', the Bantu said, 'I know it.'

If one is well versed in the codes of this friendship – by now more than a decade old – one realises that there is much more to this than the levity that seems so focal at first glance. The reference to a 'Black New Year' seems, for example, a pointed reminder that many lack the privilege to treat this day as a celebration, as a day where they have the option of absenting themselves from work. That is, New Year's day is 'traditionally' not a holiday for black workers who must work in service industries of all kinds attending to vacationing whites. Moreover, the 'Don't show me your class' anecdote – so similar to the 'Ag nee baas' or 'Messenger boy' story told to Marquard the previous year – is not so much funny as cutting, containing as it does the warning that the old

---

97 Recalling the well-known Genootskap van Regte Afrikaners (Society of True Afrikaners), which had been formed in the late 1800s to promote the Afrikaans language (Sobukwe uses an older, Dutch spelling of the word).

98 Afrikaans for 'stand still'.

intimidation tactics of white racism will no longer be countenanced without a defiant response.

A short note to Marquard on 18 January (Bd3.8) thanks her for her Christmas card and gift, relates news about his studies ('I got my legal subjects and did so well in Latin that I earned the right to write a supplementary examination in February')[99] and lets her know that 'The tribe is dispersing', which is to say that his children and visiting brother will soon be leaving after their Christmas visit. Continuing, he remarks on the weather, on recent events across the border and some less than complimentary thoughts on Idi Amin.[100]

> It's terribly hot out here and since the prayers on Monday the temperatures have been singularly high. Some people here feel we may have adopted the wrong approach in reminding God, so to speak, of his responsibilities! That's what comes of anthropomorphizing God.
>
> So we have another confrontation on the Zambesi? If Amin keeps out of it the situation[101] is not particularly dangerous. But with a madman around there's no telling what fuse may be lit.
>
> I enjoyed 'On the Sabbath, the Rabbi went hungry'[102] and have been studying Leo's thoughts on Federation. I hope to send you my comments on that.

---

99 There is humorous and self-deprecating irony here. Being granted a supplementary exam meant that one did not pass outright, but also did not do so poorly as to fail outright. Hence, one got another, supplementary opportunity to write the exam.

100 Idi Amin was the brutal and dictatorial president of Uganda from 1971 to 1979, after seizing power from Milton Obote in a military coup. He had already expelled Uganda's Asian community from the country, and confiscated their properties and businesses.

101 One cannot be entirely sure if there was a specific incident Sobukwe had in mind, save for the truth of a general 'instability' around the Zambezi River, with freedom movements in Mozambique and Rhodesia (Zimbabwe) using the area as a staging ground to mount attacks. There were, for example, two notable events in December 1972. A raid on a farm on 21 December 1972 by a Zimbabwe African National Liberation Army (ZANLA) unit is often considered the beginning of the 'second and sustained' phase (the 'Second Chimurenga') of the Rhodesian Bush War, also known as the Zimbabwe War of Liberation. Also, on 16 December 1972, the civilian population of a Mozambican village was massacred by Portuguese soldiers, leading to an escalation of fighting between Frelimo and colonial authorities in the Mozambican War of Independence. The point is that the area was a veritable powder keg which could do well without the interference of Idi Amin.

102 Harry Kemelman's mystery novel, *Saturday the Rabbi Went Hungry* (1966).

Sobukwe is effusive in his letter of 5 February to Anne Pogrund (Ba10.10), congratulating her on the birth of her son Gideon (on 6 January), and offering a few additional wide-ranging thoughts:

> Immediately I received the good news from Benjie I phoned the nursing home. But I had the 'engaged' signal every time I phoned, throughout the day. And it did not occur to me then to send a telegram; I hoped to get through. The next day I was caught up in office routine and I did not remember to phone again. And so it went.
>
> However, better late than never. We (I am using the royal 'we') are delighted at this addition to the family though we feel he could have chosen a more propitious moment for his advent; not when the cost of living is soaring, borders are being closed and terrorism, legal and illegal is the order of the day throughout the world.

Before closing, Sobukwe, perhaps casting about for a conversational topic, makes mention of the daughter of the first president of Botswana:

> I've just read this month's *Drum* and learn that Jackie Khama, Sir Seretse Khama's[103] daughter underwent plastic surgery to have her nose straightened and her lips trimmed! She married a Hollander two weeks ago and was able to put a fairly straight nose against his and fairly thin lips against his.
>
> I wonder what she will do when very full lips and broad noses become fashionable in the same way as bare breasts and 'Afro' hair – the 'wooly hair' of white novelists of a few decades ago – are becoming fashionable.

The ambition of conforming to white European standards of beauty clearly makes no sense to Sobukwe, especially given the dilemma he imagines Jackie

103 Seretse Khama was the first president of an independent Botswana, one of the most stable and successful countries in Africa. He had married a British woman, Ruth Williams, against the racial objections of both the colonial authorities and his own traditional elders. Sobukwe's comments, which highlight the unfortunate circumstances under which even a biracial child may hanker after the physical attributes of whiteness, still have pertinence today.

12. Sobukwe, in a rare visit to Johannesburg in 1973, posing in Mofolo, Soweto. (Photo by Ralph Ndawo, © Ralph Ndawo, with kind permission of Rachel Ndawo)

Khama confronting in the future: of needing to reverse course when African as opposed to European bodies are held up as ideals of beauty.

In July, Sobukwe was finally given permission to travel from Kimberley to Johannesburg to visit his son Dalindyebo, who was in hospital. The conditions for this and all of Sobukwe's subsequent trips were strict. Typically, Sobukwe was granted only 24 hours. This gave him a midnight-to-midnight window in which to make the outbound trip – which involved being driven through the night by his friend Achmat Laher[104] – to spend a few precious if fleeting hours with family and friends, and then, exhaustingly, to embark on the return journey. Sobukwe needed to check in with the police both upon departure and return.

There was an unexpected event during this visit: a chance encounter with Mangosuthu Gatsha Buthelezi[105] in, of all places, a Johannesburg clothing store.

104 Achmat Laher owned a shoe shop in Kimberley. He and his partner Fatima became firm friends of the Sobukwe family, and he proved particularly helpful to Sobukwe.

105 Initially a member of the ANC and an apartheid critic, Mangosuthu 'Gatsha' Buthelezi parlayed his royal Zulu lineage to great advantage. His increasingly vocal advocacy of Zulu identity and close ties to the Zulu monarchy would have sat uncomfortably with

13. Sobukwe, in Mofolo, Soweto, 1973. It is telling that Sobukwe is pictured alongside a car. Given that he was typically permitted to be away from Kimberley for only 24 hours, all his stop-offs in Johannesburg would have had to be kept to an absolute minimum, and he would have had to drive through the night. (Photo by Ralph Ndawo, © Ralph Ndawo, with kind permission of Rachel Ndawo)

While there is much evidence suggesting that Buthelezi had wanted to contact Sobukwe prior to this meeting – they had been contemporaries at Fort Hare in the 1940s and thus had met before – Sobukwe, by contrast, upon learning that Buthelezi was in the building, proved far more reticent. This stands to reason; although Buthelezi was an important African leader – he was both a Zulu prince and chief minister of the KwaZulu Bantustan – Sobukwe would not have wanted to confer any semblance of legitimacy on the Bantustan system that Buthelezi represented. While much awkwardness ensued – each man, it

Sobukwe. Buthelezi played a controversial role in anti-apartheid politics, because of his ethnic and Zulu nationalism as well as his willingness to work with the apartheid government, becoming chief minister of the KwaZulu Bantustan in 1977. He was branded a 'sell-out' and opportunist by the liberation movements, and public hostility to him was evinced at Sobukwe's funeral, which Buthelezi attempted to attend, only to be chased away.

14. A chance encounter. On a short trip to Johannesburg in July 1973, Sobukwe, accompanied by Pogrund, visited a Johannesburg clothing store, only to discover that Mangosuthu Buthelezi was there at the same time. Pogrund captured this image of the two men. (Photo by Benjamin Pogrund, with kind permission)

appears, waited for the other to come to him – a public meeting did follow, the two men briefly embracing and chatting with each other.

After a break of eight months, Sobukwe wrote to Mrs Marquard on 4 September (Bd3.9). He mentions that he has been in bed ill, and offers a few witty related comments:

> I fell ill [...] and have been in bed till Monday, the 27th August, 1973. It's this English flu – as sly and cunning as the people who gave it birth. How I wish we could have, just for once, a truly non-national flu, devoid of any national characteristics. I had thought I would prefer a Sotho flu: but then I remembered Moshesh's[106] cunning and wily character and felt it would be no improvement on the present scourge.

106 Moshesh, one of multiple alternative spellings of Moshoeshoe I, the first king of Lesotho, who reigned from 1822 to 1870.

> We read Leo's address[107] – an excerpt – in the *Rand Daily Mail* with pleasure and delight. It was a fine address, simple and straightforward with no Cicerian [*sic*] flourishes.[108] He got his message across all right. And of course we thought the honour long overdue.

There are a few further short comments on recent political developments, although one cannot help feeling that Sobukwe's rather circumscribed remarks are but the tip of the iceberg relative to his broader political aspirations and wishes: 'The Nats and the U.P. are becoming quite an entertaining lot of clowns. Unfortunately there is little to hope for from both Verligte Action[109] and Gerdener's party.[110] Any party that starts from the premise of separate development or multi-nationalism or whatever the new euphemism is, is a non-starter. It will be playing at white politics like the major white parties. It is our young people who will force a solution on their elders.'

While neither Verligte Action nor Gerdener's party went on to gain much traction, Sobukwe's mention of them suffices to highlight that cracks were beginning to show in the edifice of Afrikaner nationalism. Now while this might seem only a case of 'playing at White politics', the fact that rifts were opening up in the National Party was surely reason for some optimism. Significantly, both these initiatives were the result of white Afrikaners wishing to break from the apartheid party line.

Interesting also is Sobukwe's dismissal of any political party adopting the premise of 'multi-nationalism'. While in his correspondence with Marquard he has shown interest in her husband's work of federalism, even expressing a friend's support and enthusiasm for Leo's speeches and writings, here he cuts to the chase by stating quite openly that any euphemistic variation on the doctrine of separate development is 'a non-starter'. It is hard not to think of Biko and associated Black Consciousness leaders in respect of Sobukwe's

107 Leo Marquard's address on the occasion of his receiving an honorary doctorate of laws from the University of the Witwatersrand in 1973.

108 A reference to Cicero's rhetorical abilities.

109 Verligte Aksie (Enlightened Action) was a group formed in 1972 of mostly Afrikaner intellectuals and professionals who, at a time of deep division in the National Party between *verligtes* and *verkramptes* (progressives/the enlightened and conservatives), sought to advance the progressive cause and 'build bridges' within South African society.

110 In 1973 the former interior minister, Theo Gerdener, broke away from the ruling National Party and formed the Democratic Party. The party sought to attract *verligte* (enlightened) Nationalists who had grown disillusioned with the hardline apartheid government of B.J. Vorster and aimed to garner support from younger Afrikaners.

closing line ('It is our young people who will force a solution on their elders'), especially given that we know that by now Sobukwe had met with a number of such comrades, even if the immediate context of his remarks might lead the reader (or Marquard) to think he is referring to 'White politics'.

Sobukwe's last letter of the year to Marquard (on 16 October) makes reference to a series of recent events – familial, social, political – and fills her in on how things are going with his studies (Bd3.10):

> I am away from the office this week, swotting for the exams. I had overestimated my command of Afrikaans and am battling with H.J. J.M. van der Merwe's books – *Lees- en Skryftekens*; *Afrikaans Sy Aard en Ontwikkeling* and *Die Korrekte Woord*.[111] It is all a bit confusing.
>
> We are sorry to hear about Leo's misfortunes and hope he will recover completely and soon. His ideas are being taken up left right and centre and one would wish him to be in perfect health to be able to give the necessary advice and to guard against their distortion.
>
> Jack Unterhalter[112] was here last month to defend David Russel [*sic*],[113] the young Anglican priest of Dimbaza. He told me he had met you when Leo had gone for his capping to Johannesburg.[114]
>
> So we are once more in the midst of a new Schlebusch crisis[115] with rather 'big' names involved. Were it not so serious it would seem rather amusing to see these serious and studious men wearing heavy spectacles setting out deliberately to defy the law, and yet being puzzled at the intense feeling their actions have aroused in certain quarters.

---

111 Respectively, *Punctuation*; *Afrikaans, Its Nature and Development*; *The Correct Word*.

112 A lawyer and member of the Liberal Party, Jack Unterhalter was known to represent and defend anti-apartheid activists in court.

113 David Russell was an Anglican clergyman (and, later, bishop), who befriended Steve Biko and supported the Black Consciousness Movement. After moving to King Williamstown in 1970, he chose to work among the people of Dimbaza in the Eastern Cape who had been dumped in this resettlement camp by the apartheid state after being ejected from the farms and small towns of 'white' South Africa.

114 See n. 107.

115 Alwyn Schlebusch, a National Party politician, was appointed chair of the Schlebusch Commission, established in 1972 by the Vorster administration to investigate anti-apartheid organisations like NUSAS, the Institute of Race Relations and the Christian Institute. It also had the power to seize the assets and cut off the foreign funding of these organisations.

The brief note of concern for Leo was to prove, unfortunately, prescient in respect of the older man's failing health. Sobukwe's reference to their mutual friend Jack Unterhalter is of historical interest, pointing as it does to a confluence of varied anti-apartheid groups and initiatives (including the activities of the Liberal Party, and Black Consciousness developments in the Eastern Cape) gaining momentum across the country. Sobukwe signs off with a series of literary allusions:

> Yes the weather is really becoming rather petulant and fractious of late, like Pope's[116] feverish patient who tosses about in bed. Incidentally, I have just discovered that the adjective derived from Cicero is Ciceronian. So please make the necessary correction in my letter.
>
> I won't comment on the political situation either nationally or internationally. It's the same answers to the same questions: a curse on both your houses kind of situation.[117]

1974: 'We cannot feel it as the one who suffers it'

There are relatively few surviving letters from 1974, perhaps partly owing to the fact that Sobukwe was now able to speak regularly with Pogrund by telephone, thus alleviating the need to commit his thoughts to paper. Sobukwe was, of course, now far busier, pursuing his legal career and meeting with a variety of visitors – activists, journalists, international guests – who came to Kimberley seeking him out. Sobukwe sent a short note to Anne Pogrund on 27 June (Ba11.1.1), saying, 'It's been a pleasure seeing you and the kids once more,' marking thus a recent meeting with the Pogrund family.

On 1 August, Sobukwe writes to let Pogrund (Ba11.1.2) know that 'Veronica is making a rapid recovery', adding: 'It was a delight to see Gideon and the rest of your brood. You're not doing badly in your contribution to the population explosion. We had interesting talks with the gentlemen at

116 Alexander Pope, one of Sobukwe's favourite poets.

117 A reference to the line 'a plague o' both your houses', from Shakespeare's *Romeo and Juliet*.

John Vorster.[118] Will relate these to you when we meet again.' While the mention of the police headquarters of John Vorster Square is ominous, one senses that Sobukwe, by now a veteran in withstanding the intimidation tactics of the apartheid police, managed the situation without undue concern.

Perhaps the most poignant of all Sobukwe's letters to Marquard is his delayed letter of condolence, sent on 5 August (Bd3.11), following the death of her husband, Leo:

> I've found it difficult to write sooner than this because I just did not know what to say. I learnt some time ago that one cannot put oneself in another's position. We may express sympathy, feel it and even imagine the pain. But we cannot feel it as the one who suffers it. They have a saying in Xhosa that the toothache is felt by the one whose tooth is aching. I am thankful that I was able to talk to you two before Leo's death and more thankful that he died knowing how much his contribution had been appreciated.

The sincerity of his words is underscored not only by his admission that those who express sympathy do not really feel the other's pain, but also by the fact that he had experienced his own share of suffering over the preceding months: 'It has not been a good year for me. I had planned to leave with Ahmed[119] by car at one second past midnight on the 31st May and make straight for Cape Town. But these boys beat me to it. They came on the 30th May, 1974 to serve the fresh lot of bureaucratic output. Well, it's good to know that our security is entrusted to such alert people.'

The banning orders that had been imposed on Sobukwe upon his release from Robben Island expired in May 1974, only then to be immediately reinstated for another five-year period. In other words, five years after his release, the senseless obstructions and bureaucratic vindictiveness had not ceased. And while Sobukwe would no longer have been surprised by the extent to which the authorities would go to in order to

118 John Vorster Square, the police headquarters in downtown Johannesburg, an infamous site of interrogation, torture and abuse of anti-apartheid activists by the South African security police.

119 Presumably Achmat Laher.

restrict and inhibit him, these measures must now have taken their toll. He continues:

> Veronica has had a major operation as you probably read in the papers. She should have had this operation last year, but did not and the condition got worse.
>
> She has made a remarkable recovery, thanks to my very efficient and tender nursing, and has now gone back to Joh'burg for a check-up. From there she will be going to Durban to spend a week or so with her sister before proceeding to Swaziland to see the children.

So although Sobukwe was twice granted permission in June to visit Veronica and spend time with her after her operation, these understated lines nonetheless suggest his sadness and anger at not being able to be with her for longer in her time of need. Then follows a short political note prior to a further, proverbial note of consolation: 'We are breathing a little easier now that Dada Idi Amin G.C.O.[120] etc. has decided not to invade Tanzania after all. He deserves a directorship on "Punch".'[121] It is only on the last page of the letter that Sobukwe seemed finally to find the words that suited both his emotions and the note of commiseration that he wished to convey to Nell: 'The Xhosa have standard words of condolence. They say: Akuhlanga lungehlanga Lala ngenxeba (There has not occurred what has not occurred (before): LIE ON YOUR WOUND).' This resonant phrase 'lie on your wound' seems thus to apply as much to Marquard as to Sobukwe himself.

In a Christmas letter to Marquard of 21 December (Bd3.12), Sobukwe updates Marquard on the progress he has made with his legal studies, before remarking on the current global 'political boom':

> [...] I had wanted to inform you that I had passed the Practical Examination which means I have completed the legal side of my studies. But I thought I should wait until the Afrikaans results were

120 A satirical reference to Amin's practice of bestowing on himself numerous grandiose and exaggerated titles (some of the more 'colourful' including 'Lord of all the beasts of the earth and fishes of the sea', 'Conqueror of the British Empire in Africa in general and Uganda in particular', 'Field Marshal Al Hadji Doctor', 'King of Scotland'). In 1978 Amin attempted to annex part of neighbouring Tanzania, as a result of which the Tanzanian army invaded Uganda and overthrew Amin.

121 The weekly British satirical magazine.

15. Zondeni Veronica Sobukwe, in Graaff-Reinet, visiting family.
(Photo by Benjamin Pogrund, with kind permission)

out because that is what is still holding me back, *die taal*.[122] Once I get that I'll be able to practise.

Veronica and the children have gone to Graaff-Reinet for a fortnight [...]

How fast things are moving! Almost a political boom with envoys and what have you crisscrossing.[123] And there are the Arabs buying up Europe with their Petro-dollars; neo-colonialism, if there was one.

122 Afrikaans for 'the language'.

123 The so-called policy of détente, a 'charm offensive' of the apartheid government, 'reaching out' to heads of African states, particularly the Frontline States, calling for 'cooperation' and 'mutual economic benefit'. Hastings Banda of Malawi visited South Africa in 1971; and there were exchanges of views between Vorster and Kenneth Kaunda of Zambia on the question of Rhodesia (Zimbabwe) that led to the Victoria Falls Conference in 1975, which both Vorster and Kaunda attended in an effort to force Rhodesian whites and blacks to reach a settlement. On the international scene a deliberate effort was made (especially in the United States) to 'rehabilitate' South Africa's image. Whatever success this campaign enjoyed would come to a decisive end with South Africa's invasion of Angola in late 1975 and the Soweto Uprising of June 1976.

> At home, unfortunately it is the old mixture as before with now and again a bit of chutney and similar artificial flavouring. Charity, with us, does not, apparently, begin at home.
>
> We got news of you from friends and delight to hear that your spirit and sense of humour are as glorious as ever.
>
> Wishing you a blessed and rewarding Christmas and New Year.

1975: 'Whether we live or die, They will ever remember ...'

On 27 January, the *Rand Daily Mail* published a short article, credited to a staff reporter, under the headline 'Sobukwe now qualified as an attorney' (*Rand Daily Mail* 1975a). Sobukwe, the article tells us,

> received his last examination results on Saturday and is expected to apply for admission as an attorney in Kimberley, the town to which he is confined in terms of his banning orders.
>
> Even under his banning, Mr. Sobukwe has been a dominant figure looming over the political scene. At last week's talks between the Prime Minister and 'homeland' leaders, requests were made for his release from banning and the hint was given that this would be considered.

In its closing paragraph, the article draws attention to his academic accomplishments while imprisoned: 'In jail he completed a Bachelor of Economics degree through London University adding to his Bachelors and Honours degrees. His banning orders renewed for a further five years in May, were relaxed to enable him to enter courts.' Not only, then, do we have ample evidence for why Sobukwe was affectionately nicknamed 'Prof' – a nickname, incidentally, which far preceded his qualification as an attorney – but we have a demonstration that Sobukwe remained a figure of considerable public interest.

On 4 May, in a letter to Nell Marquard (Bd3.13), Sobukwe registers another point of academic success, before offering a reflection on his time as a teacher in Standerton:

> I have been going around with a feeling of guilt for over three months now, because on the day that I received the news that I had passed

16. One constant of Sobukwe's life was his love of reading. This image of 'Prof' Sobukwe captures him in Kimberley during the time of his house arrest. (Photo by Alf Khumalo, APN716963, Alf Kumalo Family Trust / African Pictures)

Afrikaans (i.e. Afrikaans Lower and the symbol was E!) I thought: 'Nell must know *immediately*. But I persuaded myself that day that I had a number of urgent files to attend to and that I would write the following day and that became the next day until the news was stale!

That, unfortunately, is the tragedy of friendship. We are so sure that our friends 'will understand' that we generally behave more rudely towards them than we would dare to do towards our enemies and strangers.

Thank you very much for your letters which are always a delight to read.

We talk of you often – i.e. Veronica and I and the Lahers and I. It is impossible, I think, for anyone who has met you to forget he has met you.

Aside from the affection and respect conveyed to Marquard here, there is something else of importance: an indication that Sobukwe had now, finally, met her in person. In a short reflection published some years later, Marquard (1986) commented both on the development of their relationship and on their first meeting: 'Our letters had begun with the slightly formal "talk" of new acquaintances, but had soon become easy, as regard developed into friendship and affection. When I eventually visited Robert in Kimberley he told me more of his experience on Robben Island than had been possible before. I found the same dignity and warmth I had got to know in his letters and a great natural gentleness.'

If there was any doubt that Sobukwe had increasingly found emotional comfort in his relationship with Marquard, it is dispelled in a subsequent section of letter (Bd3.13):

> There is a song the young children sang at their games when I was teaching at Standerton. In Zulu it went:
>
> Noma sikhona noma sesifile
> Bosala besho bethi sasikhona
>
> which being translated (as the King James Version would say) means:
>
> Whether we live or die
> They will ever remember that we once were.[124]
>
> It has always struck me as being extremely profound and apt more on the lips of philosophers than on those of little children. But then: 'out of the mouths of babes and sucklings ….'[125]
>
> By the time you receive this letter you will undoubtedly have heard that my mother died in Umtata this morning from a massive stroke. We intend burying her at Graaff-Reinet, next to my father. She was ninety.
>
> I hope to be admitted as an attorney on the 13th June, 1975. Jack Unterhalter has kindly offered to move the application before he leaves for England on the 18th June.

124 Indicative of the profundity of this memory, and the existential and political resonance Sobukwe found in these evocative lines, is that he had cited them nearly twenty years previously in an article of 1957 in *The Africanist* (see this vol., ch. 2).

125 Psalm 8: 2.

> We are all well, otherwise and are watching Galsworthy's *Strife*[126] being enacted on the political plane. Events in the East are also moving on a breath-taking pace. Reminds me of the words of a young South Africa poet[127] whose name I have forgotten but whose lines I read while a student at Healdtown in the forties. They were about the dead of war and the ruins thereof.
>
> Unaltered let them thus remain
> To show the stark stupidity of war.
>
> Very interesting articles have been appearing in *The Listener* lately.
>
> Keep well and remember that we love you very much. And that it is a pleasure loving someone like you.

We hear Sobukwe here circling back to a quieter period in his life, reflecting on his days as a young teacher in Standerton in the 1950s, sharing a memory of an event which clearly left its mark. While witnessing children singing this song may not have been particularly poignant at the time, the memory of the event certainly is so in the present, seeing that the words give such profound expression to his experience of loss. Sobukwe mentions the death of his mother – 90-year-old Angelina Sobukwe – just briefly, yet the emotional impact of her passing colours the whole of the letter. Mortality pervading his thoughts perhaps explains the confluence of themes from the past, the present and the future in the letter: memories of Healdtown and words on 'the dead of war and [...] ruins' are interwoven with reflections on the 'breath-taking' pace of recent political events, which in turn are interwoven with Sobukwe's hope of being admitted as an attorney in the coming weeks.

A *Rand Daily Mail* article of 6 May ('Sobukwe allowed to be at a funeral') confirms that Sobukwe was given permission to attend his mother's funeral in Graaff-Reinet (*Rand Daily Mail* 1975b). This would have been an exhausting journey, for the 800-kilometre trip from Kimberley to Umtata, where Angelina had died, then needed to be followed by a further 500-kilometre

---

126 John Galsworthy's 1909 play, which deals with a workers' strike at a factory.

127 How Sobukwe got to know this poem, let alone remember it, is a mystery. The poem, entitled 'Cassino: An Impression in June', appeared in *The Sable* of January 1945, a magazine of the 6th Armoured Division fighting in the Italian theatre of the Second World War. Its author was Lt J.H. Selfe of the Natal Mounted Rifles, who published *The Story of My War* in 2006. The last four lines read: 'Cassino's ruins show the awful doom / That comes of hate, the waste of toil, the cost. / Unaltered, leave it thus for evermore, / To point the stark stupidity of war.'

trip to Graaff-Reinet, itself followed in turn by a 400-kilometre direct return to Kimberley. The upshot of needing to take this marathon journey was that the Umtata–Graaff-Reinet leg took Sobukwe through King Williamstown, where, despite the considerable risks of undertaking such an illegal meeting, he met with Steve Biko. Although this was not the first of the meetings between the two men, the very fact of these two leaders – each of whom of course represented a distinct tradition or, indeed, generation in the struggle against apartheid – speaking together face to face, in conditions of privacy, cannot but pique our interest. Of all the closed-door political meetings in the history of the struggle movement in South Africa, this is surely one that most fires the curiosity and imagination of historians: what would Sobukwe and Biko have discussed?[128]

On 13 June, Sobukwe was finally formally admitted as an attorney. Four days later, Dinilesizwe and Miliswa Sobukwe (then aged 19 and 21 respectively) left Jan Smuts Airport (Johannesburg) for the United States. Their destination was Atlanta, Georgia, where they would start, in the fall semester, at Atlanta Junior College, the first step to enrolling at American universities. They were to stay initially with Andrew Young,[129] the US Congressman, who, after meeting Sobukwe in South Africa, had expressed his admiration for the former PAC president. And so, although Robert and Veronica Sobukwe had been refused a new life in the United States, their two oldest children, having finished school in Swaziland, were now afforded the opportunity.

---

128 It seems both Sobukwe and Biko agreed to keep the nature of their discussions to themselves. There were obviously pragmatic reasons for doing so, although one gets a sense that their discretion was motivated by more than political discipline. Biko seemed to give little away; in fact, he proved indignant at attempts by others to intrude. Xolela Mangcu (2012, 245) offers a related anecdote: 'Moki Cekisani, the fiery activist from Port Elizabeth, remembers getting wind of the upcoming meeting [between Sobukwe and Biko], and decided to gate-crash. Cekisani recalls a clearly annoyed Steve asking him what he was doing there.' Perhaps, despite the commonalities between Sobukwe's Pan-Africanism and Biko's approach to Black Consciousness, there were points that required the delicacy and focus that only a one-to-one meeting could provide. Another reason for the secrecy was that the two men were probably discussing how their respective organisations could be more strongly linked. Such an alignment would have proved unpopular for many PAC and BC stalwarts.

129 Andrew Young, the American politician, diplomat, activist and pastor, was a leader in the civil rights movement and a close associate of Martin Luther King, Jr. He served as a Democratic Congressman from 1973 to 1977 and was appointed Ambassador to the United Nations by President Carter in 1977.

One of the international journalists to visit Sobukwe in Kimberley at around this time was Nicholas Ashford, a correspondent for the London *Times*. His account of meeting with Sobukwe ('The silent triumph of a black South African'), published on 27 October (Ashford 1975), contains many instructive points – correctly depicting, for example, Sobukwe's views on Gatsha Buthelezi – just as it summarily refutes one of the egregiously inaccurate, yet persistent, depictions of Sobukwe (the idea that he was a proponent of 'black racialism'):

> A new sign has just been painted on the window of a small shop just inside the boundary line of Galeshewe African township on the outskirts of Kimberley. It says quite simply, 'Robert Sobukwe, Attorney'. The sign represents a personal triumph for one black South African over myriad restrictions on his freedom that would have cowed a lesser man long ago [...]
>
> Mr Sobukwe is a man of great intellectual vigour who possesses three degrees [...] A conversation with him covers not only the political situation in southern Africa but also Mr Harold Wilson's brand of socialism and the historical background of the Northern Ireland problem, with quotations from Dr Kwame Nkrumah and the Reith Lectures.[130]
>
> He talks about the early days of African Nationalism, when there seemed a real chance that the winds of change would blow as far as Pretoria. He coolly analyses the differences that developed between the all-African PAC and the ANC which, he felt, was too dependent on its white left-wing supporters. He still sees a need for an all-black nationalist movement but is worried that black racialism – a charge of which he used to be, incorrectly, accused – could develop if Africans continue to be denied political rights.
>
> He speaks with sadness of homeland leaders, many of whom he admires but who, he feels, have made unacceptable compromises. Chief Gatsha Buthelezi is an old friend, a man of intelligence and ability. But he no longer speaks on behalf of Africans as a whole, only one tribe – the Zulus. Inadvertently Chief Buthelezi has become identified with the government's policy of separate development rather than the African unity he once stood for.

130 A series of annual BBC radio lectures given by leading figures of the day.

Mr. Sobukwe is not impressed by the changes said to be taking place within South Africa. The whole apparatus of apartheid not only remains intact but has been strengthened. But he does detect a modification in white attitudes and this, he believes, could be of great significance. The 'monolithic arrogance' of the ruling Nationalist Party seems to be starting to crumble.

Small changes have struck him. Whites are now more respectful towards Africans. He has received dinner invitations from white lawyers who had never previously communicated with him. White South African journalists have suddenly 'rediscovered' him and ask for audiences. He invariably refuses because he thinks the change in attitude has been dictated by the government rather than coming from the people themselves.

He also notices a shift in emphasis from politics to economics in discussion about South Africa, inspired no doubt by the government, which constantly stresses the need to develop a middle class among the blacks. People now appear to be more concerned with economic development rather than political freedom. For instance, critics of the government's homeland policy tend to attack it because the homelands are seen to be not economically viable, rather than because the whole policy is politically and morally abhorrent.

He accepts that it is important for all people to have full stomachs, but would personally prefer to have fewer meals and more freedom.

Mr Sobukwe talks about freedom with an idealism that has not been dulled by years of repression. He wants people, both black and white, to be consulted, not just told what to do. He describes himself as a socialist but believes in consensus politics; he does not want to see one form of totalitarianism replaced by another.

His critics believe that it is already too late for his type of idealism: that the days when blacks and whites would have engaged in constructive dialogue have long since passed. But Mr Sobukwe is more optimistic. He senses that the youth of all races wants to see change. He considers that the collapse of the Portuguese regime,[131] which most Africans thought was indestructible, has raised hopes that the

131 The Carnation Revolution of April 1974, a military coup by left-leaning officers, led directly to the withdrawal of Portugal from its colonies of Angola and Mozambique.

17. Portrait of Robert Mangaliso Sobukwe. (Photo by Peter Magubane, © Peter Magubane / David Gollan)

> Nationalist government is itself not totally impregnable. He remains confident that the inexorable advance of African Nationalism will manage to reach its goal in South Africa within his lifetime.
>
> While men like Mr. Sobukwe are around there is still hope that real change may take place in South Africa without recourse to violence and bloodshed. The tragedy is that so long as he remains a 'banned person' he is inaudible to the people who ought to be heeding his words.

An important historical event in the decolonisation of Africa is mentioned in passing here, namely the fact that Portugal had withdrawn from Mozambique and Angola. That such changes were occurring so close to the borders of South Africa clearly represented a source of optimism and promise in respect of Sobukwe's aspirations for a liberated African continent.

A short letter from Pogrund on 12 November (Ba11.2.2), a follow-up to a recent phone call, delivered some rare good news to Sobukwe:

> As I told you on the phone, Randolph[132] writes: 'I am told Bob simply can't lose if he sues the publishers here.' That's good news indeed! He suggests that perhaps you would want to sue for about £15000, and adds that he could arrange the financial backing to get the case started in London.
>
> If you are happy about all this, Randolph asks that you write a letter to Henry Brown Esq., Courts & Co., Wimpole Street, London, W1, asking him (Mr Brown) to act for you in the matter. It would obviously be a good idea to sketch out what you want him to do. *The letter to Brown must be sent to Randolph,* who will make the arrangements.
>
> For once we seem to be on the side of the angels.

The reason for the excitement was that Pogrund had come into possession of a (1975) book entitled *South Africa: A Skunk among Nations* authored by a former South African diplomat, Les de Villiers, which contained a libellous depiction of Sobukwe. Sobukwe was, in an act of clear invention, miscited as advocating that other (non-African) races be cleared out of the country. Randolph Vigne, Pogrund's London-based friend, having taken legal advice, offered the above recommendations, and Sobukwe, acting accordingly, was awarded the amount of R1,500. This money would have been much appreciated as it was around this time that Sobukwe, now having been admitted as an attorney, took the step of separating himself from Nzimande's legal practice, and set up his own one-person office in Galeshewe.

1976: 'The seed must die ... the acorn becomes an oak'

On 3 February, the *Washington Post* published an article by Bernard Nossiter (1976) reporting on his recent visit to Kimberley to meet Sobukwe. Nossiter is careful throughout to avoid directly quoting Sobukwe – which would, of

132 Randolph Vigne, a publisher and member of the Liberal Party, fled South Africa in 1964 after being banned under the Suppression of Communism Act. He wrote widely on South African and Namibian affairs. In the late 1950s he maintained close relations with the PAC and with Sobukwe and supported their anti-pass campaign of 1960.

course, mean an infringement of Sobukwe's banning order – but he nonetheless effectively captures both Sobukwe's personality and his political views. Eager to associate Sobukwe with a closer-to-home exemplar of moral leadership in the fight against racism, Nossiter likens Sobukwe to the late Martin Luther King, Jr – their physical similarity, he suggests, is striking – and comments on the unequivocal certainty Sobukwe expressed in relation to the rightness of his cause and its eventual success. There are some insightful predictions offered with regard to other southern African states. For Sobukwe, who evidently had been keeping a very close eye on anti-colonial developments in neighbouring states, a crucial turning point had been reached in Mozambique, where the illusion of white invincibility had been shown up as just that: illusory, impermanent. Young black South Africans were experiencing a new degree of solidarity, or so Sobukwe implies, in his paraphrased remarks concerning how township youth routinely greeted one another with a clenched fist, that is, with the symbol of black power.

Sobukwe evidently shared a series of political predictions with Nossiter: guerrilla war was likely soon to break out in Namibia (South West Africa) and spill over into the territory of South Africa; the momentum of the black liberation struggle had grown to the point where it could no longer be halted or reversed, and Vorster's apartheid regime was entering its final days; the Popular Movement for the Liberation of Angola (MPLA) would prove victorious and Angola would become a home for the South West Africa People's Organisation (SWAPO); strikes, go-slows and sabotage would undercut the mining and manufacturing industries in South Africa; rather than a bloody revolution, South Africa's future would be one in which whites would quickly accommodate a new democratic dispensation in which each person has a vote and in which segregation would be eradicated.

It is no surprise, given the readership of the *Washington Post*, that Nossiter would have prioritised questions on regional political developments and regime change in southern Africa when visiting Sobukwe. What does seem surprising is how forthright Sobukwe was in offering such a systematic and detailed list of predictions which would clearly have perturbed the South African government.

In February, Sobukwe would share many of the same predictions with a Norwegian journalist, Jan Tystad of the *Dagbladet* newspaper, stressing that a growing political awareness and impatience were sweeping through South Africa to such an extent that many more demonstrations, strikes and instances of mass action should be expected. A further crucial prediction, perhaps the most astute of all, had already been made in June of the previous year, when Sobukwe was visited by Anthony Lewis of the *New York Times*: the youth of the country and, more particularly yet, students would be at the forefront of protest actions, which would be met by government suppression.

In a letter of 31 May to Nell Marquard (Bd3.14), Sobukwe interestingly describes details of his daily routine:

> It is true that I am kept very busy. I open at about 7.30 am to have time to read the Bible and say a silent prayer. But clients are not a particularly considerate bunch. As soon as I open, there they are with their problems which, to them are the most important problems I have to deal with. I return from court about 4.15 pm every day and have to consult until a few minutes before 7 pm. Were it not for the banning order I would be kept in that office until 9 pm daily. So it is true that nothing is totally bad!

Sobukwe's commitment to Christianity is on display here, as is his sense of humour; few others could joke in the same way about how even banning orders have a silver lining. He mentions Veronica's recent trip to visit Dini and Miliswa ('Veronica returned from the States in December. And she is certainly the better for having gone'), before discussing more of the children's American plans and experiences:

> The children in the States have closed for the summer vacations. The girl has gone to New York to attend summer school while the boy has remained at Atlanta and will attend summer school there, at Atlanta University.
>
> We have made a practice of phoning the children at least once a month. It comes out expensive but they love it and we think the expense worth it. The girl, Miliswa is at Spelman College and the boy is at Morehouse.[133] Both are predominantly black but, of course, American Blacks are more like our Coloureds here. But the black consciousness movement has, as Veronica tells me, effected a tremendous

133 Spelman is a black liberal arts college for women in Atlanta; Morehouse is a similar college for men in the same city.

> change in the attitudes of Blacks in the States. Things African are very popular. But the cultures are still different and the two groups still have to find each other.

It is not immediately clear what Sobukwe has in mind with the above comparison ('American Blacks are more like the Coloureds here') although it might point to the enduring legacy of 'black African' languages and culture in South Africa. A few comments on the progress of the twins (Dali and Dedani) in Botswana are offered alongside thoughts on 'being agitated by the Nats', prior to a series of critical remarks on the notion of 'homeland citizenship':

> Punt Janson[134] promised limited home-ownership on a thirty-year lease basis. They removed him, inserted homeland citizenship as a pre-requisite. Now we learn that we can't have offices until and unless we take out homeland citizenship. Why they always want to throw down the gauntlet, I don't know. And why they choose to believe that they are the only people entitled to have principles to adhere to, I can't understand. They ought to know that there are very many of us who, on principle, cannot take out homeland citizenship.
>
> I can't say I am enjoying my work that much. Now and again one appears before an imaginative magistrate, but, generally, the law is a depressing affair, with your shoplifters and petty thieves standing pathetically in the dock while the magistrate pontificates on the heinousness of the crime. And, of course, what is more depressing is having to tell somebody who is being endorsed out or who is being evicted from his house, that there is nothing you can do about it.
>
> I shall pass over Rhodesia in silence. Same for Mozambique and Angola. Right will still triumph over might.

The timing of Sobukwe's comments is of interest, as is the juxtaposition of his remarks on being disenchanted with his legal work and his expressed silence over political developments. One can only assume that Sobukwe's true

134 Punt Janson was deputy minister of bantu administration and education from 1972 to 1976 and made his mark in the reform of township administration in South Africa. He is credited with giving apartheid a 'human face'.

calling, that of being a political leader – and a leader, more specifically, in the struggle against white supremacy – was being frustrated. If this was the case, then events of the coming weeks would have vindicated his predictions in respect of the intensification of the struggle and of the role of the youth therein, even as it possibly touched on previous trauma. The Soweto Uprising began on 16 June in response to the insistence of the apartheid government that Afrikaans would be the medium of instruction for some subjects in local schools. An estimated twenty thousand students took to the streets that day and were met with a brutal response by the police, who opened fire on protesters, killing at least 176. The parallels between this event and the Sharpeville Massacre would have been painfully obvious to Sobukwe. While initially it appeared that the events of June might be limited to Soweto, riots started breaking out across the country, and the flashpoints of resistance shifted to the Eastern Cape and Western Cape, the latter region being the centre of particularly violent protests. By October and November – following a series of school boycotts and subsequent school burnings, in addition to political violence in the townships of Nyanga and Langa – riots had reached downtown Cape Town. As violent political protests flared up across the greater Cape Town area, it seemed as if the country had been brought to the edge of a precipice. The response of the apartheid regime was to ban all organisations in the Western Cape associated with the Black Consciousness Movement, a ban that was then extended a year later nationwide and that led directly, in turn, to the formation of the Azanian People's Organisation (AZAPO) and, a few years later, to the United Democratic Front (UDF). These events form the backdrop to Sobukwe's letter to Mrs Marquard on 9 November (Bd3.15). The letter begins with the usual salutations and family news:

> My dear Nell,
>
> I used to feel extremely annoyed when a week passed and I had not heard from you. This was when I was on the Island. And I remember with intense shame that not once did you plead pressure of work as an excuse [...]
>
> [...] We've been keeping regular contact with the children who have settled down and are doing quite well, though homesick. Benjie (Benjamin Pogrund) who knew them from the time they were toddlers is in Boston at the moment and has already visited Miliswa and phones both of them regularly [...]

Despite his yearnings for a political uprising, Sobukwe nonetheless immediately expresses reassurance: 'I have been very anxious to contact you during the past eventful days but thought I should not dramatize things. I had no fear for you whatsoever. It just did not occur to me that your life could be in danger. And I am not anxious for you now. But being fond of gossip as most mortals are I should have liked to phone and ask "How are things down there? The newspapers have us extremely worried."' This note of concern demonstrates the extent of Sobukwe's empathy. In many ways the project of his life was to overthrow the white supremacist regime of apartheid and to further the Africanist agenda of a liberated Africa. Accordingly, he must have felt great hope for what the events in Soweto might represent and precipitate as regards these goals of liberation. And yet, he is sensitive to how such events might affect his recently widowed friend. This helps explain a subtle shift in the narrative: from a recognition of what might to some feel frightening about these events to an assurance that much of promise might arise from tumultuous events:

> Events are moving fast to a climax the nature and intensity of which we cannot predict. But unless saner counsel prevails it is 'too ghastly to contemplate'.[135] Soweto and Cape Town have shown us a little of the passions that could be evoked. And the picture is very ugly. I suppose the lovers and admirers of ancient Rome felt the same when they contemplated the advance of the Barbarians on the ancient city.
>
> We are reminded: 'The old order changeth. Sic est gloria mundi,[136] but the cry that strikes a chord is: 'Where are they all: the old familiar faces.' Change is painful. The seed must die. But when it has died, the acorn becomes an oak.
>
> I am kept busy here, in court almost daily until four o'clock when I begin consultations which continue until 7 pm. Were it not for my banning order I would be kept here I suppose until 9 pm.
>
> We talk of you often and request that we [illegible][137] or two with you in Cape Town.

---

135 A phrase that Prime Minister Vorster had uttered and that was widely quoted and used.

136 Sic transit gloria mundi: Latin for 'thus passes the glory of the world'.

137 The text seems to refer to the possibility of a visit to Cape Town. Sobukwe's banning orders would have made it impossible for him to travel or visit for any other reason than a medical appointment.

He closes by updating Marquard on his brother Ernest's retirement plans and by once again expressing his dissatisfaction with the law:

> My brother, the Bishop, is retiring in a year or two and is looking around for a place to settle when he retires. He could sell the house at Graaff-Reinet for a good price and build himself another either in the Ciskei or Transkei. But I am attached to Graaff-Reinet and that particular house, and would rather raise money to assist him acquire another house. Again a question, I suppose, of the 'old familiar faces'.
>
> I have not read a single book for the past three months. I have been reading Law Reports and Journals only. I don't think I care very much for this profession. It can't compare with teaching.

1977: 'The pain remains'

There are very few surviving letters written by Sobukwe from 1977 onwards. Those that do survive are signed off by both Robert and Veronica Sobukwe, an indication either that he had very little time given the demands of his one-person legal practice (toward the beginning of 1977), or simply that his failing health was limiting his energy and his capacity to devote time to non-essential correspondence. There is an upbeat note from Pogrund on 16 February to Andrew Young (Ba11.4.1), confirming that the two oldest Sobukwe children were doing well in the States and mentioning – perhaps somewhat over-optimistically – Sobukwe's legal work: 'I am glad that I had the chance of seeing you when I was in America. And, of course, I was delighted to be able to see Miliswa and Dini and to find them so well. I was in Kimberley a couple of weeks ago and spent a day with Bob. His capacity for enjoying his legal practice is unlimited.'

Then, a lull. By June, Sobukwe had informed Pogrund that he was ailing. Unable to recover from a bad cough and an apparent bout of flu, he had consulted with doctors in Kimberley, but no satisfactory treatment seemed to be on offer. A first attempt on Pogrund's part to gain permission for Sobukwe to fly to Johannesburg for a thorough medical examination was turned down. Veronica was concerned. Pogrund visited Kimberley and, despite noting Sobukwe's persistent cough, seemed somewhat relieved. Nonetheless, upon his return to Johannesburg, Pogrund approached a doctor he trusted, Dr Bodo Koch, and started making arrangements for a special weekend appointment (so as not to keep Sobukwe away from his work for too long). The real challenge lay with securing the permission of the minister of justice, police and prisons, Jimmy Kruger,[138] to allow Sobukwe to travel.

Even Pogrund, who by now was a veteran in dealing with apartheid officials and making similar requests, seems to have been somewhat daunted by the task ahead. Nonetheless, ever industrious and tactful, Pogrund began the process, first phoning Kruger, and then following up with a letter on 29 July thanking the minister 'for the swift help you gave this week in allowing Mr Robert Sobukwe to come to Johannesburg next week for medical attention' (Ba11.4.3). Kruger was, at first at least, responsive, and a few days later, on 3 August, Sobukwe received a formal notification from the Magistrate's Office in Kimberley (Ba11.4.12):

> APPLICATION FOR RELAXATION OF ORDER: MR. R.M. SOBUKWE
>
> Your application to proceed to Johannesburg to consult Mr. Bodo Koch a medical practitioner on Saturday 6th instant is granted, on the following conditions:
>
> i) Departure from Kimberley on 6 August 1977 at 8.55 am by air and
> Departure from Johannesburg 9.30 am. on 7 August 1977 by Air.
> ii) To stay at the house of Mr. Benjamin Pogrund at 38(a) 8th Avenue, Parktown North, Johannesburg.
> iii) To consult your Doctor at above address
> iv) To communicate with and see only Mr. Pogrund and members of his household and of course your Doctor at aforementioned address.

138 Jimmy Kruger is most infamously known for his statement upon the death of Steve Biko – 'Dit laat my koud' (It leaves me cold). The callousness of the statement fuelled local protest and resentment, and the international media seized upon it as symptomatic of the government's character. The upshot was that Kruger was seen as having damaged South Africa's 'credibility' abroad, and he was fired from his cabinet post. Kruger later joined the far-right Conservative Party of Andries Treurnicht.

Negotiations followed over which flights Sobukwe could take, and as to whether he could be permitted to see Dr Koch at his medical offices rather than – as stipulated above – at Pogrund's home. Pogrund did win the latter concession, and the trip and the consultation were successfully carried out, with one exception: for a variety of reasons Sobukwe was not able to secure his previous X-rays from the Kimberley hospital and pass them on to Dr Koch. The diagnosis? A tenacious bacterial infection, which, although serious, would respond to treatment. Pogrund's (1997, 357) account of these events conveys a sense of relief, indeed of happiness, at this outcome, noting – a wonderfully informative detail – that after the consultation 'Sobukwe drank a glass of wine – for the first time in his life [...] by way of celebrating the medical diagnosis [...] But he thought it safest to remain a teetotaller.'

Intent on maintaining a clear channel of communication, Pogrund wrote to Kruger on 12 August (Ba11.4.5), enclosing the medical report by Dr Koch 'on a confidential basis', as he believed it would be helpful for Kruger to see it so that he would 'have a full understanding of Mr Sobukwe's condition'.

18. Benjamin Pogrund and Robert Mangaliso Sobukwe in Johannesburg, August 1977. (Photo by Benjamin Pogrund, with kind permission)

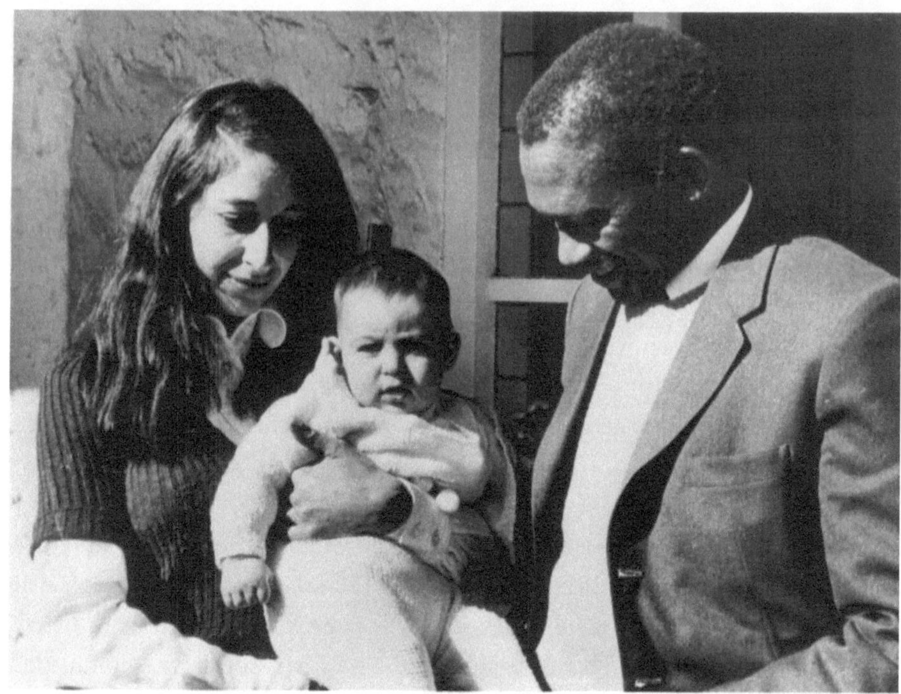

19. Sobukwe with Anne and Gideon Pogrund, August 1977.
(Photo by Benjamin Pogrund, with kind permission)

20. Robert Mangaliso Sobukwe, Anne Pogrund and Benjamin Pogrund, Parktown North, Johannesburg, August 1977. (Photo by Benjamin Pogrund, with kind permission)

Continuing, Pogrund notes: 'In layman's language, as described to me by Dr Koch, what it means is that Mr Sobukwe is suffering from a weakening of the heart muscles caused by a bacterial infection. Had this not been diagnosed at this stage and treatment immediately instituted, the gravest possible consequences could have followed.'

This was followed by a further request that permission be granted for Sobukwe to fly to Johannesburg for a further consultation with Dr Koch on the weekend of 10–11 September. The situation seemingly stable, Pogrund embarked on a planned trip to the United States. It was there that Pogrund received bad news. Having eventually obtained the X-rays, Koch spotted a sign of cancer in Sobukwe's lungs and relayed this to Anne Pogrund, recommending that surgical intervention occur at the earliest possible opportunity. Anne, in a fraught state, managed to locate her husband and inform him of this.

In the flurry of communications that ensued, Sobukwe was offered surgery in Bloemfontein. While it is difficult to assess to what extent this was offered in good faith – Bloemfontein is less than a two-hour drive from Kimberley and was thus quickly accessible – it does smack of the typical form of such gestures made by apartheid authorities to Sobukwe: yes, for the sake of public appearances, we will offer what seems to be reasonable (a job, a home, medical treatment), while still ensuring that what is offered contains within itself a further punishment of sorts (a job that would be complicit with apartheid policy; a home cut off from family, friends, associates; medical facilities not best suited to one's needs). Sobukwe himself was adamant: Bloemfontein, a conservative Afrikaner town, in which a good number of its white residents – doctors and medical professionals included – were likely to bear him some degree of animosity, would be an inhospitable location for such a procedure. For Sobukwe, according to Pogrund's (1997) telling, to undergo such an operation in Bloemfontein would mean that he would not leave the hospital alive.

Perhaps surprisingly – then again, perhaps not, given the sensitivity of the apartheid government to how it would be portrayed by the international news media – the government backed down and conceded Sobukwe's wish to be treated at Groote Schuur Hospital, Cape Town. Presumably seeing an opportunity to capitalise on a show of political largesse, Kruger announced to the press on 9 September that Sobukwe could have his choice of any doctor or hospital in South Africa in respect of his current medical needs. Pogrund was outraged at this, not only because of the grievous breach of confidentiality, but also because of the blatant attempt to score political points over Sobukwe's serious medical condition. While Sobukwe showed calm resolve in the face of what was to come, what did rankle him was the fact that the news would now reach Miliswa and Dini in the States, alarming them, before it could have been conveyed to them, more sensitively, by himself. Sections of the following communication with Kruger (on 12 September) convey the mix of desperation and fury that Pogrund must have felt at the time (Ba11.4.6):

> On returning from overseas on Saturday I was shocked to find that you had issued a statement the day before in which you made public the fact of Mr Robert Sobukwe's ill health.
>
> I cannot understand why such a statement was necessary. My letter to you of August 12, in which I gave you the then known details, was confidential and indeed (as it made abundantly clear) was sent to you entirely on that basis [...]
>
> Mr Sobukwe's illness should surely have been his own private concern until such times as he (or his family or close friends acting on his authority) chose to disclose it.
>
> [...]
>
> I feel that I must also take this opportunity to point out to you that, looking back from this stage in time, the delay during July/August in obtaining permission for Mr Sobukwe to come to Johannesburg for a medical consultation could prove to have been tragically decisive.
>
> [...]
>
> And underlying all this is the terrible thought that, had he not been confined to Kimberley but been free at any time to obtain the best possible medical advice, the exact nature of his condition could have been detected far earlier, with immeasurably better prospects for treatment than now exist.
>
> It is against this background that I wish to express the hope that he will now be allowed normal freedom to obtain medical assistance. But the medical view is that the harm has already been done.

Kruger's terse response to Pogrund on 27 September (Ba11.4.8) signalled that their relationship – and the future of any further direct communication – had now come to an end:

> I think you should have realized that I would not have issued a statement on Mr Sobukwe unless background circumstances warranted it. In any case I never disclosed the nature of his illness.
>
> The whole trend of your letter is such that in future you will have to make any representations you wish to, through the normal channels of my Department and not to me directly.

Mercifully, by the time of this letter, Sobukwe had received the operation: a lung was removed on 14 September at Groote Schuur. The circumstances of the operation showed up many of the contradictions of apartheid South Africa. Sobukwe's bedside table was constantly supplied with fresh roses, at a cost that would have eclipsed what many of his township visitors would have made in a year's wages. The hospital itself maintained segregated wards, even though the surgery team and the effective treatment of patients required that these rules needed to be temporarily suspended in everyday practice. A more glaring contradiction yet concerned the fact that a figure as significant to the history of South Africa as Sobukwe was would not even have gained admittance to Groote Schuur were it not for his standing in the eyes of the outside world and the influence of Pogrund and other donors and supporters. The disparity between what the apartheid state would have condemned Sobukwe to had no political pressure been exerted – that is, to the modest medical amenities available for 'non-whites' in Kimberley – and the world-class facilities of Groote Schuur is made all the more stark if we bear in mind that the ward in which Sobukwe was treated was overseen by none other than Professor Chris Barnard, who, ten years earlier, had achieved global renown by performing the world's first human-to-human heart transplant.

The extremes of isolation and constant surveillance that Sobukwe suffered on Robben Island were again a factor during his time at Groote Schuur, even if in a rather different form. In much pain, receiving painkillers, struggling to recover, and of course still subject to the restriction that he be with no more than a few persons at a time, Sobukwe was not able to engage with the many well-wishers: this was loneliness of a different stripe. While the around-the-clock presence of the security police was not the same as the more remote attentions of Robben Island's police guards, their proximity was an undeniable reminder of just how closely he was being watched. Despite Kruger's media-publicised claim that Sobukwe could attend any hospital in the country, there was nevertheless an awareness that Kruger would prohibit all but the most strictly limited movements when Sobukwe came to leave the hospital.

Planning for Sobukwe's care in the period after his departure from Groote Schuur brought many complications to the fore. The hope was that, after a month at Groote Schuur, Sobukwe could stay with an Anglican bishop, Patrick Matolengwe,[139] who lived close by, in his official church residence in Newlands. Several requests were directed to the minister of justice, this time by Veronica, without any forthcoming response. Alex Boraine, member of Parliament for the Progressive Federal Party and the future deputy chairman of the Truth and Reconciliation Commission, also tried to intercede, contacting Kruger's office, but, again, no clear directive followed.

On 14 October, a month to the day after the operation, Bishop Matolengwe picked up the Sobukwes and drove them to his Newlands home. The move made sense, as Sobukwe needed to return within a fortnight to Groote Schuur for the start of the radiotherapy phase of his treatment and was too weak to travel any further. One might have hoped that even the apartheid authorities would be dissuaded from intruding upon an act of Christian hospitality. And yet within thirty minutes of Sobukwe's arrival, the security police were at the door. An ugly scene followed. The police tried to force their way past Veronica, who, appalled at this incursion and desperate to shield her weakened husband, did her best to keep them from him. It mattered little; eventually the ultimatum was delivered: if Sobukwe did not immediately return to Groote Schuur, he would be booked on a flight to Kimberley. Ultimately, given Sobukwe's condition, there was only one choice: to undertake the trip back to the hospital, despite Sobukwe's dread at having to do so.

There would be multiple requests made to Kruger's office in the weeks that followed, the majority of which met with summary denials, until eventually Dr Joe (José) de Nobrega, a surgeon in the heart unit, was given permission for the Sobukwes to stay with him in the suburb of Oranjezicht. The clear inconsistency of this decision – the request made by Veronica for Sobukwe

139 As it happened, Bishop Monwabisi Patrick Matolengwe also hailed from Graaff-Reinet and was well acquainted with Sobukwe's brother Ernest.

21. Sobukwe with his family after his cancer operation.
From left: Dalindyebo, Veronica, Robert, Dini and Miliswa.
(Photo by Peter Magubane, © Peter Magubane / David Gollan)

to stay at a church house in nearby Newlands seemed, by contrast, to make more practical sense[140] – demonstrates nothing so much as the authoritarian obduracy of apartheid officials: the insistence on saying no to whatever the Sobukwe family might request.

The see-saw between moments of crisis and respite continued. The police visited the de Nobregas's house, as did many other more favourably disposed visitors, such as Alex Boraine, who knelt with Sobukwe in prayer. Sobukwe managed to attend a Methodist church service, and had the opportunity, given his temporary Oranjezicht location, of appreciating the beauty of Table Mountain up close. When the de Nobregas's house was sold, Sobukwe needed to move again, this time to a Holiday Inn, where he stayed for a short time before returning to Groote Schuur for his radiotherapy.

One figure who played a role in all this was Professor Chris Barnard. He was, to some extent, an ally of Sobukwe's. He angrily dismissed the security

140 Then again, the apartheid government would have been angered by the Anglican Church's decision to have a black man serving as the Suffragan Bishop, and so thwarting this accommodation plan may have been doubly motivated.

police from Sobukwe's ward, for example, and remonstrated with Kruger on the phone, attempting to have Sobukwe's banning restrictions lessened. And yet, perhaps enthralled by his fame, or intent on bolstering his anti-apartheid credentials in the eyes of the outside world, he was perhaps a little too willing to make Sobukwe his friend or, worse yet, a cause célèbre. Barnard, at the time a figure of considerable media interest, hoped to interview Sobukwe for a foreign television station. Sobukwe, perhaps unsurprisingly, rejected the idea.[141] While drawn to Sobukwe, Barnard was also at times exasperated by him. Sobukwe, true to form, was not about to be swayed by the ostensibly reasonable arguments of a man who would go on to profess in an interview that 'South Africa is a country more sinned against than sinning', and that 'we may have to divide South Africa into two equal divisions' (Ng'weno 1978). We should not summarily dismiss the various forms of assistance that Barnard gave to the Sobukwe family – as just one example, he paid for Miliswa and Dini to travel back from the United States for their father's funeral. And yet Sobukwe's description of the double-bind that liberals find themselves in seems to have pertained to Barnard himself. Critical of apartheid, yet antagonistic towards South Africa's opponents; seeking kinship with Sobukwe, while holding on to a hope for a 'two division' solution – do we not, here, hear the echo of Sobukwe's words: 'By his group [...] he is regarded as a renegade, a traitor. By the oppressed he is viewed [...] as the salesman of the policies of the oppressor'?

In his letter of 9 November to Andrew Young (Ba11.4.9), Pogrund provides a brief update on Sobukwe's condition:

> I am in near-daily contact with Bob Sobukwe and he has been responding to the radio-active therapy. It is a pity that, during the few days he was out of hospital the week before last, he was unable to stay with friends of his choice, but he was at least comfortable in a Holiday Inn. He is now due to be finally discharged from hospital at the end of this week and will be returning to Kimberley. I am hoping to go down to see him over the weekend of November 19.
>
> His voice is still rather weak and it is because of this that he has been reluctant to receive a phone call from you. But you will know

141 While one would not want to question Sobukwe's judgement in this respect, his decision was unfortunate at least inasmuch as there is no surviving recording of his voice. The topic of Sobukwe's voicelessness is addressed in the book's closing chapter.

> how much he is aware of and appreciates your concern. Veronica remains as steady and courageous as ever.
>
> One of the tragedies of the recent bannings, by the way, is that two of the people concerned – the Rev Theo Kotze and the Rev David Russell[142] – had become daily visitors to the hospital, praying with Bob. It meant an enormous amount to him. Now, of course, they are no longer allowed to have any contact with him.

We have here another indication of how important Sobukwe's Christianity was to him, perhaps particularly so as he entered one of the most difficult periods of his life. On 1 December, Miliswa wrote a short note to Pogrund from Michigan State University, warmly mentioning the Thanksgiving weekend that she and Dini had spent with Andrew Young's family in New York, and asking him to send her warmest regards to 'Tata and Mama' (Ba11.4.10).

On 13 December, Sobukwe dictated a letter to Veronica, intended for Jack (John) Purves, an American Mennonite working in Botswana, who had visited them in Kimberley and was on friendly terms with the family. He starts by thanking Purves for 'the delightful letters, all of which I received on my return to Kimberley from Cape Town i.e. after the 16th November, 1977', before updating his friend on family plans and responding to Purves's invitation to visit him in the town of Maun:

> Dali has been doing Matric in Lesotho [...] Veronica is desirous that he should leave for the States with his elder brother and sister who are coming home for two weeks during the Winter vacations. We expect them on the 18th December, 1977 and they return to the States on the 2nd January, 1978.
>
> Should the ban be lifted I shall certainly apply for permission to go to Maun though I do not expect such permission to be granted. You seem to have made an unfavourable impression on some people though really I cannot imagine a less anarchistic person than you. Your ideas of course are a bit unwholesome for a White man but otherwise I would think you are quite respectable.

142 The Rev. Theo Kotze was a Methodist minister who became regional director of the Christian Institute in Cape Town in 1969. Kotze was banned in 1977 along with the Christian Institute, and went into exile. On the Rev. David Russell, see n. 113.

> Thank you for the news about Maun. We wish you every success in your work.

One cannot but wonder how this relationship would have developed if Sobukwe's health had not declined so suddenly. The playful chiding – 'a bit unwholesome for a White man' – reminds one of the fondness and lightness of touch so characteristic of his letters to Pogrund. Sobukwe continues (Ba11.1.11):

> Do you hear from Gatsha? He sent me a copy of a blistering letter he had written to a journalist by the name of St John who had dared to suggest that the late Steve Biko and I were not overly impressed by Gatsha. He said, among other things, that there was nothing in our background which he could envy – we are Xhosa Commoners!
>
> I am making good progress though I have an excruciating backache that has recently made itself felt. The doctors diagnose arthritis but that does not help – the pain remains excruciating!
>
> Our love and best wishes to you and Catherine. We look forward to sharing a holiday with you.

These few lines condense a great deal. Steve Biko had died just three months earlier (on 12 September), his death the result of injuries sustained in a brutal police interrogation. The news would have come as a blow to Sobukwe, not only because of his personal relation with Biko and all the hopes he harboured for Biko's generation in rejuvenating the struggle, but also because he became aware of these events at a personally challenging time – before he was about to go under the knife at Groote Schuur. Sobukwe's characterisation of Gatsha Buthelezi would, regrettably, be proved accurate. Buthelezi's complicity in apartheid's Bantustan system, of course, marked a crucial difference between him and Sobukwe and Biko – both of whom viewed any such involvement as unthinkable – and he remained sensitive to any characterisation of himself as a less important African leader.[143] Significant also is Sobukwe's comments that 'the pain remains excruciating'. Even though offered alongside

143 After Sobukwe's death, for example, Buthelezi offered a telling remark: 'Sobukwe was great for what he suffered, and not for what he did' ('Liberal Given a Radical Drubbing by Buthelezi', *Zulu Voice* 1978).

some good-humoured remarks, this was a worrying observation, especially given that Sobukwe, typically stoic, uncomplaining, did not tend to stress his suffering.

Interestingly, the letter contains an undated handwritten note that Jack Purves had addressed to Benjamin Pogrund (Ba11.4.11), who, it seems, had requested it for purposes of research when preparing his biography of Sobukwe:

> Dear Benjy,
> Here is the letter at long last. It is probably too late for your book. I thought it was in the US but found it yesterday here in Gabs.[144] It shows Mangaliso's terrific sense of humour even in the last days.
> Best,
> Jack Purves

That Purves would speak of Sobukwe to Pogrund as 'Mangaliso' – particularly after his passing – is fitting.

Just prior to Christmas, on 20 December, Sobukwe dictated a letter to Nell Marquard (Bd3.16), thanking her for a gift – a suit for himself – and describing the difficulties of organising travel back to Cape Town and in respect of his Groote Schuur hospital bills. There is a mention of Veronica and Marquard having met: 'There is, of course, so much to thank you for but above all your considerateness which so impressed Veronica. Incidentally I am very happy you two met. I did not doubt you would get on well.'

Sobukwe had been back in Kimberley for almost a month, but despite the benefits of the privacy and comforts of home, he was still in great pain: 'For the first two weeks here I enjoyed good health. I took long walks in the morning and returned quite tired out. Then all of a sudden I developed a terrible back-ache and it is driving me crazy for nothing seems to ease it except pain killers.' There is an optimistic note for a future meeting – 'We're looking forward to seeing you' – along with the hope that 'things will be better this time' – presumably a reference to a prior visit hampered by Sobukwe's ongoing health struggles, before the sign-off: 'Affectionately, Robert & Veronica'.

144 Gaborone.

1978: 'Resolute in his beliefs'

A few days after a weekend trip to Kimberley, prompted by further worries over Sobukwe's health, Pogrund wrote, on 13 February, to Miliswa and Dini in the States (Bd11.5.1):

> As I think your Mother told Miliswa on the phone on Sunday, Anne and I were in Kimberley over the weekend. We were very worried when your Mother phoned us on Friday to tell us that Tata had been taken to the hospital there, so we drove down on Saturday.
>
> To be honest, he was very ill when we saw him that day and we were extremely concerned. But already by Saturday evening he was beginning to recover and by the time we left Kimberley, on Monday evening, he was on his way back to being his normal self. We spent many hours with him over the weekend, just sitting quietly or talking and talking. As you probably know, it seems that what happened was that he had not been able to keep down his food or liquids and this, together with the high amounts of medicines he was on, started causing kidney trouble. But the hospital put him on a drip and the nourishment quickly brought him round again. It looks as though he will be in hospital for a few days and will then be able to go home again. I spoke to your Mother on the phone a few minutes ago and she told me that Tata is now feeling a great deal better.
>
> As I know you will want to have the full details of what has been happening, I am writing this joint letter to both of you, with a copy of the letter going to Dini.
>
> We were glad to hear from your Parents that you are both keeping well. When you have the chance, will you write to us? We are always anxious to know how you are.

There was a rhythm to Pogrund's alarm over Sobukwe's health: grave concern and urgency followed by relief and hopeful (if at times unrealistic) optimism, when Sobukwe appeared to be recovering. Things were, however, very serious, and Sobukwe was soon hospitalised again, this time in

Kimberley. Pogrund had clearly been touched by what he witnessed when he visited:

> While I think of it, one of the amazing things about visiting Tata in hospital was the number of people, from Galeshewe and elsewhere in Kimberley, who were simply coming into the room to stand quietly around and then to leave quietly. It was quite a demonstration of the love and concern which so many have for Tata. I believe that when he was at Groote Schuur Hospital, exactly the same things happened, with even white porters coming in and leaving R1 or R1,50 for fruit or something to be bought. What a mad, and yet beautiful, country we have. (Bd11.5.1)

Even given the severity of Sobukwe's condition, there was consolation to be found in this: the quiet respectfulness that so many felt called upon to bestow on the former leader of the PAC.

One of the more eye-catching commentaries that appeared in the South African press on Sobukwe in 1978 featured the comments of Professor Chris Barnard. Despite the contradictions seemingly embodied in Barnard's political stance to apartheid, his remarks offer an insightful testimony to Sobukwe's personality in the last months of his life. Robert Mangaliso Sobukwe, Barnard said, was 'a humble man, a great Christian and a true gentleman': 'I was immediately impressed by the fact that here was a very friendly man, with a ready smile, a quiet-spoken and humble man who often spoke of God and who often read the Bible' (*The Star* 1978). Barnard, mindful of the government's vilification of Sobukwe, appears to have been keen here to offer a portrayal that would refute National Party depictions of Sobukwe as a reverse racist who threatened the security of white South Africa.

'What really started our friendship', he continued, 'was when we found that in our background, we had quite a lot in common. We were both Karoo boys, after all – he from Graaff-Reinet and I from Beaufort West, and in our conversations, we found that there was much that was similar in the way we grew up in our respective Karoo towns.' One can imagine Sobukwe, perhaps initially reticent, being potentially willing to connect with Barnard in this way: 'What struck me so forcibly about Sobukwe was that although here was a man who had every reason to be bitter, there was no trace of bitterness in him [...]

Even when the Security Police were concerned, he never showed any resentment or bitterness. In fact, on one occasion when I became rather cross and remonstrated with some security police at the hospital, Robert told me not to be angry, that they were just doing their job.'

Dini Sobukwe offered a similar remark. Speaking of two of the security policemen assigned to Sobukwe after he had been relocated to Kimberley, Dini noted in an interview (with Derek Hook, 29 May 2014) how his father was 'friendly with them, talked to them, spent hours talking to them. And that's about any subject at all ... he talked to them across the fence many times when they were there to see whether he was back at six.'

It is true that Sobukwe, perhaps aided by his Christian faith, was able to forgive, to avoid being dragged down to the level of those who, through fear, malice or the pure hubris of power, sought to persecute him and restrict his life. He was, without exception, more magnanimous and dignified than the representatives of the apartheid state who targeted him. And yet it would be a mischaracterisation to imply that, even at this late stage in his life, he was resigned to fate, that he had succumbed, in a kind of pacifist state, to the status quo, to a sense of 'what could not be changed'. It helps once again to refer to Dini Sobukwe, who affirmed that, despite the possibility of the Kimberley house being bugged, his father would always honestly state his political views, 'anywhere, to anyone and in any court of law':

> He was resolute in his beliefs and nothing was going to change that ... He was not going to think any differently, be told to change his mind, he wasn't going to do that ... He really believed what he was doing ... he was not going to find a way of ... sugar coating it or saying it in any way different but he was going to say it as it was and he never stepped back from that ever ... that certainty about things is what made imprisonment bearable because whatever hardships came with that ... he totally and completely believed it.

As Chris Barnard went on to admit: 'it became clear that Sobukwe was still firm in his convictions and that his views had not changed' (*The Star* 1978). If anything, this is an understatement, and it points to what was most exceptional about Sobukwe. Here was a person who, through the simple act of being himself, subverted the most basic of apartheid's premises and values. The apartheid state never could figure out what to do with him; they won

22. Miliswa Sobukwe, grieving the loss of her father, being comforted by Anne Pogrund on her arrival at Jan Smuts Airport, Johannesburg. (Photo by Benjamin Pogrund, with kind permission)

23. The memorial to Robert Mangaliso Sobukwe at his gravesite. Note both the biblical verse ('That glory may dwell in our land', Psalm 85: 95) and the quotation of Sobukwe's own memorable words: 'True leadership demands complete subjugation of self'. (Photo by Derek Hook)

many minor battles against Sobukwe, but never emerged the victor. Sobukwe did not concede, did not relent, did not compromise, and – what seemed to flummox apartheid officials and undo apartheid's internal logic more than anything else – he did so on the basis of an unyielding commitment to an Africanist humanism that he himself embodied. By means of his unrelenting dedication to the cause of Africa's freedom, Sobukwe forced apartheid's moral contradictions back upon themselves, showing, through no other 'force' than that of his own humanity, that its period of dominance, its instituted regime of white supremacy, would, inevitably, be consigned to history.

Robert Mangaliso Sobukwe died on 27 February 1978.

References

Arnold, Millard, ed. 1979. *Steve Biko: Black Consciousness in South Africa.* New York: Vintage Books.

Ashford, Nicholas. 1975. 'The Silent Triumph of a Black South African'. *The Times*, 27 October.

Brownlee, Kimberley. 2012. 'Social Deprivation and Criminal Justice'. In *Rethinking Criminal Law Theory*, edited by François Tanguay-Renaud and James Stribopoulos, 217–230. Portland, OR: Oxford University Press.

Delport, Terblanche. 2016. 'Asazi Ukuthi Iyozala Nkomoni: Robert Mangaliso Sobukwe's Historical Imagination of the Future'. *Psychology in Society* 50: 35–52.

De Villiers, Les. 1975. *South Africa: Skunk among Nations.* London: Universal Tandem.

Fanon, Frantz. 2008 [1967]. *Black Skin, White Masks*, translated by R. Philcox. New York: Grove Press.

Gerhart, Gail. 1968. 'Interview with Potlako Leballo, Nairobi 1968'. Oral History, University of KwaZulu-Natal. https://disa.ukzn.ac.za/ora19680911000009000.

Hayes, Grahame. 2021. 'On Remembering Robert Mangaliso Sobukwe'. *Transformation* 106: 68–86.

Henderson, Moira. 1981. 'Obituary: Nell Marquard'. *Sash* 24, no. 1.

Holiday, Anthony. 1968. 'The Sobukwe Ritual'. *Rand Daily Mail*, 12 June.

Hook, Derek, ed. 2019. *Lie on Your Wounds: The Prison Correspondence of Robert Mangaliso Sobukwe.* Johannesburg: Wits University Press.

Mangcu, Xolela. 2012. *Biko: A Biography.* Cape Town: Tafelberg.

Marquard, Nell. 1986. 'Robert Sobukwe: A Personal Note'. *Reality* 10, no. 3.

Ng'weno, Hilary. 1978. 'I Would Split South Africa into Two Parts – Equitably'. *Weekly Review*, 19 May.

Nkrumah, Kwame. 1967. 'African Socialism Revisited'. https://www.marxists.org/subject/africa/nkrumah/1967/african-socialism-revisited.htm.

Nossiter, Bernard D. 1976. 'Angola War Called a Harbinger for S. Africa'. *Washington Post*, 3 February.

Pogrund, Benjamin. 1997. *Robert Sobukwe: How Can Man Die Better.* Johannesburg: Jonathan Ball.

Ramose, Mogobe Bernard and Derek Hook. 2016. 'To Whom Does the Land Belong? Mogobe Bernard Ramose Talks to Derek Hook'. *Psychology in South Africa* 50: 86–98.

Rand Daily Mail. 1975a. 'Sobukwe Now Qualified as an Attorney', 27 January.

Rand Daily Mail. 1975b. 'Sobukwe Allowed to Be at a Funeral', 6 May.

Sampson, Anthony. 1999. *Mandela: The Authorized Biography.* London: Vintage.

Selfe, J.H. 1945. 'Cassino'. In *The Sable, Italian Front Edition: Official Organ of the 6th Armoured Division,* edited by L.S. Wale, January.

Slobodian, Quinn. 2023. 'The Ciskei Experiment: A Libertarian Fantasy in Apartheid South Africa'. *The Guardian,* 23 March. https://www.theguardian.com/news/2023/mar/23/the-ciskei-experiment-a-libertarian-fantasy-in-apartheid-south-africa.

The Star. 1978. 'Barnard Speaks on Sobukwe', 1 March.

Zulu Voice. 1978. 'Liberal Given a Radical Drubbing by Buthelezi', 18–20 May.

Part II: Sobukwe's Speeches, Articles and Court Testimonies

Introduction

We've mentioned earlier that our task is not to provide either a personal or an intellectual biography for Sobukwe, at least not in a conventional sense. Our aim remains for him to speak; at best, we peer over his shoulder, as in the way to which the photograph of our preface sensitised us. Even so, there are some orienting remarks we feel necessary to make, in order for his voice to resonate more clearly in the present. To that end we've alerted the reader to the importance of our footnotes – commentary or direction from the wings, as it were, or *mise en scène* providing a fuller and more meaningful understanding of the action on centre stage. We continue this practice throughout.

However, there is also some commentary that needs to be somewhat more explicit. In keeping with the metaphor of the theatre, this would be those notes printed in the handbill or programme, which provide more background, some capsule details about the performers and the performance itself, and which anticipate comments or questions the audience may have. For example, there is an eleven-year gap between Sobukwe's 'completers' social' speech at Fort Hare College in 1949 and his article in *The Africanist* in 1958. What happened in the intervening decade? This short introduction to Part II serves to provide such detail.

The section starts with the speech Sobukwe delivered, as chairperson of the Student Representative Council, to the graduating class at Fort Hare. It is remarkable for its maturity and oratory. It was also a watershed moment in Sobukwe's life, a turn at a crossroads in many ways. The career trajectory he had imagined for himself a few years earlier, and the expectation among his benefactors, was that upon graduation he would return to Healdtown Institute as a teacher. The completers' speech, however, so angered the Methodist administrators of that institution that that path was closed down – he was now a clear 'troublemaker' and 'unsuitable' for a position at Healdtown. There are indications, though, that this was not quite the disappointment such administrators may have imagined, as Sobukwe felt a gnawing pull to make a contribution on a larger stage than that of a rural teacher, the prestige and importance of the Healdtown school notwithstanding.

Principal Clifford Dent of Fort Hare wrote a cordial and rather distant recommendation, and after several months of job hunting, Sobukwe secured a teaching position at a secondary school in Standerton, a sizeable agricultural and commercial town, but still nearly 200 kilometres from the buzz and energy of Johannesburg. Sobukwe's commitment to the profession and his students was wholehearted and passionate. Indeed, so too was his immersion in the community. He organised a tennis club and a soccer team, coached a choir, and fully participated in the life and events of the community. Inasmuch as the biographer and the psychologist attempt to draw themes from a life, what is already abundantly evident is Sobukwe's unswerving, thoughtful, sincere, conscientious, dedicated and ethical commitment to a cause, project and people.

Sobukwe spent nearly three years at Jandrell Secondary School. There was no likelihood of Sobukwe settling into sedentary small-town life. Throughout his stay in Standerton, he remained politically active and in fact recruited several people from the community to join the African National Congress (ANC), some of whom would travel to Johannesburg to become actively involved there. Nationally, the apartheid government was coming into confident force, rolling out one after the other restrictive law (the Population Registration Act, the Group Areas Act, the Suppression of Communism Act and the Immorality Amendment Act, for example, were all signed into law in quick succession in 1950). One of the major responses of the ANC to the government's energetic prosecution of apartheid was the Defiance Campaign, launched on 26 June 1952. The idea was for large-scale, national acts of defiance and civil disobedience – for example, burning pass books, going into 'whites-only' establishments, sitting on benches or in bus and train sections designated for whites only, or entering areas outside curfew hours. The government response was harsh and quick. Besides a dragnet sweep of arrests of both leaders and protesters, laws were amended so that instead of relatively small fines initially levied, infractions now carried heavy fines, lengthy jail sentences and physical punishment (such as lashing and whipping). Additionally, legal restrictions on more serious charges, such as treason or incitement to violence, were modified and relaxed, allowing for easier indictments on such charges. A cost-benefit analysis of sorts prompted the ANC to suspend the Defiance Campaign in 1953.

Standerton, however, was relatively isolated from the protests that took place in many of the major urban centres. It also did not have a concentration of politicised young intellectuals, unlike Fort Hare, which was even more isolated and rural than Standerton but capitalised on the conscientised political energy of youth. Even so, Sobukwe arranged for a public meeting, to be addressed by Nthato Motlana, whom he knew from his days at Fort Hare. (Alongside his political involvements, Motlana was studying medicine at the University of the Witwatersrand at the time. Dr Motlana, in later years, would become the Sobukwes' family physician.) Cautioned not to speak at this rally by neighbourhood friends and acquaintances, Sobukwe nonetheless did so. The result was that he was reported to the Department of Native Affairs and promptly fired from his job. In a rare instance of successful pushback, however, members of the clergy and school council filed an urgent petition for the department to review and overturn its decision, singing Sobukwe's praises and commitment as a teacher.

The year 1954 was an auspicious one, personally and professionally. Sobukwe married Zondeni Veronica Mate, a young nurse he had met during the nurses' strike at Victoria Hospital in Alice, where Fort Hare was also situated. He also successfully applied for a teaching position at the University of the Witwatersrand, in the Department of Bantu Languages. Thus it was that the Sobukwes moved to Johannesburg in June 1954. The family expanded soon with the birth of their daughter, Miliswa, followed by a son, Dinilesizwe, and thereafter twin boys, Dalindyebo and Dedanizizwe. Sobukwe also embarked on postgraduate studies while he was teaching at Wits, completing his honours degree in 1958. It was, however, an achievement darkened by the government's imposition of severe restrictions on access for black students to 'white' universities. Sobukwe in fact was the last black student to graduate with a postgraduate degree from the Department of Bantu Languages.[1] Clearly it

1 In an obituary for Sobukwe, on 13 March 1978, Professor Desmond T. Cole, then head of the Department of African Languages at Wits, remarked that Sobukwe 'was the last Black student to do a BA Hons in this department before the Government's restrictions' (Cole 1978).

was a demanding time: marriage, a new home, a new job, an expanding family of four children, and a rigorous academic course of study. One may rightfully wonder whether there was time for political organisation and involvement. It seems Sobukwe not only made time, but did so energetically: 'The hibernation of Standerton was over' (Pogrund 2015, 59).

Politics within the ANC was tense, and it is worth marking a key point of contention as background for the articles and testimonies to follow. At the end of 1949, the ANC drew up a national 'Programme of Action' as the guiding document for its future activities and goals. The influence of 'Africanists' and Youth League members is clear, as it emphasised the primacy of a national struggle that was also a cultural struggle, and of unity 'under the banner of African Nationalism', as a means to abolish white domination in all forms and spheres of life. However, with the banning of the Communist Party of South Africa in 1950, and an increasing willingness among the leadership of the ANC not only to welcome former communist members into the fold, but also to forge alliances with 'white' liberal organisations and 'Indian' constituents, there was a growing feeling that the ANC leadership was betraying the principles of the 1949 Programme of Action. Such suspicion seemed patently confirmed with the adoption in 1955 of the Freedom Charter at Kliptown, an event organised by a multiracial coalition of anti-apartheid organisations. For most Africanists, the perfidy of the ANC leadership was now publicly owned and complete. The key narrative tension and plot of the articles and testimonies to follow is, indeed, the unfolding and development of these differences.

The Africanist was a newsletter started by disaffected members of the ANC, particularly in the Youth League. This newsletter was to be a powerful outlet for Africanist views and for expressing frustration, anger and difference with ANC policies and direction. Potlako Leballo, whom we will meet again in the documents to follow, was the brazen and undaunted public face of the publication, but Sobukwe was the quiet force behind the scenes, in fact closely working to ensure the success of the newsletter. Not uncharacteristically for educators and teachers especially (and a lesson learned from Standerton), early contributions to *The Africanist* were made under a pseudonym ('Nzana' being one Sobukwe used as early as May 1955). This quiet, behind-the-scenes role was to change dramatically in 1957 when Sobukwe took over the editorship of *The Africanist*. Benjamin Pogrund, in his biography of Sobukwe, writes that what he 'initially viewed as timidity' in Sobukwe was in fact 'the hesitation and doubts of an honest man struggling to decide what he should do: who was trying to reconcile the conflict between the exceptional economic and social status he enjoyed as a black man, allied with his contented family life, with his emotional and intellectual commitment to gaining freedom for blacks' (Pogrund 2015, 68). At the end of 1957, Sobukwe had decided; he knew what course to commit his life to.

References

Cole, Desmond T. 1978. 'Obituary: Mr. Robert Sobukwe'. *The Reporter*, 13 March. http://historicalpapers-atom.wits.ac.za/uploads/r/historical-papers-research-archive-library-university-of-witwatersrand/f/3/c/f3c5dbea7a395fb1f95279359fa389c1347f957e-b3a879c64ffde849a7890370/A2618-Aa17-2-01-jpeg.pdf.

Pogrund, Benjamin. 2015. *Robert Sobukwe: How Can Man Die Better.* Johannesburg: Jonathan Ball.

1. Address on Behalf of the Graduating Class at Fort Hare College: 'Completers' Social' Speech by Robert Mangaliso Sobukwe, 21 October 1949

Prof. Dent,[1] Ladies and Gentlemen, I intend to follow in my opening remarks the conventional pattern.[2] And for that reason, I will give a very brief review of our doings within the College this year. We saw at the beginning of the year the implementation of the Students' Constitution, whereby six members of the S.R.C. were elected by secret ballot at a mass-meeting of

1 Prof. Clifford P. Dent was a lecturer in chemistry, and from 1949 through 1955 he served as principal and rector of Fort Hare.

2 The 'Completers' Social' was an important event on the university calendar, attended by teaching staff, administrators, and graduating students alike, and was traditionally organised by the Student Representative Council (SRC). The event in 1949, where Sobukwe spoke as president of the SRC, caused a particular stir among the administration and benefactors alike. One casualty of the fallout was the nascent campus branch of the ANC Youth League, started just a year earlier, in 1948, which was now banned from campus. Ultimately, the university Senate resolved to recognise the 'liberty of opinion and freedom of discussion' as befitted an institution of higher learning, but to prohibit the facilities of the college for 'gatherings the purpose of which is to translate discussions into action subversive to the interests of Fort Hare' (Williams 2001, 134–135).

the students and whereby also certain[3] were delegated to the Council. Of that arrangement the worst I can say is that it seems to be working well. We witnessed also at the beginning of the year the promotion of Prof. Dent to the position of Principal of the S.A.N.C.[4] He was succeeding a man who was highly esteemed, Dr. Kerr.[5] But I do not think we lament the change, for we are concerned not with personalities, but with policies, and there has been no change in this respect. Moreover, however much we may disagree with Prof. Dent on certain issues, we cannot say that he has ever refused students a chance to state their case. And I believe it is due to this fact that there has been no trouble in the College this year. After all, even the minor demonstration we had last term was not a reaction against the administration of the College. The stimulus came from outside.[6]

But that does not mean that all is well in the College. I had occasion last year and also at the beginning of this year to comment on some features of our structure of which I do not approve.[7] It has always been my feeling that if the intention of the trustees of this College is to make it an African College or University, as I have been informed it is, then the department of African Studies must be more highly and more rapidly developed. Fort Hare must become the centre of African Studies to which the students in African Studies should come from all over Africa. We should also have a department of Economics and Sociology. A nation, to be a nation, needs specialists in these things.

Again I would like to know exactly what the College understands by '*Trusteeship*'. I understand by '*Trusteeship*' the preparation of the African

3 A printed version of the speech adds 'powers' after 'certain' but a typescript (Sobukwe Papers, Ca1) suggests 'students' was meant.

4 In 1949 the institution was still known as the South African Native College (SANC), affiliated to the University of South Africa (Unisa), which had oversight of the college and awarded its degrees. In 1951 it became the University College of Fort Hare ('associated with Rhodes University in Grahamstown'). After the passage of the Extension of Universities Act of 1959, Fort Hare became an ethnic university for Xhosa students and a concerted programme was launched to align education and student life with apartheid ideology.

5 Dr Alexander Kerr served as the college's first principal and rector, occupying that role for over thirty years.

6 This euphemistically named 'stimulus' was the election to power, a year earlier, in May 1948, of the National Party, on the platform of apartheid.

7 There are several references to these speeches of Sobukwe, in 1948, including an impressive address to the incoming freshman class at the so-called Freshers' Social. There does not seem to be an archival transcript of these speeches, however, and they are unfortunately lost to history.

ward for eventual management and leadership of the College. But nothing in the policy of the College points in this direction. After the College has been in existence for 30 years, the ratio of European to African staff is 4 to 1. And we are told that in ten years' time we might become an independent University.[8] Are we to understand by that an African University predominantly guided by European thought and strongly influenced by European staff?

I said last year that Fort Hare must be [to] the African what Stellenbosch[9] is to the Afrikaner. It must be the barometer of African thought. It is interesting to note that the theory of 'Apartheid' which is today the dominating ideology of the State was worked out at Stellenbosch by Eiselen and his colleagues.[10] That same Eiselen is Secretary for Native Affairs. But the important thing is that Stellenbosch is not only the expression of Afrikaner thought and feeling but it is also the embodiment of their aspiration. So also must Fort Hare express and lead African thought. The College has remained mute on matters deeply affecting the Africans, because, we learn, it feared to annoy the Nats[11] Government. What the College fails to realise is that rightly or wrongly the Nats believe that the Fort Hare staff is predominantly U.P.[12] So that whether we remain mute or not the government will continue to be hostile towards us. So much for the College.

8 It is not sure how much Sobukwe knew beyond rumours or wishes, but at the time there were talks afoot among administrators and donors about just such a possibility.

9 The University of Stellenbosch became the premier Afrikaner university, a *volksuniversiteit* or people's university, where ideas about apartheid were developed in the 1940s especially among academic anthropologists or *volkekundiges* (see the following note).

10 Werner Max Eiselen, the son of a German missionary couple, was an anthropologist and linguist by profession. A professor of ethnology at Stellenbosch University in the 1930s, he helped lay the foundations of the Afrikaner nationalist version of anthropology known as *volkekunde*, which ascribed an essential nature and character to every *volk* or people. By ideological extension, the university was to be a *volksuniversiteit*, serving and nurturing the nature and character of a *volk* (people). In 1948 Eiselen was appointed secretary for native affairs, serving under Dr Hendrik Verwoerd, who was minister of native affairs from 1950 to 1956. As the head of the Eiselen Commission (appointed in 1949), which recommended what became known as Bantu Education, Eiselen had immense influence as an 'apartheid engineer'. As a result of this policy, Fort Hare was placed firmly under government control, stripped of missionary and church influences, and became an ethnic university for Xhosa students.

11 Popular form of reference to the National Party by its opponents.

12 Hardly 'progressive', the United Party under the leadership of General Jan Smuts nonetheless held more 'liberal' or 'tolerant' views with respect to racial segregation, a key reason for their electoral loss to the Nationalists in 1948.

Sons and daughters of Africa, harbingers of the new world-order. What can I say to you? As you see, for the first time since the practice was started, we do not have the nurses with us on this momentous night – Completers' Social. And the reason? The battle is on. To me the struggle at the Hospital is more than a question of indiscipline in inverted commas.[13] It is a struggle between Africa and Europe, between a twentieth century desire for self-realization and a feudal conception of authority. I know, of course, that because I express these sentiments I will be accused of indecency and will be branded an agitator. That was the reaction to my speech last year. People do not like to see the even tenor of their lives disturbed. They do not like to be made to feel guilty. They do not like to be told that what they have always believed was right is wrong. And above all they resent encroachment on what they regard as their special province. But I make no apologies. It is meet that we speak the truth before we die.

I said last year that our whole life in South Africa is *politics*, and that contention was severely criticised. But the truth of that statement has been proved in the course of this year. From the pulpit in the C.U.[14] we have heard responsible and respectable preachers deplore the deterioration of race relations in this country and suggest co-operation as a solution. Dr. Bruce Gardner [*sic*] and Rev. Mokitimi are but two of a large number.[15] Professor Macmillan[16] and a number of speakers in our Wednesday assembly, have condemned this 'naughty spirit of Nationalism and non-cooperation' and have told us of the

13 The 1940s saw a number of strikes by African nurses throughout the country. Perhaps the most serious protest of all took place at Victoria Hospital in Alice, close to Fort Hare. Students helped organise the strike, which stretched into three months of defiance, and supported the striking nurses in all kinds of ways. On a more personal note, it was here that Sobukwe met a young nurse, Zondeni Veronica Mate, whom he would marry five years later, in 1954.

14 Perhaps the most iconic and recognisable building on the Fort Hare campus, the Christian Union Hall served as common room, assembly hall, and a meeting space for students, as well as a place for formal church services on Sundays.

15 The Rev. Dr James Bruce Gardiner was a prominent Presbyterian minister who spent the last five years of his working life in Alice, where Fort Hare was situated. The Rev. Seth Mokitimi was chaplain at Healdtown Institute until 1951 and became the first elected African president of the Methodist Church in South Africa, in 1964. Mokitimi was not a 'radical' politically, but he was a religious and spiritual 'radical', staunchly believing in the human dignity and equality of black people.

16 The liberal historian William Miller Macmillan was professor of history at the University of the Witwatersrand from 1917 to 1933.

wonderful things that have been done for us, forgetting, of course, that what they say has been done for the Africans the Africans have achieved for themselves in spite of the South African Government. The point I am trying to make is that that was *politics*, whether we loved it or not. So that we can no longer pretend that there is a proper place and a proper occasion for politics. During the war[17] it was clearly demonstrated that in South Africa at least, politics does not stop this side of the grave. A number of African soldiers were buried in the same trench as European soldiers. A few days afterwards word came from the high command that the bodies of the Africans should be removed and buried in another trench. 'Apartheid' must be maintained even on the road to eternity.

The trouble at the Hospital then, I say, should be viewed as part of a broad struggle and not as an isolated incident. I said last year that we should not fear victimisation. I still say so today. We must fight for freedom – for the right to call our souls our own.[18] And we must pay the price. The Nurses have paid the price. I am truly grieved that the careers of so many women should have been ruined in this fashion. But the price of freedom is *blood, toil, and tears*. This consolation I have, however, that Africa never forgets. And these martyrs of freedom, these young and budding women will be remembered and honoured when Africa comes into her own.

A word to those who are remaining behind. You have seen by now what education means to us: the identification of ourselves with the masses. Education to us means service to Africa. In whatever branch of learning you are, you are there for Africa. You have a mission; we all have a mission. A nation to build we have, a God to glorify, a contribution clear to make towards the blessing of mankind. We must be the embodiment of our people's aspirations. And all we are required to do is to show the light and the masses will find the way. Watch our movements keenly and if you see any signs of 'broadmindedness' or 'reasonableness' in us, or if you hear us talk of practical experience as a modifier of man's views, denounce us as traitors to Africa.

17 The Second World War.

18 A remarkably prescient insight, prefiguring key aspects of Frantz Fanon's and Steve Biko's insistence on the psychological liberation of the black person alongside political liberation.

We will watch you too. We have been reminded time and again that fellows who, while at College, were radicals, as soon as they got outside became the spineless stooges and screeching megaphones of 'White Herrenvolkism'[19] or else became disgruntled and disillusioned objects of pity. My contention is: those fellows never were radicals. They were anti-White. And as Marcus Garvey[20] says: 'You cannot grow beyond your thoughts. If your thoughts are those of a slave, you will remain a slave. If your thoughts go skin-deep, your mental development will remain skin-deep.' Moreover, a doctrine of hate can never take people anywhere. It is too exacting. It warps the mind. That is why we preach the doctrine of love, love for Africa. We can never do enough for Africa, nor can we love her enough. The more we do for her, the more we wish to do. And I am sure that I am speaking for the whole of young Africa when I say that we are prepared to work with any man who is fighting for the liberation of Africa WITHIN OUR LIFE TIME.

To the completers among whom I number myself, my exaltation is: REMEMBER AFRICA! I thought last year that the position was bad. I realise it is worse this year. This is a difficult period to analyse. It is a confused period, such as only a Mqhayi, or Bereng, or Dickens[21] could describe. We are witnessing today the disintegration of old empires, and the integration of new communities.[22] We are seeing today the germination of the seeds of decay inherent in Capitalism; we discern the first shoots of the tree of Socialism. In married life we see a reversal[23] to what the Missionaries condemned when they first got here – *Polygamy*. But this time it is not the African who is the culprit, and the third party is not a second wife, but a

19 From the German *Herrenvolk*, 'master race or people'. Its political and rhetorical use here, and its localisation in South Africa from the 1930s onwards, assume particular significance against the backdrop of the extensive Nazi use of the term.

20 Marcus Garvey (1887–1940) was a Jamaican-born political activist and orator who espoused a strident and unapologetic black nationalism and Pan-Africanism.

21 Samuel Edward Krune Mqhayi was a seminal isiXhosa poet, novelist and scholar. David Cranmer Theko Bereng was a Sesotho poet who produced epic and lyrical depictions of Lesotho and the life of Moshoeshoe I. Sobukwe's mention of Bereng and Mqhayi on the same footing as the English novelist Charles Dickens is consequently as political a statement as any.

22 Sobukwe is referring to the widespread independence movements of several countries from their colonial administrations, as well as the newly professed socialist forms of governments in several Eastern European countries at the time, and the socialist intentions of independence movements in Africa and South-East Asia, especially, waiting in the wings to take power.

23 i.e. reversion.

mistress. We are witnesses today of cold and calculated brutality and bestiality, the desperate attempts of a dying generation to stay in power. We see also a new spirit of determination, a quiet confidence, the determination of a people to be free whatever the cost. We are seeing within our own day *the second rape of Africa*; a determined effort by imperialist powers to dig their claws still deeper into the flesh of the squirming victim. But this time the imperialism we see is not the naked brutal mercantile imperialism of the 17th and 18th centuries. It is a more subtle one – financial and economic imperialism under the guise of a tempting slogan, 'the development of backward areas and peoples'. At the same time we see the rise of uncompromising 'Nationalism' in India, Malaya, Indonesia, Burma, and Africa! The old order is changing, ushering in a new order. The great revolution has started and Africa is the field of operation. Allow me at this juncture to quote a few lines from the Methodist Hymn Book:

> Once to every man and Nation
> Comes the moment to decide,
> In the strife of truth with falsehood
> For the good or evil side.
>
> Then to side with truth is noble
> When we share her wretched crust,
> Ere her cause bring fame and profit
> And 'tis prosperous to be just.
>
> Then it is the brave man chooses
> While the coward stands aside,
> Till the multitude make virtue
> Of the faith they had denied.[24]

The cowards are still standing aside and the brave have made their choice. We have made our choice. And we have chosen African Nationalism because of its deep human significance; because of its inevitability and necessity to world progress. World civilisation will not be complete until the African has

24 Adapted from a poem by the abolitionist James Russell Lowell (eerily and aptly titled 'The Present Crisis'), these passages were also quoted by Martin Luther King, Jr in his 'We Shall Overcome' speech of 1966.

made his full contribution. And even as the dying so-called Roman civilisation received new life from the barbarians, so also will the decaying so-called western civilisation find a new and purer life from Africa.

I wish to make it clear again that we are anti-nobody. We are pro-Africa. We breathe, we dream, we live Africa; because Africa and humanity are inseparable. It is only by doing the same that the minorities in this land, the European, Coloured, and Indian, can secure mental and spiritual freedom. On the liberation of the African depends the liberation of the whole world. The future of the world lies with the oppressed and the Africans are the most oppressed people on earth. Not only in the continent of Africa but also in America and the West Indies. We have been accused of blood-thirstiness because we preach 'non-collaboration'. I wish to state here tonight that that is the only course open to us. History has taught us that a group in power has never voluntarily relinquished its position. It has always been forced to do so. And we do not expect miracles to happen in Africa. It is necessary for human progress that Africa be fully developed and only the African can do so.

We want to build a new Africa, and only we can build it. The opponents of African Nationalism, therefore, are hampering the progress and development not only of Africa, but of the whole world. Talks of co-operation are not new to us. Every time our people have shown signs of uniting against oppression, their 'friends' have come along and broken that unity. In the very earliest days it was the Missionary (we owe the bitter feelings between the Fingoes and Xhosas to the Christian ideals of the Reverend Shaw).[25] Between 1900 and 1946 it has been the professional Liberal. Today it is again the Missionary who fulfills this role. After maintaining an unbroken and monastic silence for years

25 The history of the amaMfengu ('Fingoes') remains, to this day, an intensely fraught and controversial political (and historiographical) minefield. The Mfengu were originally disparate and scattered peoples who fled from Shaka and his Zulu armies during the Mfecane wars. Banding together, they trekked south to the Cape and, after shrewd negotiations with the British government, secured tracts of land to settle on. They were intensely targeted by British missionaries, and gave support to the British authorities in clashes with the neighbouring Xhosa, who regarded them as collaborators with the white colonial forces and administration. Closer cultural and kinship ties with the Xhosa led to a near-complete 'assimilation' and rapprochement (though there are – for better or worse – contemporary movements to 'resurrect', 'acknowledge' or otherwise 'honour' a 'unique' Mfengu history and culture, separate from that of the Xhosa. The Rev. William Shaw was a leading Methodist cleric in South Africa in the first half of the nineteenth century and pioneered missionary work in the Eastern Cape, especially among the Mfengu.

while Smuts[26] was starving the people out of the Reserves, the Missionaries suddenly discovered, when the Africans unite, that the Africans have not had a fair deal. In the same stride, so to speak, they form a 'Union wide Association of Heads of Native Institutions' for the purpose of regimenting the thoughts of students.[27] A Missionary Hospital closes even though the people are dying in its neighbourhood, and there is a dearth of Nurses throughout the country. I am afraid these gentlemen are dealing with a new generation which cannot be bamboozled. 'What you are thunders so loudly that what you say cannot be heard.'[28]

Let me plead with you, lovers of my Africa, to carry with you into the world *the vision of a new Africa, an Africa re-born, an Africa rejuvenated, an Africa re-created, young AFRICA*. We are the first glimmers of a new dawn. And if we are persecuted for our views, we should remember, as the African saying goes, that it is darkest before dawn, and that the dying beast kicks most violently when it is giving up the ghost, so to speak. The fellows who clamped Nehru into jail are today his servants.[29] And we have it from the Bible that those who crucified Christ will appear before Him on the judgement day. We are what we are because the God of Africa made us so. We dare not compromise, nor dare we use moderate language in the course of freedom. As Zik[30] puts it: 'Tell a man whose house is on fire to give a moderate alarm; tell a man moderately to rescue his wife from the arms of

26 Jan Christian Smuts, prime minister of South Africa from 1919 to 1924 and from 1939 to 1948.

27 The Association of Heads of Native Institutions had been set up to provide direction to mission schools in the areas of administration, staff appointment and curriculum content. However, just a few months before Sobukwe's speech, the association held an important meeting, to respond to increasing threats, pressure and encroachment on mission education from the apartheid government. Their worst fears were realised with the passing of the Bantu Education Act of 1953, which effectively placed all education of black students under the oversight authority of the Department of Native Affairs, which would vigorously and systematically apply apartheid ideology in education. Sobukwe's comments reflect a wider historical view – that the association clung to outmoded missionary models, and was out of touch with the 'new African' and the demands and desires of the students.

28 A quotation adapted from Ralph Waldo Emerson.

29 The reference is to Jawaharlal Nehru, first prime minister of an independent India (in 1947).

30 Better known by the moniker Sobukwe uses ('Zik'), Nnamdi Azikiwe would become the first president of an independent Nigeria, in 1963. Azikiwe was already well known for his political activism and leadership in the independence and nationalist movements in Nigeria.

a ravisher; tell a mother to extricate gradually her babe from the fire into which it has fallen; but do not ask me to use moderation in a cause like the present.'

These things shall be, says the Psalmist: Africa will be free. The wheel of progress revolves relentlessly. And all the nations of the world take their turn at the field-glass of human destiny. Africa will not retreat! Africa will not compromise! Africa will not relent! Africa will not equivocate! And she will be heard! *REMEMBER AFRICA*![31]

Reference

Williams, Donovan. 2001. *A History of the University College of Fort Hare, South Africa: The 1950s; The Waiting Years.* New York: Edwin Mellen Press.

31 At the conclusion of his speech, the assembled students gave Sobukwe a standing ovation. Staff members, on the other hand, were stunned, and some felt hurt and betrayed, their sense of goodwill and good intentions seemingly maligned. Yet, what everyone in attendance shared was the recognition of witness to the public birth of a powerful, dedicated and able new leader.

2. Forward to 1958! Editorial by Robert Mangaliso Sobukwe, *The Africanist*, December 1957

Within a month's time we shall have passed another milestone on the long and tedious journey to freedom.[1] Others, too, will have passed a milestone. But they will be travelling on the treacherous and slippery road to doom. In both cases there applies the law of inevitability. But the goals are different and so is the spirit of the travellers. The forces of 'Tokoloho ka nako ea rona'[2] are marching on, buoyant and confident, not *looking* at their hill, but *climbing* it: On the other hand, the forces of retrogression, stagnation and 'man's inhumanity to man' are administering the last desperate kicks of a dying horse. Their doom is sealed; and they [know] it. The dawn of the glory of freedom is breaking, when man shall establish control over *things* and not over other *men:* And we know it. And thus we move into 1958.

1 The reader will note the suggestive title of this newsletter, as well as the date, *before* the Africanists split from the ANC. There were in fact several newsletters, leaflets and newspapers that articulated Africanist perspectives within Congress. Apart from *The Africanist,* of which Sobukwe was editor, there was the *Voice* (later the *Voice of Africa*) and the *African Lodestar.*

2 A Sesotho phrase meaning 'freedom in our lifetime'. While Sobukwe's father was from Lesotho, and he was a scholar of 'African languages' (the subject he taught at the University of the Witwatersrand), his first language background was isiXhosa. The use of the phrase is also indicative of a practice of code-switching, in which slogans and phrases from several African languages would be woven into political speeches.

The passing year has witnessed historic events, chief among which have been the women's militant struggle against 'Passes for Women' and the militant disciplined struggle of our nurses against nursing apartheid. There have been the long-drawn-out Treason Trials[3] and the magnificent June 26th 'Stay at Home' observance. There has been the glorious Bus Boycott side by side with the abortive 'Economic Boycott of Cigarettes and Tobacco'.[4] We have witnessed during 1957 a desire for unity and solidarity among the masses and a tendency towards crippling and contemptuous bureaucracy on the part of our leaders. It is a known fact that the Bus boycott was sabotaged by some unnamed individual 'higher-up', acting under certain influences. It is equally well known that quite a number of branches in the Transvaal heard about the planned Economic Boycott after the police and the manufacturers had been informed about it by 'New Age' and 'The Star' and 'Die Transvaler' etc.[5] In fact, 1957 has been a year of 'Directives' and 'Counter-Directives' from a variety of sources. But the struggle continues.

It continues, because the African masses today owe loyalty to the movement for liberation, to the concept of a disciplined, principled struggle for freedom, rather than to a particular individual or to a particular organisation.

---

3 The Treason Trial, which ran from 1956 to 1961, was mounted by the state against 156 members of the Congress Alliance, including Nelson Mandela; in the end, all were acquitted of the charge of treason.

4 Almost all the actions listed by Sobukwe had some or other prior precedent. What was different, in 1957, was not only the frequency and variety of protest actions, but also the wider coordinating role the ANC now started to play. The tobacco and cigarette boycott, for example, was meant to target tobacco companies supportive of the National Party, and involved as well a campaign in the UK to halt the importation of cigarettes and fruit from South Africa. As Sobukwe continues, he alerts us to the dangers of such an expanded coordinating role: that of a 'crippling bureaucracy', of possible leaks and betrayals, and of thwarting the passion and spontaneity of popular protest. The Evaton (1955) and Alexandra (1957) bus boycotts, for example, were not called by the ANC, but by residents of those townships, while some later boycotts, called by a 'central', more 'distant' body, met with much less success. We glimpse Sobukwe's ability to think praxis and strategy alongside theory, policy and goal, as well as his stress on the ethical primacy of the organisation, attentive and beholden to the aspirations of the people it serves.

5 Whereas they were newspapers all, the *New Age, The Star* and *Die Transvaler* occupied quite different ideological positions. The *New Age* was decidedly 'leftist' (in fact, it was started with funds from the communist Jewish Workers' Club), *The Star* (which exists to this day) was of a more 'centrist liberal' sort, while *Die Transvaler* was an Afrikaans newspaper expressly created to promote Afrikaner nationalism.

The point we are making is that, if the people today follow the ANC, it is not because of a sentimental attachment to the name or the organisation, but because they believe it to be the embodiment of their aspirations. So long as it gives the correct lead, they will follow it. But the more it deviates, the more it concentrates on opportunistic, vaporous *activity* as distinct from planned, programmatic *ACTION*, the faster the disillusioned masses detach themselves from it and sink into the mire of despair and apathy until a new Moses appears with a gospel ringing the correct chord.

The struggle in South Africa hinges on the twin problems of land and status. And our immediate battle is for '*STATUS*', political, economic, social etc. And 1958 must be a STATUS YEAR. And having discovered that in liberatory struggles, it is the accumulation of small victories which builds up the confidence of the masses and imbues them with the sense of the inevitability of victory, we propose, for 1958, a campaign against the appellations by which the Herrenvolk[6] are pleased to know us. Next year, we are going to put a stop to the terms 'Boys' and 'Girls', which are so ungrammatically used by white South Africa. As from next year, these terms are going to be used in their strict and correct dictionary meaning. So say we. We will no longer have 'Jack', 'George', 'Nancy', 'Jane', etc. as handy labels to be attached to any black man or woman by any white man or white woman, white boy or white girl. And we will start where we pay our hard-earned money for service – be it in a private shop or in a government office.

The best would be to start with the shops. We shall here demand that we be treated as customers and ADDRESSED AS SUCH! If the white boys and girls behind the city counters feel that that is too great a demand, they will either leave the shop or we shall make it a shop 'FOR EUROPEANS ONLY'. In short, we WILL DECLARE A TOTAL BOYCOTT on that shop, and the BOYCOTT will not be lifted UNTIL THAT SHOP CLOSES DOWN! We will stand no nonsense next year. This treatment will be meted out to ANY and EVERY shopkeeper in whose shop or business our people are treated as a nuisance rather than as welcome and desired customers. Whether the shopkeeper be black or white, coloured or Indian or Chinese etc. is immaterial. We demand OUR STATUS as customers.

6 i.e. master race.

We shall elaborate on this campaign in subsequent issues of the 'AFRICANIST'. But right now, we send out to our readers, the Christmas and New Year wishes of 'STATUS AND LAND'.

There is a song they sing in the deserted villages of Africa. It goes:

Noma sikhona, noma sesifile
Bakusala besho, bethi sasikhona!
(While we live, and even after we are gone,
They will remain saying, WE ONCE WERE!)

That, MA-AFRIKA, is the meaning of our struggle!
MAYI BUYE!![7]

---

7 *Mayibuye* means to restore, resurrect, revive, come back; hence, in the popular later coupling of *Mayibuye iAfrika*, it means to restore or resurrect Africa.

3. The Nature of the Struggle Today: Article by Robert Mangaliso Sobukwe (attributed to Potlako Leballo), *The Africanist*, December 1957

There is as yet no common agreement between the Africanists and the present leadership of Congress together with its allies on the nature of the struggle.[1] To the Africanists the struggle is both nationalist and democratic, in that it involves the restoration of the land to its rightful owners – the Africans – which fact immediately divides the combatants into the conquered and the conqueror, the invaded and the invader, the dispossessed and the dispossessor. That is a national struggle. It has nothing to do with numbers and laws. It is a fact of history. And both sides are each held together by a common history and are, in the struggle, carrying out the task imposed by history. That task is, for the

1 This article appeared in the same edition of *The Africanist* as the preceding editorial, which Sobukwe clearly owned as from his pen. One can speculate as to the reasons why this contribution was attributed to Potlako Kitchener Leballo, who played a key leadership role in the ANC Youth League. Perhaps it is as simple as not wanting to dominate contributions to the newsletter, or to create the impression of a variety of leadership voices all gesturing towards a similar goal. However, it is also true that as 1957 drew to a close, Africanist disagreements with the ANC were becoming more stridently vocal, Leballo's particularly so. Political gamesmanship and manoeuvring may well have figured in the calculation to attribute authorship to Leballo publicly. It is rather interesting and telling to read this article, knowing as we do now that Sobukwe was ventriloquising Leballo; there is both a certain freedom and a constraint, some things one can say which one would not dare say in one's own voice, but by the same token some things one cannot, and some aesthetic and stylistic ways of saying one has to forgo in order for the ruse to succeed. Indeed, compared with the previous article, the criticism of ANC leadership here is much more direct and pointed, as one would expect from Leballo.

24. Potlako Leballo addressing a political gathering while Sobukwe looks on. (APN252729, Drum Social Histories / BAHA / Africa Media Online)

whites, the maintenance and retention of the spoils passed on to them by their forefathers and, for the African, the overthrow of the foreign yoke and the reclamation of 'the land of our fathers'. At the same time, our struggle is for democracy, if we understand democracy to mean the implementation of the wishes of the majority of the inhabitants of a country, as expressed in the laws of the country. A democratic struggle is essentially then, a recognition of *NUMBERS*, a National struggle is a struggle for the recognition of *heritage*. The Africans are in the fortunate position of being not only the rightful owners of the land but also the majority of the population. Our struggle, therefore, is democratic, involving as it does, the dispossessed majority against the privileged minority.

The ANC leadership and its allies are preoccupied with the latter aspect of the struggle – the democratic, to the total exclusion, nay even the open renunciation and denunciation, of the Nationalistic. And from that difference in our conception of the struggle, stem the differences in tactics and interpretation of events.

The forces involved in the struggle

Because we differ from the leadership in our conception of the nature of the struggle, we differ in our assessment of the forces for and against us. The

Congress leadership, because it interprets the struggle as one for democracy and therefore a political struggle, designed to remove legal restrictions, recognises the foe as the present Nationalist government and accepts and treats everybody opposed to the Nationalist government whatever his motives and beliefs, as an ally. The Congress leadership, therefore, if we are to judge by its actions and utterances, recognises the Nationalist government as the rightful government of the country whose policies, however, it is not in agreement with. The leadership, therefore, conceives of Congress as an Opposition party, with an alternative policy to which the people of South Africa are to be persuaded to subscribe. The difference between the United Party[2] and Congress (as conceived by the leadership) lies in the policies they advocate and in their composition. The United Party is an All-White party, standing for white leadership and supremacy while Congress, in so far as its policies, under the present leadership, are determined by all the Congress, is multiracial and stands for a democratic franchise. But both the United Party and the Congress leadership accept the Nats[3] as the rightful government of the country whose policies, however, are disastrous to the country. And both believe that the essential thing to do is to oust the Nats. Both believe that the way to do so is by appealing to the people of South Africa for support for their policies. That is why a certain 'African leader' in an issue of 'Liberation', could state that 'we (i.e. Congress) should water down our demands in order that we should muster the broadest support against the Nats'.[4]

Congress, according to the present leadership, is a political party aspiring to Parliament though, as yet, having no representative in Parliament. That is why it is so difficult to effect a boycott of the white Native

2 The United Party (UP) was the ruling political party in South Africa between 1934 and 1948, with General Jan Smuts at its helm. It lost the 1948 election to the National Party. The issue of race was central to its losses at the polls, and it could never quite articulate a clear view or policy on that score; although opposed to the apartheid policies of the NP, the UP was also not ready to give up white minority rule.

3 In 1957, the National Party had been in power for nearly a decade, with J.G. Strijdom as its leader. After coming to power, it had moved swiftly to pass and implement a slew of apartheid laws, even as worse were still to come.

4 *Liberation* was a magazine which expressly focused on 'issues of concern to South African Blacks'. Subtitled 'A journal of democratic discussion', the magazine was published from 1953 to 1959. The 'African leader' referred to here might be Walter Sisulu, who had published an article barely a month earlier about needing to forge wide linkages with a variety of organisations in order to fight apartheid policies. Leballo's disdain for Sisulu was well known.

representatives in Parliament,[5] in spite of the unambiguous statement of the Nation-Building Programme of 1949.[6] It is believed by our leaders that the number of Whites subscribing to the Kliptown Charter[7] will increase so that one day a White party committed to the Kliptown Charter will form the government and implement the hopes and wishes expressed in that document!

But the AFRICANISTS who are committed to the overthrow of white domination, club together all who stand for the maintenance of the status quo and can find no common ground with the United & Labour Parties.[8] The AFRICANISTS are aware, too, that when danger threatens the interests of the rulers, they modify their policies in order to gain support of the oppressed. That is what happened during the dark days of the last war. But as soon as the danger is past, the rulers return to their old policies with more ruthlessness in order to crush any awakened hopes. The Nationalist government has trodden on the corns of many groups and many people are prepared to go a very long way to get rid of this government. But that does not mean that they subscribe to a thoroughly democratic constitution. Many, in fact, hate the Nats, because they are threatening the status quo. We are familiar with the diversionary

---

5 After the South African Parliament abolished the qualified franchise for African voters in the Cape Province in 1936, Africans were 'compensated' by being allowed to vote for three 'Native representatives', who had to be whites, in Parliament. Mrs Margaret Ballinger was one of them, serving until 1960, when the Native representatives were abolished.

6 The difference between the Nation-Building Programme of 1949 (the 'Programme of Action') and the Kliptown or Freedom Charter of 1955 is key. Besides renewed protest in the aftermath of the National Party coming to power in 1948, the ANC convened an all-important congress in December 1949, where the Programme of Action was adopted. Much of this Programme was devised and worded by prominent 'Africanists'. A few years later (26 June 1955), at the Congress of the People, convened at Kliptown, Soweto, the 'Freedom Charter' was unveiled. The collaborative product of the ANC, the South African Indian Congress, the Coloured People's Congress and the South African Congress of Democrats (a leftist, white organisation), the Charter exemplified the very manner of its multiracial and multi-ethnic genesis in its opening statement that would become exemplary for the Africanists of the whole document, and of the direction the ANC was taking: 'South Africa belongs to all who live in it, black and white'.

7 i.e. the Freedom Charter.

8 The South African Labour Party was a small opposition party, representing the interests of white workers (against competition from black workers). After the 1948 electoral victory of the National Party, the Labour Party opposed the NP quite vocally – certainly much more vigorously than the United Party. It was precisely this new direction which ultimately led to the party's demise.

role of the Liberals. And both Mrs. Ballinger's Liberal Party[9] and Beyleveld's C.O.D.[10] fulfill that role.

Current events

I do not intend to list the numerous oppressive laws manufactured by the Nats, or revised by them. What is essential is to note their trend and the reaction of the people to them. The Bantu Education Act, the Native Laws Amendment Act, the Universities and Nurses Apartheid Bills,[11] etc., have one thing in common. They are all part of a desperate attempt to delay the Nemesis of white domination. They all aim at creating a feeling of insecurity among the oppressed and thus making them a docile labour force which accepts resignedly its inferior status. In fact the aim is to make the oppressed BELIEVE that they are incapable of equalling, let alone surpassing, the white man in any field. We must learn that we can't do without the white man. We must believe that modern 20th century technology, which is the distinctive feature of so-called western civilisation, is, like everything good in S.A., 'For Europeans only – Slegs vir Blankes'.

Take the Passes for women. As Bloom so ably illustrates in his book 'Episode',[12] when dealing with the 'Permit', every African woman, in the eyes

9 Dissatisfied with the ineffectual and half-hearted opposition of the United Party, the Liberal Party of South Africa was formed in 1953. Initially, its intent was to change the minds of the white electorate towards accepting a qualified franchise. After the Sharpeville Massacre of 1960, the party took a more unequivocal 'leftist' turn towards a 'one man, one vote' franchise within a non-racial democracy. At the time of Sobukwe's writing, Margaret Ballinger was president of the party.

10 Pieter Beyleveld, president of the Congress of Democrats, the white arm of the Congress Alliance, was a union activist. He was also a member of the Labour Party, and was one of the accused in the Treason Trial of 1956–1961. When in 1964 Beyleveld turned state witness in the trial of Bram Fischer and others, he was ostracised by his former colleagues and disappeared into obscurity.

11 The Bantu Education Act was passed in 1953, enforcing racially segregated education at all levels. The Native Laws Amendment Act of 1952 severely limited the rights of blacks to live and work in urban areas. The Nursing Amendment Act of 1957 and the Extension of University Education Act of 1959 applied apartheid to the nursing profession and the country's universities, respectively.

12 Harry Bloom was a novelist, journalist and political activist. He was also involved in black cultural, aesthetic and creative life, contributing for example to the lyrics of the landmark 'all-African jazz opera' *King Kong*. His novel *Episode* (first published in 1955 and later re-issued as *Transvaal Episode*) dramatises the ways discriminatory race relations grow, fester and erupt into violence. One wonders whether Leballo would have read or referred to these books, let alone analysed and related them to the political landscape: Sobukwe's gambit may be slipping here and in some of the following references.

of the white conqueror, is a potential prostitute, an undesirable element – not a woman, mind you, or a mother. No. An *element*! That is why, therefore, there should be nothing wrong in subjecting her to indignity and humiliation. She is not a woman, just as her husband is not a man. If the dog, the man, carries a dog-collar in the form of a reference book, why not the bitch? Anthropologists all agree that a culture progresses only through contact. Prof. Childe[13] goes further and states that a culture cannot remain static. It either progresses or retrogresses. And lack of contact leads to retrogression. And Eiselen,[14] the Anthropologist, produces Bantu Education and ethnic grouping and Tribal Colleges TO STOP CONTACT on the side of the African, while maintaining it on the European side.

Reaction of the people

But the people are not taking this lying down. The most important development in South Africa today is the militant resistance of the women to the extension of Passes to them.[15]

The opposition is sporadic but brave. It is a little disorganised but courageous. Women in the rural areas and in Nationalist strongholds have defied Verwoerd[16] and his henchmen. We praise the women for their stand and Congress for organising that stand with her limited means. But there is a danger which we Africanists foresee. And it is that we come to regard our duty

13 V. Gordon Childe, a creative and innovative archaeologist and theorist, whose stimulating ideas of cultural evolution and change were also informed and shaped by Marxist critique and insight.

14 See this vol., ch. 1, n. 10. Werner Max Eiselen, an anthropologist and linguist by profession, was, at the time of Sobukwe's speech, Secretary for Native Affairs. As the head of the Eiselen Commission, he had been responsible for the formulation of the Bantu Education Act.

15 Initially pass laws targeted black men, but their restrictions on movement were extended to black women in 1956, the consequence of which was a wholly 'surprising' resistance. On 9 August 1956, for example, twenty thousand women marched to the Union Buildings in Pretoria to register their protest. The popular anti-apartheid slogan 'You strike the women, you strike the rock' comes from a chant at this march. Scores of women refused to carry the pass, openly defying the law.

16 Dr Hendrik Verwoerd had just taken office as prime minister a few months before Sobukwe writes here, but his views on apartheid were already well known, as he had served as minister of native affairs, and authored a series of apartheid laws, including the Bantu Education Act of 1953.

and role as opposing Verwoerd's laws. The Nats are carrying out their programme and if we are going to do nothing but oppose, we will never get anywhere, for every year will bring forth, as every year has brought forth, new oppressive laws, on top of the ones we are opposing. Thus while we are fighting Bantu Education, Passes for Women come along. While we are organising against that, Universities and Nurses Apartheid come along. Our sacred duty is to carry out OUR PROGRAMME, irrespective of what Verwoerd is doing. Let us take the offensive and pursue the Nation-Building Programme of 1949, relentlessly and honestly. And white domination will collapse. Whenever any item of that Programme has been implemented, no matter how emasculated, it has drawn overwhelming and enthusiastic support from the masses and has sent the conqueror shaking in his boots. I am thinking particularly of Defiance Campaign, the One Day Stoppage of Work, the Economic and Bus Boycotts. If these had been honestly and relentlessly pursued in the spirit of true African Nationalism, we would be discussing PRODUCTION today and not oppression.

Political faith for African freedom

The salvation of the African people as a nation lies in the ideal of African Nationalism, a dynamic and most powerful philosophy with tremendous force for the overthrow of foreign domination in Africa. The late Lembede[17] emerged with his thesis on Africanism. He gave us the direction as probably no other man could have done, and in doing so, saved us as a nation. We must have faith and devotion to duty with courage and a determination to defend our cherished ideals that Africa is for the Africans, that the Cause of Africa must triumph, that we must remember Africa first, that African nationhood must be achieved irrespective of whatever odds are facing us, and that our right to determine the destiny of our Fatherland is an inherent one. The dawn

17 Anton Muziwakhe Lembede was the founding president of the ANC's Youth League, and an intellectual mentor to many of the emerging leaders, including Oliver Tambo, Nelson Mandela and Walter Sisulu. He was also instrumental in crafting the Programme of Action, adopted by the ANC in 1949, to which Sobukwe is pleading a return. Lembede died suddenly and unexpectedly in 1947, at the age of 33, but his influence and ideas were particularly inspiring to the Africanists within the ANC. As an aside, it was Nelson Mandela who rushed Lembede to hospital, where he died.

of the day must come when fascist foreign rule shall have collapsed into a rubble.

The Freedom Charter is a political bluff. It promises a little wonderful heaven if not Utopia around the corner. The question is: How to get there? The answer is: There must be immediate implementation of the Programme of Action of 1949 and the principles laid down therein, item by item, for the achievement of the aims of the envisaged little heaven or the very proposed Utopia round the corner. It is utterly useless to go around shouting empty slogans such as 'The people shall govern', 'The people shall share',[18] without practical steps towards that government. We are merely being made tools and stooges of interested parties that are anxious to maintain the status quo.

Africa wills to be a nation, both for her own sake and that of humanity. Our Programme of African Nationalism must be implemented fully to the free and full development of our faculties and powers of our intellect and our aspirations. [The] African National Congress has made a catastrophic blunder by accepting foreign leadership by the whites. How can we have leaders who are also led? If this white leadership is denied, why was one Joe Slovo[19] of the Congress of Democrats allowed to become Chairman of the A.N.C. Commission of Enquiry in 1954, into disputes involving A.N.C. policies? He presided over this A.N.C. Commission as Chairman and passed sentences of expulsion against certain members of the A.N.C. including a member of the A.N.C. National Executive, from Congress.

What Constitutional powers did Mr. Slovo have in the A.N.C.? He being a white man and a non-member of the A.N.C., why was he given such powers by Mandela's regime at the time? These are powers vested only in the constitutional authority of the National Conference of the A.N.C. Why did Luthuli[20] fail to intervene in the matter? Is this not leadership by whites?

18 These are statements from the Freedom Charter.

19 At the time of this article, Joe Slovo had just begun to rise to prominence in the ANC. When the Communist Party was outlawed in 1950, Slovo, who was an active member, became involved with the Congress of Democrats, but after the 1955 Congress of the People in Kliptown, to which he was a delegate, Slovo moved closer to the ANC.

20 Albert Luthuli was president general of the ANC from 1952 until 1967, with Nelson Mandela as his deputy (as well as leader of the ANC Youth League). Luthuli suffered continued banning orders, arrests, and harassment from the apartheid government. The intention of such restrictions was to isolate Luthuli and abandon him to relative obscurity. This was all to change in 1960, when Luthuli became the first African to be awarded the Nobel Peace Prize. Propelled now into global recognition and renown, Luthuli had

Afrika desires the progressive improvement of her sons and daughters. She reveres genius and virtue, not hypocrisy and brute force. She desires instructors not masters; the worship of truth and not falsehood and in order that a self-confident African people must exist it is necessary that they should, through action and self-sacrifice, attain political consciousness and consciousness of their destiny. This must be achieved by the Africans for the Africans. It is possible that the battles of Blood River, Keiskam[m]ahoek and Thaba-Bosiu[21] will be fought again, this time under the banner of African Nationalism; here, history must be repeated, if our African revolutionary struggle must be victorious. In this struggle for African Freedom, there can be no compromise or apology, nor collaboration, nor servitude. Here, we fight it out and to the finish. We either go under or exist as a nation. We are convinced that the struggle is between the conquerors and the vanquished and there can be no compromise nor surrender on our part, nor can we agree to go 50s with the oppressor in Afrika.

It is time that we do not cringe on our knees before the enemies or African national independence, lest we be crushed by the weight of our own cowardice. There is no bravery possible for fearful people. We either perish or survive as an African nation. Our task can never be accomplished through insincerities to our principles nor by false doctrines of expediency; but only through persistent efforts; and self-sacrifice; by ceaseless preaching of our dynamic ideas of a new Afrika. We must destroy the so-called foreign experts in African Affairs in Afrika; the foreign rule; foreign traffickers, the place-hunters and the empty slogan-mongers from the East and West. We reject inexorably and outright the petty intruders, the would-be diplomats, West and Eastern functionaries who infiltrate into our ranks to whisper 'friendliness' for the sake of white domination as preached by Strydom–De Villiers Graaff[22] axis and other non-African organisations.

---

a powerful podium from which to publicise the horrors and injustices of the apartheid regime.

21 Blood River (Ncome), Keiskammahoek and Thaba Bosiu were all sites of colonial or settler battles, in which indigenous forces of the Zulu, Xhosa and Sotho respectively were defeated. The determination to 're-fight' and even 'avenge' the loss of land and liberty resulting from these battles was a popular motif in Leballo's rousing speeches.

22 Linking the leaders of two different parties – the National Party (led by J.G. Strijdom) and the United Party (led by Sir De Villiers Graaff) – Sobukwe is arguing that there is really no substantive difference between them; they all serve white domination in one way or another.

We are putting forward to the African people with forcefulness and courage the postulates on African Nationalism, for the deliverance of our Fatherland from white fascism and win our independence from foreign rule. Together, let us seek the most active and effective method of struggle against the menace of foreign domination in Afrika. This is our urgent immediate task.

Afrika is our Fatherland by decree of Providence and Divine right. We rise to give a pledge that Afrika must be freed. Therefore, let us turn to the graves of our African martyrs, Moshoeshoe, Sekukuni, Makana, Tshaka and Dingani[23] and pray for inspiration from them and from those who died for us in the Cause.

In conclusion, we must honour the memory of African revolutionary martyrs who have fallen beneath foreign tyranny; honour the tears of African mothers for their sons in prisons, in slavery, dead and in exile. We can no longer bear evil, injustice, usurpation and foreign arbitrary rule. If we ever betray the whole or part of our principles of African Nationalism, the Gods will destroy us.

i-AFRIKA

23 All the figures listed here – Moshoeshoe, king of the Sotho; Sekhukhune, king of the Pedi; Makhanda, a Xhosa leader and prophet; and Shaka and Dingane, kings of the Zulu – were accomplished and unifying leaders and warriors. The range of names, revered among all Africans, also has the discursive effect of presenting a unified African front against the oppressor.

4. Future of the Africanist Movement: Questions and Answers by Robert Mangaliso Sobukwe, *The Africanist*, January 1959

Q. *Who are the Africanists?*[1]

A. A simple answer would be that they are the members of the Africanist Movement. But, if one wishes to go deeper into the question, one would say that they are those Africans who believe that African Nationalism is the only liberatory outlook that can bind together the African masses by providing them with a loyalty higher than that of the tribe and thus mould them into a militant disciplined fighting force.

---

1 The National Conference of the ANC took place in March 1958, 'between' the previous document and this one. Tensions between the Africanists and ANC leadership came to a dramatic and sometimes violent head. Josias Madzunya and Peter Molotsi teamed up with Potlako Leballo to deliver a spirited public challenge and critique, and at some point Madzunya stormed the platform, and supporters on both sides pushed, shoved and threw a few punches, as the meeting devolved into chaos. We mention this event here to also highlight the absence of Sobukwe from these scuffles. This was not how 'Prof' (Sobukwe's emerging nickname) operated. In the dispatches of James Fairbairn (Jack Halpern), a reporter at the conference, Sobukwe's name is not mentioned once. In fact, in those newspaper reports, Leballo is credited as the 'leader' of the Africanists. The consequence of this disastrous conference was the creation of a working group to pursue the possibility of a new political organisation (see n. 5).

Q. *How long has your movement been in existence?*

A. The germ of the Movement was there even before the advent of the European. When Moshoeshoe brought together the scattered remnants of various African tribes and moulded them into a patriotic Sotho tribe, he was engaged in nation-building. Similarly Chaka's wars whereby he sought to establish a single authority in place of the many tribal authorities of Natal, were, we say, steps in the direction of nation-building. In the Cape the House of Gcaleka[2] was recognised as the Paramount authority. There is no doubt that the pressure of social and economic conditions would in time have given rise to the Union of these territories.

As a political *organisation*, however, we trace our origin to 1912 – the year the A.N.C. was born – with 1944 the year our Movement was given that purposiveness which helps to give clear direction and power to a mass struggle. It is in that year that *Lembede* and those in his immediate circle demanded from the A.N.C.:

1. A clear outlook: African Nationalism and Africanism.
2. A basic policy outlining our fundamental postulates with respect to our social intentions, especially in the ultimate future.
3. A Programme.

The first two demands, Lembede himself met, while the third was met in 1949 when the Africanists (known as the Congress Youth League) provided the A.N.C. with the popular Nation-Building Programme of 1949.

Q. *What are your differences with the A.N.C.?*

A. First of all we differ radically in our conception of the struggle. We firmly hold that we are oppressed as a subject nation – the African nation. To us, therefore, the struggle is a national struggle. Those of the A.N.C. who are its active policy-makers, maintain, in the face of all the hard facts of the S.A. situation, that ours is a class struggle. We are, according to them, oppressed as WORKERS, both white and black. But it is significant that they make *no attempt* whatsoever to organise white workers. Their white allies are all of them bourgeois!

Secondly we differ in our attitude to 'co-operation' with other national groups. Perhaps it might be better to say we differ in our understanding of

2 Moshoeshoe, Shaka and Gcaleka are recognised as leaders who sought to unify and build the Sotho, Zulu and Xhosa peoples respectively. The task now is to broaden their inspiration to secure the unity of all Africans, irrespective of clan or ethno-cultural differences.

the term 'co-operation'. We believe that co-operation is possible *only between equals*. There can be no co-operation between oppressor and oppressed, dominating and dominated. That is collaboration, *not* co-operation. And we cannot collaborate in our own oppression! The A.N.C. leadership, on the other hand, would seem to regard collaboration and co-operation as synonymous. They seem to believe that all that is required for people to be 'equals' is that they should declare that they are equals, and lo! the trick is done.

At the present moment the A.N.C. leadership regards anybody and everybody who is against the Nationalist government (for whatever reasons) as allies.

This latter attitude is the result of a mentality that continues to speak of South Africa as though it were an island, completely cut off from the continent and, therefore, able to fashion its own policies and programmes, unrelated to and unaffected by those of the other African States. We, on the other hand, have always been acutely aware of the fact that ours is a particular front in a battle raging across the continent. We claim Afrika for the Africans; the A.N.C. claims South Africa for all. To the A.N.C. leadership the present Nationalist government is the properly elected government of South Africa whose policies, however, it does not approve of. And the A.N.C.'s main struggle is to get the Nats[3] out of power. The fact that the Nats are a logical product of past South African history and that what they stand for is approved and supported by the overwhelming majority of whites in the country has apparently escaped the notice of A.N.C. leadership.

We, however, stand for the *complete overthrow of white domination*. That means that the S.A. Act of 1909[4] – that fossilised relic of the whiteman's exclusive privileges and prejudices – must be scrapped.

Q. *What is your answer to the accusation that you are anti-white?*
A. Our reply has been officially given in a statement appearing in the Golden City Post of Sunday 7th November, 1958 signed by Mr. P.K. Leballo

3 The ruling white Afrikaner National Party.

4 The South Africa Act of 1909 was passed by the British Parliament, and provided for the establishment of the white-dominated Union of South Africa. Ironically, just two years after this article, in 1961, the 1909 Act *was* scrapped when South Africa became a Republic and left the British Commonwealth. The aim was to enshrine white privilege and prejudice even more deliberately.

(Chairman) and Mr. S.T. Ngendane (Secretary).[5] On the material level we just cannot see any possibility of co-operation. To say that we are prepared to accept anybody who subscribes to our Programme is but to state a condition that one knows cannot be fulfilled. From past history, not only of this country but of other countries as well, we know that a group in a privileged position never voluntarily relinquishes that position. If some members of the group appear to be sympathetic to the demands of the less-privileged, it is only in so far as those demands do not threaten the privileges of the favoured group. If they (the privileged) offer assistance, it is for the purpose of 'directing' and 'controlling' the struggle of the underprivileged and making sure that it does not become 'dangerous'.

Q. *But are you anti-white or not?*
A. What is meant by anti-whiteism? Is it not merely an emotional term without a precise signification? Let me put it this way: In every struggle, whether national or class, the masses do not fight an abstraction. They do not hate oppression or capitalism. They concretise these and hate the oppressor, be he the Governor-General or a colonial power, the landlord or the factory-owner, or, in South Africa, the white man. But they hate these groups because they *associate them with their oppression*! Remove the association and you remove the hatred. In South Africa then, once white domination has been overthrown and the white man is no longer 'white-man boss' but is an individual member of society, there will be no reason to hate him and he will not be hated even by the masses.

We are not anti-white, therefore. We do not hate the European because he is white! We hate him because he is an oppressor. And it is plain dishonesty to say I hate the sjambok[6] and not the one who wields it.

5 As mentioned, tensions between the ANC leadership and the Africanists in their ranks had come to a dramatic and contentious head a few months earlier. It was clear that the differences were irreconcilable. In response, an Africanist Working Group was established to explore the possibility of launching a new political organisation. Potlako Leballo was the chairman of this group, and Selby Themba Ngendane its secretary. Leballo had become an organiser for the ANC Youth League while a student at Lovedale and continued his involvement in Youth League affairs while teaching in the Transvaal; by the mid-1950s he was in charge of its Orlando East branch. Ngendane was an alumnus from Fort Hare, having graduated a few years after Sobukwe did. Ngendane, too, became involved in politics at Fort Hare, joining the ANC Youth League there and cutting his political teeth in the 1952 Defiance Campaign. Upon moving to Johannesburg to study law, he was drawn into the Africanist circle and soon rose to leadership positions.

6 Whip, symbol of white control.

Q. *Do you regard all whites as oppressors?*
A. We regard them all as shareholders in the S.A. Oppressors Company (Pty.) Ltd. There are whites, of course, who are intellectually converted to our cause, but because of their position materially, they cannot fully identify themselves with the struggle of the African people. They want safeguards and check-points all along the way, with the result that the struggle of the people is blunted, stultified and crushed.

Q. *Do you include white leftists in your indictment?*
A. There are NONE! And there have never been any in South Africa – white or black. All we have had are quacks. In fact, like Christianity, Communism in South Africa has been extremely unfortunate in its choice of representatives.

Q. *Do you think the Africanist Movement will last?*
A. Not only will it last, it will flourish. History is already vindicating our stand as far as the continent is concerned. We are in step with the continent. And the reason is that we correctly interpret the aspirations of the African people. We are not exaggerating when we say that the demand for membership is more than we can cope with.[7]

Q. *Why can't you cope with the demand?*
A. Because we lack funds. You see we do not want a blind following. We want an intelligent, informed and politically educated membership. We, therefore, require a full-time information service, full-time organisers and, above all, well-run offices. We don't want undisciplined branches mushrooming all over the country. And to maintain the necessary contact, discipline and co-ordination, we need funds.

Q. *Do you think the African people will tolerate a splinter movement at this stage?*
A. The African people want freedom and they are extremely anxious to find themselves as a Nation. They are aware of the futility of the post-1949 struggles of the A.N.C. with more and more emphasis on spectacular activity as

7 Readers in the present, and with hindsight and experience of the ANC's absolute political dominance over the last thirty or forty years, need to be reminded that the Africanists enjoyed widespread support in the late 1950s and through the 1960s. Nelson Mandela remarked, for example, that upon his arrival on Robben Island in 1962, the majority of inmates, by far, were PAC members and supporters.

distinct from principled programmatic action. That is why they have welcomed our emergence.

Q. *What is your attitude to the A.N.C.?*
A. We say, 'Let the best man win.' If the A.N.C. launches campaigns which we believe are for the good of our people, we will support them wholeheartedly. But we are not going to get ourselves involved in muddled, clumsy, senseless activity. We have the 1949 Programme to implement, and as it unfolds and its dynamism is revealed, the A.N.C. will cease to exist. Perhaps the Congress alliance may eke out a precarious existence for some time. But there will be only one organisation for the African people – and that will be the Africanist Movement.

Q. *Have you decided on a Name yet?*
A. No – not on a national level. Such matters as a name, policy, the Constitution, etc., will be finalised at the National Convention which we hope to hold in April. From then onwards we shall operate on a National level. And from then onwards we will sweep the country.

5. Manifesto of the Africanist Movement: Ratified at the PAC Inaugural Convention, Orlando, Johannesburg, 4–6 April 1959

A. A chain of reaction[1]

The significant portion of our social milieu begins with the expansion of the markets founded by the rising commercial capital of Western Europe at the turn of the fifteenth century. Succeeding years witnessed the 'discovery' of new lands by the Europeans, the Papal award of the whole of Africa to the Portuguese, increased European slave raids on Africa that denuded Africa of Africans and led to the establishment in the Americas of the greatest mass chattel slavery that the world had ever known. Africa had been successfully robbed of Africans. It was this chattel slavery that contributed substantially to the initiation of the European industrial revolution which in turn resulted in the unleashing of the forces of reaction which culminated in the rape of Africa at the close of the last century.

1 The manifesto is variously attributed to Peter Raboroko, Sobukwe and A.P. Mda – sometimes also simply to the PAC. One can reasonably assume that all these figures, as well as others even, discussed what such a manifesto should look like and contain, and it is also true that the actual writing of the manifesto might have been a collaborative or apportioned effort. What is clear, though, is the unmistakable impression of Sobukwe's rhetorical signature and intellectual thumbprint.

B. Land robbery and political subjugation

Early European settlement of Africa, especially of its southern tip, was a direct result of the rise of European commercial capital. Wave upon wave of European settlers came to Africa and their penetration of the interior involved the loss of sovereignty by the indigenous peoples and the alienation of more and more portions of their land. With the rise of the industrial capital of Europe and its increased search for raw materials and more markets, the partition of Africa went apace and the doctrine of 'effective occupation' was enunciated, a theory calculated to 'sugar coat' the bitter pills of land robbery and political subjugation. More and more settlers came into the country until today there are 5,000,000 Europeans who up to the dawn of African liberation had constituted themselves as a ruling class over the 250,000,000 indigenous peoples. Africans had been successfully robbed of Africa.

C. Established by the sword

The advent of European imperialism and colonialism to Africa brought in its wake the phenomenon of white domination, whether visible or invisible, which is characterised by the political oppression, economic exploitation and social degradation of the indigenous African masses. Throughout this historical epoch, the age of white domination, whenever the spokesmen or representatives of white domination have sprouted a conscience, they have referred to the phenomenon as the 'spread of Western civilisation' or 'the extension of Christian trusteeship'. *The undisguised truth is that White domination has ground down the status of man and stunted THE NORMAL GROWTH OF THE HUMAN PERSONALITY ON A SCALE UNPRECEDENTED IN HUMAN HISTORY.* White domination was established by the sword and is maintained by the sword.

D. Expulsion of imperialist exploiters

Significant events of the twentieth century, especially of the latter part of it, have constituted a massive challenge to Herrenvolkism,[2] a particular manifestation of imperialism and colonialism. Already European exploiters and oppressors have been dramatically expelled from such countries as

2 Master race ideology.

Indonesia, India, China, Burma, Malaya, Vietnam, etc. These are today being systematically routed and forcibly caused to retreat in confusion. The post-war world has witnessed the expulsion of the European imperialist exploiters and oppressors from large tracts of Africa and the emergence of no less than nine sovereign and independent African states. We are witnessing indeed a twilight of the tin gods of white domination – a *götterdämmerung*.

E. Decolonisation and independence

Elsewhere in Africa the progressive forces of African nationalism continue to be locked in mortal combat with the reactionary forces of Herrenvolkism. By the end of next year the peoples of Togoland,[3] Somaliland,[4] the Cameroons[5] and Nigeria[6] will have achieved freedom. The French policy of 'association' is also being rejected in favour of decolonisation and independence.

F. The liquidation of the forces of oppression

To the chagrin of the imperialists, the government of Free Algeria is a reality.[7] Tanganyika, Kenya and Uganda are on the verge of obtaining their freedom from British imperialism.[8] Contrary to their traditional policy the Belgian imperialists have been forced to accede, at least in principle, to the African people's demand for the recognition of their independence in the Congo. The policy of partnership pursued in the Central African Federation[9] has been exposed for what it is: the greatest political fraud of our times.

---

3 Togoland attained independence in 1960, as the Republic of Togo.

4 British Somaliland became independent in June 1960 and then united with the former Italian Somaliland to form the Somali Republic.

5 Cameroon, previously split into French, German and British colonies, celebrated unified independence as the Republic of Cameroon in 1961.

6 The British colony of Nigeria became independent in October 1960.

7 In 1958 the National Liberation Front (FNL), then fighting the Algerian War of Independence, formed a Provisional Government of the Algerian Republic; in the following year, Charles de Gaulle declared that Algerians had the right to determine their own future. Eventually in 1962 Algeria achieved independence from France.

8 Tanganyika (present-day Tanzania) achieved independence in 1961, Kenya in 1963 and Uganda in 1962.

9 The Central African Federation, formed in 1953, brought together Southern Rhodesia (current Zimbabwe), Northern Rhodesia (current Zambia) and Nyasaland (current Malawi), but under pressure from African nationalists in all three countries it was officially dissolved in 1963.

Even in those massive concentration camps, Angola and Mozambique, the African people have begun to reject the *status quo* in favour of their own freedom. *The liquidation of the forces of oppression is a process that not even nuclear power can halt.*

G. Right to shape own destiny

The days of European domination of Africa are numbered. Even in South Africa the writing is glaringly on the wall for those of our European rulers who can see and decipher it. For exactly three hundred and seven years today,[10] the African people have been criminally oppressed, ruthlessly exploited and inhumanly degraded. They have in the past, as they do now, declared themselves for freedom. They reject white domination in any shape or form. They are unflinchingly determined to wrest the control of their country from alien hands. They are determined to exercise the most fundamental of human rights, the inalienable right of indigenous people to determine and shape their own destiny. To the African people there can be no room in any way or in any part of Africa for any non-indigenous peoples who deny to the indigenous populations their fundamental right to control their own material and spiritual interests effectively. South Africa, which is an integral part of the continent, is the inalienable heritage of the African people and its effective control is their undoubted and unquestionable birthright.

H. No longer with the ranks of the Liberation Movement

Following the 'capture' of a portion of the black leadership of South Africa by a section of the leadership of the white ruling class, the masses of our people are in extreme danger of being deceived into losing sight of the objectives of our struggle. This captured black leadership claims to be fighting for freedom when in truth it is fighting to perpetuate the tutelage of the African people. It is tooth and nail against the Africans gaining the effective control of their own country. It is fighting for the maintenance of the *status quo*. It is fighting for the 'constitutional guarantees' or 'national rights' for our alien nationals.

---

10 Colonial settlement and oppression have traditionally been reckoned as beginning with the arrival of a Dutch party of settlers under Jan van Riebeeck at the Cape on 6 April 1652. The fact that the PAC manifesto was unveiled on 6 April resurfaces as a point of scrutiny from the magistrate in the Monyake trial (see this vol., ch. 10).

It has completely abandoned the objective of freedom. It has joined the ranks of the reactionary forces. It is no longer within the ranks of the liberation movement.[11]

I. White domination without frills and trappings

These 'leaders' consider South Africa and its wealth to belong to all who live in it,[12] the alien dispossessors and the indigenous dispossessed, the alien robbers and their indigenous victims. They regard as equals the foreign master and his indigenous slave, the white exploiter and the African exploited, the foreign oppressor and the indigenous oppressed. They regard as brothers the subject Africans and their European overlords. They are too incredibly naive and too fantastically unrealistic to see that the interests of the subject peoples who are criminally oppressed, ruthlessly exploited and inhumanly degraded, are in sharp conflict and pointed contradiction with those of the white ruling class. Citizen Toussaint[13] once remarked that: 'Whenever anybody, be he white or mulatto, wants a dirty job done, he always gets the Negro to do it.' The charterist[14] leadership, true to type, is doing the oppressor's dirty job, namely, seeing to it that the African is deprived for all time of his inherent right to control his country effectively; of seeing to it that whatever new social order is established in this country, the essentials of white domination are retained, even though its frills and trappings may be ripped off. This attitude has been labelled MULTI-RACIALISM by their white masters. They have even boldly suggested that being a multi-racialist is a virtue!

J. One race: The human race

The African people are very much proud of their race – the human race. They recognise no inescapable fundamental differences among members of even the three main branches of that race: the Caucasoids, Mongoloids and Afrinoids.

---

11 This paragraph, and the one to follow, are thinly veiled references to the ANC leadership.

12 A reference to prominent statements in the Freedom Charter.

13 François-Dominique Toussaint Louverture fought for Haitian independence from the French between 1791 and 1804. He was the most prominent general and leader of the Haitian Revolution and is known as the 'Father of Haiti'.

14 A reference to the ANC, which adopted the Freedom Charter in 1955.

They do not subscribe to the theory that there are inherent mental, emotional and psychological differences among the members of the different branches of the human species. They hold the granting of 'rights' on the basis of ethnological origin to be the entrenching of racial arrogance and the continued maintenance of contempt for human worth and disregard for human dignity.

They regard the differences that exist among various groups or subgroups of man to be mainly acquired, and they regard these differences to have been acquired in and through the individual. The African people recognize the influence of common environmental factors in the acquisition of group characters. They do not and will not tolerate any division of their country for purposes that are calculated to foster racial arrogance, and the continued contempt for the worth of the human personality, and the disregard for human dignity. The African people are fully aware that suggestions of apartheid, whether total or partial, of segregation social or political, of Christian trusteeship, white leadership with justice, of partnership etc., are all intended merely as a cloak for their continued oppression, exploitation and degradation. *They deny the foreigners any right to balkanise or pakistanise their country.* To any such schemes, programmes or policies, the African people cannot be a party. The African people are neither racists nor racialists, and they unreservedly condemn all forms of racialism, including multi-racialism. They do not nurse any crude hatred for the European peoples but they do cherish a deep-seated detestation for the Herrenvolk system.

K. Monolithic giant – Union of African States

The African people of South Africa recognise themselves as part of one African nation, stretching from Cape to Cairo, Madagascar to Morocco, and pledge themselves to strive and work ceaselessly to find organizational expression for this nation in a merger of free, independent African states; a United States of Africa, which will serve as an effective bulwark against the forces of imperialism, colonialism, herrenvolkism and tribalism, and as a sure and lasting foundation for an Africanistic socialist democracy. The African people regard the development of such a nation as essential for the preservation of their sovereignty, of their vital material and spiritual interests and for the creation of conditions under which they will be enabled to make their lasting contribution to human advancement in a free Afrika.

The African people will not tolerate the existence of the other national groups within the confines of one nation. For the healthy growth and development of the African nation, it is imperative that all individuals must owe their first, and only, loyalty to the African nation, and not to their ethnic or national groups. The African people regard the influence of material conditions in the development of a nation as being of greater significance than mere ethnic origin. Within the social environment of the African nation there will be room for all individuals who identify themselves materially, intellectually and spiritually with the African nation.

In South Africa the social force which upholds the material, intellectual and spiritual interests of the oppressed peoples is African nationalism, and the social force which upholds the material, intellectual and spiritual interests of the oppressor is Herrenvolkism. These antithetical forces shall find their final reconciliation only[15] in the synthesis of Africanism, in which the contradictory aspects shall have vanished and only the unifying factors which betray no instability shall remain. *Africanism is a social force that upholds the material, intellectual and spiritual interests of the individual.* In this way Africanism is the only logical and practical solution for the social question in Africa.

L. Social relations

The basic question confronting the African people is identical with that which has faced mankind from the beginning of time itself: the problem of man's relation to his fellowman. It is the question of how man shall live with his fellowman in fellowship, in harmony and in peace.

Man moves and has his being in a social environment. In the absence of social life the social question would fall away. Man's relation to his fellowman is determined by his primary needs. The social question, whose structural foundations are to be found in economic determinism, arises within the framework of social relations.

Man is, therefore, a social being and not an economic ANIMAL. To live in harmony with his fellowman, man must recognise the primacy of the material and spiritual interests of his fellowman, and must eliminate the tendency on his part to uphold his own interests at the expense of those of his fellowmen. It is only within

15 Another version gives 'everlasting' instead of 'only'.

such a set-up that the human personality can be developed and that respect for it can be developed.

M. Our historic tasks

The historic tasks of the African liberation movement are clearly the product of Africa's history, of the forces and factors which have made it what it is. To attain complete freedom in Africa, the historic tasks of the movement are:

To forge, foster and consolidate the bonds of African nationhood on a Pan-African basis.

To implement effectively the fundamental principle that the dominion or sovereignty over and the dominion or ownership in the whole territory of the continent vest exclusively and inalienably in the indigenous peoples.

To create and maintain a United States of Africa that will serve and provide a concrete institutional form for the African nation.

To establish an Africanistic socialist democratic social order, recognising the primacy of the vital material, intellectual and spiritual interests of the individual.

A liberation movement must find concrete expression in organisational form and substance in order that it may achieve its historic tasks. The highest organisational form and structure in which the African liberation movement has found concrete expression in South Africa is the NATIONAL AFRICANIST CONGRESS[16] and the various facets of its historic role are:

To create an organisational machinery for the galvanising of the oppressed, exploited and degraded African masses into an irresistible social force bent upon the destruction of all factors and forces that have reduced the stature of man and retarded his growth; and also bent upon the creation of conditions favourable for the restoration of man's worth and dignity and for the development of the African personality.

To establish for the liberation movement a training ground for the production of a determined, dedicated and disciplined collective leadership that will serve, not only as the symbol of national unity on a Pan-African basis, but also as the repository, guardian and custodian of the ideas, principles and methods of the movement, as well as of the policies and programmes of the organisation.

16 Later versions of the text give 'Pan' instead of 'National'.

To provide an administrative machinery for the direction, guidance and control of the national liberation movement in its grand march towards the inevitable goal of complete freedom.

N. Africanism: A third social force

Africanism is Pan-Africanistic in scope, purpose and direction. It is a social force that constitutes the third social force in the world. It serves the material, intellectual and spiritual interests of Africa, and does not in any way serve the interests of either the Eastern or the Western powers. It is continental in scope, covering the entire continent from Cape to Cairo and from Madagascar to Morocco. It is a social force functioning through the media of African social conditions, and operating to liberate Africa and to create a socialist social order, original in conception, Africanistic in orientation, socialistic in content, democratic in form and creative in purpose. Pan-Africanism became a concrete reality when African nationalists from all over the continent met at Accra. The All-Africa People's Conference, held in Accra in December 1958,[17] laid a promising organisational foundation for African nationalism on a Pan-African basis.

O. Final triumph

In its dialectical march towards the final synthesis of Africanism, African nationalism is destined to create the conditions favourable for the development of the African personality.

The final triumph of the liberation movement under the direction of the P.A.C. is assured. The movement must triumph because in their march to freedom the African people have history on their side. The militant progressive forces of African nationalism are bound to crush the reactionary forces of white domination. The movement must triumph because the P.A.C. alone has a message for the oppressed, that their salvation lies in manifest determination to unite as a nation and to struggle for the noble ends of freedom and self-determination. The movement must triumph because, having

17 Dr Kwame Nkrumah of Ghana organised the first All-African People's Conference, its primary aims being to strengthen newly independent African states and to assist independence movements in regions still under colonial rule. The conference was held in Accra, Ghana, from 8 to 13 December 1958, and was attended by over 300 delegates from 28 countries and colonies.

been purified in the crucible of oppression, the African people can demonstrate to the world genuine democracy in action, a democracy founded upon the ruin of the material and spiritual conflicts and contradictions of the existing social order, a democracy in which man shall at long last find his true self, and a democracy in which the human personality shall blossom to the full.

6. Opening Address: by Robert Mangaliso Sobukwe to the PAC Inaugural Convention, Orlando, Johannesburg, 4–6 April 1959

Mr. Speaker, Sir, Sons and Daughters of Afrika![1]

Mr. Speaker has already informed you that we had hoped that this inaugural Convention of the Africanists would be opened by

1 After the Kliptown Conference in 1955, and the adoption of the Freedom Charter, the Africanists within the ANC felt increasingly disaffected. Initially, there were attempts to pressure change from within – indeed, it was Sobukwe's preference and wish that the ANC would 'readopt' Africanist views. The ANC itself, it seems, did not foresee or imagine a breakaway, rival organisation. In truth, neither did Africanists outside the Transvaal. One should also mention a broader African Nationalism and hope: several African countries were on the verge of independence from colonial powers (Morocco, Tunisia and Ghana gained independence in 1956–1957, and there was a clear timeline for several others to follow), and a celebrated and successful Conference of Independent African States was held in Ghana, exactly a year earlier – in April 1958 – where Kwame Nkrumah officially marshalled and formalised Pan-Africanism among a community of African states. The public pronouncements and speeches of people like Potlako, Leballo and Josias Madzunya became more bellicose, and the rift was driven to the public fore by journalists and newspaper reporting. Thus it was that three to four hundred Africanists gathered in Orlando in April 1959, voting to formally constitute a new organisation, the Pan Africanist Congress, to promote Africanist ideals, ideology, and aspirations.

Dr. Kamuzu Hastings Banda,[2] failing which, by Mr. Kenneth Kaunda[3] of the Zambia African National Congress in Northern Rhodesia. Both have been unable to attend our convention, for both are now, in the language of the colonialists, 'detained' in some concentration camps because they dared to demand the right of self-determination for the indigenous African people of Nyasaland and Northern Rhodesia. The honourable task of opening this conference has, therefore, fallen to me, an Africanist, and I wish to thank the Central Committee for the honour. I am particularly grateful for the opportunity this offers me to treat briefly of certain issues relevant to our struggle which, though adequately treated in the documents that will be considered by this Convention, require to be presented to such a gathering.

I hope, then, Mr. Speaker, in the course of my address, to answer broadly questions pertaining to our stand in contemporary international politics, our relation to the states of Afrika, both independent and dependent, our attitude to the entire nationalist movement in Afrika, our stand on the question of Race in general and the so-called racial question in South Africa. Finally, I hope to outline briefly our ultimate objectives.

International scene

We are living today, Sons and Daughters of the Soil, fighters in the cause of African freedom, we are living today in an era that is pregnant with untold possibilities for both good and evil. In the course of the past two years we have seen man breaking asunder, with dramatic suddenness, the chains that have bound his mind, solving problems which for ages it has been regarded as sacrilege even to attempt to solve. The tremendous, epoch-making scientific achievements in the exploration of space, with man-made satellites orbiting the earth, the new and interesting discoveries made in the Geophysical Year,[4]

---

2 At the time of this speech, Dr Hastings Kamuzu Banda had returned to his native Nyasaland and begun campaigning against the Federation of Rhodesia and Nyasaland; he was arrested in March 1959 after a State of Emergency was declared. Banda would, in 1964, become the first prime minister and, later, president of an independent Malawi.

3 Kenneth Kaunda, having founded the Zambian African National Congress in 1958, was arrested and imprisoned for his opposition to the Federation of Rhodesia and Nyasaland, and his party was banned. He would become the first president of an independent Zambia in 1964.

4 Lasting from July 1957 to December 1958, the International Geophysical Year (IGY) was an international project of scientific collaboration and interchange between 67 countries.

the production of rust-resistant strains of wheat in the field of agriculture, the amazing discoveries in the fields of medicine, chemistry and physics – all these mean that man is well on the way to establishing absolute control over that environment.

However, in spite of all these rapid advances in the material and physical world, man appears to be either unwilling or unable to solve the problem of social relations between man and man. Because of this failure on the part of man, we see the world split today into two large hostile blocks, the so-called Capitalist and Socialist blocks represented by the U.S.A. and the Soviet Union respectively. These two blocks are engaged in terrible competition, use tough language and tactics, employ brinkmanship stunts which have the whole world heading for a nervous breakdown. They each are armed with terrible weapons of destruction and continue to spend millions of pounds in the production of more and more of these weapons. In spite of all the diplomatic talk of co-existence, these blocks each behave as though they did not believe that co-existence was possible.

Afrika's position

The question then arises, where does Afrika fit into this picture and where, particularly, do we African nationalists, we Africanists in South Afrika, fit in?

There is no doubt that with the liquidation of Western imperialism and colonialism in Asia, the Capitalist market has shrunk considerably. As a result, Afrika has become the happy-hunting ground of adventuristic capital. There is again a scramble for Afrika and both the Soviet Union and the United States of America are trying to win the loyalty of the African States. Afrika is being wooed with more ardour than she has ever been. There is a lot of flirting going on, of course, some Africans flirting with the Soviet camp, and others with the American camp. In some cases the courtship has reached a stage where the parties are going out together; and they probably hold hands in the dark but nowhere has it yet reached a stage where the parties can kiss in public without blushing.

This wooing occurs at a time when the whole continent of Afrika is in labour, suffering the pangs of a new birth and everybody is looking anxiously and expectantly towards Afrika to see, as our people so aptly put it, *ukuthi iyozala nkomoni* (what creature will come forth). We are being wooed internationally at a time when in South Africa the naked forces of savage Herrenvolkism[5] are running riot; when a determined effort is being made to annihilate the African people through systematic starvation; at a time when brutal attempts are being made to retard, dwarf and stunt the mental development of a whole people through organised 'miseducation'; at a time when thousands of our people roam the streets in search of work and are being told by the foreign ruler to go back to a 'home' which he has assigned them, whether that means the break up of their families or not; at a time when the distinctive badge of slavery and humiliation, the 'dom pass'[6] is being extended from the African male dog to the African female bitch.[7] It is at this time, when fascist tyranny has reached its zenith in South Afrika, that Afrika's loyalty is being competed for. And the question is, what is our answer?

Our answer, Mr. Speaker and children of the Soil, has been given by the African leaders of the continent. Dr. Kwame Nkrumah[8] has repeatedly stated that in international affairs, Afrika wishes to pursue a policy of positive neutrality, allying herself to neither of the existing blocs but, in the words of Dr. Nnamdi Azikiwe[9] of Nigeria, remaining 'independent in all things but neutral in none that affect the destiny of Afrika'. Mr. Tom Mboya[10] of Kenya has expressed himself more forthrightly, declaring that it is not the intention of African states to change one master (western imperialism) for another (Soviet hegemony).

We endorse the views of the African leaders on this point. But we must point out that we are not blind to the fact that the countries which pursue a

5 Master-race ideology, first associated with the Nazi Party in Germany.

6 The pass book for Africans was colloquially referred to as a *dompas*. In Afrikaans, *dom* means 'stupid' or 'dumb', hence, the reference to a 'stupid pass'. The term may also derive from, or refer to, an abbreviation for the ironic and Orwellian designation of the passbook as a '*dom*estic *pass*port', especially in light of the designation of separate 'homelands' or 'Bantustans' for Africans. Of course, these explanations need not rival each other, and both could be true.

7 Sobukwe is referring, in a calculatedly offensive and vulgar way, to the extension of pass laws from black men to black women.

8 Kwame Nkrumah led Ghana to independence in 1957, and served as its first prime minister. As keen a scholar and intellectual as he was a strategist, Nkrumah was a founding member of the Organisation of African Unity, and advocated a thoughtful political philosophy of Pan-Africanism.

9 Active in securing Nigeria's independence from Britain in 1960, Nnamdi 'Zik' Azikiwe became president of Nigeria in 1963.

10 Thomas Mboya was an activist and key figure in the struggle for Kenyan independence (declared in 1963). After independence, Mboya served in a ministerial capacity in Jomo Kenyatta's cabinet.

policy of planned state economy have outstripped, in industrial development, those that follow the path of private enterprise. Today, China is industrially far ahead of India. Unfortunately, however, this rapid industrial development has been accompanied in all cases by a rigid totalitarianism notwithstanding Mao Tse Tung's 'Hundred Flowers' announcement.[11] Africanists reject totalitarianism in any form and accept political democracy as understood in the west. We also reject the economic exploitation of the many for the benefit of a few. We accept as policy the equitable distribution of wealth aiming, as far as l am concerned, to equality of income which to me is the only basis on which the slogan of 'equal opportunities' can be founded.

Borrowing then the best from the East and the best from the West we nonetheless retain and maintain our distinctive personality and refuse to be the satraps or stooges of either power block.

Relation states in Afrika

Our relation to the States in Afrika may be stated precisely and briefly by quoting from George Padmore's book, 'Pan-Africanism or Communism'.[12] Discussing the future of Afrika, Padmore observes that 'there is a growing feeling among politically conscious Africans throughout the continent that their destiny is one, that what happens in one part of Afrika to Africans must affect Africans living in other parts'.

We honour Ghana as the first independent state in modern Afrika which, under the courageous nationalist leadership of Dr. Nkrumah and the Convention People's Party, has actively interested itself in the liberation of

11 The Hundred Flowers Campaign (from 1956 through 1957) was an attempt by Mao Zedong to invite the open expression of citizens' opinions of the Chinese Communist Party. It was a spectacular failure, and was followed by a severe crackdown on dissent.

12 George Padmore was a Trinidad-born author and thinker whose writings had a powerful impact on Pan-Africanist thought. He was a close advisor to Kwame Nkrumah, his books were widely read, and his eventual home in London became an Africanist meeting place, sanctuary, and think tank of sorts. The liberation of Africa, Padmore believed, could only come from a united and organised Pan-African movement to overthrow colonialism, imperialism and global capitalism. Education and cultural identity were to be part and parcel of the political struggle. Indeed, developing a sense of pride in Africa's heritage and history was as important a resistance tool as all kinds of political protests. One clearly sees here the inspiration for the Africanists, and even for the later Black Consciousness Movement. Padmore's book *Pan-Africanism or Communism?* was first published in 1956.

the whole continent from White domination, and has held out the vision of a democratic United States of Afrika. We regard it as the sacred duty of every African state to strive ceaselessly and energetically for the creation of a United States of Afrika, stretching from Cape to Cairo, Morocco to Madagascar.

The days of small, independent countries are gone. Today we have, on the one hand, great powerful countries of the world; America and Russia cover huge tracts of land territorially and number hundreds of millions in population. On the other hand the small weak independent countries of Europe are beginning to realise that for their own survival they have to form military and economic federations, hence NATO and the European market.[13]

Beside the sense of a common historical fate that we share with the other countries of Afrika, it is imperative, for purely practical reasons, that the whole of Afrika be united into a single unit, centrally controlled. Only in that way can we solve the immense problems that face the continent.

National movements in Afrika

It is for the reasons stated above that we admire, bless and identify ourselves with the entire nationalist movements in Afrika. They are the core, the basic units, the individual cells of that large organism envisaged, namely, the United States of Afrika; a union of free, sovereign independent democratic states of Afrika.

For the lasting peace of Afrika and the solution of the economic, social and political problems of the continent, there needs must be a democratic principle. This means that White supremacy, under whatever guise it manifests itself, must be destroyed. And that is what the nationalists on the continent are setting out to do. They all are agreed that the African majority must rule. In the African context, it is the overwhelming African majority that will mould and shape the content of democracy. Allow me to quote Dr. DuBois,[14] the father of Pan-Africanism: 'Most men in the world', writes DuBois, 'are coloured. A belief in humanity means a belief in coloured men. The future of the world will, in all

13 The European Economic Community, known as the Common Market, was formalised in 1957.

14 W.E.B. DuBois (1868–1963), an American sociologist and writer, was a pioneering advocate of Pan-Africanism, who later moved to Accra, Ghana, where he died and was buried. He is best known for his book *The Souls of Black Folk*.

reasonable possibility, be what coloured men make it.' As for the world, so for Afrika. The future of Africa will be what Africans make it.

The race question

And now for the thorny questions of race. I do not wish to give a lengthy and learned dissertation on Race. Suffice it to say that even those scientists who do recognise the existence of separate races, have to admit that there are border line cases which will not fit into any of the three Races of mankind.

All scientists agree that all men can trace their ancestry back to the first Homo Sapiens, that man is distinguished from other mammals and also from earlier types of man by the nature of his intelligence. The structure of the body of man provides evidence to prove the biological unity of the human species. All scientists agree that there is no 'race' that is superior to another, and there is no 'race' that is inferior to others.

The Africanists take the view that there is only one race to which we all belong, and that is the human race. In our vocabulary therefore, the word 'race' as applied to man, has no plural form. We do, however, admit the existence of observable physical differences between various groups of people, but these differences are the result of a number of factors, chief among which has been geographical isolation.

In Afrika the myth of race has been propounded and propagated by the imperialists and colonialists from Europe, in order to facilitate and justify their inhuman exploitation of the indigenous people of the land. It is from this myth of race with its attendant claims of cultural superiority that the doctrine of white supremacy stems. Thus it is that an ex-engine driver[15] can think of himself as fully qualified to be the head of the government of an African state, but refuse to believe that a highly educated black doctor, more familiar with Western culture than the White premier is, cannot even run a municipal council. I do not wish to belabour this point. Time is precious. Let me close discussion of this topic by declaring, on behalf of the Africanists, that with

15 Born in Rhodesia (Zimbabwe) to an Afrikaner mother and a Jewish-Lithuanian father, Roy Welensky worked on the railways, before becoming prime minister of the Federation of Rhodesia and Nyasaland. The 'doctor' Sobukwe is referring to here is Dr Hastings Banda, who, as we have seen in n. 2, opposed the Federation, and ultimately became president of an independent Malawi; he drew particular criticism from Welensky.

UNESCO we hold that 'every man is his brother's keeper. For every man is a piece of the continent, a part of the main, because he is involved in mankind.'[16]

In South Afrika

In South Africa we recognise the existence of national groups which are the result of geographical origin within a certain area as well as a shared historical experience of these groups. The Europeans are a foreign minority group which has exclusive control of political, economic, social and military power. It is the dominant group. It is the exploiting group, responsible for the pernicious doctrine of White Supremacy which has resulted in the humiliation and degradation of the indigenous African people. It is this group which has dispossessed the African people of their land and with arrogant conceit has set itself up as the 'guardians', the 'trustees' of the Africans. It is this group which conceives of the African people as a child nation, composed of Boys and Girls, ranging in age from 120 years to one day. It is this group which, after 300 years, can still state with brazen effrontery that the Native, the Bantu, the Kaffir is still backward and savage etc. But they still want to remain 'guardians', 'trustees', and what have you, of the African people. In short, it is this group which has mismanaged affairs in South Africa just as their kith and kin are mismanaging affairs in Europe. It is from this group that the most rabid race baiters and agitators come. It is members of this group who, whenever they meet in their Parliament, say things which agitate the hearts of millions of peace-loving Africans. This is the group which turns out thousands of experts on that new South African Science – the Native mind.

Then there is the Indian foreign minority group. This group came to this country not as imperialists or colonialists, but as indentured labourers. In the South African set-up of today, this group is an oppressed minority. But there are some members of this group, the merchant class in particular, who have become tainted with the virus of cultural supremacy and national arrogance. This class identifies itself by and large with the oppressor but, significantly, this is the group which provides the political leadership of the Indian people in South Africa. And all that the politics of this class have meant up to now

16 The quote is from the United Nations Educational, Scientific and Cultural Organization's declaration, in 1950, on 'The Race Question'. It forcefully argued that there is no scientific evidence for different races, or for biological or genetic attributes specific to 'races'.

is preservation and defence of the sectional interests of the Indian merchant class. The down-trodden, poor 'stinking coolies' of Natal who, alone, as a result of the pressure of material conditions, can identify themselves with the indigenous African majority in the struggle to overthrow White supremacy, have not yet produced their leadership. We hope they will do so soon.[17]

The Africans constitute the indigenous group and form the majority of the population. They are the most ruthlessly exploited and are subjected to humiliation, degradation and insult.

Now it is our contention that true democracy can be established in South Africa and on the continent as a whole, only when White supremacy has been destroyed. And the illiterate and semi-literate African masses constitute the key and centre and content of any struggle for true democracy in South Africa. And the African people can be organised only under the banner of African nationalism in an All-African Organisation where they will by themselves formulate policies and programmes and decide on the methods of struggle without interference from either so-called left-wing or right-wing groups of the minorities who arrogantly appropriate to themselves the right to plan and think for the Africans.

We wish to emphasise that the freedom of the African means the freedom of all in South Africa, the European included, because only the African can guarantee the establishment of a genuine democracy in which all men will be citizens of a common state and will live and be governed as individuals and not as distinctive sectional groups.

Our ultimate goals

In conclusion, I wish to state that the Africanists do not at all subscribe to the fashionable doctrine of South African exceptionalism. Our contention is that South Africa is an integral part of the indivisible whole that is Afrika.

17 The relationship of South Africans of Indian descent to indigenous Africans is a complex one. There is a long-standing tradition of protest within this community, starting with Mahatma Gandhi's leadership when he worked as an attorney in South Africa. However, even then, the accusation was made that these actions were self-interested. A distinction was often made between the descendants of the indentured Indian labourers brought to South Africa in the late nineteenth century and the merchant class, whose prosperity it was claimed came on the backs of local Africans. Many members of this class were, however, to be found on the side of the anti-apartheid movement.

She cannot solve her problems in isolation from and with utter disregard of the rest of the continent.

It is precisely for that reason that we reject both apartheid and so-called multi-racialism as solutions of our socio-economic problems. Apart from the number of reasons and arguments that can be advanced against apartheid, we take our stand on the principle that Afrika is one and desires to be one and nobody, I repeat, nobody has the right to balkanise our land.

Against multi-racialism we have this objection, that the history of South Africa has fostered group prejudices and antagonisms, and if we have to maintain the same group exclusiveness, parading under the term of multi-racialism, we shall be transporting to the new Afrika these very antagonisms and conflicts. Further, multi-racialism is in fact a pandering to European bigotry and arrogance. It is a method of safeguarding white interests, implying as it does, proportional representation irrespective of population figures. In that sense it is a complete negation of democracy. To us the term 'multi-racialism' implies that there are such basic insuperable differences between the various national groups here that the best course is to keep them permanently distinctive in a kind of democratic apartheid. That to us is racialism multiplied, which probably is what the term truly connotes.

We aim, politically, at government of the Africans by the Africans, for the Africans, with everybody who owes his only loyalty to Afrika and who is prepared to accept the democratic rule of an African majority, being regarded as an African. We guarantee no minority rights, because we think in terms of individuals, not groups.

Economically we aim at the rapid extension of industrial development in order to alleviate pressure on the land, which is what progress means in terms of modern society. We stand committed to a policy guaranteeing the most equitable distribution of wealth.

Socially we aim at the full development of the human personality and a ruthless uprooting and outlawing of all forms or manifestations of the racial myth. To sum it up, we stand for an Africanist Socialist Democracy.

Here is a tree rooted in African soil, nourished with waters from the rivers of Afrika. Come and sit under its shade and become, with us, the leaves of the same branch and the branches of the same tree. Sons and Daughters of Afrika, I declare this inaugural convention of the Africanists open! IZWE LETHU!![18]

18 Our land!!

7. The State of the Nation: Speech by Robert Mangaliso Sobukwe on 'National Heroes' Day', 2 August 1959

Mr. Speaker Sir, Sons and Daughters of Afrika.[1] Just over three months ago, on the 6th April, we met in the Communal Hall in Orlando, Johannesburg, to launch the ship of freedom – the Pan Africanist Congress. On that historic day the African people declared total war against white domination, not only in South Africa but throughout the continent. On that day there entered into the maelstrom of South African politics an organisation dedicated to the cause of African emancipation and independence; an organisation committed to the overthrow of white supremacy and the establishment of an Africanist Socialist Democracy.

Oppressed versus oppressor

It is just over three months that the Pan Africanist Congress has been born, but within that short space of time she has successfully pinpointed the basic assumptions in our struggle, namely that:

1. The illiterate and semi-literate masses of the African people are the key to, the core and cornerstone of the struggle for democracy in this country.

1 National Heroes Day was a day of remembrance and renewal, designated as one which all members of the Pan Africanist Congress should observe for rededicating themselves to the cause of Pan-Africanism. The actual date for Heroes Day was 31 July (originally the A.M. Lembede Anniversary) but was celebrated here on a Sunday, two days later.

2. African nationalism is the only liberatory creed that can weld these masses who are members of heterogeneous tribes into a solid, disciplined and united fighting force; provide them with loyalty higher than that of the tribe and give formal expression to their desire to be a nation.
3. The struggle in South Africa is part of the greater struggle throughout the continent for the restoration to the African people of the effective control of their land. The ultimate goal of our struggle, therefore, is the formation of a United States of Afrika.

These pronouncements have struck a responsive chord in the hearts of the Sons and Daughters of the land, and awakened the imagination of the youth of our land while giving hope to the aged who for years have lived in the trough of despair. Indeed, the aged can now truly say:

'Lord now lettest Thou thy servant depart in peace, according to Thy will[2]:
For mine eyes have seen Thy salvation.'[3]

The issues are clear-cut. The Pan Africanist Congress has done away with equivocation and clever talk. The decks are cleared, and in the arena of South African politics there are today only two adversaries: the oppressor and the oppressed; the master and the slave. We are on the eve of a continental showdown between the forces of evil and the forces of righteousness; the champions of oppression and the champions of freedom. Realising this, the oppressor is panic-stricken and is making feverish preparations for a last-ditch stand in defence of white supremacy. On the other hand, the forces of freedom are gathering strength from day to day, disciplining, nerving and steeling themselves for the imminent struggle.

Afrika for Africans

Once again, as in 1949, the African people are waiting expectantly and eagerly the emergence of a bold and courageous programme from the Pan Africanist

2 The King James Bible has 'word', not 'will'.

3 Luke 2: 29–30. This well-known scriptural passage, the Canticle of Simeon, formed an important part of worship services, across Catholic, Anglican and Methodist denominations. Religion was not only an abiding feature of Sobukwe's home environment and development, but it remained personally and intimately important to Sobukwe himself. Crucially, he was aware of the politically oppressive uses of religion in South African and was supremely able to separate his personal religious views from the political needs of the people.

Congress, an organisation that has its roots among the masses, and whose leadership comes from their loins. Not only has the Pan Africanist Congress succeeded in raising the eyes of our people above the dust of immediate conflict to the genuine democracy that lies beyond the stormy sea of struggle but it has imparted a meaning and a purpose to their struggle. The African people, therefore, are awake! They are waiting, waiting eagerly and expectantly, waiting for the call, the call to battle, to battle for the reconquest of the continent of Afrika which for over 300 years has been the prostitute of the philanderers and rakes of western capitalism. IZWE LETHU I AFRIKA (Africa, Our Land)[4] – that is the cry ringing throughout the continent. Afrika for Africans. A democratic rule of an African majority. IZWE LETHU I AFRIKA! Those are the words that spell the doom of white supremacy in Afrika.

Position in the continent

Throughout the continent of Afrika the struggle is being relentlessly waged against the historical anachronisms of imperialism, colonialism and white supremacy. Precious African blood is flowing in Algeria, where the Sons and Daughters of Afrika, under the courageous leadership of Ferhat Abbas of the government of Free Algeria[5] are paying the supreme sacrifice for the recovery of the destroyed shrines.

Greater and greater efforts are being made by the independent countries of Afrika to mould, shape and assert the African personality, and to lay the foundations for a United States of Afrika. Just recently the heads of the States of Ghana, Guinea and Liberia met in conference to discuss methods of furthering the cause of Pan-Africanism.[6]

In Tanganyika, Nyerere[7] is fighting for the revision of the multiracial constitution imposed on the African people by imperialist Britain, and is

4 The translation misses the subtle meanings involved in hearing and understanding the slogan as an affirmative and imperative, which could be 'The *land* (Afrika) is ours', or '*Afrika* is our land', or 'Afrika is *our* land'.

5 An activist for Algerian independence, Ferhat Abbas was appointed president of the Provisional Algerian Government in Exile in 1958.

6 Presidents Tubman of Liberia and Touré of Guinea, and Prime Minister Nkrumah of Ghana met in July 1959 in Liberia, where they affirmed their vision of a 'Community of Independent States', and drew up a Statement of Principles that such a federation would adhere to.

7 An anti-colonial activist, scholar and politician, Julius Kambarage Nyerere became independent Tanganyika's (later Tanzania's) first president, in 1961.

pressing for the practical application of a non-racial democratic principle of 'one man one vote'. In Uganda, as our Bulletin stated, 'British imperialism is locked in mortal combat with African nationalism'.[8] In Central Afrika tension is going high, and there is clear evidence that in the struggle between Kamuzu Banda and Roy Welensky,[9] Banda will emerge triumphant. In fact, the signs are that not only Nyasaland but also Northern Rhodesia as well, will secede from the unholy federation of Welensky and Lennox-Boyd.[10]

South Africa

Throughout Afrika, then, the forces of white supremacy are in retreat before the irresistible march of African nationalism. This is the era of African emancipation. Afrika holds the stage today. For the first time, positive action is being taken by the world against the inhuman policies of South Africa's white settler foreign minority governments.[11] And the countries that have taken the lead in this world-wide boycott of South African goods are the countries of Afrika and those governed by people of African descent. And in South Africa, what is the position? Well you all know that there has been talk from certain quarters of 'hitting the nationalists in the stomach'. We would have used the word 'belly', but responsible, moderate leaders, you see, do not use such ugly words.[12] There was such talk

8 Uganda would gain independence from Britain in 1962, with Dr Milton Obote as its first prime minister.

9 Roy Welensky was prime minister of the Federation of Rhodesia and Nyasaland, against which Dr Hastings Kamuzu Banda led a popular campaign in Nyasaland. Sobukwe's prediction proved correct: Banda would, in 1964, become the first prime minister of an independent Malawi.

10 Alan Lennox-Boyd was the British Secretary of State for the Colonies from 1954 to 1959. The 'agreement' between Lennox-Boyd and Welensky (then prime minister of the Federation) would sour, and ultimately, the Federation dissolved into an independent Malawi, Zambia and (Southern) Rhodesia.

11 Upon winning independence in 1947, India had severed ties with South Africa, as did several African countries. The ANC was gaining international sympathy and support for sanctions, and the 'Boycott Movement' was launched in London in June 1959, in direct response to ANC president Albert Luthuli's call. Sobukwe is perfectly correct in taking the temperature of a growing international sanctions movement against apartheid South Africa.

12 The 'certain quarters' are the ANC, who started to realise the power of international sanctions and boycotts of South African products, and the not-so-subtle dismissal is

then, and lists were prepared. But immediately one so-called 'nationalist concern' made certain sectional trade-Union concessions, it was no longer a nationalist controlled firm, and its products were no longer nationalist products. The old meaningless stunts are still being used by certain quarters. But there is a boycott of beerhalls launched by the courageous women of Durban[13] – a movement originating from the masses and controlled by them. Nobody doubts its success. The evidence is there for all to see. If their 'friends' do not interfere with the Durban women they will undoubtedly achieve their goal[14] – acquiring for the African in Durban the status of human beings. There is also the potato boycott[15] which, while commanding the active support of all persons because of the atrocities perpetrated by white farmers against African convict labourers, has unfortunately been handled by the quarters aforementioned.[16] The result has been that these quarters which fear the militancy of the African people more than they loathe oppression, are hoping and praying that the boycott will fizzle out before they are compelled to call it off.

---

directed at a 'moderate ANC leadership' and Albert Luthuli specifically (who said of such an economic boycott that it would 'punch them in the stomach'). Discursively and rhetorically, the message is of an ANC whose leadership has lost contact with grassroots concerns and lived experience, to which the PAC would remain attentive and beholden.

13 Several laws restricted and regulated alcohol use, including a ban on home brewing (a traditional practice was for women to brew sorghum beer) and the licensing of municipal beer halls as the only places where 'European wine, spirits, and beer' could be purchased and consumed. This ensured a steady revenue stream for the structures of apartheid. In June 1959, a group of African women protested against these laws outside the Cato Manor Beer Hall, in Natal. Over the next few days and weeks, these protests grew increasingly larger and increasingly violent. In the end, over twenty thousand women protested, several thousand were arrested, and close to thirty buildings and beer halls were burned down or damaged.

14 Another allusive reference to the ANC, which, Sobukwe intimates, swoops in to 'organise' spontaneous protests, and takes credit for them, but also is unable to direct them effectively.

15 Working conditions for black workers on potato farms in the Bethal region of the Transvaal (now in Mpumalanga) were scandalously inhumane. On 26 June 1959, the South African Congress of Trade Unions launched a nationwide potato boycott, which was very successful, prompting the government to appoint a commission of inquiry into working conditions.

16 The implicit criticism here is of the ANC. Sobukwe is implying that the ANC is stifling the revolutionary spirit and actions of grassroots protests and, because of its multiracial membership and involvement with these protests, cannot truly advance the interests and aspirations of the communities it was supposedly 'assisting'.

What of the Pan Africanist Congress?

We are met here today to commemorate our national Heroes' Day. We are, today, going down the corridor of time and renewing acquaintance with the heroes of Afrika's past – those men and women who nourished the tree of African freedom and independence with their blood; those great Sons and Daughters of Afrika who died in order that we may be free in the land of our birth. We are met here, today, to rededicate our lives to the cause of Afrika, to establish contact, beyond the grave, with the great African Heroes and to assure them that their struggle was not in vain. We are met here, Sons and Daughters of our beloved land, to drink from the fountain of African achievement, to remember the men and women who begot us, to remind ourselves of where we come from and to restate our goals. We are here to draw inspiration from the heroes of Thaba Bosiu, Isandlwana, Sandile's Kop, Keiskama Hoek, Blood River[17] and numerous other battlefields where our forefathers fell before the bullets of the foreign invader. We are here to draw inspiration from the Sons and Daughters of Afrika who gave their all to the cause and were physically broken in the struggle. We are met here, Sons and Daughters of Afrika, to take a trowel in our right hand and a shield and sword in our left, to commence the tremendous task of rebuilding the walls of Afrika.

We are gathered here, today, to reiterate our resolve to declare total war against the demi-god of white supremacy. We are here to serve an ultimatum on the forces of oppression. We are here to say Afrika must be free. We are here to make an appeal to African intellectuals and business men, African urban and rural proletariat, to join forces in a determined, ruthless, relentless and total war against white supremacy. We say to waverers and fence-sitters, choose now, tomorrow may be too late. Choose now, because very soon we shall be saying, with biblical simplicity, that He who is not with us is against us.

Pan Africanist Congress programme

The decks are cleared. The battle must be joined. Therefore, Sons and Daughters of the soil, in the name of the National Working Committee of the

17 These are all geographical sites where important battles were waged against colonial and settler forces.

Pan Africanist Congress, I announce the STATUS CAMPAIGN[18] – a campaign which once launched will not be called off until our goal is achieved. This is an unfolding and expanding campaign, involving the political, economic and social status of the African. It is all-embracing and multi-frontal, but is itself part of our unfolding and expanding dynamic nation-building Programme. Details of the campaign have already been circulated to all regions, with specific instructions that Branches be encouraged to discuss the campaign freely and frankly. I shall, therefore, not outline the campaign here, but shall deal instead with the objectives of this campaign.

Mental revolution

We have stated in the past, in all our documents, that whatever campaign is launched by any liberatory movement worth the name, must at all times be related to the ultimate objectives and must assist in building the fighting capacity of the masses.

Now for over three hundred years, the white, foreign, ruling minority has used its power to inculcate in the African a feeling of inferiority. This group has educated the African to accept the status quo of white supremacy and Black inferiority as normal.

It is our task to exorcise this slave mentality, and to impart to the African masses that sense of self-reliance which will make them prefer self-government to the good government preferred by the A.N.C.'s leader. It must clearly be understood that we are not begging the foreign minorities to treat our people courteously. We are calling on our people to assert their personality. We are not hoping for a change of heart on the part of the Christian oppressor. We are reminding our people that they are men and women, with children of their own and homes of their own, and that just as much as they resent being called 'kwedini' or 'mfana' or 'moshemane' by us[19] – which is what 'boy' means – they must equally resent such terms of address by the foreigner. We are reminding our people that acceptance of any indignity, any insult, any

18 The campaign took aim at all forms of condescending address by whites to blacks. Its purpose was also decidedly psychological (and a harbinger of Steve Biko's later emphasis on psychological liberation alongside political liberation) in that it wished to strike a blow at psychological subservience, at a 'slave mentality', and cultivate confidence and pride in blackness and one's essential humanity.

19 Terms for 'boy' or 'young man' in isiXhosa, isiZulu, and Sesotho.

humiliation is acceptance of inferiority. They must first think of themselves as men and women before they can demand to be treated as such. The campaign will free the mind of the African and once the mind is free, the body will soon be free.[20] Once white supremacy has become mentally untenable to our people, it will become physically untenable too, and will go. I am absolutely certain that once the STATUS CAMPAIGN is launched, the masses will themselves come forward with suggestions for the extension of the area of assault – and once that happens, the twilight of white supremacy and the dawn of African independence in this part of the continent, will have set in.

Soft campaign

Certain quarters have accused us of being concerned more with our status, with being addressed as 'Sirs' and 'Mesdames' than with the economic plight of the African people. Our reply is that such accusations can come only from those who think of the African as an economic animal – a thing to be fed – and not as a human being. It is only those who have been herrenvolkenised by their herrenvolk environment, people who have no idea whatsoever of the African personality, who can expect us to be lick-spittles in order to get more crumbs from the oppressor. Others, again, have said that we have chosen a soft campaign, without any risks, because we fear to challenge apartheid totally. Let it be clear that we are not fighting just apartheid. We are fighting the whole concept of white supremacy. And we are fully aware of the nature and size of our task. And we will not shirk it. Right from the beginning of the campaign, the leaders will be in front. They will picket the concerns that are to be boycotted. And they will do so under our slogan of 'no bail, no defence, no fine'. And that slogan will not be changed until we land on the shores of freedom and independence.

Clarion call

We therefore call first of all on the members of the Pan Africanist Congress who are the hard core, the advance guard that must lead the struggle and

20 The central goal of Steve Biko's later Black Consciousness Movement is presciently prefigured here.

on the African people in general. All of them, without exception, must wait for the call. They will be kept informed of every step we take. And when the call comes, we expect them to respond like a disciplined people. There is plenty of suffering ahead. There is plenty of suffering ahead.[21] The oppressor will not take this lying down. But we are ready. We will not go back. Come what may. This campaign will be maintained, unfolded and expanded until Masiza's[22] question is answered: 'Koda kube nini Nkosi Zonke izizwe zisinyasha pantsi kweenyawo?' (Until when, oh Lord, will all nations trample us underfoot?) – until we can answer 'no more'. We will go on, Sons and Daughters of Afrika, until in every shanty, in every bunk in the compounds, in every hut in the deserted villages, in every valley and on every hilltop, the cry of African freedom and independence is heard. We will continue until we walk the streets of our land as free men and free women, our heads held high. We will go on until the day dawns when every person who is in Afrika will be African and a man's colour will be as irrelevant as is the shape of his ears. We will go on, steadfastly, relentlessly and determinedly until the cry of 'Afrika for the Africans, the Africans for humanity and humanity for God' becomes a reality; until government of the Africans by the Africans for the Africans is a *fait accompli*.

We will not look back. We will not deviate, and as the heat of oppression mounts we shall become purer and purer, learning new lessons, and leaving all the dross of racialism and similar evils behind to emerge as a people mentally and physically disciplined, appreciative of the fact that:

There is only one man in the world,
And his name is All men.
There is only one woman in the world,
And her name is All women.[23]

---

21 Repeated in the original.

22 Peter Masiza (1840–1907), the first black ordained Anglican clergyman in South Africa. While clearly drawing inspiration from these words, Sobukwe's political stance highlights the importance of urgency and action. That is to say, rather than waiting for divine deliverance based upon prayer and faith, Sobukwe's response is of an actional and agentic sort, in the present.

23 From a poem by Carl Sandburg.

Sons and Daughters of Afrika, we are today on the threshold of a historic era. We are about to witness momentous events. We are blazing a new trail, and we invite you to be, with us, creators of history. Join us in the march of freedom. March with us to independence. To independence now. Tomorrow the United States of Afrika.

IZWE LETHU!![24]

24 Our land!!

8. One Central Government in Africa: Draft Article by Robert Mangaliso Sobukwe, March 1960

Nobody disputes our contention that Africa will be free from foreign rule.[1] What *is* disputed by many, particularly the white ruling minority, is that she will be free either 'within our lifetime' or by 1963, or even 1973 or 1984. However, the African nationalist movements which met at the All-African People's Conference in Accra in 1958[2] put down 1963 as the target date for African freedom.

If, however, by this date there are still parts of Africa that are under foreign rule, then certainly, they said, by 1973, every part of Africa must be free. Even though I live in South Africa, I have no doubt that this prophecy will be fulfilled. But the question is: AFTER FREEDOM THEN WHAT?

---

1 On 21 March, the Sharpeville Massacre would occur, when police fired into a peaceful protesting crowd, killing and wounding some 250 people. That this article was never finished may be related to these events, and one can only speculate on the extent to which the optimism and hope of this article was tempered or modified by the events that unfolded so rapidly after 21 March.

2 Kwame Nkrumah organised the first All-African People's Conference, its primary aims being to strengthen newly independent African states and to assist independence movements in regions still under colonial rule. The conference was held in Accra, Ghana, from 8 to 13 December 1958, and was attended by over 300 delegates from 28 countries and colonies. Tom Mboya, a trade union activist from Kenya, was elected conference chairman and captured the sentiment of the congress succinctly; it was time for the colonists, he said, to 'scram from Africa'.

The ready answer of white ruling minorities is: chaos and a reversion to barbarism and savagery. The ready answer of all Pan-Africanists, and this includes all genuine African nationalist organisations on the continent, is: the creation of a United States of Africa and the advent of a new era – an era of freedom, creative production and abundance.

To many Africans the United States of Africa symbolises the fulfilment of an emotional urge for formal African unity. What its nature and structure will be – and its role and tasks – have not been determined. But before I give an outline of the United States of Africa we envisage, I will list some of the obstacles we are bound to come across. Let us assume that by 1973, every part of the continent will be free from foreign domination. In some parts the change-over will have been comparatively peacefully achieved. In others, there will have been bitter fighting, which will leave in its wake a legacy of destruction and hate. In such countries the first ten or fifteen years will be years of re-adjustment and feverish reconstructions. There will be plenty of work to do, and the capital for that work will be forth-coming from both East and West – because there can be no greater guarantee against both political and economic instability than the final recognition of the supremacy of African interests in Africa.

By then, the older states will have passed through the first two of the four stages defined by Dr. Nkrumah, at the All-African People's Conference as:

The attainment of freedom and independence;

The consolidation of that freedom and independence;

The creation of unity and community between the free African independent states; and

The economic and social reconstruction of Africa.

These States will probably act as Big Brother to the younger States, but of course we will have recalcitrants. I am certain that some of the leaders of the African States who are 'great' – either because the press has made them so or because they are one-eyed dwarfs in a land of blind dwarfs – will advance a number of excuses to put off complete unification of the African continent for fear of losing their 'greatness'. Others, while paying lip-service to the concept of Pan-Africanism, will probably demand autonomy for each State with the object of remaining in the public eye. Fortunately, all African nationalist leaders on the continent are Pan-Africanists, and are not likely to allow personal ambition to hamper the cause for which they have laboured and suffered so long in their countries throughout Africa.

On the structure of the United States of Africa, there appears to be no clear agreement yet among African nationalists. At the Accra Conference,[3] Dr. Nkrumah stressed the necessity for such a communion of our own to give expression to the African personality. The conference adopted the late George Padmore's[4] outline of an initial federation of states on a regional basis, finally merging into a federal United States of Africa.

The Pan Africanist Congress, though it has adopted the same outline, is not enamoured of federations because they entail compromise, sometimes on vital issues. Federations tend to kill effective unity, because inherent in them is the idea of 'trial for a period' and the threat of ultimate secession by one State or another. So it is a unitary constitution that the Pan Africanist Congress envisages for the United States of Africa, with all power vested in a central government, freely elected by the whole continent on the basis of universal adult suffrage. In such a set-up, only continental-wide political parties committed to a continental programme cutting across sectional ties and interests, whether of a tribal or of a religious nature, are possible.

This will in turn promote the idea of African unity, and the concept of a free and independent African personality. The potential wealth of Africa in minerals, oil, hydro-electric power and so on, is immense. By cutting out waste, through systematic planning, a central government can bring about the most rapid development of every part of the State. By the end of the century the standard of living of the masses of the people will undoubtedly have risen dramatically under an African Socialist Government. Subsistence farming will have disappeared and a huge internal market will absorb a very large percentage of the industrial and agricultural products of the continent.

All nationalist movements on the continent aim at wiping out racialism, imperialism and colonialism in all their manifestations. In a United States of Africa there will be no 'racial groups' and I am certain that with freedom of movement from Cape to Cairo, Morocco to Madagascar, the concentration of so-called minority groups will disappear.

---

3 Lofty as the ideal was, there were only three All-African People's Conferences. Besides Accra in 1958, conferences were hosted in Tunis in 1960 and Cairo in 1961. The Organisation of African Unity, established in Addis Ababa on 25 May 1963, was inspired by the All-African People's Conferences that preceded it.

4 On George Padmore, see this vol., ch. 6, n. 12. Padmore's writings had a powerful impact on Pan-Africanist thought. The liberation of Africa, Padmore believed, could only come from a united and organised Pan-African movement to overthrow colonialism, imperialism and global capitalism.

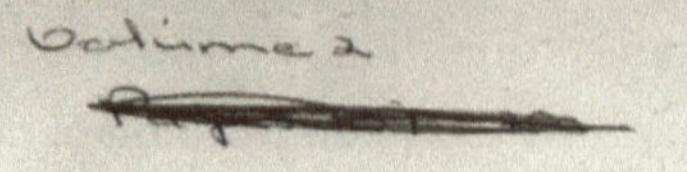

CASE NO. L 173/60.

DATE: 4/4/1960.

IN THE MAGISTRATE'S COURT FOR THE REGIONAL DIVISION OF SOUTH TRANSVAAL, HELD AT: JOHANNESBURG.

BEFORE: MR. J. de K. DU PLESSIS.

REGINA versus: (1) ROBERT (Mangaliso) SOBUKWE.

2. KITCHENER LEBALLO (Potlako.)	3. JACOB NYAOSA.
4. SEPHANIA MOTHOPENG.	5. SELBY NGENDANA (Themba)
6. LENNOX MLONZI.	7. ROSETTE NDZIBA.
8. JOHN WALAZA.	9. DANIEL KHUNOU.
10. WELLINGTON RANGAKA.	11. JOSIAS MADZUNYA.
12. SOLOMON MATHOPA.	13. ZACHARIA MTUNZI.
14. ABRAM MOGALE.	15. ABE KGARE.
16. JAMES THAMAE.	17. JOHANNES PHASHE.
18. LUCAS MATLOU.	19. GEORGE NDHLOVU.
20. JOSHUA MACHABA.	21. GEORGE SIWISA.
22. LANCELOT MAKGOTI.	23. JOHN MAKGETE.

CHARGE: As per Charge Sheet attached.

PLEA: All the Accused REFUSE TO PLEAD.

FOR THE CROWN: Mr. J. Robinson.

FOR THE DEFENCE: All the Accused - IN PERSON.

TRANSCRIBERS: Mesdames: McKenzie, Kuhn, Sykes & Vos.

INTERPRETER: Douglas Rasmen.

---------oOo--------

25. The covering page of the transcript of the court record for *R. vs Robert Mangaliso Sobukwe and Others* (Historical Papers Research Archive, Wits University)

9. R. vs Robert Mangaliso Sobukwe and Others, April 1960

Case No. L.173/60[1]

Date: 4/4/1960[2]

In the Magistrate's Court for the Regional Division of South Transvaal, held at Johannesburg

Before: Mr. J. de K. Du Plessis

REGINA[3] versus:

1. ROBERT (Mangaliso) SOBUKWE
2. KITCHENER LEBALLO (Potlako)

---

1 This chapter was prepared on the basis of original court transcripts produced at speed by the court stenographer. There are thus typographical inconsistencies in the text. It seems unnecessary, for example, to render 'White Parliament' or 'Police' in capital letters. There are other occasions where capital letters should have been used, as in the case of 'African nationalism' (which clearly should be rendered 'African Nationalism'). There are also varying designations for 'Pan-Africanism'. Ultimately, we have opted to stay as close as possible to the historical materials we had to work with – the original transcripts – rather than overwriting and correcting all these inconsistencies. In the case of incorrect spelling of names, we have either corrected the spelling, or made corrections in the footnotes.

2 Sobukwe submitted himself for arrest on the morning of 21 March 1960, some hours before the Sharpeville Massacre occurred. Initially, his case was scheduled to be heard on 23 March, but the prosecutor asked for a postponement to 26 March. Upon appearing on that day, a Saturday, Sobukwe petitioned to attend the funeral of those killed at Sharpeville, which, inexplicably and uncharacteristically, was permitted. Hence the trial formally got under way on 4 April 1960.

3 Prior to South Africa becoming a Republic and leaving the British Commonwealth, criminal cases were prosecuted by the State in the name of the Sovereign – 'Regina', or the reigning Queen.

3. JACOB NYAOSA
4. SEPHANIA MOTHOPENG
5. SELBY NGENDANE (Themba)
6. LENNOX MLONZI
7. ROSETTE NDZIBA
8. JOHN WALAZA
9. DANIEL KHUNOU
10. WELLINGTON RANGAKA
11. JOSIAS MADZUNYA
12. SOLOMON MATHOPA
13. ZACHARIA MTUNZI
14. ABRAM MOGALE
15. ABE KGARE
16. JAMES THAMAE
17. JOHANNES PHASHE
18. LUCAS MATLOU
19. GEORGE NDHLOVU
20. JOSHUA MACHABA
21. GEORGE SIWISA
22. LANCELOT MAKGOTI
23. JOHN MAKGETE

CHARGE: As per Charge Sheet attached.[4]
PLEA: All the Accused REFUSED TO PLEAD.[5]

---

4 Sobukwe was charged on two counts. The first was 'incitement' of persons 'to commit an offence by way of protest against a law or in support of any campaign against any law, or in support of any campaign against any law or in support of any campaign for the repeal or modification of any law or the variation or limitation of the application or administration of any law'. It is worth noting that this version of the law was passed in 1953, in response to the Defiance Campaign of 1952, purposely written quite broadly to make protest against any (apartheid) law a prosecutable offence. The sentencing guidelines were for imprisonment up to five years and a whipping of up to ten strokes, at the discretion of the magistrate. The second charge was violation of the pass laws, which included destroying a passbook, refusing to produce one on demand, falsifying or fraudulently using one, or being without possession of one.

5 The slogan 'no bail, no defence, no fine' summarises the PAC approach. They would not enter a plea, nor appoint a lawyer. Before the trial started, and upon the magistrate asking for a plea, Sobukwe responded as follows: 'Your Worship, without impugning your personal integrity and honour we refuse to plead. Because our contention is that the law under which we are charged is a law made exclusively by the white man, specifically for

FOR THE CROWN: Mr. J. Robinson.
FOR THE DEFENCE: All the Accused – IN PERSON.[6]
TRANSCRIBERS: Mesdames: McKenzie, Kuhn, Sykes & Vos.
INTERPRETER: Douglas Rasmen.
[...]

Cross-examination of Robert Mangaliso Sobukwe

THE COURT. You are the Accused No. 1 in this case?

SOBUKWE. Yes, Your Worship.

THE COURT. Yes – you may carry on now.

SOBUKWE. I am president of the Pan-Africanist Congress, elected to that position unanimously at the inaugural convention of the Pan-Africanist Congress ... For the same reason, thinking on a continental level, we stand for government of the Africans, by the Africans, for the Africans, with everybody who owes his only allegiance to the Continent of Africa and is prepared to accept the democratic rule of an African majority being regarded as an African. Our analysis of the South African situation has led us to the conclusion that we can best achieve our objectives by clearly defining our ultimate goals and drawing up a programme of action which we shall faithfully pursue instead of reacting to the legislation of the White Parliament as it flows from that Parliament. We decided to bring about the immediate abolition of the Pass Laws because that was the immediate needs of the African people. That was their demand. Before I proceed with the present case, Your Worship, I would like to give a picture of the structure of our organisation. Right at the bottom of the organisation, forming the nucleus so to speak of the organisation, are the general members of the Pan-Africanist Congress, fifteen or more of them constituting a branch. Each branch elects a Branch Executive.

the oppression and suppression of the blacks, and the officers who administer that law are themselves white, and in this whole drama only the accused are black and we don't feel that justice can be done under these circumstances and we therefore refuse to plead.' The court entered pleas of 'not guilty'.

6 Sobukwe ('Accused no. 1') would be the spokesperson for the group, ask questions of state witnesses, and answer questions of the court and the prosecutor on behalf of the group, except where the court wished to question or hear any other of the accused specifically.

A number of branches within a specified area constitute a region and each region elects a Regional Executive. Above the Regional Executive stands the National Executive which is responsible for the implementation of decisions of the National Conference, during the periods of course when the National Conference is not meeting. From among the members of the National Executive a specified number are elected and they constitute what we call the National Working Committee. Above all these sub-organs stands the National Congress which is the only body that can make policies and the only body that can take decisions on a national level. It meets once a year. At the National Conference then of the Pan-Africanist Congress which met on the 19th and 20th of December, 1959, a resolution was taken that the organisation should take positive and decisive action against the Pass Laws. The actual planning of the campaign and the nature that that campaign should take, those were left solely to the National Executive and because, as I have already explained, the National Executive really is scattered throughout the country, this particular task then devolved upon the National Working Committee. The campaign, Your Worship, in connection with which we are appearing here to-day was first made known on the 18th of March, on a Friday, the 18th of March, 1960. It was made known through me at a Press Conference. Immediately the nature of this campaign and the details of this campaign became known, the Alexandra branch of the Pan-Africanist Congress dissociated itself from that campaign through its chairman, Mr. Josias Madzunya,[7] in no uncertain terms. As a

7 Josias Ratshilumela Madzunya cut quite a visible figure, sporting a sumptuous beard and often a long black coat. Add to this an expansive and fiery personality, 'uncontrollable like a "wild steer"' (Gerhart interview, ch. 11, this vol.) and one could hardly ignore the man. He was often portrayed in the mainstream media as the firebrand face of the Africanist movement and, as often to a sinister end, an embodiment of the looming Africanist bogeyman. Behind the scenes, and within the Africanist movement, he was tolerated at best and exploited at worst. Madzunya enjoyed large support among the Venda and in Alexandra (where he played a leading role in the Alexandra bus boycott of 1957), but it was also his 'tribalist' notions that were off-putting and in fact anathema to the Africanist position. Madzunya, according to the Africanist inner circle, was distrustful of educated people and did not quite grasp Africanist philosophy. (In the interview with Gail Gerhart in this volume, Sobukwe notes that Madzunya 'was not an educated man. He probably didn't grasp the full import of our philosophy.') Madzunya himself seemed oblivious of such views of himself, and fully expected to be elected to the executive of the PAC, even to become its president. He was not elected to a single office. Many believe this snub was at the heart of his subsequent opposition. By the same token, though, it was not out of

result – because of powers split between me and the constitution, I expelled him from the Pan-Africanist Congress. As I've said, then the campaign was made known on the 18th of March. Circulars were printed and distributed to the members of the organisation and on the 21st of March, on Monday, in obedience to a resolution that they had taken the members of the Pan-Africanist Congress surrendered themselves at various Police Stations throughout the Country.

[...]

Sobukwe cross-examined by Selby Ndengane

NDENGANE.[8] Do you know anything about the membership of the Pan-Africanist Congress?

[...]

SOBUKWE. I cannot give precise figures as that is the duty of the National Secretary but it is close to 200,000.

NDENGANE. Close to 200,000?

SOBUKWE. Yes.

NDENGANE. Do you read newspapers?

SOBUKWE. Yes, I do.

NDENGANE. What papers do you read?

SOBUKWE. I read *The Star*, the *Daily Mail*, *Contact*, the London *Observer*, the *Manchester Guardian*, some overseas American papers like *Liberation*. I subscribe to journals like *Science* and *Freedom*, I read occasionally the

character at all for Madzunya to stubbornly go his own way. The reader will note that this testimony is delivered in Madzunya's presence – he was Accused no. 11.

8 Because the PAC members did not employ a lawyer on their behalf, they were responsible for their own defence. Selby Ngendane (Accused no. 5) questioned Sobukwe so as to make their case. A fellow alumnus from Fort Hare, Selby Themba Ngendane graduated just a few years after Sobukwe did. He, too, became involved in politics at Fort Hare, joining the ANC Youth League there and cutting his political teeth in the 1952 Defiance Campaign. Upon moving to Johannesburg to study law, he was drawn into the Africanist circle and soon rose to leadership positions. Commentators sometimes refer to the handsome, dapper figure he cut, always smartly dressed and somewhat of a 'playboy', but such descriptors belie his articulate intellect and passionate, unswerving commitment – one, however, which also wrought internecine tensions for the hardline (some might say authoritarian) manner in which he argued it. In fact, conspiracy theories notwithstanding, evidence points to Ngendane's assassination in 1990 by members of his own party.

Afrikaans papers such as the *Vaderland*. I read *The World* and almost all the papers, the *Post*.[9]

NDENGANE. You said the membership is close to 200,000, do you remember what figure was issued by the Pan-Africanist Congress for its membership for December 1959?

SOBUKWE. I do.

NDENGANE. What is the December figure?

SOBUKWE. Some papers reported 31,000, others 35,000 as our membership.

NDENGANE. Would you say therefore that these figures released through the Press were figures that were released from your office?

SOBUKWE. The 35,000 correct.

NDENGANE. If in December membership was 35,000 do you mean therefore that within two months membership rose from 35,000 to nearly 200,000?

SOBUKWE. I don't mean that.

NDENGANE. Can you give an inference of about what it is to mean – how did it come about that if in December it's about 35,000 members and to-day you report 200,000 within two months?

SOBUKWE. The 35,000 were figures we deliberately released to the Press but at that time we had already gone beyond the 100,000 mark, in fact to be precise, I think at that stage our membership was 100,095.

NDENGANE. Do you know all the accused?

SOBUKWE. Yes.

NDENGANE. Did you know them before they appeared in this Court?

SOBUKWE. Yes.

NDENGANE. Would you say therefore that they are all members of the Pan-Africanist Congress?

[...]

SOBUKWE. Not all ...

NDENGANE. Do you recognise any as members?

---

9 One is struck by the wide range of Sobukwe's reading. *The Star* and the *Rand Daily Mail* (edited by Laurence Gandar) were liberal English newspapers published in Johannesburg; *The World* (famously edited in the 1970s by Percy Qoboza) and the *Golden City Post* (founded in 1955 by Jim Bailey), owned by white publishing companies, were aimed at black readers. The *Manchester Guardian* (or, as it is now known, *The Guardian*) and *The Observer* are well-known left-liberal London papers. *Contact* was the journal of the Liberal Party of South Africa. *Liberation* was an American 'new left' and independent monthly, published till 1977. *Die Vaderland* was an Afrikaans nationalist newspaper, unapologetically supportive of apartheid.

SOBUKWE. Yes.

NDENGANE. Now, in your evidence you've mentioned something about the structure of the Pan-Africanist Congress?

SOBUKWE. Correct.

NDENGANE. And if I've got you correctly the structure you referred to was that you've got a branch, a Branch Executive, a Regional Executive, National Working Committee, National Executive Committee, and then the Conference?

SOBUKWE. Correct.

NDENGANE. Would you say then that the Accused are members of the – of these various structures?

SOBUKWE. They belong to various structures in the movement.

NDENGANE. Don't they belong to one structure, like National Executive or Branch Executive or Regional Executive?

SOBUKWE. They don't.

NDENGANE. Do these various structures then even ever meet as a block to take decisions about the organisation?

SOBUKWE. They never.

NDENGANE. Do you imply they work independently?

SOBUKWE. The body that gives directives in implementation of the decisions of the National Conference is the National Working Committee, acting on behalf of the National Executive.

NDENGANE. Does your organisation have branches in places like Orlando, Western Native Township, George Goch, Jabavu, Germiston.[10]

SOBUKWE. It does.

NDENGANE. Would you say therefore that those branches also have directives about the campaign?

SOBUKWE. Correct.

NDENGANE. Were those branches present at the conference which you held in Orlando according to you on the 19th and the 20th of December?

SOBUKWE. They were represented.

NDENGANE. Were they a party to the resolution passed there?

SOBUKWE. They were.

NDENGANE. You said in evidence that the National is responsible for the implementation of the decisions of the conference?

10 These are all areas in and around Johannesburg where Africans lived.

SOBUKWE. Correct.

NDENGANE. Are those numbers staying in the same town – are they all in Johannesburg to start with?

SOBUKWE. No, the National Executive.

NDENGANE. The National Executive Committee?

SOBUKWE. No.

NDENGANE. Would you say they are all over the country?

SOBUKWE. Correct.

NDENGANE. How far in the country are they?

SOBUKWE. Natal, in the Cape, in the Transvaal.

NDENGANE. Has this committee ever met since December 20th, 1959?

SOBUKWE. It has not.

NDENGANE. You said this is the Committee that decides to implement decisions of the Conference, would you say therefore it is the same Committee that implement the decisions of this – I mean of that Conference of the campaign if it didn't meet since December, 1959?

SOBUKWE. I said in my evidence that the National Working Committee who are composed of a specified number of members of the National Executive is the body that acts on behalf of the National Executive because the National Executive is scattered throughout the country.

NDENGANE. As President is it your duty to dictate to the members what line of action to follow?

SOBUKWE. No, ours is a Democratic movement.

NDENGANE. If any decision is to be taken or any campaign such as this one is to be implemented, who must decide on the campaign, whether there should be a campaign or not?

SOBUKWE. The National Conference.

NDENGANE. How is this constituted?

SOBUKWE. It has representatives from each branch of the movement, one member representing every fifteen members in a branch as the delegates to Conference.

NDENGANE. About this campaign, this pass campaign would you say this is the decision of – this is your decision or the decision of your National Working Committee or that of the members of the Pan-Africanist Congress?

SOBUKWE. That there should be taken positive and decisive action against the Pass Laws was the decision of the National Conference but the nature of that campaign was left solely in the hands of the National Working Committee.

NDENGANE. In your evidence you stated that, I'm quoting out your words, 'We decided to end the Pass Laws.' Who were you referring to when you said: 'We decided', who are 'we'?

SOBUKWE. I referred there to the members of the Pan-Africanist Congress.

NDENGANE. Members of the Pan-Africanist Congress?

SOBUKWE. Correct.

NDENGANE. In your evidence again you mentioned these words: 'That the decision was, the nature of the campaign was first made known on the 18th of March', is that correct?

SOBUKWE. Correct.

NDENGANE. You meant therefore that the actual date of launching was not made known before the 18th of March?

SOBUKWE. It was not.

NDENGANE. Who knew about the date before the 18th of March?

SOBUKWE. I was the only man who knew about the date.

NDENGANE. If anybody says that he knew about the actual date of launching, say about the 7th of March, would you say that person is telling a lie?

SOBUKWE. I would say so.

NDENGANE. I wish to question you about the statement, about the evidence you've given about the Alexandra branch. According to your evidence they learnt about the nature of this campaign on the 18th of March?

SOBUKWE. Correct.

NDENGANE. What was their decision – at the branch?

SOBUKWE. They decided not to participate in that campaign. In fact, in a press statement through their chairman they condemned the campaign.

[...]

NDENGANE. Do you know of any people who participated in this campaign who are not members of the Pan-Africanist Congress?

[...]

SOBUKWE. I do not. I'm sorry, may I put this correctly though, that as I've already stated in evidence, there is the man we have expelled from the movement[11] but he did not participate in the campaign. All those who participated in the campaign were members of the Pan-Africanist Congress.

11 Sobukwe is referring to Josias Madzunya.

NDENGANE. NO FURTHER QUESTIONS.

[...]

Sobukwe cross-examined by Rosette Ndziba[12]

NDZIBA. You said in your evidence that leaders of the Pan-Africanist Congress were originally members of the A.N.C.?

SOBUKWE. Correct.

NDZIBA. I suppose you're also one of the A.N.C. members?

SOBUKWE. Correct.

NDZIBA. Did you attend any public meeting under the auspices of the A.N.C.?

SOBUKWE. Correct.

NDZIBA. Did you ever discuss passes in your public meetings?

SOBUKWE. Correct.

NDZIBA. What was the feeling of the people in those meetings about passes?

SOBUKWE. They were completely against the Pass Laws.[13]

NDZIBA. What action did they take against passes?

SOBUKWE. They launched in 1952 what was known as the Defiance Campaign. In 1950, on the 1st of May, they had some action against the passes, they took some action against the passes. As recently as last year they organised a potato boycott as an indirect method of fighting against these laws.

NDZIBA. Now you spoke about one of your aims in the organisation, that is the complete overthrow of White Domination. What do you mean by 'White Domination'?

SOBUKWE. By White Domination I mean exclusive control of all legislative, administrative, economic and military power in the hands of a minority of Whites.

---

12 Questioning now passed from Selby Ngendane to Accused no. 7, who was Rosette Ndziba, a schoolteacher and active member of the PAC founding group. In fact, Ndziba was the person delegated to deliver the letter listing Africanist concerns at the disastrous National Conference of the ANC, which took place in March 1958. At that meeting, Ndziba narrowly escaped a beating by several ANC loyalists incensed with him and the Africanists.

13 This is important, historically and for the present. The PAC has steadfastly maintained that the organisation had reached out to the ANC to collaborate and participate in the pass campaign, but that the ANC refused. In the aftermath of the Sharpeville Massacre, and the tremendous political mobilisation that arose from it (domestically and especially internationally), the ANC – to varying degrees – 'claimed' or 'appropriated' the pass protests for itself.

NDZIBA. You spoke of a government of the Africans by the Africans and for the Africans, could you elaborate on that a bit, what do you mean by that exactly?

SOBUKWE. Briefly put it means government of the majority, irrespective of one's colour or creed. It means loyalty of course of everybody to the Continent of Africa. It means Democracy as we have been taught it by the West.

[...]

Court resumes after an adjournment

NDZIBA. Was the Alexandra branch against the Conference resolution?

SOBUKWE. No, it was not.

NDZIBA. Now why did they not take part in the campaign – any reason?

SOBUKWE. Because they were not satisfied with the nature of the campaign, so they said.

NDZIBA. You have said that the campaign was made known to your branches on the 18th of March at a Press conference?

SOBUKWE. Correct

NDZIBA. Could anyone have organised this campaign before the 18th of March, 1960?

SOBUKWE. No.

NDZIBA. Were the meetings held in Alexandra Township and elsewhere along the Reef in support of this campaign?

SOBUKWE. No.

NDZIBA. But passess were discussed at these meetings, not so?

SOBUKWE. Correct.

NDZIBA. In what connection were they discussed at these meetings? ...

SOBUKWE. They were condemned, [...] it was just a way of giving vent to the genuine grievances of the African people against Pass Laws.

NDZIBA. Do you imply the usual condemnation of the passes?

SOBUKWE. Correct.

NDZIBA. Now you said you belong – you're the President of the Pan-Africanist Congress, not so?

SOBUKWE. Correct.

NDZIBA. Who are allowed to join your movement?

[...]

SOBUKWE. All Africans over the age of sixteen.

NDZIBA. What is an African?

SOBUKWE. An indigenous person of this land, of Africa.

NDZIBA. How would you classify the extinct Bushmen and Hottentots and Coloureds?

SOBUKWE. They are Africans.

NDZIBA. Because they are in—?

SOBUKWE. Because they are indigenous.

NDZIBA. Because they are indigenous?

SOBUKWE. Yes.

THE COURT. You say they are also of the Coloureds?

SOBUKWE. Yes, Your Worship.

NDZIBA. How many races are there in South Africa?

SOBUKWE. There is only one race, the human race.

NDZIBA. There is only one race?

SOBUKWE. Correct.

NDZIBA. The human race?

SOBUKWE. Correct.

NDZIBA. Do you imply that the Africans, the way you have described them now, and the Whites of this country belong to this race?

SOBUKWE. Correct.

NDZIBA. You told us that – in your evidence, that on the 8th of November, 1958, you seceded from the African National Congress, why did you secede from this organisation?

SOBUKWE. There were a number of reasons, but it was generally on a question of ideology, principally on a question of ideology that we differed because the African National Congress at that stage, having adopted a programme known as the 'Freedom Charter' stood for what is known as multi-racialism which we have condemned because we say that multi-racialism simply means a transfer of the prejudices and the bigotry that applies in the present society to a new society. The African National Congress differs with us on the question of African nationalism which we regard as the essence really of our creed. There were certain aspects also of the Freedom Charter on which we disagreed, particularly the preamble to that Charter which we regarded as dishonest because it claims that we the people of South Africa, white, and black, brothers, countrymen and I don't know what … friends, I think, and our contention was that a slave and his master could not be equals, a slave and his master could not be countrymen. We said that was a dishonest assertion in the Charter. Then the Charter said the land belongs to all who live in it and as I have already pointed out, our contention is that South Africa is an integral part of the Continent of Africa which historically and geographically belongs to the African people.

NDZIBA. Is that true?

SOBUKWE. Yes.

NDZIBA. Who are the slaves in your opinion – you referred to?

SOBUKWE. The African people.

NDZIBA. And who are the masters?

SOBUKWE. The white people.

NDZIBA. And who else – and Indians and Coloureds, who are they?

SOBUKWE. They are oppressed peoples too except that among the Indians there is a class that we regard as being tainted with the virus of cultural superiority and national arrogance, that is the merchant class.

NDZIBA. You told us that African Nationalism is the essence of a political creed?

SOBUKWE. Correct.

NDZIBA. Now, is a Nationalism, is your African Nationalism – do you narrow visualistic [*sic*] and socialistic Nationalism?

SOBUKWE. No.

NDZIBA. Could you give me a brief exposition of your African Nationalism – a very brief exposition?

SOBUKWE. Our contention is that the African people on the Continent of Africa are a nation by virtue first of all of their origin and secondly through the fact that they have a sad historical experience – an experience of dispossession by the Whites from Europe. It is also our contention that they have a common destiny, that as a nation they have to contribute to the fund and wealth of human culture and civilisation.

NDZIBA. NO FURTHER QUESTIONS

[...]

Cross-examination by the Public Prosecutor[14]

PROSECUTOR. Now, I want to read to you an extract here. I'm going to put it to you as being the extract from the National Conference held on the

14 J. Robinson.

19th and 20th and if you find that it is incorrect, just say so: 'At the Conference the following Resolutions were put forward, the following are the Resolutions submitted by the Resolutions Committee were unanimously adopted by the Conference.' I think you indicated earlier to His Worship that it was a unanimous decision at this Conference, is that correct?

SOBUKWE. Correct.

PROSECUTOR. Now, the first one is: 'That the National Executive be instructed: (a) To call the nation on a positive, decisive action against the Pass Laws.' Is that the correct …?

SOBUKWE. Correct.

[…]

PROSECUTOR. '(b). That the Pan-Africanist Congress should embark immediately on a campaign of intensive organisation in order to get the nation ready at the earliest possible time.' That is (b), is that correct?

SOBUKWE. It is.

PROSECUTOR. 'That the nation be alerted immediately and be advised to be ready for the call and be ready for any positive action as from now.'?

SOBUKWE. Correct.

PROSECUTOR. 'That the Pan-Afrianist Congress members be taxed £1.2.6d. per member to establish a National Fund to finance the campaign.'?

SOBUKWE. Correct.

PROSECUTOR. 'That whatever form of action the National Executive decide upon, the slogan of: "No bail, no defence, no fine" should be strictly adhered to.'?

SOBUKWE. Correct.

PROSECUTOR. 'That the National Executive Committee be instructed to implement the status campaign as part of an unfolding program but that action against Pass Laws be given priority in that action.'?

SOBUKWE. Correct.

PROSECUTOR. 'That the continental salute of the Pan-Africanist Congress should be the right hand raised up, the palm facing forward.'?

SOBUKWE. Correct.

PROSECUTOR. Like that (*P.P. demonstrates*). 'This to be adopted as the National salute of the Pan-Africanist Congress.' Is that correct?

SOBUKWE. Correct.

[…]

PROSECUTOR. Now, these Resolutions were accepted at the National Conference?

SOBUKWE. Correct.

PROSECUTOR. And at this National Converence you had – I think you've indicated earlier on – representatives from all the branches?

SOBUKWE. Correct.

PROSECUTOR. Was it one representative for each fifteen members or one representative for each branch of more than fifteen members?

SOBUKWE. For each fifteen members in a branch.

[...]

PROSECUTOR. You addressed the meeting at the beginning, the Conference at the beginning and then later I think you also rendered a vote of thanks, can you remember it?

SOBUKWE. I addressed the Conference and then we had a session later on I think when we had a rally, that's where I spoke.

PROSECUTOR. Pardon?

SOBUKWE. I spoke at a rally.

PROSECUTOR. At a rally?

SOBUKWE. That's right.

PROSECUTOR. Not at the Conference itself?

SOBUKWE. I gave the Presidential address of course.

PROSECUTOR. That's right and then subsequent to that a vote of thanks – I think towards the tail end of the Conference?

SOBUKWE. I won't deny it but I can't remember.

PROSECUTOR. I'll read it to you and perhaps it will strike a chord: 'I wish to thank all speakers and those who attended this Conference, very much. I thank the Conference for the mandate it has given us. I wish to appeal to all the masses not to divulge the secrets of our movement to white people. We are not going to disclose our methods of fighting Pass Laws, status campagin etcetera, otherwise everything can be a colossal failure like the potato boycott.' Do you recall that?

SOBUKWE. I don't talk such nonsene.

PROSECUTOR. Pardon?

SOBUKWE. I don't think I'll be capable of talking such nonsense.

[...]

PROSECUTOR. Can you recall in this address whether you used words very similar to the following or the following nature: 'Go and call the masses that 1960 is the year in which the African men and women will cease to carry passes in this country.' Have you at any state ever indicated that 1960 would be the year when Pass Laws would be abolished?

SOBUKWE. We regarded 1960 as the year which will see the beginning of an unfolding program for liberation.

PROSECUTOR. And would that first step of that unfolding program, would that have been the abolition of the Pass Laws or the necessity of the Natives to carry a pass law?

SOBUKWE. That would be according to the decision of Conference. As I said earlier on it is Conference that decides on whatever campaign has got to be pursued.

PROSECUTOR. Yes, the Conference makes the decisions according to the evidence you have given, I appreciate that but subsequent to the Conference there has been considerable reference made to 1960 as being the year in which the Pass Laws will be abolished?

SOBUKWE. 1960 was the year on which we shall launch definitely, that is right, it was decided that we'll launch in 1960.

PROSECUTOR. That was the decision?

SOBUKWE. I beg your pardon?

PROSECUTOR. That was the decision which was made?

SOBUKWE. Yes, within this year.

PROSECUTOR. And was it also stated then that the law would be abolished this year?

SOBUKWE. I said that top priority should be given to a campaign – top priority should be given really to action to bring about the – what can you call it – top priority should be given to decisive and positive action to be taken against the Pass Laws, I think that's how ...

PROSECUTOR. That is the furthest that you've taken it, I mean the Executive – have they taken it any further – have they taken it any further and said 'well listen, by the end of 1960 Pass Laws must be abolished'?

SOBUKWE. That was the general feeling of the members, yes.

PROSECUTOR. That was the general feeling?

SOBUKWE. That is, now.

PROSECUTOR. And that was then?

SOBUKWE. It was then, yes.

PROSECUTOR. Now, you mentioned earlier on the National Working Committee, who was the National Working Committee, who stood at the head of it?

SOBUKWE. I do.

PROSECUTOR. And how many other members did it consist of ?

SOBUKWE. Four, I think – or six ... four.

[...]

PROSECUTOR. Now, I want to refer you to certain Exhibits which have been found in the possession of some of the Accused [...] I think you have seen some of them. 'The Africanist' ...?

SOBUKWE. That's right.

PROSECUTOR to THE COURT. Your Worship, the document marked 'No. 8' of 'Exhibit AT', it is marked: 'The Africanist, volume 6, No. 1, February/ March, 1960.'

PROSECUTOR to SOBUKWE. Is this the official organ of the Pan-Africanist movement?

26. Sobukwe with fellow members of the PAC on the day of the anti-pass campaign, 21 March 1960. There is a sense, in the expressions of Sobukwe and those around him, of the exuberance of the moment. (Photo by Peter Magubane, © Peter Magubane / David Gollan)

27. Making history: Sobukwe and PAC comrades, mid-salute, heading to the Orlando police station to present themselves for arrest. (Photo by Peter Magubane, © Peter Magubane / David Gollan)

SOBUKWE. 'The Africanist' , yes.

PROSECUTOR. Yes, 'The Africanist', is that the official organ of your organisation, the Pan-Africanist Congress?

SOBUKWE. Yes.

PROSECUTOR. Now, what was the official organ of the A.N.C., the African National Congress?

SOBUKWE. 'Lode Star' I think, I'm not too certain.

PROSECUTOR. You say you're not certain? ...

THE COURT. The?

SOBUKWE. 'Lode Star', I know that was the organ of the A.N.C. Youth League.

[...]

PROSECUTOR. Now tell me, at this initial conference that you held in April, 1959, I take it a draft constitution was then prepared – I'm using the word 'draft constitution', I think you used some other word for it?

SOBUKWE. Draft constitution.

PROSECUTOR. Did you use the word 'draft constitution'?

SOBUKWE. Yes.

PROSECUTOR. And it was then decided I think at that same conference what the name of your organisation would be?

SOBUKWE. Correct.

PROSECUTOR. Prior to that I think it was called 'The Africanist Movement'?

SOBUKWE. Correct.

PROSECUTOR. Which was a break-away from [...] the African National Congress?

SOBUKWE. Shall I put that right though?

PROSECUTOR. Yes, correct me if I'm wrong there.

SOBUKWE. The Africanist Movement and the Pan-Africanist Congress are different movements, the point I want to make here is after the break-away, those who had broken away comprising a number, mind you, of the men here now – constituted then what became known as the Africanist Movement, that's right, but when on the 1st of April when we met on the 4th of April, it was those who were known to be Africanists really who attended that meeting. From all over the country. It was members of the Africanist Movement themselves.

PROSECUTOR. Yes?

SOBUKWE. Who attended the movement because they were Africanists but at that meeting then it was decided that the name of the organisation should become the Pan-Africanist Congress with a constitution for the Pan-Africanist Congress which was not the constitution of the Africanist movement.

PROSECUTOR. Yes well, I think you have put it very similarly to the way I've put it except I probably put it in a – not quite the terminology that you used, but is it correct that – who actually led the break-away from the African National Congress?

SOBUKWE. Who actually?

PROSECUTOR. Led the break-away?

SOBUKWE. I can't specify any particular individual.

PROSECUTOR. If I submitted to you that it was in fact Accused No. 11?[15]

SOBUKWE. It would be incompletely ... that would be wrong.

PROSECUTOR. That would be wrong?

SOBUKWE. That would be wrong, that's right.

15 Josias Madzunya.

PROSECUTOR. In an item marked No. 5 of the same Exhibit 'AT' that I referred the Court to earlier on there is a document here which reads at the top: 'Draft Constitution of the Africanist Liberation Congress', was that the document which you subsequently changed and amended before drawing up your sub-constitution? [...]

SOBUKWE. It's similar to it.

[...]

PROSECUTOR. Now, do you know this organisation known as the Africanist Liberation Congress?

SOBUKWE. It doesn't exist.

PROSECUTOR. Can you perhaps give me any information on it?

SOBUKWE. It never existed.

PROSECUTOR. Was it a proposed organisation?

SOBUKWE. Never, it was – we had a number of suggestions really as to the names.

PROSECUTOR. Oh, I see.

THE COURT. Was that one of the names suggested?

SOBUKWE. That's right.

PROSECUTOR. Discarded?

SOBUKWE. Yes.

[...]

PROSECUTOR. Now you mentioned in your evidence that you did in fact hold a press conference on – I think the 18th or 19th of March?

SOBUKWE. Correct.

PROSECUTOR. When it was decided that the date would be the 21st of March, that is how you actually – how you publicised the date as being the 21st of March. Now did you – at this press conference that you referred to, did you in fact give it to the 'The New Age'[16] as well?

SOBUKWE. There were a number of pressmen present.

PROSECUTOR. I'm going to read to you from an extract of 'The New Age'. Thursday, March the 24th, 1960. Reads: 'Top left ...' – refers to a number of pictures there, you can refer to them just now. The heading is 'Sobukwe states his case. Johannesburg. The Pan-Africanist President, Mr. Mangaliso R. Sobukwe, announced at a press conference held last

16 *New Age* was a leftist newspaper published in Cape Town between 1954 and 1962, when it was banned.

Friday that his Congress would start a sustained disciplined, non-violent campaign against the Pass Laws on Monday, March the 21st. Mr. Sobukwe told newspaper reporters as long as the campaign is on, nobody will go to work. Africans would leave their passes at home and would surrender themselves at chosen Police Stations under the leadership of local Pan-Africanist Congressites. The leaders will tell the Police: "We do not have passes. We will not carry passes again. Millions of our people are arrested under the Pass Laws as you had better arrest us all now." They then thickened the print slightly: "These are my orders" said Mr. Sobukwe "and if we must win, these orders must be faithfully carried out." Asked how long the campaign would last Mr. Sobukwe said: "Till our demands are met. Nobody would call off the campaign except the National President himself, who would do so at public meetings of the people." Mr. Sobukwe said if passes were left at home this would mean the people had divorced themselves mentally from the passes.' Now is that – what I've read up to then, is that correct?

SOBUKWE. That's a report by 'The New Age'...

PROSECUTOR. Yes, but is that correct on what you actually said to them at the time?

SOBUKWE. With the exception of the latter portion I would say it's correct.

PROSECUTOR. Which is that – the portion about ...?

SOBUKWE. That if they'd leave their passes behind they'd divorce themselves mentally – that's a stupid statement in any case.

PROSECUTOR. Yes well I'm reading on, I want you to interrupt me as soon as you find something which is not correct: 'The Africanists' demands were for the total abolition of the Pass Laws, a minimum wage of £35.0.0d. per month or £8.3.4d. a week throughout the country. A guarantee that no worker would be dismissed as a result of this campaign and an assurance that leaders would not be victimized as a result of positive action by the African people.'?

SOBUKWE. Correct.

PROSECUTOR. 'As a change from their former policies of go it alone and not being interested in fighting, isolated issues, the Africanists have sent letters to the African National Congress and to the Liberal Party inviting them to create history by taking part in the campaign.'?

SOBUKWE. Correct.

Prosecutor. 'Mr. Sobukwe said he offered an opportunity to all these non-African individuals and groups who have expressed themselves to be bitterly opposed to the Pass Laws to participate in this noble campaign. A letter to the Commissioner of Police from Mr. Sobukwe announced the start of this campagin and asked for instructions to the Police to do nothing that would lead to violence and not to give impossible commands to the people. The usual mumbling of a Police officer of an order requiring the people to disperse within three minutes and almost immediately after a baton charge deceives nobody and show the Police up as sadistic bullies. The Police should have no difficulty,' says the letter, 'we will surrender ourselves to the Police for arrest.' The letter ends: 'Hoping you will co-operate to try and make this a most peaceful and disciplined campaign.' 'Leaflets issued by the Pan-Africanist ...' – well this actually I think is not a portion of what you said to them, if it was ... I'll just read it to you: 'Leaflets issued by the Pan-Africanists say: if one man is arrested for not having a pass you will stop there and then and tell the people you do not have passes either. Demand that they arrest you all. At this stage of the campaign all men will go to gaol under the slogan: "No bail, no defence, no fine." The women will be assigned their historic role. In the first stage of the struggle they must see to it that all men go to goal.' [...]

Court resumes after an adjournment

Prosecutor. Now tell me, is it also one of the aims and objects shall I say of the Pan-Africanist Congress for complete freedom in 1963?

Sobukwe. Correct.

[...]

Prosecutor. Now, I want to show you [...] Exhibit 'BC', it's got an African language on the front and on the reverse side it is in English [...] Now, I notice at the top is it – it is also one of the shall I say mottos of the Pan-Africanist Congress that the campaign would be 'No bail, no defence, no fine'?

Sobukwe. Any campaign.

Prosecutor. Any campaign relating to this – now you have already indicated, if you'll look at that first paragraph there, 'anyone who gets the circular should keep it. He will get hold of history. These are the elected leaders of the nation, dedicated to the cause of African freedom, freedom and independence by 1963.' That is also in accordance with the Pan-Africanist Congress aims and objects, not so?

SOBUKWE. Correct.

PROSECUTOR. Now then there is a decision of the nature: 'The conference of the Pan-Africanist Congress held on the 19th and 20th it was resolved that the President should call the nation to take positive, decisive action against the Pass Laws any time this year.' Now that I take it was in accordance with that resolution passed?

SOBUKWE. Correct.

PROSECUTOR. And I think it was also the donation, in the next paragraph, of £1.2.6d., that was also one of the resolutions?

SOBUKWE. Correct.

PROSECUTOR. Now, further on there is referred specifically to the resolution and then they give an order or they ask – the order goes out: 'The President will call upon the nation very soon to honour his resolutions. The order that goes out to the nation therefore is (a) Save money. Save food. Save money immediately! Which is also in accordance with the proposed campaign?

SOBUKWE. Correct.

[...]

PROSECUTOR. [...] and then they say: 'Keep the circular, remember these leaders, they will lead you into action, the order will come from them only.' That is still, I take it, in accordance with the resolution?

SOBUKWE. Correct.

PROSECUTOR. 'Be ready for the call. Know what we are fighting for, it is a noble and glorious struggle calling for the service, sacrifice and suffering from the Native people. This is going to be a disciplined mass campaign.' Well that is also, I take it, that is now paragraph (c), first line?

SOBUKWE. Correct.

PROSECUTOR. This is also in terms of your resolutions. Now you see what I'm getting at – I haven't gone right through it – is that this particular pamphlet contains all the resolutions which were referred to at the conference in December, on the 19th or 20th?

SOBUKWE. Those weren't resolutions, you can't say it contains all the resolutions ...

PROSECUTOR. Not all the resolutions, no, no, but these were resolutions, some of them were?

SOBUKWE. They weren't resolutions as such really, there's no resolution to the effect that people should save food, nor was there any resolution as to their keeping these particular circulars.

PROSECUTOR. Yes?

SOBUKWE. All the people knew was that the National Working Committee would decide on the nature of the campaign and that the President would give the call.

PROSECUTOR. Yes – no, I appreciate that but what I'm really getting at – I perhaps worded it badly, I don't mean that all these relative paragraphs in this circular (Exhibit 'BC') that they are all resolutions, some of them are resolutions, some of them are decisions made by the National Working Committee, some of them are your general requests which you did issue?

SOBUKWE. There was only one resolution in connection with the Pass Laws. That's right – top priority be given to that.

PROSECUTOR. I appreciate that – no, but what I'm getting at is that this was the policy which was adopted?

SOBUKWE. We could say that is the pegged line.

PROSECUTOR. The pegged line, that's what I'm getting at, that's probably better worded than what I have …

[…]

PROSECUTOR. Now, earlier on you mentioned that – I think it was in your examination in chief probably or when you were cross-examined by one of the Accused, when you were cross-examined by one of the Accused you indicated that only you knew the date?

SOBUKWE. Correct.

[…]

PROSECUTOR. Now, can you tell me whether it is an actual fact they – rules or advice which had been given to the Pan-Africanist Congress leaders that they should destroy all original or signed documents?

SOBUKWE. I beg your pardon?

PROSECUTOR. Is it a rule applied by the Pan-Africanist Congress that they should destroy all original documents bearing signatures of leaders and so on?

SOBUKWE. No.

PROSECUTOR. Has that been given – has that advice however been given to them?

SOBUKWE. I beg your pardon?

PROSECUTOR. Has it alr— have they in fact been advised to do so, however?

SOBUKWE. No, what they were advised to do was to make sure that personal correspondence did not come into their files, because what we want to face is a charge concerned with the movement, not personal opinions of individuals.

PROSECUTOR. Now tell me, when you say you decided that, did you sort of convey it to the members of the Executive, the various Executives, was it done by circular or was it done by way of an address, can you perhaps recall?

SOBUKWE. It was conveyed to members of the National Working Committee by myself, I think.

[...]

PROSECUTOR. You mentioned earlier on that the general terms of the proposed campaign might have been known, namely that it involved imprisonment. When you say the general terms, what do you really mean by that?

SOBUKWE. As I was trying to explain earlier on, every one of our members, as I said, knew that it couldn't be a violent campaign, that's right, and if it wasn't a violent campaign it would entail the contravention of an established Law of the white Parliament of this country and that would entail our arrest and therefore we were prepared, whatever campaign we launched, not to pay any bail, not to engage any lawyers, not to pay any fines, should such be imposed. It was known also that probably we would be away for a long time – for a period of years, in imprisonment, so that those who were going to participate are members who would have saved food and so on.

PROSECUTOR. Yes, so that is what you actually meant by the general ...?

SOBUKWE. Correct.

PROSECUTOR. General terms, in other words I take it it would also include walking with the leaders to hand themselves over?

SOBUKWE. No, what it would entail was that the leaders would be in front.

PROSECUTOR. They would be in front – I used the word walking, I actually meant the leaders would be in front?

SOBUKWE. Correct.

PROSECUTOR. So they had knowledge that their leaders, whatever campaign, whatever the nature of the campaign, the leaders would be in the front, that they would be imprisoned, did they have any way of knowing ...?

SOBUKWE. Yes.

PROSECUTOR. I think – can one accept too that assuming that it was – they did in fact know it was a non-violent campaign?

SOBUKWE. Correct.

PROSECUTOR. So I take it they could also accept that they would have to hand themselves over to the Police?

SOBUKWE. It's possible.

PROSECUTOR. It is possible – thank you, Sir.

PROSECUTOR. NO FURTHER QUESTIONS.

THE COURT to ALL THE ACCUSED. In view of the further evidence given by Accused No. 1 in cross-examination, I want to give the rest of you the opportunity, if you wish, to ask him further questions arising out of the cross-examination. I think I have already explained to you that if the Crown has succeeded, only if the Crown has succeeded in proving a conspiracy between you, as set out in the charge sheet, then any statement

28. Sobukwe with members of the PAC at the Orlando police station on 21 March 1960. He is to the right of the image, standing between two white policemen. (Photo by Peter Magubane, © Peter Magubane / David Gollan)

29. Sobukwe, having arrived at the Orlando police station, speaks with comrades. The fence is a foreshadowing of what is to come. (Photo by Peter Magubane, © Peter Magubane / David Gollan)

30. Security police officers escort Sobukwe to his home in Mofolo, Soweto, after his arrest. (Photo by Peter Magubane, © Peter Magubane / David Gollan)

by any one of you would be evidence against all of you, all those involved in the conspiracy. Has anybody got any further questions?

Cross-examination by Ndengane

NDENGANE. You have referred to circulars which have gone out – to who were these circulars referred?

SOBUKWE. To members of the Pan-Africanist Congress.

NDENGANE. You stated then that those circulars were a call – to quote your actual words 'to the Nation' and the word in the circulars: 'All men must go into action', what do you understand by the term 'Nation'?

SOBUKWE. The term 'Nation' really depends on the ideology – a definition of the term is ideological, with the African National Congress, for instance, the South African Nation would include all people in South Africa whereas with the Pan-Africanist Congress, 'Nation' would mean people of – who are indigenous to the con … the African nation would refer to people who are indigenous in the continent of Africa, so that the term 'Nation' I think, the definition of that term, depends on the ideology that the people hold – the particular group …

THE COURT. Confine yourself to the Pan-Africanist Congress?

SOBUKWE. I see.

THE COURT. How do you mean it refers only to African people?

SOBUKWE. That's right, with the Pan-Africanist Congress the term 'Nation' is a term understood to refer to the African people but because we are the only people who use the term in that sense we have come to use the term 'Nation' as synonymous with Pan-Africanist members.

NDENGANE. Am I correct now assuming therefore that when you use the word 'Nation' you are using it as it is understood by the Pan-Africanists?

SOBUKWE. Correct.

NDENGANE. Were you therefore referring to the nation as it is in the Pan-Africanist Congress?

SOBUKWE. Correct.

NDENGANE. You stated then that you sent letters inviting other organisations to participate in this historic campaign, did you get any replies from these organisations?

SOBUKWE. Yes, I did.

NDENGANE. Did you get a reply from the A.N.C.?

SOBUKWE. Yes, I did.

NDENGANE. What was the reply?

SOBUKWE. They refused to associate themselves with any campaign.

NDENGANE. In your further evidence you made mention of the fact that the National Executive Committee of the P.A.C. implements the decisions of Conference? ... How often does this Executive Committee meet?

SOBUKWE. Constitutionally, once a year.

NDENGANE. Seeing that the P.A.C. is one year old as you stated, how often then did the National Executive meet?

SOBUKWE. They met only once – in September in Bloemfontein.

[...]

NDENGANE. May I refer you to the potato boycott some time last year ... or thereafter, do you know anything about the potato boycott?[17]

SOBUKWE. Yes.

NDENGANE. Do you remember circulars which were issued against the boycott which were alleged to have been issued by the Pan-Africanist Congress?

17 On the potato boycott of 1959, to protest against working conditions of black workers on potato farms in the Bethal region of the Transvaal (now Mpumalanga), see this vol., ch. 7, n. 15.

SOBUKWE. Yes.

NDENGANE. Had your Congress in fact issued these circulars?

SOBUKWE. No, in fact we issued a statement subsequently denying any association with those leaflets.

NDENGANE. Do you know whether those circulars then came from the Pan-Africanist Congress?

SOBUKWE. I don't know but we have our suspicions, and we had them then.

NDENGANE. What did you suspect?

SOBUKWE. We suspected that the thing had been done by the Police.

[...]

NDENGANE. You stated that you knew from the onset that it would be a non-violent campaign?

SOBUKWE. Correct.

NDENGANE. What do you understand by a non-violent campaign?

SOBUKWE. By a non-violent campaign, I mean where the people who will participate in the campaign would not use any method of violence, would use any weapons with which to inflict wounds or so on. That they would themselves be prepared to suffer.

[...]

THE COURT. You said you understood by a non-violent campaign is where you say the people would not use any weapons or any violence of any nature?

SOBUKWE. Correct.

THE COURT. And would be prepared to suffer?

SOBUKWE. Correct.

THE COURT. To put it shortly, even at the hands of the Police?

SOBUKWE. That's what one would expect, Your Worship.

THE COURT. Do you say that the people would be prepared to suffer, even at the hands of the Police?

SOBUKWE. I said that's what I would expect when I call for a non-violent campaign.

NDENGANE. When your organisation thought of a non-violent campaign, did they perhaps have in mind what had happened in the past when non-violent campaigns, like the Defiance Campaign, had been launched?

SOBUKWE. Correct.

NDENGANE. Do you know of any instances during the past where violence was in fact meted out to the people?

SOBUKWE. In the Mayday Campaign of 1950, in the Defiance Campaign of 1952, June the 26th, I think 19 … I'm not too certain of the year, it's either '57, '58. I'm not sure.

NDENGANE. What was your Congress prepared to do then in case of such instances?

SOBUKWE. It first of all drilled the members themselves on the conception of non-violence –what it entails – appeals to them not to allow themselves to be provoked, even by the Police and then sent subsequently, finally a letter to Colonel Rademeyer,[18] appealing to him to assist in making this a peaceful campaign.

NDENGANE. Is your organisation a pacifist organisation?

SOBUKWE. Definitely not.

NDENGANE. Do you refer to non-violence then as a policy of the organisation?

SOBUKWE. Not at all.

NDENGANE. What did you mean by non-violence in this particular campaign – if you're now positive?

SOBUKWE. It was a tactic – because of the situation which …

THE COURT. I didn't quite …?

SOBUKWE. It was a tactic, Your Worship, a strategy to be applied, because of the nature of this struggle at the moment.

NDENGANE. In other words, you regard non-violence merely as a tactic?

SOBUKWE. Correct.

NDENGANE. Not as a policy?

SOBUKWE. Not as a policy.

NDENGANE. NO FURTHER QUESTIONS.

[…]

Cross-examination by Ndziba

NDZIBA. Do you know of any organisation except your own movement that supported your campaign?

SOBUKWE. No.

18 Sobukwe's letter to the police commissioner, Colonel C.I. Rademeyer, is appended at the end of chapter 10 in this volume.

NDZIBA. It was alleged that you contend one of your objects is that you must have freedom in 1963?

SOBUKWE. Correct.

NDZIBA. Freedom from what?

SOBUKWE. From white domination.

NDZIBA. That is, you would like everybody to have a say in the state of … Government?

SOBUKWE. I would like to see established a non-racial Democracy.

[…]

THE COURT. Is there anything else you wish to say?

SOBUKWE. No, Your Worship.

[…]

JUDGMENT by Mr. J. de K. Du PLESSIS: In all the circumstances set out above, the Crown has clearly proved that all the accused, except only accused Nos. 8, 20, 22 and 23, took part in the conspiracy set out in the charge.

There is a strong suspicion that accused Nos. 8 and 22 also participated but the Crown has not pressed for conviction in their cases and in the circumstances outlined they are given the benefit of the doubt. The only evidence that they were members of the Witwatersrand Regional Executive is that of accused No. 1 who has also stated that Regional Committees were not advised of the nature of the campaign. It is not clear what the functions of that body were. There is no other evidence that they took part in the incitement.

There is no evidence at all that the two members, Nos. 20 and 23, participated in any way.

Accused Nos. 8, 20, 22 and 23 are accordingly found NOT GUILTY and DISCHARGED. I would ask them to keep their seats in the meantime.

In regard to the remaining accused, there is no doubt that the Crown has proved that they are GUILTY of the main charge. I find them GUILTY on the Main charge in respect of inciting pass-carrying Natives to commit the offence of contravening section 15 sub-section (1) paragraph (a) of Act 67 of 1952.

SENTENCE by Mr. J. de K. Du PLESSIS: Your offence is a serious one. Apart from the fact that Parliament has enacted very heavy penalties, namely, a maximum of a fine of £500 or imprisonment for 5 years or both for persons who incite other persons to commit offences by way of protest against existing

Laws etc. the nature of the offence you incited the Native people to commit, coupled with the manner in which the campaign was to be carried out, was potentially far reaching in its consequences, particularly on the Rand with its large Native population and vast Native labour force.

Not only was it your object to flood the gaols with the impressionable masses of the Native people, but in that manner you intended to paralyse trade and industry and so undermine the economy of the country in order to compel the Government to change its Laws. Whether a Law is unjust or is considered unjust or not, the Law of the land must be obeyed.

The harm done by you, both politically and economically, is difficult of accurate assessment. This Court must accordingly impose adequate sentences, not only as a punishment to you but as a deterrent to others who may be similarly minded.

I have already set out the manner in which each of you participated in this offence. This has weighed with this Court in assessing the sentence to be passed on each of you.

As far as No. 1 Accused is concerned, I must also take into account that in terms of paragraph (f) of exhibit 'BD' issued by the National Working Committee i.e. the pamphlet 'Calling the Nation', no one can call this campaign off but he as National President. This does not appear to have been done; on the contrary exhibit 'BG' has been produced here being the note handed to Accused No. 4 in the Police cells at Marshall Square by a visitor to the effect that the campaign is being continued.

In all the circumstances Accused No. 1 will be sentenced to THREE YEARS IMPRISONMENT.

Accused Nos. 2, 3, 4, and 5 – all members of the National Working Committee responsible for giving effect to the National Conference resolutions in this campaign, are each sentenced to TWO (2) YEARS IMPRISONMENT.

I have carefully considered the parts played by the remaining Accused Nos. 6, 7, 9, 10, 11, 12, 13, 14, 15, 16, 17, 18, 19, and 21 and find it would be unjust to differentiate between them as far as sentence is concerned. Each of them has played his part in inciting the masses in terms of the Pan Africanist Congress plan to ensure the success of the campaign. Each of these Accused will be sentenced to EIGHTEEN (18) MONTHS IMPRISONMENT.

M.J. De K. Du Plessis
REGIONAL MAGISTRATE

10. Robert Mangaliso Sobukwe's Testimony in R. vs Monyake and Others, September 1960

Accused no. 39, David Ramodibe, calls Robert Mangaliso Sobukwe[1, 2, 3]

THE COURT to PROSECUTOR. I am making a request, I am not making an order, that the witness' leg irons be removed.[4] It is only when I receive

1 As in chapter 9, inconsistencies in the original transcript have not been corrected in this chapter.

2 Johannes Monyake, an executive member of the Transvaal PAC, was the first person to be arrested on 21 March 1960, before the Sharpeville Massacre took place. He was characterised as one of the 'main inciters' of the gathering crowd. In total, 76 people were charged with 'public violence', as well as more 'minor' contraventions. Some of the accused employed their own attorneys, many of whom consequently managed to have the charges against them dismissed. The public prosecutor then revised the charges, mainly to allow as well for a clearer series of related counts of 'contravening the pass laws', to which the remaining 23 or so (from the initial 76) were asked to plead. PAC members, in general (including Monyake and David Ramodibe), refused to plead, arguing that the laws were immoral and illegal, enacted as they were by a parliament from which they were excluded. Pleas of 'not guilty' were entered by the court on their behalf. The hearing commenced on 29 September 1960 in Vereeniging (evidence was concluded on 15 May 1961 and a verdict delivered on 22 June 1961).

3 The accused managed their own defence, and called Sobukwe as a defence witness. Accused no. 39 was David Ramodibe, elected as spokesperson for the group. Ramodibe had been a law student at the University of Cape Town.

4 At the time of the Monyake trial, Sobukwe was himself imprisoned (hence the leg irons), and just before he was to take the stand, there was some negotiation about access to witnesses – the police argued that a police person had to be present when the accused, if a prisoner, consulted with his or her witness; while the accused maintained that a police presence compromised the rights to strategise and otherwise plan a sound defence. At the suggestion that the police be stationed outside the room if there was a door, or outside a window, the police countered that their fear was not simply escape in the moment, but that something might be passed to the prisoner which might enable escape later. In the end, the judge ruled that a 'Bantu police person' be in the room, and said he would not entertain any breaches of the defence's right to confidentiality.

an assurance to the contrary, that it is essential that we must have the leg irons, that I will permit them to be left on. Now, is the witness going to give evidence in English?

PROSECUTOR. Yes.

SOBUKWE. English.

THE COURT. Before we go on, I have now requested that the leg irons be taken off you. I hope you realize that as far as this Court is concerned, you will not cause any trouble on that account. Will you give me that understanding?

SOBUKWE. Correct.

THE COURT. Now accused No. 39 in the case will conduct the examination in chief on behalf of the five undefended accused.

RAMODIBE. Mr. Sobukwe, what was your occupation before the 21st of March, 1960?

SOBUKWE. I was lecturer in Bantu languages at the University of the Witwatersrand.

RAMODIBE. What was your educational standard?

SOBUKWE. I'm a B.A. of the University of South Africa, B.A. Honours, Witwatersrand.

RAMODIBE. Do you know an organisation called the Pan African Congress?

SOBUKWE. Correct.

RAMODIBE. Are you a member there?

SOBUKWE. I was the President of the Pan Africanists Congress.

RAMODIBE. How old was the organisation before the 21st of March, 1960?

SOBUKWE. Just on 11 months. It was founded on the 6th of April, 1959.

THE COURT. Is there any significance in the fact that it was founded on Van Riebeek day?[5]

SOBUKWE. I don't know.

RAMODIBE. Mr. Sobukwe, was P.A.C. a registered organisation before the 21st of March?

SOBUKWE. African political organisations are not registered.

RAMODIBE. Can I put the question this way. Was the P.A.C. organisation known by the Government?

SOBUKWE. Correct.

5 White South Africa celebrated 6 April as a national holiday, to commemorate the arrival of the first Dutch settlers at the Cape in 1652 under the command of Jan van Riebeeck.

RAMODIBE. Before the campaign I realized that certain pamphlets were delivered by the P.A.C. [...] When was the last pamphlet delivered, or issued?

SOBUKWE. It should be round about the 18th of March, the Friday prior to the riots.

RAMODIBE. What information did it carry to the people?

SOBUKWE. It outlined the nature of the campaign and also gave the date on which the campaign would start.

RAMODIBE. Can you tell the Court in short how the campaign was to be conducted?

SOBUKWE. The instructions were that in every township and village, under the leadership of the Pan Africanists Congress, all African men would move to the Police Stations, there to surrender themselves for arrest. The leader of each group had been instructed to inform the police when he met them, that the gaols were in any case full of Africans arrested for Pass Laws ...

THE COURT. Just go slowly. The leader of each group was to inform the police that ...?

SOBUKWE. That the gaols in this country were full of Africans arrested for Pass Laws, and therefore the police may just as well arrest that group as well.

THE COURT. You mean the police may just as well arrest them all?

SOBUKWE. Just as well arrest them all. Strict instructions were given against any possible use or encouragement of violence.

Court resumes after an adjournment

RAMODIBE. Mr. Sobukwe, I was still on the very same question where I asked you to explain how the Pan African Congress launched this campaign on the 21st of March?

SOBUKWE. I think the points I've made were that under the leadership of the Pan Africanists Congress, individual villages and townships, the men would go to the Police Stations and surrender themselves, and what the various leaders would say to the police when they encountered them, and also that strict instructions were given to them with regard to the possible use and occurrence of violence. That is as far as I got. It was stated further in these circulars that the campaign would be called off by me alone, and nobody else. Further, with regard to women, I think it was stated that they will be ascribed their historical role later on. I think that is what was stated in the circulars.

THE COURT. You say their historical role?

SOBUKWE. Correct.

THE COURT. Not hysterical role?[6]

SOBUKWE. Not hysterical. I think our demands are set forth there too in that same circular: Total abolition of the Pass Laws and a minimum wage of about £35 per month.

RAMODIBE. Mr. Sobukwe, do you think that certain undisciplined elements could have done anything to cripple the campaign of the Pan African Congress on the 21st of March. By this I mean certain other people who could for instance have forced the people to get to the Police Stations, or have prevented the people somehow not to go to work by forceful means?

SOBUKWE. That could happen. It could happen in any mass organisation. In fact, my very specific instructions about the possible occurrence of violence were intended to forestall such elements. One was quite aware that such elements might creep into a struggle such as ours, and it was one of our ways to try and forestall their activities, to call on those who were the leaders to try and see that no violence occurred, but they could succeed at this stage.

RAMODIBE. Mr. Sobukwe, in all the meetings of the P.A.C., particularly in Johannesburg, did P.A.C. ever advocate violence?

SOBUKWE. Not at all.

RAMODIBE. Do you know of a man named Josias Lezunja [*sic*]?[7]

SOBUKWE. Correct.

RAMODIBE. How do you know him?

SOBUKWE. He was Chairman of the Alexandra Branch of the Pan Africanists Congress. But towards the middle of March, just towards the week when we were about to launch the campaign, it came out in the newspapers a strong line against the campaign, as a result of which I expelled him from the movement.

RAMODIBE. What did he say about the passes in connection with the 21st of March campaign of the P.A.C.?

---

6 One suspects the magistrate was completely serious here. This confusion between 'historical' and 'hysterical' occurs later in the hearing too.

7 On Josias Ratshilumela Madzunya, see this vol., ch. 9, n. 7.

SOBUKWE. I wouldn't be able to answer that question unless I knew in what reference. He addressed a number of meetings in Johannesburg, as came out in our indictment, where he strongly condemned the Pass Laws himself, very strongly indeed. I wouldn't know what particular reference you want me to …

RAMODIBE. I think I'll put it this way. Do you think he could have done anything to sabotage the campaign of the 21st of March?

SOBUKWE. As I said earlier, he issued statements in the Press against the campaign of the P.A.C. It was because of the statements he had made, that I expelled him from the P.A.C.

RAMODIBE. Did the senior police officials know about the campaign of the 21st of March?

SOBUKWE. Well, I wrote a letter to the Commissioner of Police,[8] it was then Colonel Rademeyer, I think, informing him about the campaign, and asking that the police should co-operate to make sure that this was a peaceful campaign. I assured them that on our side we will see to it that no violence occurred.

RAMODIBE. Does that mean that you wanted to make sure that the police did not intimidate – I mean, force the people to violence?

THE COURT. What is the question?

RAMODIBE. By writing him a letter, did you want to make it clear to him that the people were not going to violate …

THE COURT. The people themselves were not going to commit violence?

RAMODIBE. Commit violence?

SOBUKWE. I was trying to prevent any occurrence of violence, in fact, I did state in my letter that the practice by the police of giving the people generally three minutes or so to disperse and after which shooting on the masses, was not a practice that could take in anybody at all, and I precisely asked him that the people are given enough time to disperse and I assured him that if they were asked to disperse, our people would disperse, if they're given reasonable time to disperse.

RAMODIBE. Mr. Sobukwe, can you tell me who actually distributed the pamphlets?

THE COURT. Who actually?

RAMODIBE. Distributed the pamphlets in connection with the campaign?

8 The letter is reproduced at the end of this chapter in an appendix.

SOBUKWE. In this area here, the people who were in charge of the distribution of leaflets were Mr. Nana Mahomo and Mr. Peter Malutse [*sic*],[9] of the National Working Committee.

THE COURT. Just a moment. Repeat these two names?

SOBUKWE. Nana Mahomo and Peter Malutse.

THE COURT. Of – what did you say?

SOBUKWE. Of the National Working Committee.

RAMODIBE. So by that, if I understand you correctly, does it mean that the distribution of the pamphlets were solely to be delivered by these gentlemen and by no others personally?

THE COURT. Accused No. 39, you are now examining your witness, you are not cross-examining the witness. I cannot allow you to put into his mouth what you want him to say. You must ask him questions in such a manner that you do not suggest what answer you want, particularly on controversial points like this. You will remember that the evidence, if I remember correctly, in regard to distribution of pamphlets, affects you – that is the Crown's case. What you can ask this witness is what were these two men to do about it, how were they to set about the distribution of it. Will you answer that please?

SOBUKWE. There were no particular instructions given to them regarding that. Their duty was to see to it that the circulars were distributed.

THE COURT. Were they too inhabitants of this area?

SOBUKWE. No, they were Johannesburg people.

THE COURT. They were not inhabitants of Vereeniging?

9 Nelson 'Nana' Mahomo was a former member of the Transvaal Congress Youth League who sided with the Africanists within the ANC and subsequently left that party to join the PAC. He was elected secretary for culture in the PAC in 1959 and was in addition a member of the organisation's National Executive Committee. Peter Molotsi had a similarly long track record of activism, and was also the editor of *The Africanist* before Sobukwe took over that role. He was a founding member of the PAC and became its secretary for Pan-African affairs. Molotsi left South Africa with Mahomo on the eve of the Sharpeville Massacre, managing to stay just a step ahead of the South African police. After an extended journey through Malawi and Tanzania, they ended up in Ghana, where they set up PAC offices in exile. A while later, Mahomo left for London, to set up offices there, while Molotsi took responsibility for organisation in Africa. Molotsi also served as a representative of liberation movements to the United Nations, and actively petitioned for Sobukwe's release from prison. While serving in this role in the United States, Molotsi – who left South Africa with a Standard 6 education – completed bachelor's, master's and doctoral degrees at Rochester, Fordham and New York universities.

SOBUKWE. No, they were from Johannesburg.

RAMODIBE. Mr. Sobukwe, did you hold any conference on the 19th and 29th of December, 1959?

SOBUKWE. Correct.

THE COURT. In the Communal Hall in Orlando?

SOBUKWE. Correct.

RAMODIBE. Mr. Sobukwe, did delegates who were at the conference – I'll put it this way. Did you know any delegates who were at the conference?

SOBUKWE. Did I personally know these people – I'm not too certain – or did I know the areas they came from or did I know the individuals who came as delegates?

RAMODIBE. I mean the individuals?

SOBUKWE. There were quite some people I knew, quite a number that I knew.

RAMODIBE. What is meant by this saying 'Africa for the Africans'?

SOBUKWE. That is the political line of the P.A.C. The political demand made after analysis of the situation, is to the effect that the Government we would like to establish in a free Africa would be a government of the Africans, by the Africans, for the Africans.

THE COURT. Did you say Government by the Africans?

SOBUKWE. Government of, by, for.

THE COURT. Of the Africans?

SOBUKWE. And by the Africans.

THE COURT. For the Africans?

SOBUKWE. Yes, and we have gone further to say that all those who accept the democratic rule of an African majority, and their only allegiance to Africa, will be regarded as Africans. It is in that connection that we used 'Africa for the Africans'.

RAMODIBE. By that, do you mean that the P.A.C policy was different of that of the A.N.C.?

SOBUKWE. Oh absolutely. We differ in a number of ways, our concept, our concept of the struggle as such, the way in which the struggle should be conducted, our ultimate goals are absolutely different from those of the A.N.C.

RAMODIBE. Did the P.A.C. have any flag at all?

SOBUKWE. Correct.

RAMODIBE. Can you describe to the Court how it was?

SOBUKWE. It was a flag with a green background and in the centre was a black map of Africa, with a yellow lodestar on the North-West where geographically Ghana would be situated, with rays radiating from that centre throughout the Continent of Africa.

RAMODIBE. Can you, without entering too much into detail, describe the policy of the P.A.C.?

SOBUKWE. The best probably would be to start at its aims. We have five basic aims, the first is to organise the African people under the banner of African Nationalism. Secondly, to overthrow White domination. Thirdly, to establish a new social order which we described as original in concept, Africanist in orientation, socialist in contents, democratic in form, creative in purpose.

THE COURT. Which we describe as?

SOBUKWE. Original in concept, Africanist in orientation, Socialist in content, democratic in form, creative in purpose. In that order we call it an Africanist Socialist Democracy. Fourthly, to strive for the realization of a United States of Africa, stretching from Cape to Cairo, Morocco to Madagascar. And fifthly, to promote the concept of the African personality, and Pan Africanism, in which Society was stated, would be emphasized the primary supremacy of the material and spiritual needs of the individual.

THE COURT. Just repeat that last bit, please? In which Society would be emphasized?

SOBUKWE. The primacy of the spiritual and material needs of the individual. These are the five aims that we set ourselves. We have therefore taken the struggle – I'm still going to the body, I don't know if that is necessary, whether that answers the question or whether I can go further?

THE COURT. It depends on what the accused wants?

RAMODIBE. I think you can go further?

SOBUKWE. So that was then that the struggle would be Continental and not merely local, our view being that South Africa cannot solve her problems in isolation from, and in utter disregard of, the rest of the Continent. We are an integral part of the Continent and we must live as such. That the so-called race question …

THE COURT. Just a moment, what has that got to do with the case?

RAMODIBE. I think I was just about to stop him. That answers the question.

THE COURT. That answers your question. Very well, the next one?

RAMODIBE. Mr. Sobukwe, was it ever the aim of the P.A.C., after achieving all that it wanted, to throw the White men into the sea?

SOBUKWE. That is nonsense. It is a nonsensical statement repeatedly made by certain elements, for what purpose one just doesn't know.

RAMODIBE. NO FURTHER QUESTIONS

[...]

Sobukwe cross-examined by defence advocate Jack Unterhalter[10]

UNTERHALTER. Mr. Sobukwe, was there a slogan that the Pan Africanists had?

SOBUKWE. Correct, in connection with a particular campaign we were launching, is that it?

UNTERHALTER. Yes that, and generally?

SOBUKWE. There was.

UNTERHALTER. Will you tell His Worship what it was?

SOBUKWE. No bail, no defence, no fine.

THE COURT. Just a moment. No fine – was that in connection with?

SOBUKWE. That was in connection with any campaign we would launch. That if we went into action it would be under that slogan of 'No bail, no defence, no fine'. Another was this one of 'Africa for the Africans', I don't know if I ...

UNTERHALTER. Perhaps I'll make it a little clearer. Let me put it from another point of view. Was any particular gesture adopted by members of the Pan Africanists to indicate solidarity among themselves, or used as a form of greeting?

SOBUKWE. They had a salute, accompanied by certain words, of course.

UNTERHALTER. Was the 'thumbs-up' sign their salute?

SOBUKWE. No.

UNTERHALTER. It is correct, is it not, that the thumbs-up sign is a gesture that has gained currency among African people through the influence of the African National Congress over a period of years?

SOBUKWE. Correct.

---

10 Whereas the PAC executive members conducted their own defence, several of the other accused employed a professional advocate, Jacob (Jack) Unterhalter. A member of the Liberal Party, Unterhalter was known to defend political activists and appear on their behalf in court.

UNTERHALTER. It wouldn't necessarily indicate, would it, that the person making the gesture was a member of the African National Congress, it was, so to speak, common coin among African people today?

SOBUKWE. Correct.

UNTERHALTER. The use of the word 'Africa', just as an exclamation, was that a slogan of the P.A.C.?

SOBUKWE. In the case of the P.A.C., it was in response to what would have gone before, 'Iswelethu',[11] the one would say, and the reply would be 'E Africa'.

UNTERHALTER. If used by a member of the A.N.C. at, say, a political meeting, the greeting would be 'Mayabuya Africa'?[12]

SOBUKWE. Correct.

UNTERHALTER. But the use of the word in isolation, 'Africa', again, I suppose, is almost current coin among African people through its popularity over the years?

SOBUKWE. Correct.

UNTERHALTER. Now, the organisation of the P.A.C. was about eleven months old, you've told us, when the campaign in March, 1960, was launched?

SOBUKWE. Correct.

UNTERHALTER. I take it, Mr. Sobukwe, that although it had gained a fairly large membership, at that date the membership was not to be counted in hundreds of thousands?

SOBUKWE. On the 21st of March?

UNTERHALTER. Of 1960?

SOBUKWE. It was just under 200,000.

UNTERHALTER. That is the total number for the whole of the Union of South Africa?

SOBUKWE. Correct.

UNTERHALTER. In many townships, villages, and so on, there were of course very many people, I take it, who had not joined the P.A.C., and who had either continued to be members of the A.N.C or were not members [illegible] …

SOBUKWE. Correct.

---

11 'Izwe lethu' or 'Izwe elethu', a common slogan meaning 'Our land', or 'The land is ours'.

12 As common a slogan as 'Izwe lethu' was 'Mayibuye', especially in the collocation 'Mayibuye iAfrika', meaning 'Come back, Africa', or 'May Africa return'. In their early usage, as Sobukwe indicates here, these slogans functioned as something of a shibboleth, to distinguish Africanists from ANC supporters.

UNTERHALTER. In any fairly well populated township, would it be fair to say that the majority of people living there were still not members of the P.A.C.?

SOBUKWE. It would depend on the particular Province one was dealing with.

UNTERHALTER. In the Transvaal?

SOBUKWE. Those who were politically minded, as a point of argument, as the majority of people probably wouldn't belong to any particular organisation in any event, but in certain areas in the Transvaal, of the politically minded, that's what I'm trying to say, a large number would belong to the P.A.C., but the greatest majority of the people still would probably belong to no particular organisation at all.

UNTERHALTER. Mr. Sobukwe, would it be fair to say that so far as the township of Sharpeville is concerned, that the majority of people who resided there were not members of the P.A.C.?

SOBUKWE. Correct.

UNTERHALTER. I take it, in regard to the demonstration concerning the Pass Laws last year, it was not the policy of the P.A.C to advocate or encourage the burning of the passes?

SOBUKWE. Correct.

UNTERHALTER. If that were advocated at all, it was advocated by a group that was, so to speak, competing with the P.A.C.?

SOBUKWE. Correct.

UNTERHALTER. NO FURTHER QUESTIONS

Sobukwe cross-examined by the Public Prosecutor

PROSECUTOR. Mr. Sobukwe, to get the record straight, is it correct that in April of last year, you were charged jointly with a number of persons, the charge being that you incited, together with the other co-accused, persons to commit offences against the Pass Laws by way of a protest, as a campaign against the Pass Laws?

SOBUKWE. Correct.

PROSECUTOR. And you were ultimately found guilty and sentenced to three years' imprisonment?

SOBUKWE. Correct.

PROSECUTOR. Now, I'd just like to go through the accused who were with you in that trial.[13]

[...]

PROSECUTOR. I think the best thing would be to – your organisation, the P.A.C., was founded when you were elected President of this inaugural conference on the 6th of April, 1959, is that correct?

SOBUKWE. Correct.

THE COURT. 1959?

PROSECUTOR. 1959. It was founded essentially by a splinter group of the A.N.C.?

SOBUKWE. Correct.

PROSECUTOR. Who felt that the A.N.C. wasn't achieving as quickly what it should achieve?

SOBUKWE. No.

PROSECUTOR. Not that?

SOBUKWE. There is another reason.

PROSECUTOR. Was it because it was a multiracial organisation which was being used as a tool to lull the Africans into a sense of false security?

SOBUKWE. That was one of the reasons, but basically it was ideological, I think.

[...]

PROSECUTOR. Now, you also had a motto, S.S.S. I'm not sure which order it goes, but you mentioned Service, Sacrifice, Suffering?

SOBUKWE. Correct.

THE COURT. What does that stand for?

SOBUKWE. Service, Sacrifice, Suffering.

PROSECUTOR. And your National salute – Iswelethu – that was the National salute?

SOBUKWE. There were words that accompanied it. The verbal words accompanying it.

THE COURT. Well now, as you are a lecturer in bantu languages, give us the correct spelling please?

SOBUKWE. Izwe Lethu.

13 The prosecutor proceeded to present a lengthy list of names (including, for example, P.K. Leballo and Zeph Mothopeng), asking not only if Sobukwe knew them, but what their positions were in the PAC, and what court sentences they had previously received. At some point in this lengthy exposition, even the magistrate grew weary, telling the prosecutor that much of it was 'unnecessary'.

[...]

PROSECUTOR. Now, throughout, the tenor of the speeches which were made in Johannesburg, it would appear that only Africans were eligible for membership in the beginning, in the elementary stages of the P.A.C.?

SOBUKWE. Correct.

THE COURT. I'd like to know what kind of Africans, because you've given a definition of Africans just now, when you were dealing with the slogan 'Africa for Africans'?

SOBUKWE. Correct.

THE COURT. What kind of Africans were eligible for ...?

SOBUKWE. The indigenous people.

THE COURT. Only the indigenous people?

SOBUKWE. I there may qualify to say that in our analysis, even the so-called Coloureds are regarded as Africans.

THE COURT. The Whites of course are not regarded as indigenous?

SOBUKWE. And the Indians.

THE COURT. They are not regarded as ...?

SOBUKWE. No.

[...]

THE COURT. And the Indians?

SOBUKWE. No.

THE COURT. What about Arabs?

SOBUKWE. Well, they are not a problem here, they're probably a problem where they are. They don't fall into our analysis here. We've made just that broad analysis of National groups.

PROSECUTOR. And was an oath of allegiance taken by members on the following lines: 'On my life, honour and fortunes I solemnly pledge and swear that I shall always live up to the aims and aspirations of the P.A.C. and shall never, under any circumstances, divulge any secrets, plans, of the organisations, nor betray an Africanist, and that if I dare to divulge and secrets of the P.A.C., or betray a member of the cause or use the influence of the P.A.C. for my own personal interests or advertisements, I do so at my own risk and peril. I will obey and act upon the orders, commands, instructions and directions of the National Executive Committee of the P.A.C. I will always serve, sacrifice and suffer anything for the cause for which the P.A.C. stands, and will at all times be ready to go on any mission that I may be called upon to perform. I will make it my duty – my aim and duty to foster the cause for which the P.A.C. stands in any organisation that I may become a member of. I accept the leadership of the P.A.C.'?

SOBUKWE. That is provided for in the Disciplinary Code. As to whether it was ever taken in the general, I cannot vouch for.

[...]

PROSECUTOR. Now, obviously, for any organisation to recruit members, it will be futile to recruit members on the basis of 'Join the P.A.C. for National Unity', I mean, you wouldn't get many people coming for just a theoretical National Unity, you had to find some common ideals to weld the people together, to say 'We must achieve this'. Is that correct?

SOBUKWE. Unity is one of them, correct.

PROSECUTOR. Unity is one, but I think you will agree that amongst people, to solicit people to join an organisation merely for unity, will not succeed unless unity is backed to achieve a purpose.

SOBUKWE. In our case we just put across what we stood for, the aims and objects of the organisation.

PROSECUTOR. That is right, and the aims and objects were divided into three parts, really. First of all, the total abolition of the Pass System?

SOBUKWE. That is not part of our aims and objects. That was a campaign. It isn't part of the P.A.C. structure at all. The Pass issue was just an issue that flows – as part of a program to be carried out.

PROSECUTOR. Yes, but your program was in three steps – we can call it three stages. First of all you were going to abolish the Pass system by 1960. That is what the P.A.C. had set out to achieve?

SOBUKWE. They'd never stated that.

PROSECUTOR. I see, we'll come to that later. Coupled with the Pass campaign, there was the Status campaign.

THE COURT. The?

PROSECUTOR. Status campaign. Would you agree with that?

SOBUKWE. That was one of the campaigns that was going to be launched.[14] No date was set for that either.

PROSECUTOR. And the final phase was the substitution of White rule in this country by 1963 by a democratic form of Government by the Africans for the Africans?

14 This campaign was announced in 'The State of the Nation' speech of 2 August 1959 (see this vol., ch. 7) and took aim at all forms of condescending address to black people.

SOBUKWE. That wasn't stated in such words. It was probably the implication of what was said, but it wasn't stated in that fashion. All that was stated was that the P.A.C. wanted to achieve independence by that date.

PROSECUTOR. Obviously, what your society was aiming at was one vote, one man?

SOBUKWE. Correct.

PROSECUTOR. And obviously the Africans in South Africa outnumber the Europeans, or the Whites, we'll call them, 5 to 1, isn't it?

SOBUKWE. About.

PROSECUTOR. So on that basis there would obviously be an African majority?

SOBUKWE. On that basis probably the majority of people would be black, but they wouldn't necessarily vote black, if that is what you mean.

PROSECUTOR. No, but assuming for the moment that each man voted black, then that would be the position, there would be an African majority?

SOBUKWE. I beg your pardon?

PROSECUTOR. If every man voted black, there would be an African majority?

SOBUKWE. Correct.

PROSECUTOR. And the target for the achievement of independence was set for 1963?

SOBUKWE. Correct.

PROSECUTOR. So, in order – to get back to membership, in order to recruit members, you had to, first of all, have a campaign to get the people to weld themselves together. You had to look for something which was common to all the people, to attract them to your society?

SOBUKWE. We didn't have to look for it.

PROSECUTOR. Well maybe that is not perhaps the right word, but you chose the abolition of the Pass system as a method whereby people would be attracted to your society by means of a campaign for recruitment of members?

SOBUKWE. Not at all. We moved into the Pass campaign because that is what the people demanded.

PROSECUTOR. Well, in other words, you looked for something that was in demand, and then formed a society to satisfy the need of that demand?

SOBUKWE. We responded to demands.

PROSECUTOR. And, briefly put, the culmination of your campaign, the Pass campaign, was this, that on the 21st of March, 1960, all people would leave their passes at home and under the leadership of P.A.C. officials, surrender themselves for arrest at the Police Stations?

SOBUKWE. Correct.

PROSECUTOR. And obviously, to do this, they had to tell prospective recruits what they stood for and what the policy of the P.A.C. was?

SOBUKWE. Correct.

PROSECUTOR. There was personal campaigning by the members, public meetings were held, and literature was published and sold to anybody, advocating the policy of the P.A.C. and its drive for membership?

SOBUKWE. Correct.

[...]

PROSECUTOR. Now, the *Africanist* being the official organ, would obviously express the policy and aims of the P.A.C.?

SOBUKWE. Not necessarily, because quite a number of people wrote for *The Africanist*.

PROSECUTOR. Who was the editor of *The Africanist*?

SOBUKWE. I wonder if it is necessary for that information to be divulged?

THE COURT. Yes, will you reply to the question please?

SOBUKWE. I was.

THE COURT. You were?

SOBUKWE. Correct.

PROSECUTOR. And, Mr. Sobukwe, the function of an editor – what would you say the function of an editor of a magazine such as this was?

SOBUKWE. To edit the articles that are submitted, invite criticism and so on.

PROSECUTOR. Putting it conversely, anything which you did not approve of, you would see that it was not published?

SOBUKWE. Not at all, the paper didn't belong to me. It had to publish what was of interest and value to the people, not necessarily to me alone.

PROSECUTOR. Would you publish in this organ, *The Africanist*, Josiah Mejunja's[15] call to people to destroy their books forcibly?

SOBUKWE. Definitely would have, and criticized him very severely for it.

THE COURT. You will publish Mejunja's views and criticize them?

SOBUKWE. Correct.

THE COURT. Did you do so?

SOBUKWE. We didn't publish an issue of the *Africanist* after that.

15 Josias Madzunya.

THE COURT. There was no edition of *The Africanist* issued at that time, in March?

SOBUKWE. Correct.

PROSECUTOR. Wasn't there a February/March 1960 issue of *The Africanist*?

SOBUKWE. Correct.

PROSECUTOR. But, obviously, in fairness to you, Mejunja's trouble came to a head on the 20th of March, is that correct?

SOBUKWE. In fact, all his statements came after *The Africanist* had been issued and published.

PROSECUTOR. Now, in the *Africanist* for January, 1959, there is a questionnaire which is headed 'The future of the Africanist movement' and it is answered by means of question and answer?

SOBUKWE. Correct.

PROSECUTOR. That was written by you?

SOBUKWE. I would like to see it.

[...]

PROSECUTOR. Well here the question is posed to the reader: 'Who are the Africanists', and the answer is given concisely...

THE COURT. 'Who are the ...?

PROSECUTOR. 'Who are the Africanists', and the answer is given as: 'A simple answer would be that they are members of the Africanist movement, but if one wishes to go deeper into the question, one would say that they are those Africans who believe that African Nationalism is the only liberatory outlook that combine together the African masses by providing them with a loyalty higher than that of the tribe and thus meld them into a militant, disciplined, fighting force.' It sounds like something you might have written?

SOBUKWE. Correct.

PROSECUTOR. And you agree with that?

SOBUKWE. I do.

PROSECUTOR. Then, in the same issue it was stated: 'African nationalism, the people's liberatory outlook: The black people of Africa (Southern) are suppressed as a national group. They suffer national oppression. The direct and immediate goal of their struggle is national freedom. A position or state where they can shape their own destiny as a people without let or hindrance. Where the people are oppressed as a national group it is inevitable that they should wage a national struggle.' Do you agree with these sentiments?

SOBUKWE. I agree.

PROSECUTOR. And apparently – do you recognize that as being your writing or not?

SOBUKWE. No, I wouldn't go that far, not to the latter at any rate.

PROSECUTOR. The writer continued and he said, 'The growth of African nationalism is rooted in the history of the African Continent. It is a continuation of the fierce, patriotic resistance which was begun by our forebears in this country about 300 years ago, against the foreign invaders. It is a synthesis of different tribal nationalities, Xhosas, Zulus, Zechuana,[16] Pedi, etc., with more powerful and organised political weapons and new forms of struggle for the establishment of a better and higher political and economic organization.' Do you agree that the struggle of the Pan Africanists Congress was a struggle that was embarked upon by leaders such as Chaka and Moshesh, 300 years ago?

SOBUKWE. It is a matter of opinion, isn't it? If you wanted my opinion, you could get it, if the Court is interested in my opinion.

PROSECUTOR. I'm asking you if you agree with these sentiments which I'd just expressed, or not?

SOBUKWE. As an individual, yes I do.

PROSECUTOR. And as an editor of this organ you must have agreed too?

SOBUKWE. It was not for me to agree or disagree.

PROSECUTOR. Now, did you and your organisation regard the White man in South Africa as a foreigner?

SOBUKWE. Correct.

PROSECUTOR. You see, there has been reference in the same article, how people arrived at this rich country some 300 years ago, and any resistance they encountered from the unsuspecting and peaceloving Africans was avoided by shooting them – dead men tell no tales – and ere long reports were sent to starving and sick and diseased in Europe that with the aid of gunpowder and handcuffs, Africa is a continent flowing with milk and honey for Whites. More scum was sent from Europe to inhabit this country. They came in their hundreds; they came in dozens. They arrived by night, they arrived, they carried bibles, they carried gunpowder. Is that part of the sentiments of your organisation as well, that the European came to this country and has unfairly, by means of unfair laws

16 Bechuana or Batswana.

and superior weight of power, military power, and by means of the Bible, suppressed African masses?

SOBUKWE. Correct.

PROSECUTOR. So then ultimately your organisation must consider the position in Southern African to be that of the African defending himself against an aggressor?

SOBUKWE. That would have been the history at a particular stage. At the present moment the aggression is stabilized. The African is more or less in the position of subject people.

THE COURT. That is the position of the Africans.

PROSECUTOR. But the whole concept of the position and the picture that was sought to be painted by your organisation, was that the existing position in South Africa – I'm talking about up to the 21st of March, 1960. What transpired after that has nothing to do with this case. The position in South Africa was considered as the African defending himself against the foreign aggressor?

SOBUKWE. It couldn't be, because the aggression was complete. He couldn't be defending himself any more. The aggression was completed in the 19th century.

PROSECUTOR. Didn't Chaka defend himself against aggression?

SOBUKWE. That is what I mean, it is complete. There is no aggression now continuing. The people were dispossessed. The African people were dispossessed and dispossession is a fait accompli today.

PROSECUTOR. It is in a state of continuance. Once you're dispossessed you remain dispossessed until you repossess yourself, isn't that so?

SOBUKWE. Correct, but there is no particular aggression being fought, I mean, there is no war of aggression now, that we are thinking of.

PROSECUTOR. So this dispossession wasn't voluntary, it was forcible?

SOBUKWE. Correct.

PROSECUTOR. That constitutes an aggression?

SOBUKWE. At that stage, yes.

PROSECUTOR. And that aggression continues up till this day by legal means, according to you and your organisation?

SOBUKWE. I don't think I stated that.

PROSECUTOR. But don't you consider that to be the case?

SOBUKWE. What we have said is that we are oppressed as a national group today, and our struggle is a national struggle.

PROSECUTOR. Now, you have mentioned in your evidence that the P.A.C. sought to overthrow White domination?

SOBUKWE. Correct.

PROSECUTOR. How do you define White domination, as the President of the P.A.C.?

SOBUKWE. White supremacy, White 'baasskap', the entrenchment of a particular group in the economy, military power, political power of the country, just by virtue of its pigment.[17]

[...]

Court resumes after an adjournment

[...]

PROSECUTOR. Now, at that particular conference,[18] some resolutions were adopted?

SOBUKWE. Correct.

PROSECUTOR. They were passed unanimously by all the delegates present?

SOBUKWE. Correct.

PROSECUTOR. Were the resolutions to the following effect – I'll hand you the paper to read in a moment – 'That the National Executive be instructed (a) to call a motion on a positive decisive action against the Pass Laws; (b) that the P.A.C. should embark immediately on a campaign of intensive organisation in order to get the nation ready at the earliest possible time; (c) that the nation be alerted immediately and be advised to be ready for the call and be ready for any positive action as from now; (d) that the P.A.C. members be taxed £1.2.6. per member to establish a national fund to finance the campaign; (e) that whatever form of action the National Executive decide upon, the slogan of 'no bail, no defence, no fine' should be strictly adhered to; (f) that the National Executive Committee be instructed to implement the state of campaign as part of an unfolding program but the action against the Pass Laws be given priority in that action' [...]

---

17 Here Sobukwe deftly parries the prosecutor's attempt to link the PAC to violence and incitement to violence, for which the accused were on trial. *Baasskap* is Afrikaans for master-ship, i.e. white domination.

18 The prosecutor is referring to the inaugural conference of the PAC. For Sobukwe's inaugural speech at that conference, see this vol., ch. 6.

THE COURT. Well, is it correct that resolutions to that effect were passed?

SOBUKWE. Correct.

PROSECUTOR. Now further you have mentioned that violence was something that your organisation anticipated or took into account when planning its campaign?

SOBUKWE. That we took into account, the possibility.

PROSECUTOR. As a matter of fact, at that particular National Conference, of which Jacob Nyesi [*sic*][19] was the chairman, the question of violence was discussed there?

SOBUKWE. It wasn't discussed. The question was put to me to explain what our position was with regards to violence.

PROSECUTOR. Can you recall saying the following at the Conference: 'The second question was whether or not we stand for violence or non-violence. Our attitude has been that it is foolish to reveal our method.' Can you recall saying that?

SOBUKWE. I recall what I said on that occasion, and I think I could say what I said.

PROSECUTOR. Do you recall saying what I read to you?

SOBUKWE. Not at all, I didn't say it.

PROSECUTOR. Can you recall an unknown speaker from the floor putting to you 'Our leader has spoken to us of violence and that the violence we are resorting to is that of self defence'. Can you recall the question being put?

SOBUKWE. There was no question of that nature put, in fact, I was wondering if you would allow me to tell you what my answer was, in connection with violence, so that we know what we are talking about.

PROSECUTOR. Yes?

SOBUKWE. The question was put to me as to what our attitude was towards violence, and I said there were three views of violence current. The first is the pacifist view of violence, of giving the other cheek and that we just have nothing to do with. The second view of violence is the view accepted by all civilized countries, and that is the view that one can resort to violence in defence of one's property and life, and the third is the view that violence is a necessary instrument of struggle, and my answer was that we have not yet come to such a conclusion regarding violence. We inclined

19 Jacob Nyaose came from a trade union background. He was a founding member of the PAC and was elected its secretary for labour on its National Executive Committee in 1959.

towards the second view of violence. That would probably explain why the man then spoke in terms of our using violence in self defence.

PROSECUTOR. Could you have put it as follows: 'That the third view of violence is where violence is organised as an instrument of action, where people organize violence in order to obtain their freedom'?

SOBUKWE. Not at all.

PROSECUTOR. You don't recall those words?

SOBUKWE. I didn't use them.

PROSECUTOR. Can you recall saying, after the Secretary for Resolutions Committee had had his say about the Status campaign, and the Continental salute, then there was a speaker, Mashabane, who wanted action taken then, and then you said 'We must learn to keep our secrets. We must learn not to beat our breasts, not to beat our chests and raffle our secrets, and tell the world in advance that on such and such a day we're going to do this and that. It is foolish for a boxer to tell his opponent to take a left.' Can you recall using these words?

SOBUKWE. That I wouldn't wonder, because that is what I'd been saying all along, right from the inaugural convention, you see. One wouldn't know whether one said it on this occasion or not.

PROSECUTOR. Can you remember concluding and saying 'All our energy as from today must be directed towards the final complete and decisive overthrow of the Pass Laws'?

SOBUKWE. I probably could have said that.

PROSECUTOR. And you received a magnificent ovation after that was said?

SOBUKWE. I don't notice ovations.

PROSECUTOR. Now, four circulars were issued in respect of this particular campaign, that is as far as we are aware. The first one, I think, has been called 'The dawn has come, or the great awakening has started'. Would that be correct?

SOBUKWE. I wouldn't know the order.

PROSECUTOR. I'll show them to you and perhaps we can establish the order. Have a look at Exhibit 47, that is titled 'The great awakening has started, the dawn has come'. Would that be the first in the series of these circulars that were sent out?

SOBUKWE. Correct.

PROSECUTOR. And apparently – I don't want to bind you down to a fixed date – approximately what date would that have gone out?

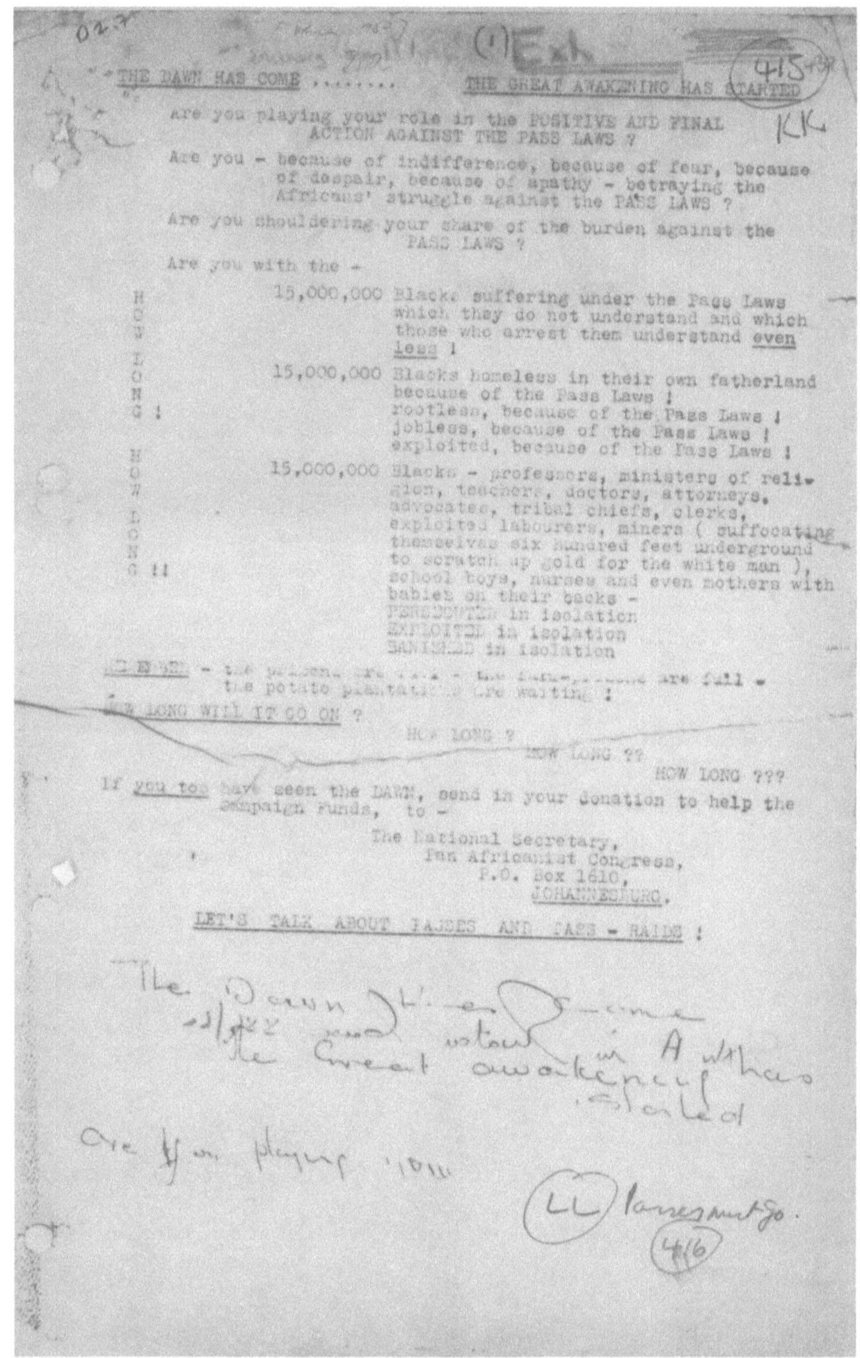

THE DAWN HAS COME .... THE GREAT AWAKENING HAS STARTED

Are you playing your role in the POSITIVE AND FINAL ACTION AGAINST THE PASS LAWS ?

Are you – because of indifference, because of fear, because of despair, because of apathy – betraying the Africans' struggle against the PASS LAWS ?

Are you shouldering your share of the burden against the PASS LAWS ?

Are you with the –

HOW LONG ! HOW LONG !!

15,000,000 Blacks suffering under the Pass Laws which they do not understand and which those who arrest them understand even less !

15,000,000 Blacks homeless in their own fatherland because of the Pass Laws !
rootless, because of the Pass Laws !
jobless, because of the Pass Laws !
exploited, because of the Pass Laws !

15,000,000 Blacks – professors, ministers of religion, teachers, doctors, attorneys, advocates, tribal chiefs, clerks, exploited labourers, miners (suffocating themselves six hundred feet underground to scratch up gold for the white man), school boys, nurses and even mothers with babies on their backs –
PERSECUTED in isolation
EXPLOITED in isolation
BANISHED in isolation

[illegible] – the prisons are [illegible] – the farm-[illegible] are full – the potato plantations are waiting !

HOW LONG WILL IT GO ON ?

HOW LONG ?

HOW LONG ??

HOW LONG ???

If you too have seen the DAWN, send in your donation to help the Campaign Funds, to –

The National Secretary,
Pan Africanist Congress,
P.O. Box 1610,
JOHANNESBURG.

LET'S TALK ABOUT PASSES AND PASS – RAIDS !

31. Three leaflets issued by the PAC for its anti-pass campaign in March 1960, which were later produced as court exhibits. 'The Dawn Has Come'. (Historical Papers Research Archive, Wits University)

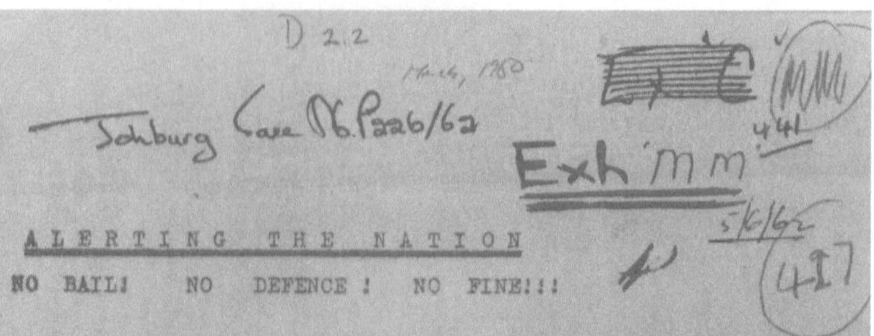

ALERTING THE NATION

NO BAIL! NO DEFENCE ! NO FINE!!!

Anyone who gets this circular should keep it. He will have got hold of history. These are the elected leaders of the Nation, dedicated to the cause of African Freedom and Independence by 1963!

DECISION OF THE NATION:

At the conference of the Pan Africanist Congress held on the 19th and 20th December, 1959, it was resolved that the President should call the Nation to take Positive, Decisive action against the Pass Laws any time this year.

It was resolved, also, that each person should make a donation of £1. 2. 6d. This money will be used to care for the Widows and Dependants of the Nation.

The President will call upon the Nation very soon to honour its resolution. The Order that goes out to the Nation, therefore, is:-

(a) Save food, save money imediately.

(b) Send your donations, immediately, to The National Secretary, Pan Africanist Congress, P.O. Box 1610, JOHANNESBURG, Transvaal.

(c) Keep this Circular. Remember these leaders. They will Lead you into action. Your orders will come from them only.

(d) Be ready for the call. Know what we are fighting for. It is a noble and glorious struggle calling for service, sacrifice and suffering from the African people.

(e) This is going to be a disciplined, mass campaign. Orders must be carried out faithfully. If we all play our part, if we all cling together, no force can defeat us . We will win.

(f) We will do away with Pass Laws once and for all. There is no doubt about that. There is no need for any of our people to die from police bullets to achieve this. Discipline and an Iron will are what we need.

Children of the Soil, we are on the side of history. In 1960, we take the first step - in 1963 the last!

Issued by the Pan Africanist Congress, P.O. Box 1610, Johannesburg

32. 'Alerting the Nation: No Bail! No Defence! No Fine!!!'

(Historical Papers Research Archive, Wits University)

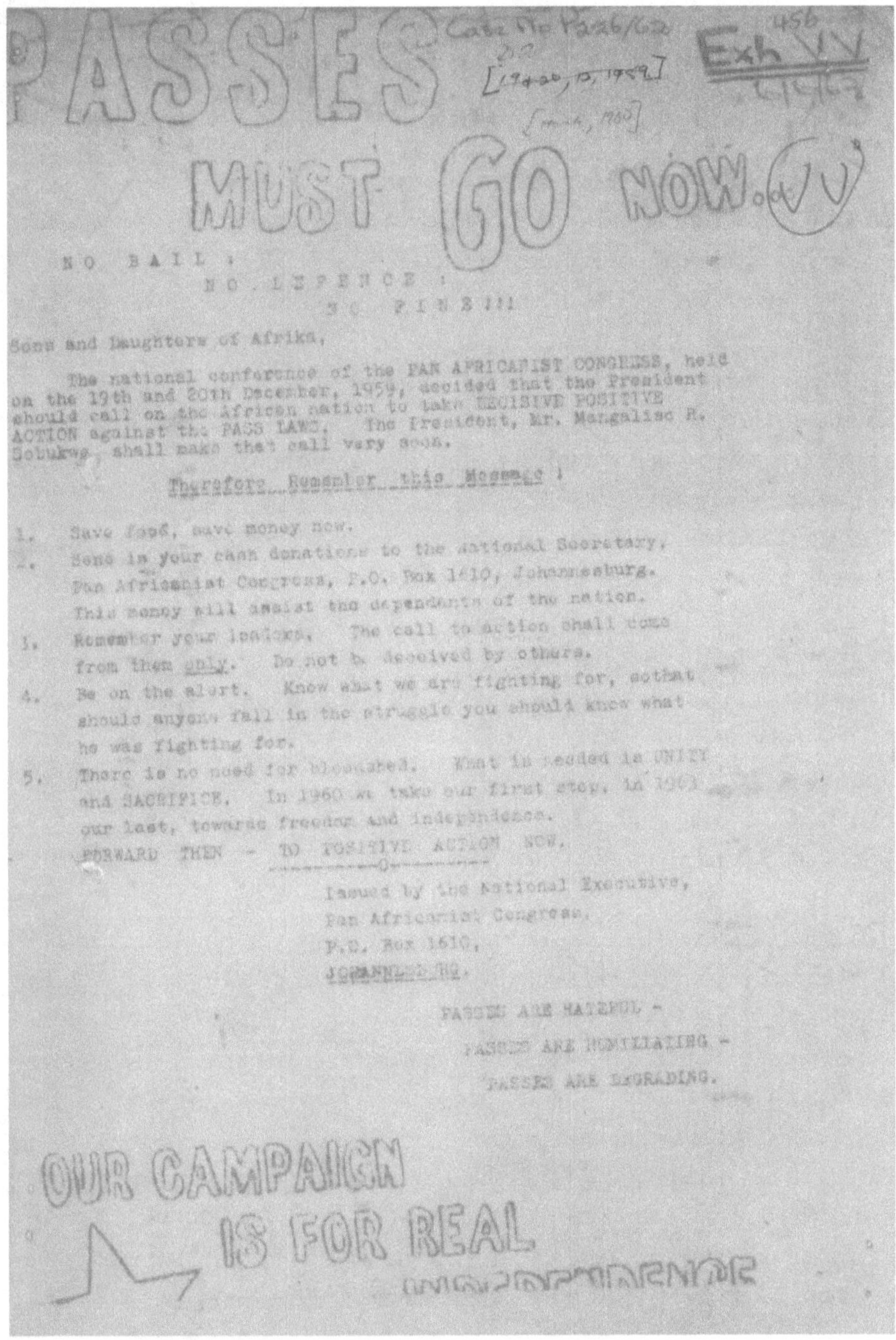

PASSES MUST GO NOW.

NO BAIL!
NO DEFENCE!
NO FINE!!!

Sons and Daughters of Afrika,

The national conference of the PAN AFRICANIST CONGRESS, held on the 19th and 20th December, 1959, decided that the President should call on the African nation to take DECISIVE POSITIVE ACTION against the PASS LAWS. The President, Mr. Mangaliso R. Sobukwe, shall make that call very soon.

Therefore Remember this Message!

1. Save food, save money now.
2. Send in your cash donations to the National Secretary, Pan Africanist Congress, P.O. Box 1610, Johannesburg. This money will assist the dependants of the nation.
3. Remember your leaders. The call to action shall come from them only. Do not be deceived by others.
4. Be on the alert. Know what we are fighting for, sothat should anyone fall in the struggle you should know what he was fighting for.
5. There is no need for bloodshed. What is needed is UNITY and SACRIFICE. In 1960 we take our first step, in 1963 our last, towards freedom and independence.

FORWARD THEN – TO POSITIVE ACTION NOW.

Issued by the National Executive,
Pan Africanist Congress,
P.O. Box 1610,
JOHANNESBURG.

PASSES ARE HATEFUL –
PASSES ARE HUMILIATING –
PASSES ARE DEGRADING.

OUR CAMPAIGN IS FOR REAL

33. 'Passes Must Go Now'. (Historical Papers Research Archive, Wits University)

SOBUKWE. I'd make it early in March. I'm sorry, I can't state the date.

PROSECUTOR. Have a look at Exhibit 49 'Passes must go now'. That would have been the second circular in the series to have gone out?

SOBUKWE. Correct.

PROSECUTOR. How long after the first one, days or weeks after the ...?

SOBUKWE. Probably a matter of more than a week. I wouldn't say two weeks or so, but it would be more than a week.

PROSECUTOR. Now Exhibit 6, headed 'Alerting the nation', that was the third of the series that went out. Would that be correct? First of all you alerted them and then you called them into action?

SOBUKWE. Correct.

PROSECUTOR. And that would have gone out approximately a few days to a week after Exhibit 49?

SOBUKWE. That would have gone out a few days or so before the final one.

THE COURT. A few days or so before the 21st?

SOBUKWE. Before the final circular of the 18th or so.

THE COURT. Oh, the final circular.

PROSECUTOR. The final circular was Exhibit 5, that is the one headed 'Calling the nation'?

SOBUKWE. Correct.

PROSECUTOR. That went out on the 18th of March, I think you said?

SOBUKWE. Round about, yes.

[...]

PROSECUTOR. Now the Exhibit I'm about to show you, another *Africanist*, February/March, 1960 – that would be Exhibit 121. There, on page 1 of the *Africanist*, I think reference is made to the 'Dompas'.[20] Is that a colloquial term which was attached to the Reference Book?

SOBUKWE. Correct.

THE COURT. What is that word please?

PROSECUTOR. A 'Dom pas'. Would that be your article, Mr. Sobukwe?

SOBUKWE. Correct.

PROSECUTOR. And another Exhibit, 122, would this be your letter to Major General Rademeyer of the Police at Cape Town?[21]

SOBUKWE. Correct.

---

20 Translates as stupid pass. See also this vol., ch. 6, n. 6.

21 See Appendix to this chapter.

[...]

PROSECUTOR. Now, according to this letter, you and your organisation must have realized that the Police authorities were going to be embarrassed by a vast crowd gathering round their Police Stations?

SOBUKWE. Not at all.

THE COURT. You say you did not realize that?

SOBUKWE. In fact, we didn't have any such fears or doubts.

PROSECUTOR. Well, let's clear that up. You and your organisation realized that with the membership at your disposal, vast crowds were going to be at the Police Stations to offer themselves for surrendering?

SOBUKWE. We realized that quite a number might not even reach the Police Stations, because there was no telling where the police would stop them on the way or not, but we did expect numbers to converge on the Police Stations.

PROSECUTOR. And it was realized by you and your organisation that this was going to cause embarrassment to the Police Authorities, so much so that they were going to have to request the crowds to disperse?

SOBUKWE. I wonder if the word embarrassment is correct. In fact, it would be something the Police authorities wouldn't want, if that is what you mean, and would therefore disperse the crowds, seeing that the demonstration would in any event be what they would regard as an unlawful demonstration.

PROSECUTOR. Well, an awkward situation would be created by many people gathering round the Police Stations, or an unwanted situation?

SOBUKWE. An unwanted situation.

PROSECUTOR. Now you, yourself, have a very high standard of education, you concede that?

SOBUKWE. I'd make it reasonable.

PROSECUTOR. And your colleagues who were in the executive positions of the P.A.C., would you say that they were reasonably educated, not like Lebaka [*sic*],[22] for example?

SOBUKWE. They were graduates, many of them.

THE COURT. What is your reply?

SOBUKWE. Most of them are graduates.

PROSECUTOR. Most of them are graduates?

22 P.K. Leballo.

SOBUKWE. Correct.

PROSECUTOR. And will you agree that the general standard of education attained by most Africans is lower than that of Europeans, generally speaking?

SOBUKWE. I don't like to make such comparisons. I'd make it that numbers of them haven't probably been able to reach standard six.

PROSECUTOR. Yes, perhaps the opportunities aren't there, but will you make that concession?

SOBUKWE. I will say there are more Whites educated, is that what you mean?

PROSECUTOR. Yes.

SOBUKWE. Correct.

THE COURT. Would it be correct to say a bigger percentage?

SOBUKWE. The bigger percentage of Whites, yes.

THE COURT. Are educated than of non-Whites?

SOBUKWE. Correct.

PROSECUTOR. I mean, that is quite clear. When your organisation appeals to people about the Pass Laws, you see, say, a speaker were to say 'This is a degenerate system of legislation', it wouldn't carry as much weight to the ordinary classes whom you're addressing as if you said 'This is a dirty stinking piece of legislation'?

SOBUKWE. We don't indulge in invectives in our meetings, just describe things as they are. The Pass itself doesn't need any embellishments at all, the people know what it is.

PROSECUTOR. What I'm driving at is this, that surely it must have entered, or have been taken into consideration by you and the organisers of this campaign, that awkward situations were going to be created by the police, when unwanted crowds offered themselves for arrest on the 21st of March?

SOBUKWE. I think my reply was there that the police probably wouldn't want such demonstrations. Whether they would regard that as awkward or undesirable is a different matter. They would probably regard it as undesirable.

PROSECUTOR. What was the object of having masses of people surrender themselves at any particular Police Station for not having a pass in their possession?

SOBUKWE. To get themselves arrested. As I've said in the instructions …

THE COURT. What is the object of getting themselves arrested, I think that is what the Prosecutor wants to know?

SOBUKWE. Correct, and as I've said, I've stated in my circular that there are already so many thousands arrested for this particular offence, that there is no reason why others shouldn't be arrested if they didn't have the passes. That was our idea. Fill the gaols with these people, if you want to.

PROSECUTOR. Can I put it to you this way – well, you've answered it, but the idea behind this campaign was to fill the gaols with as many people as possible, and as such force embarrassment on the authorities who had limited accommodation in the gaols?[23]

SOBUKWE. That would be one aspect of it, but I think we also stressed the industrial aspect of it.

PROSECUTOR. Yes, by doing that, having a large number of arrests and people in detention under the 'No bail, no fine, no defence' scheme, would mean that vast supplies of labour would be withdrawn from the so-called White capitalists ...?

SOBUKWE. Correct.

PROSECUTOR. And the Government would be deprived of its manpower?

SOBUKWE. All it would mean is that industry would be paralysed.

PROSECUTOR. And in this way your organisation hoped to force the Government to capitulate and withdraw the Pass Legislation?

SOBUKWE. Correct.

PROSECUTOR. Now there's one thing I can't understand. Can you recall an article in one of the *Africanist*, I haven't got it to hand at the moment, where reference is made to the fact that the Pass was being extended from the African male dog to the African female bitch. Is that your writing?

SOBUKWE. It is mine.

PROSECUTOR. Now, why the use of the double genitive?

SOBUKWE. I see, it is probably poor knowledge of English, because what I meant is it is the dog that means the collar, and if it is being passed to our women as well, it is being passed to the bitches, that is all I wanted to say.

PROSECUTOR. Isn't it correct that to anybody, reference to anybody as a dog, or as – anybody in any section as a bitch, is highly derogatory?

SOBUKWE. It is.

PROSECUTOR. And were you as such trying to bring the Pass into as much contempt as you could, by associating it with the terms dog and bitch?

---

23 The continued return to a sense of 'embarrassment' or 'humiliation' provides rich interpretative fodder. Phenomenologically, such a humbling always involves an other, an audience, to whom one is shown to have been lacking, to have made mistakes, or to have lost control. There is of course the audience that is the white populace, but there is also an international audience, and to have been 'embarrassed' – or, worse yet, 'humiliated' – by a 'lesser' adversary, viz. blacks, adds salt to an already smarting wound.

SOBUKWE. Not [illegible]…. exactly what the Legislation makes out of the people whom it affects.

PROSECUTOR. Do you concede that the use of such terminology is likely to inculcate in a person feelings of wrath?

SOBUKWE. I didn't think about that, I was expressing what I felt.

PROSECUTOR. The P.A.C. also paid homage to its past heroes and also had a heroes day, is that correct?

SOBUKWE. Correct.

PROSECUTOR. And I think one of the prominent heroes was Limbede [*sic*]?[24]

SOBUKWE. Correct.

PROSECUTOR. Would this be your …

THE COURT. One was – what was his name?

PROSECUTOR. Lembede, sir. Would this be writing of yours: 'Who then are our national heroes? African men like Chaka, the black military genius, Mosheshoe, the shrewd strategist and statesman, Sekukuni, the soldier, Hintsa, 'Makwakeman'[25] – I can't pronounce the name – who fought against van Riebeek's land robbers, Humedi, Makata, Platjie, and Tsimeng,[26] who were the founders of pure African nationalism, men whose lives were dedicated to the saving and salvaging the land from foreign invaders; men whose blood was blood spilled in the cause of Africa by bitterly trying to shake off White domination.' Would that be your writing?

SOBUKWE. The writing is not mine, although the views wouldn't be against mine. It is not my article, at any rate, but I have nothing against what he expressed …

[…]

PROSECUTOR. Now, did you and your organisation liken the present struggle to the struggle of those men of the past?

---

24 Anton Muziwakhe Lembede was the undisputed intellectual wellspring of Africanist thought. His inspiration was not limited to Pan-Africanists, but also included a whole cadre of ANC members, including Nelson Mandela. Indeed, Lembede was the driving force behind the creation of the ANC Youth League, and served as its first president.

25 Shaka, king of the Zulu; Moshoeshoe, king of the Basotho; Sekhukhune, king of the Pedi; Hintsa, king of the Xhosa; and Maqoma, nephew of Hintsa and Xhosa chief and military leader, are all outstanding indigenous leaders of the nineteenth century, who resisted white colonisation and expansion.

26 Josiah Gumede, S.M. Makgatho, Solomon T. Plaatje and Selby Msimang were leaders of the African National Congress in its early years.

SOBUKWE. The point is, I think I said earlier that this is a phase of our history. We recognized that phase, when our forefathers had to fight in defence of their land. That is a phase of African history that we recognize.

PROSECUTOR. Wasn't it part of your present policy to liken the Pass struggle, in the light of nationalism, with the present struggle?

SOBUKWE. In what way, because as I've said earlier, we think in terms of a continental struggle, where theirs was a tribal struggle, various tribes fighting isolated battles. We are thinking in terms of a giant nation standing together in a modern age. I don't see how we could compare the two.

PROSECUTOR. Didn't you have a common invader?

SOBUKWE. The invader is that of the past who probably persisted in the present, if that is what you mean. If I could get the question correctly, I wouldn't hesitate to answer it.

PROSECUTOR. No, I concede that. You see, I'll put it to you bluntly what my view is, the Crown's, is that mere lip service was paid to your term of non-violence; that by reference to your past heroes and the shedding of blood and instances where blood was shed; instances where violence took place, that that was the true nature of this particular campaign, even though you only paid lip service to 'We shall not have violence'?

SOBUKWE. I would say that is absolutely untrue.

[...]

PROSECUTOR. You mentioned in your evidence in chief the historical role of women. What would be the hysterical [*sic*][27]role women would play?

SOBUKWE. In fact, they would be allowed to participate in the campaign. There were pressure from them, they wanted to come into the campaign at the time and we didn't want them to.

PROSECUTOR. Now, women have from time immemorial, as far as the African is concerned, played a historical role in this respect, that they have always, or nearly always, urged the men into battle with a high pitched shrill type of warcry. Do you agree?

SOBUKWE. It is not said by history books.

THE COURT. Mr. Sobukwe, what is meant by the word 'hysterical' [*sic*]. What you have said now, that they wanted to join in this campaign, is very recent history. What was then their hysterical [*sic*] role?

27 See n. 6.

SOBUKWE. Correct. There we meant the role that would get them known in history, that would make them known in history at a future connotation, not the past.

PROSECUTOR. You see, do I understand you to say the historical role women would play, would be such that it would ensure them a nitch [*sic*][28] in future history?

SOBUKWE. Correct.

PROSECUTOR. You see, I don't follow you there because your circular Exhibit 5, that is the one 'Calling the nation', in paragraph (e) says 'All men will go to gaol under the slogan "No bail, no defence, no fine"'. The women will be assigned their historical role that in the first phase of the struggle they must make sure that all men go to the gaol?'

SOBUKWE. Correct.

PROSECUTOR. In other words, they were being assigned a historic role, a role which was something of their history?

SOBUKWE. Not at all. They were being assigned a role which would assure them a place in a future, in the house of history. As I said a few moments ago, the women were pressing, they wanted to participate in the campaign, and we didn't want them in at that stage, so we had to keep them off, so in the early stages then their chief task was to see to it that the men went to gaol, and then their historical role would be when they themselves participated in the campaign.

PROSECUTOR. Weren't they to assist by seeing that the men went to gaol, by perhaps making a derogatory remark and calling a man a coward, and saying 'Come on, get in there, fall in the line'?

SOBUKWE. They would help organising, to make sure the men went.

PROSECUTOR. You agree that women are emotional creatures, more so than men?

SOBUKWE. I think that is a reflection on them.

PROSECUTOR. The strict instructions which you mentioned, which were given against the possible use of violence, they were contained solely in the circular, and the resolutions taken at the conference?

SOBUKWE. And in *The Africanist* itself, in fact, it is stated there that the only people who would benefit by violence, would be the Government and the police, not the African people at all.

---

28 i.e. niche.

[...]

PROSECUTOR. In one of your *Africanists* too, it was mentioned that you wanted an African Democratic Socialistic State, once the independence had been achieved. Did you write that portion?

SOBUKWE. I wouldn't know, unless I were to see *The Africanist* concerned.

PROSECUTOR. I think your organisation realized that it was assured a large amount of success because nobody wants to carry your Pass ...?

SOBUKWE. Correct.

PROSECUTOR. What would be the object of one person, for example, crying out 'Africa', and somebody else responding with 'Izwe Lethu'?

SOBUKWE. It is a form of greeting that we employed, in fact, it was probably a method of distinguishing us from many other African organisations. All you have to do is 'Izwe Lethu', with the requisite sign, and then he replies 'E Africa', with the same salute. This probably is not even a watchword really, it is merely a form of greeting, and one would make it.

PROSECUTOR. Anyway, the two organisations, the A.N.C. and the P.A.C., have one thing in common and that is the dislike and the wish for the abolition of the pass system?

SOBUKWE. I won't just prescribe it to the organisation as such. The African people in general does.

PROSECUTOR. Yes, but if your organisation hadn't organised the campaign, it is hardly likely that the Africans would have gone along, without any pamphlets, to surrender themselves, would they?

SOBUKWE. Probably not.

PROSECUTOR. So it is as a result of the leadership and the campaign instituted by the P.A.C. that people went to the Police Stations?

SOBUKWE. Correct.

PROSECUTOR. NO FURTHER QUESTIONS

Sobukwe re-examined by David Ramodibe

RAMODIBE. Mr. Sobukwe, I take it that the P.A.C. had means whereby it wanted to [make] clear to the people that it was never its intention to use violence at all, and thereby devising such things as 'N'kosi Sikelele Africa'?

Sobukwe. I wouldn't take that as the property of the P.A.C. That is the national anthem that dates back to the early part of the 20th Century, 'Nkosi Sekelele [*sic*] Africa', probably as early as the 1918s, thereabouts.[29] It has been accepted as a national anthem, not only in South Africa but it is sung also in the Rhodesias, in the languages of those areas. But the song as such does reflect a religious outlook more than probably a political one. It represents the days when people believed in prayer probably more than in active struggle for political rights.

Prosecutor. Would you say that a group of people singing 'Nkosi Sekelele Africa', do not mean to do any harm at all?

The Court. Would you say that?

Ramodibe. ... Any group of people singing 'Nkosi Sekelele Africa' do not intend to do any harm at all?

Sobukwe. Honestly speaking, really, I'd probably have to be a psychologist to know what they're thinking about, whether they sang it honestly or not. Some people sing hymns without in any way meaning them, but you would take it generally that a political party singing that and knowing what it was singing, would be a party that didn't intend any violence at all.

Ramodibe. NO FURTHER QUESTIONS.

[...]

The Court. Exhibit 122, please, the letter to the Commissioner of the Police, put it before the witness. Now, did you think that you were going to get the co-operation of the police by writing that letter?

Sobukwe. Correct.

The Court. You wanted their co-operation, did you?

Sobukwe. Correct.

The Court. What did you expect the police to do – what did you expect the police would do to co-operate with you in this campaign?

Sobukwe. They would arrest those who came to submit themselves, or if they didn't want to arrest them, they would just tell them to disperse.

The Court. To either arrest those who came?

Sobukwe. Correct.

The Court. Or to disperse them?

Sobukwe. Or to disperse them.

29 The ANC anthem, 'Nkosi Sikelel' iAfrika' (God Bless Africa), was composed first as a hymn by Enoch Sontonga in 1897.

THE COURT. And if the police ordered them to disperse, what would they do?

SOBUKWE. What I've said, they would disperse, given sufficient time to the people themselves ...

THE COURT. Just a moment, please, just a moment. Where, in all your circulars, do you tell people to disperse if the police tell them to disperse? Where in all your pamphlets do you tell them that?

SOBUKWE. I'm not too sure that there is a circular where I've done so, but every member knows that I've said it at almost every public meeting, that that will be done.

THE COURT. Would you care to go through the copies of the four pamphlets you've got here, and tell me where you tell the people 'If the police tell you to disperse, please go home'?

SOBUKWE. I hope you remember this part on the letter here ...

THE COURT. I don't want to argue with you, answer my question now. Do you want the opportunity to look through those four pamphlets and show me where you tell your people to 'Obey the police when they tell you to disperse'. Now I'll adjourn and when you've read through them, send for me and tell me?

SOBUKWE. Yes.

Court resumes after an adjournment

THE COURT. I allowed you an opportunity now of going through the pamphlets, the four that were mentioned. Is there anything in them in which you tell the people to obey the police orders to disperse?

SOBUKWE. No.

THE COURT. Now, you were about to add something else. What was that?

SOBUKWE. This is what I wanted to say, that not every order appears in the circulars.

THE COURT. All orders were not in the circulars?

SOBUKWE. Correct.

THE COURT. Yes?

SOBUKWE. Quite a number of things that one said, one said at a public meeting, and so on.

THE COURT. Did you in any public meeting or public meetings tell the people to disperse on police orders?

Sobukwe. Correct.

The Court. Where and when?

Sobukwe. At Cape Town I did, at a public meeting there.

The Court. You did it in Cape Town. Anywhere else?

Sobukwe. At meetings of the P.A.C. as such, I've instructed all leaders that once this was done, once the police told them to disperse, then they would ask for reasonable time.

The Court. Well, how did you convey that to all leaders now? Did you have them all together?

Sobukwe. It was in meetings of Regions.

The Court. Mr. Sobukwe, I don't understand you, because if they obeyed such police orders, that would surely defeat the object of all your demonstrations.

Sobukwe. In fact, if Your Worship recollects correctly, you will remember that in Cape Town, itself, at the time the people were told to disperse …

The Court. Mr. Sobukwe, I know nothing about Cape Town yet. You can tell me what you said in Cape Town, if you wish to, but that is 1000 miles from Vereeniging?

Sobukwe. I get that. I was going to give that a bit of information, that in Cape Town when the people were told to disperse, the leader, in accordance with my instructions, went up to the police there and asked for a reasonable time, because they were given three minutes within which to disperse, and he said that that was not reasonable for a crowd of that size to disperse within three minutes, but the police were not in the mood for argument, I think.

The Court. Now, I'm going on to another point, I must put this to you …?

Sobukwe. Please.

The Court. Do you think that after you've said these insulting things to the Commissioner of Police about his men, that you would get co-operation?

Sobukwe. I didn't think they were insulting.

The Court. Did you think you would get co-operation by insulting the police?

Sobukwe. I didn't regard it as an insult at all.

The Court. You didn't regard your letter as insulting?

Sobukwe. Not at all.

The Court. You did not regard your letter as insulting the police, is that right now?

Sobukwe. Correct.

THE COURT. Firstly, you ask the Commissioner to instruct the police to refrain from actions that may lead to violence?

SOBUKWE. Correct.

THE COURT. So you are there saying the police may do things which may lead to violence?

SOBUKWE. Correct.

THE COURT. 'It is unfortunately true that many White policemen brought up in the racist hothouse of South Africa, regard themselves as champions of White supremacy and not as Law officers.' Is that not insulting?

SOBUKWE. Correct, I don't think it is insulting.

THE COURT. That is not insulting?

SOBUKWE. That is a statement of fact.

THE COURT. Listen, a statement of fact may be true, but it still may be insulting. Don't you regard this as insulting?

SOBUKWE. I do not.

THE COURT. 'In the African they see an enemy, a threat, not to law and order, but to their privileges as Whites.' That is not insulting?

SOBUKWE. Not at all.

THE COURT. 'The usual mumbling by a police officer of an order requiring the people to disperse within three minutes and almost immediately ordering a baton charge, deceives nobody, and shows the police up as sadistic bullies.' Do you regard that as insulting?

SOBUKWE. Not at all.

THE COURT. 'We cannot be expected to run helter-skelter because a trigger-happy, African-hating young White police officer has given thousands or even hundreds of people, three minutes within which to remove their bodies from his immediate environment.' Is that not insulting?

SOBUKWE. I wouldn't regard it as.

THE COURT. Mr. Sobukwe, I can only say that you have peculiar ideas as to what is insulting and what is not insulting. Are you saying so now?

SOBUKWE. Yes. Could I have a chance to answer?

THE COURT. Yes.

SOBUKWE. The position is that after all, everybody we say is a product of his environment. He need not necessarily be a 100% product, but he is affected by his environment, and we say that the police in South Africa are no different from the ordinary human beings that non-police people are, and the prejudices that Whites have, who are not policemen, the policemen also share because they have been brought up in that environment. Therefore, if there is African hatred on that part of some Whites, and these policemen who have been brought up in South African conditions, must of necessity share those prejudices and there is, to my knowledge, no education that they receive to see to it that they are purged of such prejudices. Shall I proceed?

THE COURT. No, I'm not going to allow you to make any further speeches, thank you. You may sit down.

***

Afterword

Of the 76 people who were originally charged alongside Monyake, only 19 were eventually tried, and of these all were acquitted apart from Monyake and three others, who were found guilty.

The judge's lengthy summary of the case and the evidence of the witnesses who came forward provide a remarkable account of the events surrounding Sharpeville. In the understandable attention to Sobukwe's case, historians

34. The burial of those who had been killed at Sharpeville on 21 March 1960, with a PAC presence. (Photo by Benjamin Pogrund, with kind permission)

and commentators have largely neglected the Monyake trial, which till now has remained wholly unpublished, its historical riches unmined.

***

Appendix: Letter of Sobukwe to the Commissioner of Police, 16 March 1960

Robert Sobukwe
to Major-General C.I. Rademeyer,
Commissioner of Police,
Cape Town, 16 March 1960

Sir,

My organization, the Pan Africanist Congress, will be starting a sustained, disciplined, non-violent campaign against the Pass Laws on Monday the 21st March 1960. I have given strict instructions, not only to members of my organization but also to African people in general, that they should not allow themselves to be provoked into violent action by anyone. In a Press Statement I am releasing soon, I repeat that appeal and make one to the police too.

I am now writing to you to instruct the Police to refrain from actions that may lead to violence. It is unfortunately true that many white policemen, brought up in the racist hothouse of South Africa, regard themselves as champions of white supremacy and not as law officers. In the African they see an enemy, a threat, not to 'law and order' but to their privileges as whites.

I therefore, appeal to you to instruct your men not to give impossible commands to my people. The usual mumbling by a police of an order requiring people to disperse within three minutes, and almost immediately ordering a baton charge, deceives nobody and shows the police up as sadistic bullies. I sincerely hope that such actions will not occur this time. If the police are interested in maintaining 'law and order', they will have no difficulty at all. We will surrender ourselves to the police for arrest. If told to disperse, we will. But we cannot be expected to run helter-skelter because a trigger-happy, African-hating young white police officer has given hundreds of thousands of people three minutes within which to remove their bodies from [the] immediate environment.

Hoping you will cooperate to try and make this a most peaceful and disciplined campaign.

I remain

Yours faithfully,
Mangaliso R. Sobukwe
President
Pan Africanist Congress

Part III: Interviews

11. 'We Africanists': Gail Gerhart Interviews Robert Mangaliso Sobukwe, 1970

This interview was conducted by Gail Gerhart, who at that time was a graduate student at Columbia University. It took place during the mornings of 8 and 9 August 1970, in a rental car on the outskirts of Kimberley. Because of police surveillance and Sobukwe's banning order, no notes were made during the course of the interview. Gerhart audio-recorded her best recollection of what was said immediately after the meeting.

GERHART. When did you first become interested in politics?

SOBUKWE. My first awareness of politics was in 1948 at Fort Hare when I took a course in Native Administration. This course was taught by Ntloko[1] and there was a text by Hanley(?).[2] I had always known most of the facts as such, for example that Africans had three representatives in Parliament, but up to then I had merely accepted these as facts which one had to learn, to memorize, without thinking of their implications. During this course I began to realize what the reality was, for example that these white MPs had no effect on policy, in spite of the fact that they were eloquent speakers.

1 Cecil Ntloko was a lecturer in 'Native Administration' at Fort Hare. His inspiring and mentoring influence on the young Sobukwe cannot be overstated. Often discussions and issues from Ntloko's lectures would spill over among students into lengthy conversations well into the night. A graduate of Healdtown, Ntloko studied at Fort Hare as well as the University of Cape Town before returning to Fort Hare, where he remained until 1958.

2 Probably *An African Survey: A Study of Problems Arising in Africa South of the Sahara* (first published in 1938) by William Malcolm Hailey, 1st Baron Hailey, which became a standard text for British colonial administrators.

Ntloko was an AAC man,[3] and the AAC was very influential at Fort Hare in those days. Most of us agreed with what the AAC stood for, except we didn't like the fact that they were not African nationalists. The Nationalists' victory in 1948 helped politicize me.

Godfrey Pitje[4] and I started the Youth League at Fort Hare. Pitje was the one who had had a connection with the early Youth League in the Transvaal. He was our link. He had known Lembede.[5]

GERHART. Did Pitje give you documents drawn up by the early Youth League, or statements of Lembede?

SOBUKWE. No, we never saw these. We drew up our own documents. It was all conveyed to us through conversation and discussion.

GERHART. Did you favor the efforts in the late 1940s to reunite the AAC with the ANC?

SOBUKWE. Yes, very strongly. We wanted total unity, though; not a federation. We always felt that federations were inherently weak. This was also the case with the Africanists later when Madzunya's[6] group wanted to federate with us. We wanted unity, not a federation.

The ideas of the AAC were good, but we knew they could never be counted upon to act. They believed that no action could be launched until

---

3 The All African Convention (AAC) took place from 15 to 18 December 1935. It gathered together notable black figures across a wide political spectrum and was convened to provide a united response to three parliamentary bills (the so-called Hertzog bills) that would drastically reduce Africans' rights. From this initial aim, the AAC expanded and became involved in broader political conscientisation, mobilisation and activism.

4 Godfrey Mokgonane Pitje was one of the very few black teachers at Fort Hare, lecturing in anthropology and African studies. After obtaining a law degree, Pitje left Fort Hare for Johannesburg, where he worked in Mandela and Tambo's law firm. In 1972 Pitje earned a doctorate in law and in 1975 became the first black vice chancellor of the University of the North (now the University of Limpopo).

5 Anton Muziwakhe Lembede was the undisputed wellspring of Africanist thought. A towering intellectual and influential activist, Lembede qualified as a lawyer and also completed postgraduate work in philosophy. His inspiration was not limited to Pan-Africanists, but also included a whole cadre of ANC members, including Nelson Mandela. Indeed, Lembede was the driving force behind the creation of the ANC Youth League, and served as its first president. He died at the age of 33.

6 Josias Ratshilumela Madzunya was born in the northern Transvaal, the son of a Venda-speaking peasant farmer. He moved to Johannesburg where he joined the ANC in 1947 and became chairman of the Alexandra branch. He played a leading role in the Alexandra bus boycott of 1957 and among Venda-speaking people, but it was also his 'tribalist' notions that were off-putting and in fact anathema to the Africanist position. He failed to win a seat on the executive committee of the PAC when it was formed in 1959.

the people had been 'properly educated'. Only they could say when this had been achieved. We felt this would take forever, and anyway that it was only through action itself that the people would come to understand fully the nature of the struggle.

GERHART. What was your role at the time of the 1949 Program of Action?

SOBUKWE. The Program of Action was drawn up 'at Fort Hare by Pitje and myself'. Of course Z.K. Matthews[7] was also there and was consulted. Our draft was then taken to the Cape ANC provincial annual conference in Queenstown in June 1949 where it was approved by the conference. The province was then under the leadership of Calata[8] and Matthews. Both at Queenstown and at Bloemfontein I spoke in favor of the program as we had drafted it.

GERHART. Did people come to Bloemfontein from the Transvaal and other provinces with other drafts for consideration?

SOBUKWE. Not as far as I can remember. I don't recall any other versions offered, from the Transvaal or elsewhere. The final version adopted was ours, except for one clause which was inserted at Bloemfontein, the clause calling for a one-day strike. Ironically, I think Calata proposed this clause.

We went to Bloemfontein from Fort Hare feeling that Xuma[9] was still our man. We thought he was a good leader and could be kept if he could be 'tied' to a program. He was in the habit of acting very independently, on his

7 Zachariah Keodirelang ('ZK') Matthews was an intellectual powerhouse. A graduate of Fort Hare (in 1923, the first black graduate in South Africa), Yale University, and the London School of Economics, Matthews was appointed to teach social anthropology and law at Fort Hare in 1936. In 1944 he became head of the Department of African Studies. Active in politics, he was a leading figure in the ANC, being elected to the National Executive Committee in 1943, and was a driving force behind the proposal that led to the drafting of the Freedom Charter. Matthews's father, the Rev. John Matthews, was a founding member of the ANC in 1912.

8 James Arthur Calata was an ordained Anglican clergyman, and an active member of the ANC – in fact, he served as Cape ANC president for nearly two decades, and as secretary general of the ANC from 1936 to 1949. James Calata was the grandfather of Fort Calata, one of the so-called Cradock Four, brutally murdered by the South African police in 1985.

9 Alfred Bitini ('AB') Xuma was the first black South African to qualify as a medical doctor, in 1927. He was also a political activist and served as president of the ANC from 1940 to 1949. Under his leadership the Youth League was established, though the League would later consider Xuma too 'conservative' and careful, not aggressive enough in challenging the apartheid state.

own judgment. We went there prepared to support him, but found to our surprise that the conference rejected him.

GERHART. Was there opposition to the Program from the left?

SOBUKWE. We went to Bloemfontein expecting that they would oppose it, but in fact they didn't oppose it; they supported it.

GERHART. Did you feel that the 1952 Defiance Campaign followed correctly from the Program of Action?

SOBUKWE. No. By this time the Program was already being compromised. The struggle was always to bring the ANC back to the Program. During the 1950s it strayed far away. If the Program had been followed we would all be living different lives today. Deviation began with the strikes in 1950.[10] These were concocted by the left wing. We felt that they had nothing to do with us but were merely protests at the banning of the Communist Party. A split was already beginning in our ranks; the Youth League was on the decline. Some were going over to the Communists.

The main thing we didn't like about the Defiance Campaign was the leadership role taken by Indians and whites. It was a lesson we had learned, that whenever these groups were involved in any action, you had the Africans just 'taking a back seat', sitting back and letting these people run things. We felt this had to be overcome and that Africans had to learn to take the initiative, to do things for themselves. I recognized there were some non-Africans who fully identified with us and were prepared to sacrifice, but as a matter of principle we couldn't let these people take any part because of the bad psychological effect this had on our people.

One reason some Africans welcomed Indian and white support was that as of the time of the Defiance Campaign it became clear that campaigns would always end in everyone needing a lawyer and money for defense. This increased dependence on non-Africans.

When the split began, we knew that Sisulu[11] had gone over and Mandela had gone over. Tambo, we knew 'was resisting'. We saw this

10 On 1 May, a general strike was called to protest against all discriminatory laws and for full franchise rights for blacks.

11 Walter Sisulu, Nelson Mandela, and Oliver Tambo were all actively involved in the creation of the Youth League. As such, they all advocated a more assertive approach to the apartheid struggle. Sobukwe's characterisation here is of how the Youth League distributed their loyalties in terms of the emerging tensions between nationalist and Africanist views. Sisulu served as secretary general of the ANC from 1949 to 1954.

happening in the Youth League. I myself was national president – no, national secretary. Pitje was president. We were elected in December 1949 at the ANC conference. We saw this split happening, but we were just too weak to prevent it.

When J.B. Marks[12] ran for President of the Transvaal, we were opposed to him. We backed Selope Thema.[13] We knew that if Thema became president, we – the nationalists in the Youth League – would be able to use him to promote our line. But Marks was very popular, partly because he was well known from the 1946 mine strike, and he won. It didn't make sense to most people to oppose him simply because he was a Communist.

GERHART. What was it about communism that attracted Africans of your generation?

SOBUKWE. First, it was 'the militancy' of Communists. They had a press that vigorously aired the grievances of Africans, exaggerated them, in fact; just as the *Post* and *The World* nowadays exaggerate murder and rape. This impressed us.

Secondly, we knew that if someone was a Communist it meant he had no color prejudice. He accepted you as another human being, this you just knew. A Communist would listen and frankly criticize what an African said, treating his arguments on merit, showing where they were weak. The liberals were different. They never wanted to risk hurting anyone's feelings, so if they were critical of what an African said, they'd just keep quiet, and that was no help to anyone. But we knew the Communists would never accept nationalism, and that is what we held against them.

The split began around 1950, and it centered in a way around the competition between Marks and Thema. It was hard for us to attack

12 John Beaver Marks had a prominent communist and trade union pedigree – presumably factors that figured into the opposition of the Africanists to his presidency. He was elected president of the Transvaal ANC in 1951 but later lost the position to Mandela. He played a leading role in organising the African mine workers' strike of 1946. Subject to banning orders and continued police surveillance, Marks left South Africa in 1963 for Tanzania, from where he coordinated ANC activities in exile.

13 Richard Victor Selope Thema was a teacher and journalist, with impeccable organisational credentials. He was also a founding member of the All Africa Convention and first editor of the influential newspaper *Bantu World* (later *The World*). When J.B. Marks became president of the Transvaal ANC, Thema organised a National Minded Bloc that opposed both cooperation with the Communist Party and the increasing turn to militancy in the ANC.

Marks. The people didn't care that he was a Communist; he was popular and a good speaker. He was a strong leader and a very 'hard working' man.

At this time I was in Standerton but I was coming frequently to Johannesburg, as early as 1950. We had the Bureau of African Nationalism[14] circulating our ideas. I received the Bureau's sheets from Leballo,[15] and I contributed pieces. I don't remember actually meeting Leballo until 1954. Cape people were also involved in the Bureau.

By 1950 the Youth League was declining, being absorbed into the ANC, and the split was starting. The League no longer had the strength it had had in 1949. You had people like Duma Nokwe[16] who had gone over. We knew he was attending Communist meetings, of the 'Communist Youth League'. They were operating here and there, and at St. Peter's School.[17]

One issue where we differed strongly with the Communists was on the question of boycotting the Advisory Boards, parliamentary elections and so on.[18] They opposed the boycott because they were sometimes able to get their people elected. This was in direct contradiction to the

14 An early grouping of Africanists, with A.P. Mda as the organisational force behind it, the Bureau of African Nationalism also disseminated *The Bulletin* as well as pamphlets around the country.

15 Potlako Kitchener Leballo was a persuasive orator and indefatigable organiser. He assumed a key leadership role in the Youth League of the ANC. However, he was also known to speak his mind, and when tension with the ANC leadership emerged, his was a harsh and unflinching critical voice.

16 Philemon Pearce Dumasile Nokwe was secretary general of the ANC from 1958 to 1969. A graduate of Fort Hare (with a BSc degree and teacher's diploma), Nokwe taught at a high school in Krugersdorp, but was summarily dismissed after his arrest for participation in the 1952 Defiance Campaign. Thereafter he proceeded to study law, and in 1956 became the first African advocate admitted to the Supreme Court. He was also at one stage chairman of the Orlando branch of the Communist Youth League. Nokwe left South Africa in 1963 to continue his political work for the ANC from Zambia, where he died in 1978.

17 St Peter's, Rosettenville, was a prestigious high school for African boys and girls run by the Anglican order of the Community of the Resurrection, until it closed in 1956 because of the Bantu Education Act.

18 After the Hertzog bills abolished the franchise for Cape Africans, various government bodies were set up to channel African political aspirations, such as Advisory Boards in the urban areas and the Native Representative Council, to which Africans could be elected. There was much debate on the issue of whether to participate in these bodies.

Program of Action. Moretsele,[19] for example, was on an Advisory Board. But we had the people with us on this question. They had seen the uselessness of these bodies. But Congress just 'dilly-dallied' on the issue.

According to Mokhehle,[20] the Communists have used the same type of technique in Lesotho, tactics of infiltration. They've tried to get people into positions of influence, by hard work.

GERHART. Why do you think some Africans were attracted to the left while others weren't? Was it circumstances, personality or what?

SOBUKWE. It was mainly a matter of 'contact' between these people and Communists, in Johannesburg. Firstly, there was the appeal of Communist philosophy; it's a doctrine that no one can object to philosophically. It's for the poor, it's against wealth, it's for equality. No one can quarrel with the kind of society communism holds out in theory. We ourselves didn't so much oppose Communist philosophy, but we could see in the states that were Communist that the ideal couldn't be put into practice, in Russia and China. First you had the party – supposedly the dictatorship of the proletariat, but really the dictatorship of the party. Eventually, as with Stalin, this became the dictatorship of the leader, one man. We could see this was the case. Milovan Djilas confirms it in his book, *The New Class.*[21]

But it was hard to object to the principles of communism in the abstract. Once a person was invited to the homes of these white Communists, he couldn't then raise any objections to Communist practice, in Russia for example, because it would have seemed impolite or irrelevant. Such Africans got to know these whites as friends, and participated in their discussions. And one could always be sure that these whites

19 Elias Phakane Moretsele was an entrepreneur – in fact, he became the first black person to own a cafe and a hotel in Johannesburg in the early 1900s. He joined the ANC in 1917, and remained politically active, leading marches and demonstrations, especially during the Defiance Campaign. Moretsele succeeded Nelson Mandela as Transvaal ANC president in 1953, and in fact was the person who, by dint of that position, opened the Congress of the People in Kliptown, where the Freedom Charter was adopted in 1955.

20 Ntsu Mokhehle was an activist and politician in Lesotho. He also studied at Fort Hare, and befriended Sobukwe while a postgraduate student. Although he joined the ANC, and the Youth League in particular, his attention turned to politics in Lesotho on his return there. He served as the third prime minister of Lesotho from 1993 to 1998.

21 Milovan Djilas was a prominent politician and communist in Yugoslavia. He grew disillusioned with the communist leadership and the book Sobukwe refers to, published in 1954, highlights such criticisms, notably the growing bureaucratic and privileged class that was forming within the ruling party, and the increasing detachment of that class from the ordinary people. Djilas was expelled from the Communist Party and imprisoned.

were unprejudiced, and ready to accept Africans on their individual merits. This was the immediate thing; the reality of Russia was far away.

GERHART. When you were at Wits,[22] you and other Africanists had the opportunity to accept such invitations. Why didn't you?

SOBUKWE. We had already seen too many people corrupted; we had their example to learn from. It began as early as 1950. So we declined the invitations, and eventually our sympathies became known and we weren't invited anymore. We were shocked at what had happened to staunch fellows like Mandela, who were so opposed to communism at first. He just went over. We felt he 'lacked backbone'. In the case of Sisulu, everyone could see what had happened. While he was secretary-general, there was one period of about six months when the ANC was so poor that the phone and electricity were cut off in the office. These Communists from the Indian Congress – Dadoo and Cachalia[23] – came and supplied the ANC and Sisulu with money. Also Sisulu's business[24] was in trouble. You couldn't blame him for being grateful to these men. Sisulu even said this openly himself to us, that what else could he do?

GERHART. Did you consider Sisulu an intelligent man?

SOBUKWE. Well, I don't think so really. He was very hard-working and devoted to the ANC, but he lacked education, and this made him defer to the opinions of more educated people. When he got into discussions with more educated people, he would usually just accept their judgments.

Mandela was one man I never really knew personally until I was already in prison. We were never friendly, although I had heard him address meetings and had met him. He is a very 'arrogant' man. He lacks a common touch. I remember him at one meeting around the time of the Defiance Campaign. People had gone there still undecided if they were going to participate.

---

22 The University of the Witwatersrand.

23 Yusuf Mohamed Dadoo was a medical doctor by profession. His family in Krugersdorp had a history of political involvement reaching back to Gandhi's protests in South Africa. He himself became politically engaged as a medical student at the University of Edinburgh in the 1930s and continued his activism on his return to South Africa. He quickly became involved in the ANC, the South African Indian Congress (SAIC), and the Communist Party of South Africa. Yusuf Cachalia rose to prominence within the SAIC and was particularly instrumental in forging organisational bridges and alliances between the Transvaal and Natal Indian Congresses and the ANC. As such he started to work closely with prominent ANC leaders in planning the Defiance Campaign.

24 Walter Sisulu was an estate agent in Johannesburg and brought his conveyancing business to Tambo and Mandela's law firm.

Mandela got up and said very peremptorily, 'All those with us, come forward; all others get out.' And most people just got out. They were put off by his manner. Mandela was strong among the leaders, although we always recognized Tambo as superior in intelligence. Mandela had a way of attacking people very viciously if they disagreed with him, and were a 'smaller' person than himself. He could reduce them to a 'shriveling' mass, then he would 'pat them on the head and draw them to him', and thereafter they would be his men, always deferring to him, looking up to him. If he came across any man who wouldn't look up and defer to him and acknowledge his superiority (e.g. myself, implied) then he wouldn't have anything to do with that person. Mandela could always attract weak people; but he could never get on with another strong person. In any relationship, he had to dominate. But he was an engaging person. He could always crack a joke, make you laugh; he always had a story to tell. But I was never friendly with him.

Tambo was closer to our point of view, but his loyalty to the ANC was just too strong. Of course he already had a high position in the ANC, from the earliest days, so he felt obliged to defend it. Tambo and Mandela never got on well together. Tambo is a much quieter man, but very intelligent.

GERHART. Is it true that Mandela was betrayed by the Communists because he came back from his Africa tour rejecting multiculturalism?

SOBUKWE. We could never get a straight answer out of him in prison about this. We did get the idea he had had some falling out with 'Ruth First and that group'.[25] He was very impressed by what he saw in Africa. He met Oginga Odinga[26] and was impressed by him; he met Kenyatta, waving his

25 Heloise Ruth First was a scholar and prominent member of the South African Communist Party. Alongside Joe Slovo, to whom she was married, she became a leading force in the protest actions of the 1950s. Mercilessly harassed by the apartheid state, and listed as a banned person, she was so restricted in her political activities that she opted to leave South Africa for London, from where she continued to speak out and work against apartheid. In 1978, she became the director of research at the Centre for African Studies at the university in Maputo, Mozambique. There she was assassinated in 1982 by a parcel bomb sent by the South African police.

26 Jomo Kenyatta led Kenya to independence from Britain, and served as its first prime minister and president. Jaramogi Ajuma Oginga Odinga was a prominent figure in Kenya's struggle for independence, serving as vice president in Kenyatta's cabinet. Ideological differences would later lead Odinga to form an opposition party to Kenyatta's Kenya African National Union (KANU). It is unclear whether these differences between Odinga and Kenyatta were apparent to Mandela, but they would have been of interest to Sobukwe: Kenyatta seemed to favour forging alliances with the Soviet Union and China, whereas Odinga was supportive of the United States and the West more generally.

flywhisk. These people affected him more than the white leaders he had met. But it was clear that Mandela was a Maoist.[27] We got to know this in prison. I don't know if he finds Mao especially appealing because he is a non-white. Mandela was very well read up on Mao. In a sense, though, he is really a Titoist, that is he believes in some reconciliation of communism and national peculiarities. Philosophically, Mandela has always been an 'opportunist', going from one theory to the next, taking out what seemed most likely to be impressive to other people, most likely to boost his own prestige. Oddly, he also showed tendencies in jail of being a tribalist. He used to wear a ——.[28] We used to criticize him for this.

GERHART. What did you mean when you said that all Communists in South Africa were 'quacks'?

SOBUKWE. I meant that they were only intellectual communists. The type of lives they led – the whites and Indians – precluded their being considered practicing communists. They had too many privileges. They were wealthy and they used and enjoyed their wealth. And deep down they actually believed in the perpetuation of these inequalities. Communists in South Africa 'have never been really revolutionary'. They are merely communists and revolutionaries intellectually. They were always well-read on communist theory and literature, and could recite it back at great length. But none of them were willing to materially come down to our level, or to accept the possibility that roles might someday be reversed.

GERHART. Would most Communists have been willing to accept an African government?

SOBUKWE. No, they would have always opposed it, opposed any nationalistic government. We Africanists made a point of reading Lenin and Marx to

---

27 Some of the more prominent differences between communism of the Leninist and Maoist varieties involve the importance of a 'vanguard party' in the revolution (Lenin) as opposed to the revolutionary potential of the peasantry (Mao), and the need for a strong, centralised socialist state (Lenin) as opposed to the 'continuous revolution' of vigilance against the emergence of a new bourgeoisie (Mao). Titoism was the unique form or adaptation of socialism in Yugoslavia under the leadership of Josip Broz Tito, and featured a non-aligned foreign policy, maintaining diplomatic relations with both Western and Communist blocs, and a market-driven socialism. In many ways Sobukwe's observations are particularly prescient: it was indeed so that the anti-apartheid movement of the eighties, under the 'Charterist' banner of the United Democratic Front (UDF), proposed a Leninist analysis particular to South Africa, 'Colonialism of a Special Type' (CST).

28 Sobukwe was apparently referring to some form of Xhosa dress, the name of which Gerhart didn't catch.

learn the vocabulary of communism. Then we used their terminology to support our own arguments. This had a way of really disarming them.

Gerhart. What was your role in the Defiance Campaign?

Sobukwe. I had spoken publicly in its favor. Once Tambo came to Standerton and we addressed a meeting together. 'I didn't launch.' We had received instructions from Johannesburg to wait and we were about to launch within a few weeks at the time when the Campaign was called off. I had in the meantime been dismissed from my post for speaking out.[29]

The campaign was called off because the leaders got cold feet. When these laws were passed, it became clear that they weren't actually prepared to make sacrifices.

Gerhart. When you first came to Johannesburg from Standerton, did you want to get into politics?

Sobukwe. When I got to Johannesburg I met P.K.[30] and his group. I felt that we were up against strong forces and we shouldn't make ourselves targets until we had built our strength. P.K. was already getting expelled and so forth. I didn't want to get expelled. But 'P.K. was a fighter!' [said with admiration]. He was always for barging ahead. He could never hold his tongue when he was provoked.

This group had begun *The Africanist* and they invited me to be the editor. Peter Molotsi[31] had been the editor up to then.

In trying to put our point of view across in Congress we were very frustrated because of the leadership situation in the ANC. By this time the real leaders were banned and couldn't speak openly. Therefore we couldn't directly attack them personally, and there was no way they could personally reply to us in public. We knew, however, that it was they who were responsible for the course of events in the ANC. While these banned men were behind the scenes, men of much lesser caliber – total 'fools' – were actually in the leadership positions in Congress. We had no respect for any of these people; yet there was no point in personally attacking them, because they were simply carrying out instructions from the

29 Sobukwe was dismissed from his teaching post in Standerton.

30 P.K. Leballo (see n. 15).

31 Peter Molotsi was a journalist and political activist. He was a member of the ANC Youth League and became part of the circle of militant nationalists around P.K. Leballo. He became editor of *The Africanist* in 1955, being succeeded later by Sobukwe. He joined the PAC on its foundation and became its secretary for Pan-African affairs.

banned leaders, saying what they'd been told to say by the big boys. They tended to be dogmatic and there was no point in trying to engage them in argument. Our tactics in the face of this were to try to use every meeting and conference to speak directly to the people, to 'hammer home' our 'line' with all the persuasiveness we could. Pretty soon they got wise to this and began to exclude us from conferences.

But we were up against a situation that has always existed in South Africa, namely that the masses will automatically follow a leader or organization that they have a loyalty to, without thinking about the wisdom or weakness of particular policies they are told to support. This is particularly true of the women. Oh, the women!

'We knew that our numbers were small' and that it would be hard to put our views across. I was ANC chairman in Mofolo,[32] and their tactic there was to have their own man with a rival branch, and when conferences came they would recognize him as a delegate instead of me.

We didn't put much faith in Lutuli.[33] He was a gentle old man, but he didn't have much political sense. He was politically naïve. I don't suppose there was ever a speech of Lutuli's delivered at a conference that was in the original form in which Lutuli had drafted it. Leaders like Mandela had a 'cynical' attitude to Lutuli.

At one ANC annual conference – probably 1955 where the Freedom Charter was debated – there was a violent fracas. Calata[34] was presiding. The Charter was finally shelved on the grounds that it was contrary to the constitution of the ANC to adopt it. They postponed it and then called a special conference the following April to adopt it. The conference was actually meant to consider another issue – passes for women – but this wasn't discussed. People were just brought there to ratify the Charter.

The people running the ANC by this time were a very mediocre lot. One couldn't engage them in argument because they didn't themselves understand the policies they were supposed to defend. Just as in the

32 In Soweto.

33 Albert Luthuli was president general of the ANC from 1952 until his death in 1967. Inspired by his Christian faith and the non-violent methods of Gandhi ('The path to freedom is via the Cross'), Luthuli was at odds with the growing turn to militancy and armed struggle in the ANC in the late 1950s and early 1960s. He was awarded the 1960 Nobel Peace Prize.

34 The Rev. James Calata (see n. 8).

earlier days, we felt the ANC was only reacting to moves made by the government. It had abandoned the Program of 1949 altogether. Our aim was always to bring the ANC back to the Program of Action. We would be living different lives today if the ANC had stuck to that Program.

GERHART. Do you think there was any element of cynicism in the ANC regarding the alliance? A belief that it was tactically wise, practical in terms of getting money and organizational help (while leaders were actually nationalists at heart)?

SOBUKWE. No, they were actually convinced of the correctness of multiracialism.

GERHART. Was the Freedom Charter attacked more as a symbol of the Alliance or because of what it actually said?

SOBUKWE. We objected to the whole thing. Raboroko[35] wrote an excellent rebuttal to it, emphasizing the impossibility of whites and Africans being considered 'brothers' in South Africa. We knew that every white person – no matter how sympathetic he was to us – benefited from the South African set-up, and enjoyed privileges based only on color. Whites would say to us, 'What can I do? Give up my salary? My house?' And what could we say to them? We had no answer for them, but we knew they could never be seen apart from the material situation.

The Freedom Charter said something ridiculous about how the land has been taken from us, we blacks and whites together. But how could they try to avoid the issue of whose land had been taken by whom? They were trying to gloss it over.

Sometimes when I discussed these problems with Benjie and Patrick Duncan[36] we tried to come up with another word, some new term that would crystallize the idea of non-racialism as opposed to multiracialism. We could never think of a good word, other than 'non-racialism' itself. We hated the word 'multiracialism'.

---

35 Peter Nkutsoeu 'Rocks' Raboroko served as secretary for education in the newly formed PAC. A theoretician and sharp writer, Raboroko did not shy away from written debate and polemic. He wrote several articles outlining Africanist thought, and played a major role in crafting the PAC manifesto.

36 Benjamin Pogrund and Patrick Duncan. The son of a former governor general of South Africa, the latter participated in the 1952 Defiance Campaign and joined the Liberal Party in 1955. His sympathy with African Nationalism and his strong anti-communism led him to support the PAC's anti-pass campaign in 1960. After going into exile, he became the first white member of the PAC in 1963.

We knew that the Freedom Charter wasn't actually drafted at the Congress of the People. It had been drafted by 'Slovo[37] and his circle'. People just arrived there and found the thing already printed up.

GERHART. Why did you believe the Africanists would be able to prevail eventually?

SOBUKWE. We thought this for a long time. At the time I came to Johannesburg there was still no feeling that there might have to be a break and a separate movement.

Another thing about the ANC that we objected to strongly was the Consultative Committee[38] with its system of representation. Only two from the ANC and two from each of the other, much smaller, groups. In any arrangement like this we knew the ANC would be taking a back seat even though it represented millions.

GERHART. Why did the Africanists try to run Madzunya[39] for Transvaal president in 1958?

SOBUKWE. I don't recall the exact sequence of events here. Madzunya was never part of the inner group in the Africanist movement. He had a following of his own. He had been important at the time of the 1957 bus boycott in Alexandra, and he was a critic of the ANC. He wanted to be with us. But he was uncontrollable, like a 'wild steer'. He was actually backed for this election by an odd collection of people like the late P.Q. Vundla[40] and B. Legwate,[41] people who sympathized with us but were only on the periphery of our movement. We didn't accept them as members, but they suggested that Madzunya run, and we thought he could be 'used'. We thought we could let him draw the fire of the enemy, and use him to test our strength.

Madzunya was not an educated man. He probably didn't grasp the full import of our philosophy. His thinking was rather 'primitive' – he wanted to put spears and shields on our flag! [laughter]. He didn't trust

37 Joe Slovo's close and intimate association with the ANC, indeed his unassailable commitment to that organisation, and his membership of the Communist Party, are both well known. In addition to his being white, his communist bona fides and background were points of contention for many Africanists.

38 Of the Congress Alliance.

39 On Josias Madzunya, see n. 6.

40 Philip Qipu Vundla was an active ANC member and organiser. He was secretary of the Mine Workers Union and one of the key organisers of the mine workers' strike of 1946. In 1952 Vundla was elected to the National Executive Committee of the ANC.

41 B. Legwate was a journalist with *The World*. His column, 'Let's Talk Politics', was a popular and regular feature of the paper.

middle class educated people like the rest of us. He said such people would never be able to suffer and sacrifice.

GERHART. What was Mda's[42] position during this time?

SOBUKWE. Mda was one man we have always admired for his 'brilliance' and clarity of thought. He has a great gift for language, a way of using words to express ideas with complete clarity, He can 'untie mental knots'. One could go to him with any problem, and he would analyze it for you, untie it. We tended to always accept his advice on any subject. Compared to Mda, all of us were 'political babies'. He had been around much longer. He had more knowledge of the South African situation than anyone. He had read very widely. He knew much more about communism than we did, for example. We could always go to him and get a clear 'analysis of the situation'. That was his great strength. He could also advise on action and organization. He advised us to organize secretly, through cells, to 'build up our strength before coming out in the open'. He was very much influenced by the writings of Lenin.

GERHART. Did he actually cite Lenin?

SOBUKWE. Yes. We were always amused at how he could oppose communism so strongly, yet use the principles of Marxism to prove his case for nationalism [laughter]. In the fights with the AAC it was always A.P. who could outline to us the line of argument. I first met him when I was at Fort Hare.

But A.P. was bitterly against the breakaway. He told us how all the other breakaways had failed – Mosaka's[43] ADP and so on. He also disagreed with us when we decided to launch. He wrote me a critical letter, saying that our view of the situation was too 'apocalyptic'.

---

42 Ashby Solomzi Peter ('AP') Mda played an outsize role in articulating, refining and spreading Africanist ideas and thought. Despite difficult personal circumstances, Mda obtained a BA degree. Eventually securing a job at a primary school, Mda proceeded to study law through correspondence with Unisa. His insight and intellectual prowess were noticed in the ANC, and he was instrumental in the formation of the Congress Youth League. Lembede, in particular, was a close friend, intellectual sparring partner and equal. After Lembede's premature death, the intellectual mantle of Africanist thought and theorising passed to Mda.

43 Paul Ramotsoane Mosaka was a Healdtown and Fort Hare alumnus and teacher. An active participant in the Alexandra bus boycott, Mosaka had close affinities with ANC policies, but nonetheless sought to form his own political organisation, the African Democratic Party (in 1943), which he hoped would work closely with the ANC, even be affiliated to it. A.B. Xuma, then president of the ANC, would have nothing of it, and the ADP was forced to strike out on its own. A mere three years after its formation, the ADP folded.

In the days of the Africanist movement our nationalism was mainly 'emotional'. We needed A.P. to help us intellectually to work out our position.

GERHART. Many people seemed to have hero-worshipped Mda. Did you share this feeling toward him?

SOBUKWE. This was certainly the case. Even P.K. felt this way toward Mda. Myself? Well, I don't know. A.P. is a great student of revolution. At our conference of September1959 he kept pointing out how Mao hadn't done such and such a thing in China.

Around the time of the break I was going down to the Cape – was I going to Grahamstown to work on my riddles?[44] – and I went by Engcobo[45] to look for Mda. I forget who was accompanying me. We didn't find him home. I don't recall exactly when this was. But we decided we would just have to go ahead with what we were doing without consulting him. Even P.K. said this, and he was a great admirer of Mda. But A.P. wrote us to say he disapproved of the break.

GERHART. How did you feel about the fact that by 1959 paths had diverged with Mda?

SOBUKWE. I suppose we regretted it, but by this time the situation had changed. The younger men didn't know A.P.; he wasn't widely known. He was only known to the early Youth League men. So it wasn't so widely discussed. We knew A.P. was busy doing his law, and that physically he was not strong. And we knew that he himself would never go to jail.

GERHART. Did you feel he was out of date? Out of touch?

SOBUKWE. Yes. We just had to go ahead without him. We still respected him, but his opinion wasn't sacrosanct any longer. We still saw him as the repository of our ideas. I think it was 1957 when I went to Engcobo to look for A.P. In September 1959 we got him to attend our NEC[46] meeting in Bloemfontein. He was quite impressed with our success at that time, even though we didn't yet have the 100,000 members we had predicted. He was impressed with the success of our Inaugural Conference. He didn't attend that, but he was in Johannesburg at the time. He gave us a wonderful talk that night at Bloemfontein on organization. A.P. had

44 Sobukwe's research on Xhosa riddles was eventually published as 'A Collection of Xhosa Riddles', *African Studies* 30, no. 2 (1971): 117–150.

45 In the Transkei, now part of the Eastern Cape.

46 National Executive Committee.

a power over words. He could manipulate words so that they said more than just their surface meaning. Like the slogan of the Youth League – Africa for Africans, Africans for humanity, humanity for God.

GERHART. Who formulated the later slogan that anyone who owed his first loyalty to Africa and accepted the rule of an African majority would be considered an African? Was the ambiguity of this intentional?

SOBUKWE. I suppose it was [laughter]. This came from the earlier Youth League slogan, from the first clause of it – Africa for the Africans. That was the part that had always received all the attention. This was our formulation.

GERHART. Yours?

SOBUKWE. Yes. It was so funny, because by this time Benjie and I were already friends, and he used to really get after me about this one. Also, the late Patrick Duncan. They argued that you couldn't promote exclusivism then hope that tomorrow the people you had organized exclusively would turn around and begin recognizing these other non-Africans as Africans. I could see this argument, but I still felt that history would bear us out and that we were choosing the correct course.

We knew many people agreed with us. When we were setting up the PAC, we tried to persuade Matthews, for example, to come with us. But we couldn't get anywhere with him. He was too much an ANC man, although we knew he agreed with a lot of what we were saying. [This said a little wistfully as though they'd been disappointed or hurt by Matthews's reaction.] But regardless of what our strength was, we had to stand on our principles.

I know it is true that there were times when we simply were not clear in our own minds of how to deal with the situation. [These were not Sobukwe's exact words; but the idea was definitely expressed.] This is why sometimes our slogans were misunderstood or ambiguous. This perhaps reflected confusion in my own thinking, but I was always certain of certain basic principles.

It was hard to fight an established organization like the ANC. I can remember when I gave a speech at Fort Hare in 1948 to the graduates, I told them to always make politics part of their lives. I said if you're a doctor, don't just treat the patient for his physical ailment, also send him down to join the ANC. If you're a teacher and you see your children coming to school nearly naked in winter, tell yourself, and tell the parents, what the cause of that is. Link it to politics. This was the kind of spirit we had in those days.

Being up against the ANC was like being up against a church. It was like a religion to its followers. Your father had belonged, so you belonged. People like Z.K. Matthews knew the appeal of the ANC in this way, and would never leave it. It had the tradition and aura of a church.

In the days of the early Africanist movement we had cells in the Rand area, East London. We were weak in Natal because the ANC was very strong there; we were weak in PE,[47] weak in the Western Cape.

When we got to PE on our tour in 1960, you could only whisper that you were there from PAC [laughter] because the ANC was so strong there. You were more afraid of the ANC than of the police in PE! It was like a religion, and religion was strong there too. Cape Town had no organization at all. We felt strongly that if we could build our strength in the Transvaal, then other things would follow.

By the time of the break, I had accepted the necessity of it and the fact that we weren't going to be able to capture the ANC. Our numbers were too small, and their methods were too successful.

One reason we couldn't make direct attacks on the banned leaders in the late 1950s was that we had to uphold the slogan of 'We stand by our leaders' in the Treason Trial. You just couldn't attack them while that was going on.

Tambo felt that some opposition within Congress wasn't necessarily a bad thing. He didn't favor expelling the Africanists. All this time that the ANC was making these unwise moves in the 1950s, the Africanists were the only ones willing to speak up frankly and criticize. Once we were out, there was no one left inside to criticize or question.

GERHART. When you came to Johannesburg in late 1954 were your ideas any different than they had been in 1949? Had you rejected anything, e.g. from Lembede's philosophy, or added anything?

SOBUKWE. No, I hadn't rejected anything. But I was hesitant to draw attention to myself as a critic of the ANC.

GERHART. Can you trace the development of your own attitude towards personal involvement in politics?

SOBUKWE. At the time I first came to Johannesburg, I still didn't see myself as an activist particularly, not of the Leballo-type anyway. I saw myself more as an intellectual who could help back up this movement and give it some

47 Port Elizabeth, now Gqeberha.

theoretical strength. P.K. and his group were 'mainly emotional' in their nationalism; they needed firmer theory, more 'academic' grounding. The articles that were appearing in *The Africanist* were a bit wild and diffuse, without much educational value. I felt that in at least every issue there should be one educational article, explaining the nature of the struggle to our people. So I was offered the editorship by P.K. and I was glad to take it up. I saw this as a way I could make my contribution, and also stay behind the scenes. But as soon as I became the editor, naturally the critics singled me out for attack. I became openly identified as an Africanist. I was never hesitant to take part, but unlike P.K., I believed we should build our strength before inviting such open attack. I wasn't hesitant to participate. I was so very critical of the ANC, and believed so strongly in what we stood for.

GERHART. I've been told that Leballo thought your family life held you back from full-time political work.

SOBUKWE. No. Leballo would say this because we have different views of our wives. Zeph Mothopeng[48] and I believed in treating our wives like other human beings, devoting time to them. Leballo believed his wife was just there to feed him, mind the children, etc. He gave every minute of his time to politics. I can believe that P.K. spoke about 'petticoat government'.

I can remember in my days at Fort Hare Pitje and I considered this problem, and we took a vow that we would never marry because it would interfere with fulfilling our political tasks. Pitje was the first to break that vow! [laughter] My family life didn't conflict, but my job sometimes did. When these stay-at-homes were called,[49] what could I do? The professors and students were there waiting for me, but naturally I couldn't be seen boarding the train in Mofolo. So I'd always have to make up some excuse of why I couldn't go to work or couldn't stay home.

GERHART. Is it true that you favored opening membership in PAC to poorer Indians?

SOBUKWE. This is true, but the others just wouldn't accept it. There were a lot of very poor Indian workers. They didn't come to South Africa of their

48 Zephania Mothopeng was a teacher and political activist, and a founding member of the PAC. He married Urbania Lonake in 1941.

49 A common form of protest organised by the ANC in the 1950s.

own free will, they have no other home, they were themselves exploited, and there was no way in which they exploited Africans, unlike the Indian merchant class. The merchant class is prejudiced against Africans, and they are oppressors. Of course, we considered the coloureds as Africans. A.B.[50] was so strongly against this thing of including Indians!

GERHART. Hypothetically speaking, if PAC had come to power and then found that Indians persisted in preserving their own ethnic subculture instead of identifying with Africans, what would you have done?

SOBUKWE. I wouldn't have been bothered by this, because I know that such changes take time. People would have been allowed their own customs, foods, and so forth. But we would have legislated against all racial discrimination – in housing, schools, everywhere. Eventually barriers would break down, with children going to school together and people living together. There would be 'black spots' in white areas at first, and gradually merging would take place. Some Africans would move to Hillbrow; 'Benjie would move to Soweto' [laughter]. Of course there would be people who would cling to their prejudices. We would have to be patient.

I think Nixon[51] is right in saying that children shouldn't be bused to force integration. This is going too far. You couldn't pass a law that a white man, for example, had to carry Africans in his car. You would, I think, at first also have to allow whites to maintain exclusive clubs if they wanted to. It would all take time. But you would immediately do away with all discriminatory laws. I am critical of what the Kenyans have done to the Asians there. If we had succeeded in bringing change I know we would have found, even in the first generation of Indians and whites, that there were people willing to come in with us wholeheartedly. We would have accepted them fully, as equals, as Africans with us. We would have 'absorbed' them immediately. Others would come in more gradually.

GERHART. To what extent is it true that PAC believed in violence or rejected non-violence?

SOBUKWE. We didn't have any faith in non-violence, passive resistance, because the penalties had become too high. People were unwilling to engage

50 Abednego Bhekabantu Ngcobo worked as a trade unionist while he completed his bachelor's degree at the University of Natal. He began law studies thereafter. He became provincial secretary of the ANC Youth League and, later, treasurer general of the PAC. He ultimately fled the country for Swaziland and Zambia.

51 President Richard Nixon.

in it, and it was no longer a useful technique. We did, however, believe in the potential power of massive 'non-collaboration'. Philosophically, we didn't hold to nonviolence. Is it DuBois[52] who said that there are three types of beliefs about violence? One is the Communist one, that no change can be accomplished without violence. The second is the pacifists' view that violence is never justified, no matter what. And the third, which was our view, was that violence might sometimes be necessary and couldn't be ruled out altogether. I didn't think in 1960 that we were in any position to launch violence, or that our people were prepared for it.

Passive resistance, we felt, could only succeed in more advanced 'modern' countries, where demonstrations have been shown to bring results. In the U.S., for instance, I am critical of black radicals who have gone beyond the use of nonviolent methods. After all, protest is legal in the United States, and brings results. Why go beyond it? This isn't justified. But in South Africa, the use of passive resistance has been ruled out by the harshness of the laws against it. Students can't even stage a march without being penalized. Other means then become legitimate. I think I came to this conclusion only after going to prison.

It is not true to say that PAC promoted violence. We always stressed non-violence. We urged the police not to provoke violence by mumbling orders like 'disperse in three minutes'. Philosophically, we were not in favor of taking lives. We thought we could win by means that fell short of this.

GERHART. When you said 'We are ready to die for our freedom, but we are not yet ready to kill', did you mean 'not ready' philosophically, or did this have the double meaning of 'we do not yet possess the means of killing'?

SOBUKWE. [Laughter]. I know what you mean. I think I meant philosophically we weren't ready. We knew if there was violence it would only work against our cause. We believed that if we followed our plan, with the leaders in front, with sincerity, conviction, and strength, that the power of our example would be enough to mobilize the masses to action, to non-collaboration. [Sobukwe acknowledged that the distinction between non-violence and non-collaboration was vague here, but this wasn't further pursued in the course of the interview.]

52 W.E.B. DuBois, the American sociologist and writer (of, inter alia, *The Souls of Black Folk*) and advocate of Pan-Africanism.

We believed that Africans could eventually succeed if they could break their psychological dependence on whites and non-African leadership. An example of African dependence on whites was one incident at Newclare when there was a women's demonstration against passes.[53] We went there to try to persuade the police to grant bail for the women. Because we were Africans, the police just told us to *voetsek*.[54] Then a certain white arrived on the scene, a man named Vincent Swart. He had started some small organization for African rights. Because he was white, the police agreed to talk to him, and naturally the friends and relatives of the women there just 'flocked' to this man, pleading with him to help with bail.

We always opposed the participation of whites in any kind of action because we wanted to get the point across to our people that by their own efforts – and by these alone – change could be brought about. It was a psychological thing. When the pass laws actually were suspended[55] and Africans had the sensation for those few days of not living in fear, we knew this would have a big psychological impact. People could see this had been done solely by African effort. Of course, I wasn't allowed to see newspapers during this time, so I wasn't able to follow developments closely. I did know there was undisciplined violence in the Transvaal. This was because the leaders were locked up.

GERHART. What did you say to young men who demanded they be given a chance to fight the whites?

SOBUKWE. This question never really came up, because right from the beginning we had promised action, we had told people that passes were to be the target, the leaders were going to be in front, and that this was how we were going to do it. This would be sufficient to bring us victory. We always stressed publicly that we were non-violent. After all, we had a responsibility to protect our followers from the consequences of possible violence, retaliation from the authorities. I myself never favored the idea of anyone being killed. I sincerely believed that determined non-collaboration could do the job, since the whole system, the whole economy, rests on the cooperation of our people. In prison I revised my views in that

53 Newclare was a black township on the outskirts of Johannesburg.

54 Afrikaans for 'scram'.

55 After the Sharpeville Massacre, the government announced the temporary suspension of the pass laws, but they were reintroduced later.

regard, however. Now that the penalties, even for passive resistance, are so high, up to three years, we can no longer ask our people to engage in this kind of action. The return is too small.

We believed at the time of our campaign that a determined lead from us would bring success. Ordinary Africans – like Madzunya's followers – didn't believe that we were prepared to suffer. We thought that, just as in the ANC where the people were willing to follow the leaders almost blindly, in our case they would also follow when we had given the example. The government was always hammering on this point – that the big leaders called people into action, then let them go to jail and suffer while they stayed outside 'riding around in big cars'.

GERHART. Were there ever divisions in the National Working Committee over matters of policy, for example, over the decision to launch?

SOBUKWE. No, everyone was in agreement over the launching.

GERHART. There are various theories about the launching. One theory is Ngubane's,[56] that you were pressured into it by the others.

SOBUKWE. I have read Ngubane's book,[57] and that man has some very strange ideas. What he says is not true on this. Ngubane made us believe that he was with us and he had offered to get our three circulars printed for us in Durban, at an Indian press there. We just had no money, and so we agreed. The first leaflet was the alert, the second was the one telling people to save food, save money; then the last one. Our original plan was to launch in January, as soon as we got back from our tour of the Cape. I hadn't gone back to my job at Wits because I expected the launching to be soon. Ngubane had promised to have the circulars ready. I don't exactly recall the sequence of events. P.K. and J.D.[58] and I went to Durban to see to this printing, before we set out on the tour of the Cape. We met with

56 Jordan Khush Ngubane was a distinguished journalist who developed an early interest in politics. Together with Lembede, Ngubane wrote the lion's share of the ANC Youth League manifesto. Not in sympathy with either the left or the extreme nationalist wings of the ANC, he was drawn to the Liberal Party, whose national vice chairman he became in the late 1950s. He attended the inaugural convention of the PAC and became known as sympathetic to that organisation. Both Mda and Luthuli later fell out with Ngubane as his politics started to gravitate towards liberal, 'malleable' and inconsistent positions. Ngubane left South Africa in 1969 for the United States and returned to South Africa in 1980 to throw his support behind Buthelezi's Inkatha Freedom Party.

57 *An African Explains Apartheid* was first published in 1963.

58 P.K. Leballo and Jacob Dumdum Nyaose, who came to the PAC from a trade union background (see this vol., ch. 10, n. 19).

Ngubane. A.B.[59] wasn't there because he and Ngubane weren't on speaking terms. We asked Ngubane why these things hadn't been sent to us. He took us to meet the Indian editor of his paper,[60] I don't recall his name, but it wasn't Manilal Gandhi. It was funny, us all sitting there when we were supposed to be so anti-Indian! [Laughter]. We had a long discussion, and we tried to press him with the seriousness of our intentions. Ngubane wasn't convinced by our arguments. We left, and later I wired him to urge him to send the circulars. He replied with a long letter saying he just couldn't provide them.

This was really our undoing. There was no going back. I told Ngubane we were going ahead whether we had the leaflets or not. Ngubane's letter said he thought the campaign was unwise. About this time I also had a letter from A.P. saying the same thing.

GERHART. Was Ngubane in touch with Mda?

SOBUKWE. I think so, but I'm not certain. So we proceeded with our tour. I was very impressed with our following in Cape Town. I knew Cape Town would respond well to the call. You had the men there living in bachelor quarters. Some reliable source said the ratio of men to women there was 25 to 1. People's grievances were very strong in Cape Town. I also knew we could be sure of Sharpeville.

GERHART. Why?

SOBUKWE. People there had some local grievances, especially against the location superintendent. The leaders there had assured me that the people were ready; we had nothing to worry about there. They could have launched with success in January, even though demonstrations were forbidden there. Ngubane really let us down. Boys had come up from Cape Town to get the circulars, and we just had to send them home empty-handed. We gave them a sample and told them to make their own. We sent a model to East London and told them to make their own, also Port Elizabeth.

GERHART. How did you decide on the date for their launching?

SOBUKWE. The main thing was that the ANC was about to launch its own pass campaign. We knew this would be another three-day affair, the people's

59 A.B. Ngcobo (see n. 50).

60 *Indian Opinion*, of which Ngubane was assistant editor from 1952 to 1957. Manilal Gandhi, the son of the Mahatma, remained in South Africa after his father returned to India and was in fact editor of *Indian Opinion* from 1920 until his death in 1956.

energies would be exhausted, and we would be unable to act. So we had to launch first; that was the main thing. We would have launched earlier if we had gotten the circulars. We had promised the people that they were going to get action.

The response was poor in Johannesburg the day of the launching because of the lack of the leaflets. Also, Johannesburg has often lacked militancy, partly because the city administration there has always been relatively progressive. Africans in Johannesburg are less idealistic, more materially-oriented also.

GERHART. If the launching had resulted in widespread chaos and violence, do you think progress would have been made?

SOBUKWE. No, I was against this. That is why I told the police not to provoke the people by giving impossible orders, like disperse in three minutes. Privately, on the Cape tour and at other times in preparing for the campaign, I had told leaders that if the police ordered crowds to disperse, then they should be ordered by the leaders to disperse.

GERHART. Do you think the leaders in Cape Town acted correctly, then, at the time of the big march?

SOBUKWE. Yes, I do. They were carrying out the orders that I had given. Naturally I hadn't made it public that if police told us to disperse, we were going to disperse. That would have undermined the people's confidence. But I had ordered this privately. In Cape Town, had I been there, I would have done the same thing.

Perhaps Ngubane acted the way he did because he was resentful that we had rejected his advice. Something made him vindictive, and I think that is why he printed in his book that thing about my appeal. This was unfair. He wasn't in a position to appreciate the circumstances. The police had divided us into two groups: the followers and the leaders, who were tried separately in a batch of 22. Some of the men included in this leaders' group – people like Lennox Mlonzi and Rosette Ndziba[61] – objected to their being included as leaders. They wanted to be in the other group. They felt that with us their sentences were going to be too heavy. So, they wanted to appeal; perhaps a majority in our group wanted to. Then I consulted Joe Slovo, and he advised me that it would be impossible for only

61 Both Mlonzi and Ndziba were active members of the PAC who took part in the 1960 anti-pass campaign.

part of the group to appeal, since we had all been tried together. It was all or nothing. So I agreed, but only on condition that the appeal was on the merits of the case, not merely against the severity of the sentences. I had been in favor originally of dividing us into leaders and non-leaders because I had hoped they would only sentence the leaders and let the rest go free. They would have been able to carry on the campaign outside.

GERHART. Do you think P.K. or the others misled you about the preparedness of the people?

SOBUKWE. No. P.K. and I always worked very closely together, and I knew everything he knew. There was no question of my being deceived. Everyone knew that P.K. always exaggerated. 'He would add a nought to every figure.' If there were 25 people at a meeting, P.K. would come and tell you there were 250. But we always knew to allow for this [laughter].

GERHART. What was the basic strategy of the pass campaign? How did you envision the 'unfolding' stages?

SOBUKWE. By filling the jails we believed we could bring the economy to a halt. If the defiance had gone on and on, eventually they would have been forced to negotiate with us. The women were told to stay home, to keep things going while the men – the backbone of the economy – went to jail. Eventually we thought the women would join too. We believed the people were ready, if a clear lead was given. They would see that we were ready to give up jobs – good jobs, too – and they would be convinced by our example.

GERHART. If it had come to negotiations, what would you have demanded?

SOBUKWE. Firstly, the things we had specified in our propaganda – the abolition of the pass laws and the minimum wage of one £ a day. The whole system of control is built on the pass laws, so this is crucial.

GERHART. What would have come next?

SOBUKWE. Well, probably the next thing would have been the vote. I was prepared to acknowledge that this would take time. I would actually have accepted a qualified franchise, as long as it was equal for all races. This would have been hard for them, perhaps impossible, because it would have disqualified some white voters. But the vote would have been next.

GERHART. Do you think the high morale of the Working Committee ever clouded anyone's evaluation of political reality?

SOBUKWE. I wouldn't say so. Except for P.K., they were a rather 'cautious' lot. It was a 'strange' group. They were always raising reasons why something or other couldn't be done. P.K. was always optimistic about success, but the rest were cautious.

GERHART. In planning the Campaign, did you discuss any lessons of the 1952 Defiance Campaign?

SOBUKWE. Yes, definitely, at length. We felt the Defiance Campaign had failed because the leaders had let the people down by calling the thing off when the going got rough for them personally. They engaged lawyers, particularly Moroka.[62] And we saw that these new laws – the Public Safety Act, etc. – were a threat to their interests. The campaign was still going strong, and the people were prepared to continue, but it was the leaders who backed down. That was the lesson of the Defiance Campaign – failure of the leaders. So we knew we weren't going to repeat this error; that is why we asserted the slogan of 'no bail, no defense, no fine' – to convince the people that we were serious this time.

GERHART. Did you or your men ever refer to the proposed action as 'revolution' in the literal sense? [Sobukwe offered no direct answer to this, moving on instead to other topics, and the question was not returned to.]

GERHART. Was there any feeling that the government might be a false front, apparently strong but actually weak, ready to fold like the Belgians in the Congo?

SOBUKWE. No, not among the leadership. But remember when the campaign was launched, there was massive support in Cape Town and then rioting in Johannesburg. The police were paralyzed. They just didn't know what to do for a while. The pass laws were suspended.

GERHART. Who did you consider the strongest members of the Working Committee?

SOBUKWE. The hardest worker was always P.K. For all his weaknesses, this was one man I always liked. One had to admire his energy, his ability.

62 James Sebe Moroka was a medical doctor (he qualified at the University of Edinburgh, and later also trained as a surgeon at the University of Vienna though he was prevented from using the surgical facilities of the Bloemfontein hospital on his return to South Africa). The All Africa Convention was politically conscientising, and Moroka became more and more politically involved – eventually he was elected president of the ANC from 1949 to 1952. He enjoyed substantial support from the Youth League but his reputation suffered a devastating blow when he was arrested with 21 others in 1952 but proceeded to distance himself from his co-accused by securing his own counsel, entering a plea of mitigation, and identifying the others as communists. After leaving the ANC, he concentrated on his medical practice and community medicine.

I had confidence in him, and I relied on him heavily. He was always ready to sacrifice everything he had for our movement. More than anyone else, he was always willing to put the party's interests above his own.

GERHART. Do you think he ever fancied that he should be president instead of you?

SOBUKWE. No. I'm sure he didn't. P.K. is not such a highly educated man, not as much as others in our group. He knew these limits. He was very happy to be secretary; he never saw himself as number one. Nana[63] hated him though. Nana even opposed his becoming secretary. One of P.K.'s weaknesses was a tendency to try to build up a personal following. The others criticized him for this. There was conflict whenever Nana was around.

P.K. also tended to always pick out one person that he didn't like. In the Working Committee he picked Ngendane[64] as his target. If Ngendane said something was white, 'P.K. would feel constrained to argue that it was black'. Ngendane was a 'playboy', a fancy dresser. He often was absent from Working Committee meetings, or he would come and have his girlfriend waiting outside. It was only later when I got to know him much better in prison that I myself began to appreciate the quality of Ngendane's mind, and the sincerity of his devotion to our cause.

One of Leballo's strengths was that there could never be any doubt that he was prepared to suffer, prepared to go to jail. He was a 'fire-eater'. He raised money and he never spent a penny on himself. I had to give money to 'the wife' because P.K. wouldn't give her money for food. He put everything he had into the organization. This is why I can hardly believe the stories of P.K. 'squandering money' on the outside, because he never did that when I knew him.

---

63 Nelson 'Nana' Mahomo was a former member of the Transvaal Congress Youth League who sided with the Africanists within the ANC and subsequently left that party to join the PAC. He was elected secretary for culture in the PAC in 1959 and was a member of the organisation's National Executive Committee. Mahomo did much to build the PAC in the Western Cape.

64 Selby Themba Ngendane was an alumnus of Fort Hare, graduating a few years after Sobukwe. He, too, became involved in politics at Fort Hare, joining the ANC Youth League there and cutting his political teeth in the 1952 Defiance Campaign. Upon moving to Johannesburg to study law, he was drawn into the Africanist circle and soon rose to leadership positions. It was common for commentators to refer to the handsome, dapper figure he cut, always smartly dressed and, as Sobukwe mentions, somewhat of a 'playboy'. Such representations belie his articulate intellect and passionate, unswerving commitment.

One of his weaknesses is that in any group he will pick one person to attack, one person that he doesn't like, like Ngendane. If there are three people, he'll join with one against the third. If there are five people, he'll get three with him against the other one. In the National Executive he picked out Nyaose as the one he didn't like.

GERHART. Why is he like that?

SOBUKWE. P.K. by nature is 'an oppositionist'. He's always got to be in opposition to something. He'd never be a good member of a government. P.K. was expelled various times from the ANC because of being this way. I myself didn't want to be expelled. Although I was known as an Africanist. I was merely regarded as someone on the 'right wing' of the ANC.

In the PAC, I drafted many of the letters that went out over P.K.'s name.

GERHART. Did you also write the pieces that appeared in *The Africanist* over his name?

SOBUKWE. I don't recall ever doing this. He wrote those pieces himself.[65] There was only once I can recall when I got angry at him for overstepping without consulting me. He put something in *The Africanist* about how A.K. Harden had written to denounce a certain South African 'half caste' named Michael Hommel who had been exposed in Ghana as a spy. P.K. put this into *The Africanist* without showing me first, and I had to take him to task for using the term 'half caste'. Since we were supposedly accepting coloureds as Africans, naturally we couldn't use such derogatory terms to refer to them.

P.K. and I always worked very well together. But another one of his weaknesses was that he could never be trusted to keep a secret. The others always tried to hide things from him for the sake of secrecy.

Nana was a backroom boy, not a good platform man. He did a good job of organizing in Cape Town, organizing the Task Forces there, one for each area of the townships. These boys did the distribution of leaflets and jobs like that.

Nyaose was not a politician; he was just a 'hard working trade unionist'. Philosophically, he wasn't part of our Africanist movement, but his union – the Bakers – had opposed Communist leadership.

65 One possible exception to this is 'The Nature of the Struggle Today', which was attributed to Potlako Leballo, and which appeared in the December 1957 issue of *The Africanist*. There is evidence to support the claim that Sobukwe authored this article (see Karis and Gerhart 2013).

We nationalists had virtually written off trade unions. Their administration was so weak, and they were so easily dominated by Communists. African unions were mere puppets. There were only a few exceptions – Nyaose's Bakers Union, which was very well run and had actually negotiated and won concessions from employers, like a real union; and Lucy Mvubelo's[66] Women's Garment Workers Union. Not the men's Garment Workers – they were Communist-led. Only the women were strong and independent, African-led.

GERHART. Is it true that Nyaose opposed the launching of the campaign?

SOBUKWE. No, this isn't true. In fact he even exaggerated to me the strength of his own supporters, their numbers. He wouldn't have done this if he opposed the launching.

Molotsi[67] was a 'hard worker', not lazy, but he had a tendency to want to discuss things at great length on an academic plane. In abstractions. He had a very sharp tongue, both he and Z.B.[68] Both were good 'platform men'.

Mahomo wasn't such a good platform man, but whenever he came up from Cape Town he always brought some good ideas, like the idea of the task forces. That was Nana's idea. It was our way of using the '*tsotsi* element'.

The best brains in the NWC were Rocks,[69] Z.B. and Molotsi. They were the idea-men, the 'original' thinkers. Rocks had the weakness of not being able to resist the bottle, but he is a 'brilliant' man. Z.B. is also highly intelligent, but 'a little lazy'.

GERHART. How important were the executive members who lived outside the Transvaal?

SOBUKWE. These men were quite far removed from the action. We sent them reports and copies of statements, but naturally they were quite cut off.

---

66 Lucy Buyaphi Mvubelo qualified as a teacher but left to work in the garment industry. She soon became general secretary of the Garment Workers Union and was a founding member of the South African Congress of Trade Unions (SACTU).

67 See n. 31.

68 Zachius Botlhoko Molete was particularly taken with A.P. Mda, whom he met in 1949, and who inspired him to embrace a politically committed African Nationalism. After graduating from Fort Hare and a brief teaching stint, he took up law studies and entered the orbit of P.K. Leballo and the group of active Africanists. Molete was elected as secretary for publicity and information when the PAC was formed.

69 Peter Raboroko (see n. 35).

I knew them less well. We only met together once. We had agreed that we would meet at least once a year, but in the end we were only able to meet once.

Morley Nkosi[70] 'never took politics seriously', even in South Africa. He was working for some company then. He was supposed to launch and we were very angry when he didn't. He became enemies with Ellen Molapo[71] when they were trying to operate after the emergency.[72] If Nkosi wants to be helpful now, he should look around and not wait. Ngendane and Mothopeng are in need of help – they have no prospects of employment. Pokela[73] is doing 30 years on Robben Island, and his family needs help.

Ellen Molapo convinced us that women were capable of understanding our philosophy. Lucy Mvubelo also convinced us; she was a strong figure. She and her union sided with the ICFTU[74] against the other trade union federation in Africa – the leftist one. But in general we knew that women were more conservative politically than men.

GERHART. After the breakaway, did Tambo or others try to bring about a reconciliation?

SOBUKWE. Yes, there was some effort, but not much.

GERHART. Do you think the common man in the street understood your explanation of nonracialism? [Sobukwe's answer is somewhat vague; the general gist of it seems to have been 'no'.]

SOBUKWE. There was nothing one could say that could really cut through the fact that most people were simply anti-white. I wrote somewhere that our people don't hate the sjambok; naturally they hate the man who wields it, because he is an oppressor. This summed up how most people feel.

---

70 Morley Nkosi was a member of the PAC who left South Africa for the United States in 1960. There he earned his doctorate in economics and had a successful academic career.

71 Ellen Maposholi Molapo cut her political teeth in the Garment Workers Union. She joined the ANC and later the Basutoland (Lesotho) Congress Party, of which she was the first woman member elected to party leadership. During her time in the PAC, she served as its treasurer.

72 The State of Emergency declared after the Sharpeville Massacre.

73 John Nyathi ('Poks') Pokela shared a rather similar path to Sobukwe's, graduating from Healdtown and Fort Hare to teach thereafter in Standerton and join the ANC. He left the ANC with Sobukwe, serving as the acting secretary general of the newly formed PAC. Pokela was subsequently involved with Poqo, a militant and armed wing of PAC supporters.

74 International Confederation of Free Trade Unions, set up in 1949, after seceding from the World Federation of Trade Unions, which was allegedly communist-dominated.

But I always pointed out whenever I got the chance that when foreign white teams came to play against South Africa, we always rooted for them. Therefore, we couldn't say that we were against all whites everywhere as such, only whites in South Africa. It wasn't really a question of skin color; it was a question of who is the oppressor.

The strength of anti-white sentiment was a major factor in our calculations. We knew that the vast majority of Africans are simply anti-white; the *tsotsis* and right on up, everyone. Whenever the press called us anti-white, we felt this was to our advantage.

GERHART. You were actually glad?

SOBUKWE. Yes [laughter]. This was our surest way of getting the people with us. I didn't say such things openly, of course. That was P.K.'s role, to play to these sentiments. He had no hesitation about doing it.

Another weakness of P.K. is that as soon as he sees his name in the newspaper, he tends to get carried away, and to do something else to get his name back in the paper again.

All the papers were hostile except *The World*. Even Benjie[75] sometimes printed things against us.

Intellectually, I didn't believe in drawing the conflict along strict color lines. We were opposing a racially exclusive policy, and I realized the contradiction of preaching the same line ourselves. But we were not the oppressors. I actually believed in seeing it more from a Marxist point of view in terms of the material interests that were at stake. I couldn't sell this fully to my colleagues. People from Natal were especially adamant about any matter concerning Indians. But I was conscious of the fact that we had to come up with a way of expressing our position that would be acceptable to varying types of people. We worked very hard to do this.

GERHART. Were you influenced by the views of Pogrund and Duncan?

SOBUKWE. Yes, I was. But I also knew that ordinary Africans, the people in the streets, the people who attended our conferences, were motivated plainly and simply by 'naked anti-white feeling'. 'All of our people are anti-white, anti-Indian, even anti-coloured. Our people are anti-everything.' Our people hate the whites, and there is no point in denying it. We had to attract these people to us; of course we had to take their sentiments into account. I couldn't say this kind of thing publicly, of course.

75 Benjamin Pogrund.

GERHART. Did PAC ever consider trying to ally with any of the separatist churches?

SOBUKWE. We did think of them as our allies, definitely. We saw them as recruiting grounds for us.

GERHART. How?

SOBUKWE. We approached the leaders. But they were always hostile to people who were still members of non-separatist churches. Occasionally we would get opportunities to address congregations. P.K. addressed a few congregations (of the African Methodist Episcopal?). Bishop Dimba was with us, and so was Rev. Tantsi,[76] though I don't know if he ever actually became a PAC member. The feeling in these churches was very anti-white; it was the whole basis of their existence. [Laughter here over the story of the conference where some Basotho 'Russians' (gang members or *tsotsis*) were told by ANC leaders to rough up the Africanists, before they were told that the Africanists were the ones who wanted to 'drive the white man into the sea', after which they refused to attack.]

GERHART. To which groups in the African population did you expect PAC to have the most appeal?

SOBUKWE. 'Students and intellectuals'. But actually we didn't think in terms of appealing to particular groups. We felt our appeal was to everyone. And we didn't believe that there was a true African middle class, or true classes at all among Africans. All Africans have to carry passes, live together in the townships, and so on, and this puts them on the same level.

GERHART. Did PAC particularly attract *tsotsis*?

SOBUKWE. Yes, this was true. They are the most bitterly anti-white element, anti-everything, especially in Johannesburg. In Johannesburg you do have classes in a way, and many Africans are quite 'bourgeois', materialistic. The *tsotsis* aren't, and there is friction between them and the bourgeois element. We recruited entire gangs by getting together with their leaders and persuading them to work for us instead of fighting each other. They were some of our strongest supporters in the Transvaal.

76 Walter M. Dimba was a minister in the African Congregational Church from which he broke away to form his own church, the African Congregational Church. Nimrod Boyce Tantsi was a presiding elder of the African Methodist Episcopal (AME) Church. While he had been president of the Transvaal ANC during the Defiance Campaign in 1952, he attended the inaugural convention of the PAC and was, like Dimba, openly sympathetic to the organisation.

Anyone in the PAC leadership could walk through the townships at midnight, and no *tsotsi* would lift a finger against him. Ngendane once nearly got himself in trouble, though, because he was such a sharp dresser. One night some *tsotsis* stopped him and roughed him up a little. They didn't beat him up, they just warned him that Sobukwe had said that the high were going to be made low and vice versa. They didn't say this in words; they gestured with their hands, showing that high was going to be low [laughter]. Their concept of politics wasn't very sophisticated, but they had grasped basically what we stood for.

Of course, we wanted to appeal to workers, but every African is a worker, more or less. We couldn't hope to use trade unions to any great extent, because they have never been strong. We hoped to appeal to workers directly, as individuals rather than union members. Port Elizabeth was always a stronger trade union center than the Reef.

GERHART. How strong was FOFATUSA?[77]

SOBUKWE. It was in the same position as PAC – very new. The Bakers and the Women's Garment Workers were the strongest. We didn't use FOFATUSA directly; we didn't address its meetings, for example. We just knew that the members would join as individuals. Whenever we spoke to FOFATUSA union officials, we realized that their main concern was benefits – of a trade union type – for workers, though they saw the importance of politics.

GERHART. Why did you assert the slogan of 'independence in 1963'?

SOBUKWE. [Laughter] This rightly could be called 'propaganda'. Of course, none of us believed this was really possible. This was simply an effort to hold out to people the prospect, the hope, of a reward for their efforts. We wanted people to have a goal, something they would achieve if they followed us. We figured that by the time 1963 actually came, we would by then have achieved enough that the people would be completely with us. The ANC would be eliminated altogether. We wanted to just do in the ANC completely, by the sheer force of our numbers. They would be swept off the map by us. We would start by trying to convert their members to our side, but eventually we would be enrolling completely new people, more members than they had ever had, because we would attract people who had been 'uncommitted'. The slogan was simply propaganda.

77 The Federation of Free African Trade Unions of South Africa, formed in 1959, was linked to the PAC.

GERHART. Do you think most people – e.g. the *tsotsis* – grasped the idea of Pan-Africanism? Or of a United States of Africa? Was this all propaganda, or did you believe it?

SOBUKWE. Oh yes, we sincerely believe(d) in this. And even schoolboys – and many *tsotsis* were schoolboys – understood perfectly well the idea that Africa was one. This wasn't beyond them, and it was very appealing.

GERHART. Is it true that you felt that anything Nkrumah said was 'the gospel'?

SOBUKWE. Yes, in a way we did. Nkrumah was tremendously important to us. He was the first leader of an African state, a modern African state. Just at this time you had Welensky attacking Banda,[78] saying he couldn't even run a municipal office. We were always being reminded that Ethiopia and Liberia were the least developed countries in Africa, because Africans were incapable of doing anything for themselves without European guidance. There was a constant degradation of our people in this way, and naturally we in South Africa were affected psychologically by this.

Then Nkrumah came and showed that Africans could run a 'modern' state, not like Ethiopia or Liberia. Anything Nkrumah said naturally seemed like the ultimate wisdom. Our real gospel actually was George Padmore's[79] book, *Pan-Africanism or Communism?* We got this when it first came out – I don't recall just when. A few copies (or one?) was passed around until it was dog-eared. It was 'compulsory reading' for the Africanists. No other book was comparable in influence.

At that stage we knew that we couldn't count on other African countries for material aid. We knew they were weak, that they couldn't give military help. But we looked to them for inspiration.

GERHART. What was the origin of PAC's connection with the BCP?[80]

SOBUKWE. It was my friendship with Mokhehle, dating back to when we were together at Fort Hare. He began the BCP along the lines of the original

78 Roy Welensky was prime minister of the Federation of Rhodesia and Nyasaland from 1956. In Nyasaland (later Malawi), African opposition to the white-ruled Federation was led by Dr Hastings Banda, who had returned to his country from the UK in 1958.

79 George Padmore was a Trinidad-born author and thinker whose writings had a powerful impact on Pan-Africanist thought. The liberation of Africa, Padmore believed, could only come from a united and organised Pan-African movement to overthrow colonialism, imperialism and global capitalism. His book *Pan-Africanism or Communism?* was first published in 1956.

80 The Basutoland Congress Party, led by Ntsu Mokhehle.

Youth League. I was invited to speak at their opening conference in 1957, and again in 1958.

GERHART. Was there anything in the claim made by some that ANC was more an Nguni party and that PAC spoke more for the Sothos, or attracted the Sothos more?

SOBUKWE. No, this isn't true. How would one explain the allegiance of Cape Town to PAC? There were many non-Nguni leaders in the ANC – Moses Kotane, J.B. Marks, Elias Moretsele[81] weren't Ngunis.

GERHART. Leballo[82] told me that one reason Sharpeville was so militant was because it was nearly all Sotho and he could speak to them in the vernacular and they looked to him as one of them.

SOBUKWE. That may be true, but one couldn't generalize. It would even be difficult to say to which group I myself belong. My father's father was a southern Sotho who moved from Basutoland into the Transkei. My mother was a Xhosa. My wife – I found out after marrying her – is a Zulu. My children have schooled in Lesotho and they speak Sotho best.

Tribalism is our 'enemy number one'.

We had no regard for this factor when we chose our National Executive or our leadership at any level. Oddly enough, intellectuals in South Africa tend to make more of the tribal issue than do ordinary Africans. An ordinary man accepts anyone as his equal and doesn't care where he comes from. Intellectuals look for ways to use the tribal factor to their own advantage. They play it up. And of course, the government wants to play it up too, to manipulate tribal feelings for their own ends. People are susceptible to this, unfortunately. But ordinary people will always accept a leader and judge him by his ideas, not his tribe. Take the example of an outsider like Clements Kadalie.[83]

It is also worth noting that quarrels are often most bitter, not between Nguni and Sotho, but between peoples who are most closely related – the

---

81 Moses Mauane Kotane was an ANC member but left to work with the trade unions, and later joined the Communist Party, of which he became the general secretary. For Marks and Moretsele, see nn. 12 and 19.

82 See Gerhart 1968.

83 Clements Kadalie was born in Malawi but his parents migrated to Cape Town in South Africa in search of employment; hence Sobukwe's reference to Kadalie as an 'outsider'. Kadalie became the founder and head of the Industrial and Commercial Workers Union (ICU), which, with over a hundred thousand members, was at one time the largest trade union on the continent.

Zulu and the Xhosa, the Sotho and the Tswana. Whatever one may say about Nkrumah, one must give him credit on this question. Nkrumah wiped out tribalism in Ghana, consciously and thoroughly. [There is an agreement between Sobukwe and Gerhart that Kenyatta seemed to have missed his opportunity to do the same in Kenya.]

I remember at the 1949 Bloemfontein conference that everyone spoke in his own language and there were no interpreters. But Xuma always used English. He refused to use Xhosa or to be identified in any way with one ethnic group. Intermarriage between tribes has always been the ideal for nationalists. If the PAC had come to power, we would have eliminated this problem of languages. English would be made the national language because it is most widely understood in Africa.

GERHART. How was it decided that Molotsi and Mahomo would leave on the eve of the launching?

SOBUKWE. I decided this; it was my idea. No one opposed it that I can recall. If P.K. later claimed that he opposed it, he was probably just looking for ways to discredit them.

GERHART. When you were in jail, could you communicate with the outside at all?

SOBUKWE. At first I could, but I never felt assured that my orders would get to the right people.

GERHART. What was your reaction when you heard about Poqo?[84]

SOBUKWE. This thing was 'undisciplined'. No movement can succeed without discipline. I could see that once the leaders were in jail, things had gotten out of control. There was no way of guiding this (Poqo) thing; it was the '*tsotsi* element' taking over.

I don't think Leballo should have made the statement that PAC and Poqo were the same, because they weren't, really. Poqo had about the same relation to PAC that Mau Mau had to KANU.[85] They weren't the same thing.

I had always known that we had people who believed in blowing up things, in sabotage. When we were organizing for the campaign, people

---

84 Poqo, which means 'pure', was a military formation set up while Sobukwe was imprisoned and the PAC banned. Established before the ANC's Umkhonto we Sizwe, in the early 1960s it targeted suspected police informants or government 'stooges', who were then murdered. There were also some attacks on whites, the aim being to foment a revolutionary uprising and the overthrow of the apartheid government.

85 The Kenya African National Union (see n. 26).

came to me and asked for permission to derail trains and things like that. I told them no, that we could probably succeed without that. But I did think that at some later stage of the campaign we might have to do this, to hit at the economy by derailing trains that carried workers into Johannesburg, for example. But I myself took no part in this, I thought I could leave it to those people (who knew how to do it). We never considered blowing up pylons. We didn't think there was any point in hitting any targets except the government itself – transport, perhaps 'municipal buildings'. We didn't believe in taking anyone's life.

***

Further notes by Gail Gerhart on her interview with Robert Mangaliso Sobukwe, 8 and 9 August 1970

Sobukwe is a rather ordinary-looking man, about 5′ 10″, slightly stooped in his walk, energetic and jaunty. He chain-smoked through both our conversations. He has a warm laugh, a ready smile, a pleasant voice and eyes that light up – very small eyes with no lashes or brows. His speech is completely fluent; he rarely searches for words. Like A.P. Mda, he has a wide command of English idiom (Nana and P.K. 'didn't hit it off'). He used the word 'academic' several times to describe his own approach to analyzing problems. Has he perhaps picked up some things from his studies in prison that he now applies to things with hindsight? There was no point asking in the interview when it seemed likely that something was being given an ex post facto interpretation.

Talking about the *tsotsis,* he made a revealing statement to the effect that he never ever had doubted his own ability to convince any African of the rightness of his point of view. All he needed was a chance to talk to a person, e.g. any *tsotsi.* In effect he was saying he had such complete confidence in his own principles that he felt they were self-evident to anyone who would stop to give them consideration. This came up in the context of how he might have fared in the U.S. had his application for an exit permit been successful. He was saying that, in effect, he was confident of being able to win anyone's respect. He noted that the police in Kimberley 'respected him' and that he was 'respectful toward them'.

He never expressed the sentiment 'my life's work may be finished, but I've done what I could', nor did he say anything to the effect that the struggle still goes on and I'm part of it still. He made no summary statements about his own life as it stands at this point.

The second day we were parked near a path off the main road and two teenage boys passed, carrying sticks, wearing blankets, their faces painted white. He didn't know what tribe they were, but he said he remembered going through the same initiation process, with his face painted white. He remarked they had been in this condition for some time because their hair had already grown out from being shaved.

The novel he is writing is not at all political. It draws characters from his childhood in Graaff-Reinet. The people in it are partly urban, not really still tribal; they are confused about their lives. The book has no moral. If it has any point, it is summarized by a saying in Xhosa that you must 'sleep on your wounds'. If you are hurting, never let anyone see it.

The University of Wisconsin has offered to send him linguistics books. He is going to write and ask if there is any way he can do the degree and be examined by an external examiner appointed by them. He was amazed that Roosevelt University was prepared to pay him $2 000 just to lecture once a week. He didn't know that Roosevelt was a black school.

He thinks the police are leaving him alone more since the denial of the exit permit. He said if he ever left 'it would be by the front door', though it would be easy enough to escape from Kimberley since it's so near the border. (Pogrund thinks the police are actually watching to see if he'll run.) Our first day we were followed short distances by 2 traffic police cars, and I was questioned by a plainclothes man at my hotel.

A white friend in Kimberley took him a few days before to the nearby white resort of Riverton. Sobukwe went in as the 'boy'. But that's risky since he is easily recognized. At least every African in Kimberley recognizes him.

Veronica (his wife) has taken the denial of the exit permit very hard. She has even been sick, which he thinks is psychological. She was so excited about the chance of going that she knew the average temperature in Wisconsin was something like 50 degrees. Sobukwe said he never expected to get the permit.

Their two oldest children are in a boarding school in Lesotho in Form I (St. Agnes?) They have a woman Peace Corps teacher there in English. The twins are in Std 5 and 6, and they live with friends in Lesotho. They have lived with them for a long time. It is good that in Lesotho there is at least some contact with the outside world and a strong emphasis on learning English from native speakers.

Veronica had a job for about a month in Kimberley as a nurse. But their names were still so much in the papers that she was singled out there for different treatment and she didn't like it. The matron wouldn't give her any direct orders; she would give the orders through another person, right in her presence.

Pogrund and Raymond Tucker[86] want to take the permit case to court and argue that either the government must grant the permit or pay him a sum of money equivalent to what he would have been paid at Wisconsin and Roosevelt Universities.

References

Gerhart, Gail M. 1968. 'Interview with Potlako Leballo, Nairobi 1968'. Oral History, University of KwaZulu-Natal. https://disa.ukzn.ac.za/ora19680911000009000.

Karis, Thomas G. and Gail M. Gerhart. 2013. *From Protest to Challenge: A Documentary History of African Politics in South Africa, 1882–1990*, vol. 3: *Challenge and Violence, 1953–1964.* Auckland Park: Jacana.

86 Raymond Tucker was one of the few attorneys in Johannesburg who was prepared to defend victims of apartheid.

12. 'He Was the Intellectual, Completely': Derek Hook Interviews Joe Thloloe, 2014

Joe Thloloe was one of the founding members of the Pan Africanist Congress (PAC), having joined at the time of the November 1958 break with the African National Congress. Thloloe played a crucial part in the anti-pass campaign of 1960 which led to the Sharpeville Massacre and which resulted in his imprisonment. He was incarcerated first at Stoneyard Prison in Boksburg and then at the Stofberg Prison in the northern Free State, where, with fellow PAC detainees, he was exposed to many of the harshest disciplinary measures of the apartheid system. It was during prison that Thloloe turned to journalism.

After release, Thloloe worked at *The World* and then at the *Rand Daily Mail* as the first black journalist of the township edition; a second period of incarceration followed the Soweto Uprising in 1976. Thloloe was banned under the Suppression of Communism Act in 1981 and arrested and imprisoned several more times by the apartheid government. In 1988 Thloloe was appointed the managing editor of *The Sowetan*.

Thloloe served as chairman of the South African National Editors' Forum (SANEF) and president of the Union of Black Journalists and Media Workers Association of South Africa. He was the South African Press Ombudsman from August 2007 to January 2013. In 2012 he was awarded the Order of Ikhamanga for his contribution to the liberation struggle, literary writing and journalism.

Thloloe was a long-time associate of Robert Mangaliso Sobukwe, and it is his memories of Sobukwe and the early days of the PAC that form the focus of this interview, conducted in 2014.

HOOK. Joe, you were a member of the PAC, if I understand correctly, very early on? 1959?

THLOLOE. I joined in 1958, on the 2nd of November 1958. That's the day the Africanists broke away from the ANC.

HOOK. What was the feeling among the PAC people at that time? I mean it must have been one of excitement and enthusiasm?

THLOLOE. What had happened was that there was the Transvaal Congress of the ANC, and it started on the Friday night with Luthuli giving an address to the Congress. And at the end of that address, the Africanists who had spread themselves throughout the hall, started firing questions at him and discrediting him with what they called 'multiracialism' at the time. It was only later that the ANC got to use the PAC terminology of non-racialism. But they then went attacking his [Luthuli's] multiracialism, saying that the ANC has been taken over by the Congress of Democrats and the Indian Congress. Decisions were no longer being taken by the ANC, they first had to be passed by the Congress Alliance, and then brought to the members as finished decisions. So that ended up very rowdy. On the Saturday, 2 November, when congress was supposed to resume, the Africanists found at each gate of the hall, the Orlando Communal Hall, at the gates there were groups of people, gangs called the Russian gangs. These were Basotho men clad in blankets carrying kieries[1] and other weapons. And they had been recruited to guard entrances. And with them were senior ANC people who were saying to them, 'Let that one come in, this one doesn't come in. Let that one come in, that one doesn't come in.' And the Africanists who were then excluded, couldn't get into the congress, then walked to a house nearby, where Potlako Leballo used to stay, number 142 Orlando East. They went to that house, and said, 'What do we do in wake of the fact that we are being excluded from the congress? If we try to force our way in, we will in fact be assaulted by these thugs.' So they then agreed on a letter, pulling out of the ANC, saying that they were not going to descend to the level of the ANC and try and fight.

1 Clubs.

So the Africanists were now going to charge their own way. And this letter was given to Rosette Ndziba[2] to go and deliver. Rosette didn't go to any of the gates. He jumped over one of the fences, went through the back door, into the hall, but on the estate side of the hall, and delivered the letter. And when people saw him, they rushed for him, trying to assault him, and he dashed out again and jumped over the fence. He was helped because the security police who were around that area, one of them shot into the air. And the people who were chasing Rosette then stopped, and he was able to jump over and get out. Now, I was passing at that time, and there were crowds outside watching this, and I asked, 'What is happening here?' And somebody told me that these were the Africanists. I had been reading about them, and I had been fascinated by them, and I had always wanted to find out where they are so that I could go and join them. So I went over to them and said, 'Hey, chaps, I believe in what you stand for!' And somebody gave me a membership card. It was an ANC membership card. I paid two shillings and sixpence – it was before we converted to rands and cents – and I got this membership card. But written across the membership card was the word 'Africanist' to show that in fact it wasn't a membership card of the ANC. And from that day on I was a full-fledged member of the PAC, the Africanists, although I was still a student at the time.

HOOK. Joe, do you have memories of the anti-pass campaign? And particularly those crucial days when Sobukwe and other PAC leaders handed themselves in for arrest and the events that followed after that?

THLOLOE. I was with him on the day that he was arrested, in fact I was arrested on the same day. What had happened was that the PAC had then issued the statement that every man over the age of 16 should leave his pass at home on the 21st,[3] go to the police station nearest to us, hand ourselves over, and tell them that we are not carrying our passes, we are no longer prepared to carry any passes, and they should arrest us. So we woke up that morning, and all over the townships we had people walking with us and we had people marching towards the police station. But then the police were in their vans and they started harassing the crowds that were forming. I mean they would come driving straight into the

2 On Rosette Ndziba, see this vol., ch. 9, n. 12.

3 21 March 1960.

crowds, and we would spread. And when we got together, we were fewer than we were before. And that continued all morning from about three in the morning until about six or seven in the morning. And we walked up to Orlando Police Station, and we stood outside the police station, and we waited for the group with Sobukwe (that was the group from Orlando West) to come too. And they also came through and joined us, and we then walked into the police station, and we said, 'We have come to surrender. We are not carrying any passes.' And the police refused to arrest us. They just refused. So they chased us out, and we went instead and parked right in front of Orlando Police Station. And we sat there singing, and women would come and give us coffee and tea. And while we were seated there, two things happened. The first is that the security police from Gray's Building,[4] that was the headquarters of the police at the time, drove into the police station. They went in there, and after a while one of the seniors came through and he had a list of names. They read out all the names of the National Executive members,[5] as well as of the Regional Committee members. And they then took these people into the police station.

And the next thing is that we saw them all drive out, they were sitting in the back of those cars, and they were taken away from the police station. We remained seated, and of course the journalists were there taking pictures. But after a while they started taking their things and running to their cars, and we were asking, What is happening? And they were telling us there is a massacre at Sharpeville, and they raced off. And slowly we got to get stories about the shootings at Sharpeville, where apparently as the crowd walked towards the police station, the police panicked and opened fire on the crowd, believing that they were under attack. So some of the journalists that came back then told us the stories of what had happened, how many people had been killed, etc. It was frightening. We only got to know the full story when we were taken into the cells the next day and we got the newspaper. That is when we got the full story of what had happened at Sharpeville. I remember sitting in the cells at Johannesburg Court and weeping when seeing the pictures of the people who had been killed. We were fortunate that we were not killed. But then after our

4 Gray's Building was at the time the headquarters of the security police in Johannesburg.

5 Of the PAC.

arrest, we were then put in the same cells as Sobukwe and his executive at the Johannesburg court. They were charged in the Regional Court, we were charged in what was then known as the Bantu Affairs Court, where all the pass cases were heard.

HOOK. What was … you say you saw Sobukwe on the day in March, in the beginning of the anti-pass campaign. How would you describe him? What was his mood?

THLOLOE. Very angry, very frustrated. In fact I have seen Sobukwe cry only three times in my life. The first time was on the day that we decided we were going to embark on this anti-pass campaign. It was in December 1959. And the women were parading in front of us, and saying we [the men] are scared, we the men are scared. We should give them our trousers, they should wear the trousers, because we don't want to confront the apartheid monster. When Sobukwe stood up to respond to the debate, he was saying, 'This is going to be a long and bloody road, but we are ready to take that road.' He was accepting the mandate to then formulate the anti-pass campaign and lead the nation into that campaign.

The second time I saw him cry was on this day when he spoke to us, and we saw these pictures. And he was saying to us, I did warn you it was going to be a long and bloody road, and it is going to get worse, but, with determination, Africa will be free. And the third time I saw him cry was after we were sentenced to three years in prison or £300. And on the day that we were convicted, they took away our private clothing that we had been wearing, they shaved us clean, they made us wear those shorts and red shirts with our clean-shaven heads. And at breakfast, Sobukwe was coming out from his cell, and he saw this mass of people in red, and again I saw tears come down his face.

HOOK. He was crying there because of what you had been made to wear and what you had been forced to undergo?

THLOLOE. No, just seeing what we were undergoing is what shocked him at the time. These were tears of anger and frustration, but it didn't make him break in his resolve, that we are going to continue. And his speeches throughout our period in prison, his one theme was Africa is going to be free. Nobody is going to stop us.

HOOK. Were there other things that he used to say? I mean that's one example, but were there other slogans?

THLOLOE. He was the intellectual, completely. But he was able to translate his thoughts into everyday language. He could speak eloquently in Xhosa, eloquently in Sesotho, and eloquently in English, and every time his message was very clear: 'We are going to liberate this country.'

HOOK. I was wondering whether you might be prepared to share with me some of your experiences at Stoneyard Prison in Boksburg?

THLOLOE. Before Stoneyard we were taken to Pretoria[6] for so-called observation, which was in fact torture. And then after about a month, they released the people to Stoneyard. When we got to Stoneyard, Sobukwe's crowd which had just been convicted in the Regional Court also arrived at about the same time. So we were meeting again after a month's parting. Now in the month that we were away, we were taken to a man[7] in Pretoria. It was pretty cold that year in Pretoria, and they gave us each one of us a pair of socks, and a very flimsy red shirt. They removed the blankets and the mats during the day, so we had to walk around the cell all the time to keep warm. This was what they called observations. And for every little infringement of prison rules, they would stop your meals, or stop three meals, or six or nine that you would need. So it was essentially torture, although they called it observations for classification. But we were then classified as group C, in other words, we could get one visit every six months and we could get one letter after six months. So we joined Sobukwe and his crowd – his were the national leaders of the PAC, as well as the regional leaders of the PAC. They were convicted in the Regional Court.

On the first day that we arrived there, a fascinating thing happened. We were all again given short pants to wear and red shirts, very flimsy again. And we were given old shoes, so each one had to look for a pair that was as near as possible to their normal size. And after we had all been given our share of clothing, some senior officer came in and said, 'Wie is Sobukwe?'[8] and pulled him out in front of us. And he brought him a long pair of pants, a jersey and fairly decent shoes. I don't know where they got them from. And he said, 'These are for you.' And of course Sobukwe said, 'I am not going to accept them unless my colleagues also get the

6 Pretoria Central gaol.
7 i.e. all of the men.
8 Who is Sobukwe?

same.' And their response was 'Ja, jy is 'n parmantige k----r,'[9] and they walked away. So from the time that we got to Stoneyard, Sobukwe was doing exactly the same, had the same privileges as us, ate exactly the same things that we did, and he refused to accept any form of privilege because he was Sobukwe. And that is one of the reasons why I respect him.

HOOK. Did you have any other memories or experiences of Sobukwe at Stoneyard?

THLOLOE. For the time that we were at Stoneyard, we were not given any chores to do except to clean our cells and the yard where we were imprisoned. And then we managed to smuggle stuff into the cells, we managed to smuggle pieces of paper, pencil stubs, and we could send messages outside using the black warders who were quite supportive of us. This continued until one day there was a massive raid on our section, probably all the personnel in the prison came there, and they pulled us all out of our cells and they started searching each cell, and they found these pencil stubs and these pieces of paper, etc., etc. And what they then did is they pulled out Sobukwe and the members of his executive and the regional executive – they pulled them out and sent them to Cinderella Prison,[10] which was a tougher prison than Stoneyard, so we were again parted with them.

But we continued smuggling stuff, in fact that is where I first started to learn my journalism. Matthew Nkoana,[11] who was a *Post* and *Drum* reporter at the time, would sit with a few of us telling us about journalism, telling us how they write stuff, how they write stories and [they would] give us assignments to practise, etc. But that was the period that we spent at the Stoneyard. And then we met Sobukwe again when they took us to a space in the Free State, what do you call it now ...?

HOOK. Oh yes, it was in the northern Free State if I remember?

THLOLOE. Ja, northern Free State.[12] That is where we reunited with Sobukwe and the executive members of the PAC, and for the rest of that year we were together, but during the times that we were together, there were political lessons where the members of the executive would come around to our cells and they would talk to us about Pan-Africanism, about world

9 Yes, you are a cheeky k----r.

10 In Boksburg.

11 On Matthew Nkoana, see this vol., part I, n. 63.

12 Stofberg Prison.

politics etc., etc., and Sobukwe was a part of that rotation, where he would come into our cell and he would talk about all the history of the PAC, the history of the ANC, the history of blacks in this country. And then, while we were there, we were put into teams to go and work on digging a dam on the prison premises. Picks and shovels. I was lucky, I suspect, because I was the youngest, or not the youngest but had the smallest body ... so I was left in the cells to do the cleaning and the dishing up of food, etc. And I watched these guys go down into the fields, and they would work all day digging the dam. The first two days were very bad, people would come in with bruises on their hand, with bleeding hands, and when they went to complain, they were then given mercurochrome[13] on their hands, and the next day they were expected to go back there and continue digging. And the warders, this time it was gloves off. The warders would insist that people work. If they tried to rest for a while they would say, 'Kom, kom, kom, jong',[14] otherwise you get punished if you refuse to continue working.

HOOK. Was this the 'battle of the pickaxes'?

THLOLOE. Ja, it was the same, that battle of the pickaxes happened there. In fact I was standing on one of the top floors looking through the windows down at the crowd at the bottom. What happened that morning is that some of the prisoners would take two teaspoons with their porridge in the morning. They would ask me to give them one teaspoon, and they would then wrap the second teaspoon and keep it with them to use at lunchtime or at dinner, and use it on their porridge at that time. So on this day, the sugar fell from one of the prisoners as he was bending down, and the warder asked him if it was tobacco – because tobacco was banned – and he came very aggressive towards the prisoner. And we had a way that if any of us was threatened, we would all sort of get together and defend the person that was being threatened. Now this was a holiday, I think it was October 10th, that used to be the old Kruger Day.[15] So it was just skeleton staff that was working. So this one warder who panicked, ran out of the yard, went to the office and hit the alarm, and then the next thing was

13 A topical antiseptic.

14 Come on, boy.

15 Apartheid-decreed national holiday honouring Paul Kruger, president of the Transvaal Republic, who symbolised the Boers' resistance to British aggression at the time of the Anglo-Boer War (South African War).

that the whole place was filled with off-duty warders. When they came in they went to the office and they were all given pick-handles. Now the pick-handles had a hole at the back, and they had a leather strap to assist in handling, and they all marched to the yard, and started lashing out, left, right and centre. They did not even ask what the matter was, they just started lashing out at people. And they drove that whole crowd back into the yard where we were kept, and as they were coming in, all those that were injured were set aside. The rest who were not injured were sent to their cells and ... [told] you are going to miss three meals.

Now those who were injured were taken to the single isolation cells, where you stayed alone in your cell. They were all locked up in the single cells, and the next day there was a trial where they were accused of revolt. And they were sentenced to lashes, and to something like twenty days without food, or thirty days without food. After the trial, they went back to their single cells, and the following day the prison doctor, who used to drive an old Volkswagen, came in and all the people that were being sentenced were taken to him. He looked at them, looked at their injuries and said they were fit to be lashed. And the lashing at that time was the most cruel punishment you could ever imagine. I had watched it happen here at the Johannesburg court, and I had been watching it over at the other prisons, and it was the most brutal form of punishment that one could get. So these guys were whipped. And for days after that, they could hardly wear their pants because of the wounds on their backs. So they would lie there all day, and they wouldn't want anything, not even a blanket to touch anywhere near where the lashes had been given. And every day they would get a dose of mercurochrome over their wounds until they healed. But in the meantime, they then had to start their fasting. It was two days of no food whatsoever, and on the third day they would get a mixture of rice and water, a very strange mixture. Now what happened, as they were cooking the rice, before it even ripened, they would scoop up the rice with some of the water in that rice. You couldn't even eat that stuff. They would be given half a ration of that. And then I got to a point where I managed to steal some mielies[16] – that was our lunch there – they had brought out boiled mielies. So I would take those mielies and I would take a sheet of paper, and lay it out on the sheet of paper, and slip it under

16 Corn.

the door of each one of the prisoners' cells. I was very lucky I was never caught. And I think the warders were also surprised that these guys are refusing to take even the boiled rice so there must be something they are taking, but they never found out how these people managed to survive those days and weeks in solitary confinement. That was the battle of the pick-handles. So they were accused of revolt, when in fact it wasn't true. They had never revolted, it was just that one young warder that got into a panic and said there was a revolt.

HOOK. The picture you paint, Joe, is one of extraordinary cruelty and suffering. You must have seen Sobukwe during these times. I wondered if you could maybe describe how he appeared to you? And I know it sounds like a silly question, because you know one can see pictures of him ... But it would be interesting to hear a physical description of him from someone who had seen him in those situations.

THLOLOE. He was quite tall, probably about the height of Mandela. And also just as imposing, very impressive and extremely handsome. He had this very wide grin on his face, but he could get very serious and he could get very funny. He told stories all the time. He was trained in African literature, so he told some of the stories that we did not pick up in our own education, and he would show exactly what they meant for Africans and why those stories were important to us. How they formed part of the culture of Pan-Africanism, to remember our roots. He had a way of ... every time there was an issue to discuss, he would throw the ball up and get what people were saying. At the end of it, he would strike his one palm with his other hand, with the blade of his other hand. And he would say 'so we are agreed', and then he would sum up what he believed to be the consensus of that meeting.

HOOK. That is a very striking picture, it really conjures up an image of him. Do any other memories stick with you, particular incidents maybe, of Sobukwe interacting with other people?

THLOLOE. I had one particularly interesting conversation with him, when I went to ask him why he was a Methodist preacher. I said, 'You can't be worshipping the gods of white people, when [you are] helping the oppressed.' He laughed at me and said, 'You are still a young man. One day you will learn who God is and what he is.' And I tried to argue, and I was saying, 'There is absolutely no proof that God exists,' and all the usual teenage debates. And he wouldn't tackle me on any of those issues.

He said, 'My boy, I am not going to argue with you, you are going to learn as you grow up,' and that's how he got rid of me. But ultimately I got to understand then that he was deeply religious. Besides being a Methodist preacher, he as a person was religious. I was talking to Dini[17] the other day and he was telling me that every time he went to Robben Island, every night the whole family would get together and he would read the Bible and pray, and every morning he would do exactly the same thing. So he believed very earnestly.

Hook. Do you think the time of imprisonment had effects on Sobukwe? I mean, I was particularly struck because you saw him at a number of different times during his imprisonment. Did he seem changed? And do you think the time on Robben Island had a lasting effect on him?

Thloloe. No, absolutely none. His resolve remained the same. I went to see him in Kimberley shortly after he was released from prison, and he was still preaching the same story of Pan-Africanism. In fact at the time he was grappling with whether he should do his articles as an attorney. Remember he qualified as an attorney ... he had done his examinations while he was in prison. Now he was yet to do his articles to qualify as an attorney. And he was agonising with having to go and do articles, saying that he had stood in court saying that he doesn't recognise the court, he doesn't recognise the laws of the country, so how could he with a clear conscience go and become an officer of the court? And it was quite agonising for him, and our argument was that when he goes into a court of law, he will not be going in there on the side of apartheid, he would be going in there defending the oppressed. It was another arena for the struggle, so ultimately he did do his articles, and was admitted to the side bar. But at that time, he was still committed to liberation and he was still committed to Pan-Africanism. In fact it was not surprising that he was listed as a co-conspirator in the Bethal Treason Trial.[18]

Hook. Could you say a bit more about that, Joe?

Thloloe. No, the Bethal Trial was in fact a trial of ... the main accused there was Zephania Mothopeng. He was accused of putting the PAC together

17 Robert Mangaliso Sobukwe's son.

18 A trial of 18 PAC members, including Zeph Mothopeng, accused under the Terrorism Act inter alia of fomenting the Soweto Uprising; the trial, which was held in camera, began in 1977 and ended in 1979.

again after the government had thought they had wiped it out completely, and I think he was sentenced to something like fifteen years in prison ... no, I can't remember the actual number of years. But in that time, Sobukwe was listed as a co-conspirator, but he died during that period.

HOOK. Is there something that really needs to be remembered in today's South Africa, something that is particularly crucial about Sobukwe's life and his politics?

THLOLOE. If you go through his speeches, he talks about total liberation, not just physical, but mental and economic etc., *total liberation.* And I think those ideals haven't been achieved yet. We still have problems. So it would help us to go back to some of his writings and take stock where we stand.

HOOK. Thank you again for your time.

Part IV: Conclusion

The Afterlife of Robert Mangaliso Sobukwe

Robert Mangaliso Sobukwe's name has begun to appear with increasing frequency in South Africa today. To cite just one prominent example: the Robben Island Museum declared 2023 the year of Robert Sobukwe. What is it, then, that underlies the growing public interest in the figure of Sobukwe? Why this renewed enthusiasm for a man whose political and intellectual legacy has remained dormant for the better part of the last four decades? The question that the famous Jamaican-British cultural studies scholar Stuart Hall (1996, 12–13) posed more than twenty-five years ago in respect of the decolonial theorist and revolutionary Frantz Fanon deserves to be recast in contemporary South Africa, asked in respect of this fellow opponent of the colonial order: 'Why *Robert Mangaliso Sobukwe*? Why *today*?'

This, to be sure, is not a line of questioning concerned exclusively with Sobukwe himself. It is an enquiry also into the particular social and political circumstances of the contemporary post-apartheid era; it is a questioning, furthermore, of the emerging – or re-emerging – conditions of political desire that have occasioned this revitalisation of Sobukwe's memory. Sobukwe, as powerful political image, as historical legacy, as icon of the struggle against white supremacy, as a profound identification with African Nationalism and Pan-Africanism, is representative of a great many political aspirations. In pursuing the above line of questioning (Why *Sobukwe*? Why *today*?) we should therefore remember that multiple constituencies call upon Sobukwe, that what Sobukwe has come to stand for might differ in some important respects from what is contained in the biographical narrative, the details of the historical

35. Portrait of Robert Mangaliso Sobukwe, Johannesburg, August 1977. (Photo by Benjamin Pogrund, with kind permission)

persona, or indeed Sobukwe's own speeches and writings contained in earlier parts of this book. There are many portrayals of Sobukwe, many uses made of his legacy, and to survey a cross-section of these depictions and utilisations of Sobukwe, as we do, does not mean that they all cohere or even that they all need to be agreed upon. Having paraphrased Stuart Hall once, we can do so again: 'Rather than trying to recapture the "true" [Sobukwe], we must try and engage the after-life of [Robert Mangaliso Sobukwe]' (Hall 1996, 14). This is not, of course, to foreclose the prospect of close and diligent readings of Sobukwe's own words and writings – the first section of this book hopes to facilitate precisely such an undertaking – just as it is not to sideline the importance of ongoing archival work on the documents concerning his life. Similarly, it is not to ignore the existing literature concerning Sobukwe, be it chiefly biographical (Hook 2019; Ntloedibe 1995; Pheko 1994; Pogrund 2015; Plaatjie 2019), more broadly historical (Gerhart 1978; Karis and Gerhart 2013; Lodge 1983, 2011), or focused on the rise and decline of the Pan Africanist Congress (Kondlo 2009).

What do we speak of when we speak of Sobukwe?

The pertinence of the question we are asking here can be underlined with a perhaps inevitable comparison. A decade ago, Nelson Mandela was laid to rest amidst near universal acclaim, in a commemorative spectacle virtually unprecedented in South Africa. Robert Mangaliso Sobukwe, by contrast, a man who was for a significant period a more potent repository of radical hopes and dreams for liberation across the African continent, was, at the time, afforded only the most meagre space of public commemoration. How are we to understand the relationship between these differing modes of memorialisation? It would seem the more Mandela was elevated to a messianic status, the greater was the necessity to remove from history those who might challenge Mandela's role as the most crucial protagonist in the history of the anti-apartheid struggle.

So, to return to the question posed above: Why has Sobukwe's name returned after such a lengthy period of neglect, and, as significantly, why now particularly? Why are we *re*-membering differently now? Of course, to speak of Sobukwe is to speak of a good deal more than the biography and historical importance of the man himself. It is to join a series of debates and critical injunctions that have been alive in South Africa in some or other form since at least the 1940s. To speak of Sobukwe as such is to invoke a series of revolutionary ideas, to revisit a Pan-Africanist vision, to recall the African Nationalism espoused by Anton Lembede, Potlako Leballo, A.P. Mda and others. It is, moreover, to recall a form of radicalism that took an uncompromising stance against not only colonialism and white supremacy, but against white liberalism and, notably, against the political direction of the African National Congress after it had incorporated the ideals of the Freedom Charter in 1955. The name Sobukwe thus serves as representative of a cluster of ideas and aspirations routinely excluded – even repressed – from political debate in the post-apartheid public sphere. What else, though, does the name Sobukwe represent? What other aspirations and hopes are present when his name is pronounced?

Without voice

We can begin our discussion with a preliminary biographical observation. 'According to his wife, Victoria', reports Xolela Mangcu (2012, 118), Sobukwe 'had started forgetting how to speak by the end of his sentence [on Robben Island].' This condition of being rendered unable to speak has, regrettably, continued. It proves a recurring theme not only within the context of Sobukwe's life – certainly so, given the multiple banning orders and restrictions of association placed upon him – but also retrospectively: it applies still today in a variety of contexts in which Sobukwe's voice has been forgotten, over-written, silenced, or even (as we will see) appropriated. Dini Sobukwe, the former PAC leader's son, who did so much to commemorate his father's memory, spoke in an interview with Derek Hook (29 May 2014) of his frustration in trying to locate recordings of his father. Given how extensive the security police surveillance of Robert Mangaliso Sobukwe had been during the course of his life, it seems impossible – so Benjamin Pogrund (2015) says – that no recordings were made. How are we to make sense of what appears to be the systematic erasure of Sobukwe's voice, an elimination that indicates a larger project of historical erasure? The point is made by Thami ka Plaatjie (interview with Derek Hook, 23 August 2014):

> Why can't we, when Sobukwe died in 1978, get an audio of Sobukwe? Where is the audio? Sobukwe was appearing in court, he was a lawyer, he spoke in court, the transcripts of prisons were there, where's

> the audio? Where's the voice of this man? And why is it in someone's interest that we must not have access to it? Steve Biko's voice is there, Mandela was recorded by the BBC, the audio, the footage is there, but where is the material on Sobukwe ...? And why would Mandela's speech at [the] Rivonia [trial be historically documented] ... and not Sobukwe's in 1960?

Sobukwe's silencing is apparent also in what might be called a systematic failure of commemoration. 'South Africa', says Benjamin Pogrund (2015, 410–411), 'has not been kind to Robert Sobukwe. The magnitude of his deeds and beliefs is largely ignored. The African National Congress has done much to airbrush him out of the freedom struggle. He is seldom referred to ... The anniversary of Sharpeville, on 21 March, is officially Human Rights Day, but to watch and read references to it is to believe that it was really an ANC effort. Sobukwe has not been honoured with any major public naming of public institutions.'

Mcebisi Ndletyana (2013) points out how opportunities to honour Sobukwe's life are repeatedly met with silence. This silence is telling, he argues, for it is 'an ironic expression of an anomaly. Silence does speak. It too has a voice. The silence tells us, in its own unique way, of an official quest to forget Sobukwe.' More forthrightly yet: 'Attempts to erase Sobukwe's memory in our public consciousness are indicative of how those in power legitimise themselves. They only tell and memorialise narratives that cultivate popular acceptance of their ideas' (Ndletyana 2013). Steve Lebelo (2014) argues, similarly, that literature dealing with the history of the struggle in South Africa mostly focuses on the ANC and its alliance partner campaigns. There appears, he continues, to have been a deliberate effort to undermine the contributions of Sobukwe and the Pan Africanist Congress. Rapule Tabane (2012) claims that Sobukwe is being 'culled from our history'. More forcefully yet, Bennie Bunsee (2013) proclaims: 'It is well-known that the ANC went out of its way to crush the PAC.'

Sobukwe, we can thus say, has been the subject of a form of historical amnesia in South Africa for at least the last thirty years. This type of motivated forgetting has at times no doubt been intentional, strategic – indeed politically motivated – and, at other times, perhaps less than conscious or deliberate, although no less systematic for that. The irony of the situation is that steadfast political opponents have come to be united in this respect, joined in a virtual consensus of forgetting. Whereas Julius Malema's Economic Freedom Fighters (EFF) are clearly an exception, the hegemonic voting publics of the African National Congress and the Democratic Alliance appear to agree on this point: Sobukwe's political legacy is best consigned to history.

The reason for such an unlikely alliance of forgetting is not difficult to surmise. As already intimated, Sobukwe's vision of African Nationalism offers debilitating critiques of key ideological commitments underpinning both the Democratic Alliance and the ANC (that is to say, the largely white conservative or neo-liberal and the Charterist) constituencies. Sobukwe, in short, clearly attacked the self-serving interests of paternalistic white liberalism. Yet he was highly critical of the ANC's turn – by means of the Freedom Charter – to a politics of multiracialism. The sad and paradoxical result of this consensus of forgetting is that Sobukwe, a man known for his utopian vision of a Pan-Africanist future, was better known during, rather than after, apartheid.

Remembering so as to better forget

We should be cautious of the claims we are making. While Sobukwe's voice has been erased, his name has not completely disappeared from the history books. Sobukwe has not been eradicated from histories of the country or accounts of the struggle against apartheid. His name regularly appears in the indexes of historical overviews and textbooks, and yet the space afforded any discussion of the nature of his role is, as a rule, minimal, amounting to little more than a few lines noting his leadership of the anti-pass campaign that directly preceded the 1960 Sharpeville Massacre. This itself is part of a broader project of repression. We might put it this way: yes, we remember some historical fragment of Sobukwe, so as to better attend to the work of structural forgetting.

A more performative example of this principle is to be found in the experience of many visitors to Robben Island. Despite the prominent images of Sobukwe displayed at the tour's departure point on the Victoria and Albert Waterfront, the guided tour of the Island itself typically sidelines the role of the former PAC leader. As opposed to the lengthy guided tour of the main prison block – the highlight there for many being Mandela's cell – the modest building where Sobukwe was kept in isolation between

1963 and 1969 often tends to be neglected. Pogrund (2015, 404) describes the situation: 'These days buses stop for a few minutes outside the fenced-in compound ... But visitors remain in the bus and do not see the interior of the Robert Sobukwe House. It cannot be said whether this is for political reasons in downplaying Sobukwe's historical role or if it is because of the rushed nature of the tours.'[1]

Ndletyana (2013) offers an insightful remark: 'Where an official gesture has been made to recognize Sobukwe's memorial site, it has also been accompanied by acts of concealment.' A further example: '[Sobukwe's] law office in Galeshewe [township, Kimberely] is recognised and concealed at the same time. The front wall bears an inscription about the building, with signage nearby pointing towards it. But, no attempt is made to keep the building visible to a curious eye. Hawkers stack-up their trolleys against the wall hiding the plaque. One really has to look hard to find the building' (Ndletyana 2013).

What holds for public spaces reserved for the commemoration of Sobukwe's life holds also for the space afforded him in official or popular histories of the country. It is as if an agreement exists in many historical texts on South Africa: Robert Mangaliso Sobukwe's historical role cannot be denied – he is undoubtedly part of South African history – yet both he and the Pan-Africanism that he championed are not – in the final analysis – worthy of further exploration. Such brisk dismissals are typically associated with an accompanying gesture: the reduction of Sobukwe's political philosophy to little more than a crude form of anti-whiteism or, worse yet, a type of apartheid in reverse. In view of the latter, we might cite a telling example drawn from Chana Teeger's research on high-school history education in post-apartheid South Africa, in which a high school teacher at Glenville High School in

1 A rather personal anecdote may be appropriate here. In the late 1990s, not long after tours to Robben Island started, one of the authors, Leswin Laubscher, had occasion to visit the Island, led by considerably younger former inmates than is the case today. Stopping at Sobukwe's house, in exactly the way Pogrund describes above, the guide intoned, 'And here was kept the most dangerous man in South Africa, Robert Sobukwe.' To which a member of a small group of high school students from the Cape Flats exclaimed, 'Who was he?' The embarrassment was exacerbated by another response, one spoken with what could only be an American accent, 'He was the leader of the PAC.' (As became apparent later, this was said by an exchange student at the University of Cape Town, visiting from an American university.) It was hard to miss, in the moments that followed, the first student silently mouthing to her companion, 'What's the PAC?'

Johannesburg (Mr Pretorius) asks his students about the Pan Africanist Congress:

Mr Pretorius. Remember what the PAC stood for?
Students. Reverse Apartheid.
Mr Pretorius. Yes. And what race was only allowed to be in the PAC?
Students. Blacks.
Mr Pretorius. Yes ... It was trying to reinforce apartheid – just vice versa. (Teeger 2015, 1175)

As Teeger remarks, such treatments of South African history not only hinder students' abilities to make connections to the past, but they also effectively insist upon the irrelevance of that past.

White anxiety

The tendency to reduce Sobukwe's political stance to little more than a strident anti-whiteism is apparent even in the work of eminent South African historians. Take, for example, the case of Hermann Giliomee's *The Afrikaners*, which is often cited as an authoritative text of South African history. Giliomee (2003, 519) refers to Sobukwe only once, and reduces his political position to the threat to drive whites into the sea, a notable mischaracterisation – certainly so when taken in comparison with Sobukwe's own writings – one which, arguably, speaks more of Giliomee's own reaction to Sobukwe than of any close reading of Sobukwe's own comments on this issue.[2]

A similar and equally telling example can be found in David Welsh's *The Rise and Fall of Apartheid*, where Welsh scrutinises a remark made by Anton Lembede – Sobukwe's clear ideological forebear – while discussing

2 It is worth noting both Giliomee's tone and the accompanying threat of violence contained in an extract in which Giliomee describes an exchange between Sobukwe and Nic Olivier, a Stellenbosch University academic tasked with assessing the attitudes of African leaders to the apartheid government's policies of separate development: 'Robert Sobukwe, leader of the PAC, warned that if whites continued to pursue [the policies of separate development] ... they would all risk "being driven into the sea". A heated exchange followed between him and Olivier, who warned that whites lacked neither the will nor the resources to resist such a challenge' (Giliomee 2003, 519).

the development of the African Nationalism that played so crucial a part in the formation of the PAC. He cites Lembede's argument that 'Africans are fighting for Africa; but other sections are fighting only for their rights to trade and extract as much wealth as possible from Africa', before adding the following in parentheses: 'The snide, not to say racist, comment at the end of this quotation was aimed at Indians as much as any other group. Another comment in the same article, asserting that "Indians have India as their motherland; they are only here in Africa as traders", could have been written by any white Natalian anti-Indian bigot' (Welsh 2010, 43–44). Given that Welsh's text is populated by a great many apartheid ideologues and leaders who can quite legitimately be characterised as bigots, it is surprising that Lembede is singled out for such a treatment. The point here is not so much to defend Lembede – although the characterisation of the initially quoted segment, 'Africans are fighting for Africa', as racist is questionable – but simply to note the gratuitous nature of Welsh's characterisation. We witness, in this parenthetical comment, the measured tones of the scholarly historian giving way to something more defensive. It is as if Welsh feels compelled to respond to Lembede by way of attack, as if in fact he feels his own position to be somehow under threat by the African Nationalism or Pan-Africanism advanced by Lembede and Sobukwe some sixty years earlier. We edge closer here to a sense of Sobukwe as a type of symptom – or point of anxiety – within white South African discourse.

Admittedly, we are only offering a few select examples here – although more could be cited – but the point seems clear enough: the topic of Sobukwe (or Lembede or African Nationalism) still touches a nerve, raises the hackles of many white historians. We can say, then, that in popular versions of South African history the name Sobukwe has often tended to elicit a nervous – and, indeed, defensive – reaction. In fact, virtually all the basic types of psychological defensiveness can be witnessed here. Mention of Sobukwe is enough to induce projection (it is *Sobukwe/Lembede themselves* who are racist); denial (Sobukwe is *not really significant* in the history of South Africa); reversal (rather than attacking apartheid, Sobukwe himself *reinforced apartheid*); disavowal (Sobukwe was, admittedly, historically significant yet, simultaneously, decidedly *not*); and reduction to one single irrational feature (Sobukwe as embodying anti-whiteism).

An interesting study waits to be written in respect of the last of these considerations, one exploring how, in popular accounts of South African history, Sobukwe and the PAC so often come to be reduced in just such a way – that is, to a single and powerfully exaggerated signifier: anti-white. One might even entertain possibilities of such a future study by referencing Malcolm X in the United States (who was similarly branded) and Steve Biko (who was not, or not quite). How is it that the insistence on black agency and self-reliance, on the exclusion of involvement – and, indeed, the diluting and ultimately undermining influence – of whites from African politics came to be read as necessarily and essentially anti-white?

To be sure, this apparent equation (Sobukwe = anti-white) was not always straightforward or direct. Take, for instance, the qualification noted in Leonard Thompson's *A History of South Africa*: 'Sobukwe ... did not hold the extreme views of some of his followers. Ultimately, according to Sobukwe, Whites might become genuine Africans; but since they benefitted from the existing social order, they could not yet identify with the African cause' (2014, 211). This more ostensibly balanced view is accompanied by a quote from an unidentified 'African journalist': 'The masses do not hate an abstraction like "oppression" or "capitalism" ... They make these things concrete and hate the oppressor – in South Africa the White Man' (Thompson 2014, 211). And so, although Sobukwe is momentarily freed of the stigma of anti-whiteism, the threat remains present by means of an association with an unnamed journalist. The irony of all this is that the journalist's quote could quite easily be attributed to Sobukwe himself.[3] These are the words with which Sobukwe responds to the question 'Are you anti-white?' in an interview published in January 1959 in *The Africanist* (this vol., ch. 4): 'In every struggle ... the masses do not fight an abstraction. They do not hate oppression or capitalism. They concretise these and hate the oppressor, be he the Governor-General or a colonial power ... or, in South Africa, the white man.' What has been lost in Thompson's presentation of this view are the lines that immediately follow: 'They hate these groups because they associate them with their oppression! Remove the association and you remove the hatred. In South Africa then, once white domination has been overthrown and the white man is no longer "white-man boss" ... he will not be hated even by the masses.'

It is odd for a well-regarded historian to omit such a crucial qualification. Then again, in light of what we have noted above, such an omission is not surprising. Another example, then, of how the name Sobukwe

3 It is unclear whether Thompson was aware of this.

represents something of an anxious condition in white accounts of South African history.

Sobukwe's Mandela

Let us shift from the theme of white anxiety to modes of repression that come to operate in relation to the history of the ANC and the biography, more particularly, of Nelson Mandela. We are now familiar with the comparison: Mandela's legacy – although increasingly contested and conflictual – remains undeniable, while Sobukwe's, until very recently, has languished to the point of near non-existence. The problem with such observations is that they are, as a rule, followed by little in the way of sustained analysis of the dynamic of memory on display. In other words, they stop short of exploring how the image of Mandela might itself be reliant on the repressed memory of Sobukwe. Let us take up this line of analysis, and ask in what ways Mandela was indebted to Sobukwe.

There is a telling moment in Mandela's *Conversations with Myself* (2011, 118), in which Mandela and Ahmed Kathrada discuss Sobukwe in relation to the preparation of Mandela's autobiography, *Long Walk to Freedom*:

MANDELA. No, I was never confrontational towards Sobukwe. You must remember that Sobukwe was my client. I was his lawyer, and we respected each other very much, Sobukwe, because he was a very pleasant chap.

KATHRADA. Ja.

MANDELA. And a gentleman and there was never any confrontation and I got on *very well* with him in prison.

This brief exchange seems innocuous enough. It is followed on the same page[4] by a series of Mandela's thoughts on the concept of nonracialism:

4 It may help to add a little biographical context here. In *Long Walk to Freedom*, Mandela clearly expresses his respect and even fondness for Sobukwe. Mandela's feelings toward the PAC are, however, far less sanguine. On the same page of his autobiography in which Mandela praises Sobukwe – 'His … willingness to pay the price for his principles earned my … respect' – he also castigates his political rivals, led of course by Sobukwe: 'Many of those who cast their lot with the PAC did so out of personal grudges or disappointments, and were thinking not of the advancement of the struggle, but of their own feelings of jealousy and revenge … I found the views and behaviour of the PAC immature' (Mandela 1994, 215).

> We have never accepted really multiracialism. Our demand is for a non-racial society, because when you talk of multiracialism, you are multiplying races; you are saying that you have in this country so many races. That is a way to perpetuate the concept 'race', and we preferred to say we want a non-racial society … We discussed and said exactly what we are saying, that we are not multiracialist, we are nonracialist. We are fighting for a society where people will cease thinking in terms of colour. (2011, 118)

This seems an extraordinary – if unintentional – reference back to Sobukwe and Pan-Africanist thinking, one that begs comparison with Sobukwe's own words. Consider the following, an extract from Sobukwe's opening address to the PAC's inaugural convention (this vol., ch. 6), delivered in 1959, fifty years before the publication of Mandela's words: 'To us the term "multiracialism" implies that there are such basic insuperable differences between the various national groups here that the best course is to keep them permanently distinctive in a kind of democratic apartheid. That to us is racism multiplied, which probably is what the term truly connotes.'

How are we to respond to what appears to be an example of political plagiarism? It perhaps helps to bear in mind here that with these words Sobukwe was precisely setting the Africanists against the multiracial, Charterist ethos of the ANC at the time. In other words, we are not dealing with a minor or pedantic historical issue, but with a question that lay at the heart of the rift between the ANC and the PAC.

The above example is not an isolated occurrence. In his 2014 Sobukwe memorial lecture, Motsoko Pheko insisted that Sobukwe was a 'pace setter' in determining political strategy, and stressed how other political parties often followed the precedents he had set. Pheko's key example concerns Sobukwe's court appearance on 4 April 1960, where he reminded the magistrate: 'Your Worship, it will be remembered that when this court began we refused to plead because we felt no moral obligation whatsoever to obey laws which are made exclusively by a white minority … an unjust law cannot be justly applied … We are not afraid of the consequences for our actions and it is not our intention to plead for mercy' (Pheko 2014). Two and a half years later, notes Pheko (2014), a 'rival political leader' – he means, of course, Mandela – used the following words in his defence in a Pretoria court: 'I challenge the right of this court to hear my case. Firstly I fear that I will not be given a fair trial.

Secondly, I consider myself neither legally nor morally bound to obey laws made by a parliament in which I have no representation.' Another facet of the repression of Sobukwe comes into view here. Again, it is not a case of outright silencing: Sobukwe's (or the PAC's) message persists even though it has been appropriated and, arguably, diluted. Sobukwe's voice has been overwritten, credited to some other political party and historical figure.

Psychologically, the argument is sometimes made that what is remembered is contingent upon what has been forgotten – a reversal of the more intuitive idea that the forgotten plays little or no part in what is actively remembered (see Worby and Ally 2013 for an application of this argument to the post-apartheid era). Put in more straightforward terms: what is elevated to the level of conscious memory is in a continual relation with what one does not wish to remember. That is to say, one response to disruptive or upsetting memories or histories is to latch on to a good image – or historical persona – that screens our more disturbing recollections. The good image, such as that of Mandela, becomes all the more cherished and celebrated as a result: it shields us from a more threatening alternative. The consolations provided by the various political myths of Mandela can be seen as in part the result of the repression of a murky subset of threatening political values coalescing around the signifier Sobukwe.

In short, then, the affectionate attachment to Mandela can be understood as a type of over-compensation that shields from view the more genuinely revolutionary changes that Sobukwe's name represented. If this seems at first unlikely, consider the political situation in 1950s South Africa as sketched by Karis and Gerhart (2013, 121–122):

> Sensitivity to racial tensions and white fears had always exerted a restraining influence on the ANC and had caused it throughout much of its history to project African aims in ways that would minimize white backlash. In their anxiety not to be guilty of racism in any form, Congress leaders had many times found themselves constrained by the tendency of whites to label any suggestion of an African takeover of power as 'black racialism' or 'apartheid in reverse' ... To the young PAC militants, no such political taboos or considerations of white opinion seemed relevant ... The PAC's executive took no pains to avoid the question of how they wanted ... political power distributed ... Africans would rule.

This account helpfully stresses how Sobukwe may have been a threatening embodiment of freedom not only to whites but also to those within the Congress Alliance who wished to distance themselves from the apparently extreme aspirations of the PAC. The ANC (and the image of Mandela) can thus be said not merely to play their part in repressing Sobukwe, but to have profited from such a repression. We are a short step here from concluding that Sobukwe and the PAC came, in fact, to be derogated by Mandela's ANC precisely as a way of legitimising itself in the eyes of whites. Recall the famous words uttered by Mandela (1994, 354) at the Rivonia Trial: 'I have fought against white domination, and I have fought against black domination', a statement which implies a problematic symmetry between apartheid and the Africanists of the PAC (who are, one presumes, the representatives of 'black domination').

Sobukwe as the return of the repressed

We might also have titled this section 'Sobukwe as the return of the calls of the oppressed'. It serves to illustrate that complicated and interrelated dynamic between the times and the psychology of the times, between memory and the needs of memory in a particular material context and circumstance. We have spoken of the historical circumstances underlying the repression of Sobukwe, and of the ways in which Sobukwe can be said to trouble white, liberal and Charterist sensibilities. What then might be said in respect of the challenge that the memory of Sobukwe poses to the political status quo of a 'post-Mandela', 'loadshedding present' South Africa?

During the celebrations of Sobukwe's 90th birthday in Graaff-Reinet (on 5 December 2014), the coincidence with the first anniversary of Mandela's death (also on 5 December) was mentioned more than once. 'What are the gods trying to tell us?' intoned poet Don Mattera quizzically, his implication being that a symbolic passing of the baton was by now well overdue. This coincidence of anniversaries seems suggestive: does Sobukwe's re-emergence correspond with the decline of the Mandela era? This seems apparent in many of the more overtly polemical appeals to Sobukwe's name: 'It has now become known that Mandela gave the country back to the colonialists, and today they are fighting to retain those privileges. The colonial and imperialist world has turned Mandela into an icon and there is now a preposterous cult of the man. Sobukwe, who spent almost eight years alone, separated from the other political prisoners on Robben Island, is given secondary importance. Why?' (Bunsee 2013).

Sipho Seepe (2008) makes a similar point: 'As we enter the period of disillusionment with the so-called rainbow nation that excludes the centrality of African content, we need to ... reclaim our heroes, learn from the our past ... Sobukwe's literary and political contributions are a necessary antidote to the meaningless but intoxicating language of rainbowism.'

A word of caution is called for here. The scholar Grahame Hayes (pers. comm., 14 October 2014) has warned of the danger of turning Sobukwe into nothing more than a project against the ANC. And it is true: Sobukwe is a good deal more than an anti-Mandela figure or the embodiment of anti-ANC sentiment. He was, of course, we should always remember, a member of the ANC's Youth League, a group which was itself arguably essential to Sobukwe's (and the PAC's) development. We should, nevertheless, note that both the societal and political crises of the present and the associated decline of the ANC's political hegemony have provided important historical conditions of possibility for Sobukwe's re-emergence.

One of the reasons that the image of Sobukwe gains as much traction as it does among leftist critics of the ANC has undoubtedly much to do with the moral integrity that Sobukwe is seen as embodying. It is perhaps not going too far to say that in the scandal-fatigued realm of the South African public sphere, such an image of an uncompromised and ethically unbending figure strikes us as something from an altogether different world, where political leaders might still be incorruptible. Part of what has occasioned the return to Sobukwe today is undoubtedly just such a crisis of leadership. Kwandiwe Kondlo (2019, 125) makes this argument emphatically: 'The character of leadership exemplified by Robert Sobukwe is what South Africa doesn't have today.' Sobukwe, says Kondlo, lived a reflective life of principle and sacrifice. In his short tenure as president of the PAC and, indeed, in the moral courage and guidance he demonstrated in the years that followed, Sobukwe exemplified a '"political spirituality" of leadership ... "another kind of leadership" and "another kind of politics" – a shift from "a politics of precarity", of a precarious existence, to a politics of devotion, a desire-less politics of sacrifice' (124). Kondlo (135–136) elaborates his position by means of a crucial distinction:

> In our situation and context in South Africa ... the 'precarity of our politics' is more about the rent-seeking behaviour of political elites

36. Poster for Sobukwe's 90th birthday commemoration project, 5 December 2014, Graaff-Reinet. (Photo by Derek Hook)

> leading government and business entities, and that is threatening the overall legitimacy of the democratic state. Patronage networks are so pervasive in our political space. The political party, rather than being a tool of the people ... is instead a conduit between the government and private capital ... Getting us out of the 'politics of precarity' requires ... a political leadership that has moral authority. It is in this context that the leadership of Robert Sobukwe becomes critical.

Kondlo notes how Sobukwe's leadership connected 'the purpose, politics, unyielding perseverance and acceptance of pain as part of a "self-surrendering self"' (135–136) and points to the inscription on Sobukwe's tombstone: 'True leadership demands complete subjugation of self, absolute honesty, integrity and uprightness of character and fearlessness, and above all, a consuming love of one's people.' Were it not to sound too cynical and pessimistic by far, we might note: more often than not, it is exactly the opposite of these characteristics that we see on display in many of the country's most prominent political leaders and personalities.

As is by now apparent, appeals to Sobukwe's legacy make it possible to bring into perspective – to pinpoint – many of the failings and social contradictions apparent in today's South Africa. A biting commentary is offered by PAC spokesperson Dumisani Methula (2014), who calls on Sobukwe as a means of condemning

> the elitist transition founded on racial capitalism and the philosophical ideology of political neo-liberalism that took place in 1994, that secured the interests of white oligarchs and the emerging black bourgeoisie at the expense of the majority of African[s] ... [Sobukwe's] struggle was not about cosmetic political reforms or about cheap reconciliation not founded on justice and an egalitarian society ... his struggle was about structural change and the total overthrow of the entire colonial apartheid system which was rooted in institutional violence, racist policies, the economic marginalisation of blacks.

Sobukwe, Methula continues, 'would have spoken against the property clause in the constitution, that legalized land theft and justified land robbery and resulted in South Africa being notoriously the most unequal country in world'.

The land issue is a factor of considerable importance in the repression of Sobukwe's legacy. As Ndletyana (2013) stresses: 'Because Sobukwe reminds us of land dispossession, his memory is uncomfortable for a society that seems intent to forget the past. This fake amnesia endangers our future. Sobukwe is a necessary reminder of the need for social justice.' Sobukwe's presence certainly can be felt in those arguments which link the land issue to diluted forms of anti-racism that fail to address the severity of structural disparities between white and black in South Africa. The fundamental link between these issues is often understated or sidelined. The prospect of an authentic non-racialism for Sobukwe, the future hope of moving beyond racial categories, remains contingent on concrete material considerations of social justice, encapsulated most forcefully in the land issue. Sobukwe's Africanist vision of non-racialism thus insists on material and structural transformations as a necessary historical condition of possibility. One appreciates why, in his analysis of the persistence of racism in post-apartheid South Africa, Andile Mngxitama (2016) foregrounds what he – clearly borrowing from Sobukwe – takes to be two of the crucial underpinnings of continued white supremacy: a commitment to the Freedom Charter's notion of 'nonracialism' and the associated insistence that 'the land belongs to all that live in it'.[5]

> Racism is institutionalised in South Africa – it has become a way of life ... The key philosophical foundation that prevents blacks from recognizing racism is the notion of 'nonracialism', which is contained in the Freedom Charter and has found its way into the Constitution. The Charter declares a common humanity without demanding accountability for colonialism. This nonracialism without justice traps whites and blacks inside a lie mistaken for a common brotherhood and limits our understanding of ... the institutionalised racism whose foundation is colonialism and which dates back to 1652 with the arrival of Europeans, who dispossessed Africans of their land ... To end racism, we have to go back to the beginning. This is the conversation the ruling party is not willing to have. White supremacy in South Africa was created from land theft. A return of the land as part acknowledgement and part reparation would break the back of white racism at the economic level, and at the symbolic level.

While we have no way of knowing exactly where Sobukwe would stand in respect of particular policies and procedures of land redistribution in present-day South Africa, there can be no doubt that the question of reclaiming the land was crucial for him. In respect of claims and demands such as those cited above, it would seem a case of the times having finally caught up with Sobukwe, with the oppressed calling on Sobukwe from and for a future he imagined more than a generation ago.

5 To avoid confusion: the radical historical form of non-racialism espoused by Sobukwe and the PAC is to be distinguished from the ostensibly inauthentic 'nonracialism' of the Freedom Charter in that the latter more closely resembles an instance of multiracialism that retains existing racial categories.

This discussion of the Freedom Charter provides us with an opportunity to return to Sobukwe's thinking on race. While we have already noted Sobukwe's rejection of multiracialism, it is worth briefly returning to this issue so as to emphasise how his position remains radical and contrary to much progressive and ostensibly commonsense thinking about race still today. One problem with equating the notion of non-racialism with anti-racism more generally, or with seeing it as tantamount to a critique of white supremacy, is that something crucial gets overlooked. Sobukwe's target, in his rejection of multiracialism, is not only racism, but the whole notion of race; indeed, it is racial thinking as such. As Emma Daitz (2022, 112) has recently pointed out, only rarely have anti-racist 'intellectuals or activists framed race *both* as the outcome of political arrangements amenable to change *and* imagined a common future in which we would be permanently liberated from its violence'. Race, she continues, is, for many – those on the left included – an immovable fact of social life in the twenty-first century. As she observes: 'At the heart of the imaginary the [Freedom] Charter ... is not the radical dissolution of race but a situation in which races can coexist peacefully under just conditions. As the concept of races exists only to justify racism, it is difficult to imagine a just future premised on multi-racialism as the Charter, and indeed the imaginary of our present [South African] constitution, does.'

With this historical backdrop in place, Daitz turns directly to Sobukwe so as to differentiate his position from that of others in the liberation struggle:

> Sobukwe ... understood race to be made primarily through conquest and sustained through a combination of political arrangements and personal aspirations (that is ... [as] the outcome both of structure *and* agency) rather than as something that is found in nature and that he imagined a future in which people could belong not to races but as Africans. Much of how the opposition to apartheid imagined the future was characterized by some form of racialism. Sobukwe, however, was, to his core, a non-racialist. Treating race as made not found, meant that ... Sobukwe could, and did, propose a future without races. (Daitz 2022, 115)

This returns us to the topic of white anxiety. One could say that whites were right to be perturbed by Sobukwe, that Sobukwe's preference *would* have been for there to be no more whites in South Africa. The obvious qualification here is that Sobukwe preferred that there would be no races at all in a future non-racial democracy, believing, as he did, that a move beyond multiracial thinking – which, of course, invariably reinscribes racial categorisation and thereby racism – would be possible (see also Dladla 2017 and Soske 2015).

A coalescence of struggles

Repression does not always necessitate complete forgetting. It works also by separating and dispersing ideas, disconnecting them, so that such a fragmentary array of thoughts cannot meaningfully coalesce into a single discourse. This is part of what is done in referring to Sobukwe today: this disconnection is reversed, in such a way that a range of ostensibly circumstantial social, economic and structural problems come to be viewed as symptoms of a far broader failure. While we have no actual recording of Sobukwe's voice, appeals to his name are enabling of a voice. That is to say, referring back to Sobukwe provides a kind of narrative coherence, a means of drawing together and speaking out against a multiplicity of structural factors of oppression that remain historically unchanged. Consider the following pronouncement by Malaika wa Azania (2014):

> There is a rapture happening in our country. There is an awakening of black people. There is a sense of consciousness that is slowly but surely creeping into our communities ... The increasing number of service delivery protests ... are a result of disenfranchised masses fighting for the right to humanness. These are people who are refusing to continue living in squalor, to being accessories to corruption, maladministration and mediocre leadership, obese with immorality and a lack of integrity ... These are Sobukwe's disciples, blacks who refuse systematic dehumanisation.

What becomes clear in this rendering of Sobukwe's vision of liberation is that the series of seemingly disconnected failures in social administration, leadership, governmental resources and so on are not just arbitrarily arising issues of incompetence or mismanagement, but are all connected components of a greater legacy of oppression that continues into the present. This, then, is part of what it means to advance Sobukwe's name today: it makes it possible that a number of seemingly isolated political grievances and desires might start to cohere into an overarching political rationality. With this in mind, let us turn to the words of Aubrey Mokoape (2014), Sobukwe's former comrade and veteran of the struggle:

> The big question today ... is what would Sobukwe say today when ... our people have to rely on grants ...? Sobukwe would be seriously disappointed ... I think he also would remind us that the signs were ... already there earlier on ... when the PAC broke away ... when the [PAC] was expelled [from the ANC] ... [for insisting] that this is a National struggle ... Those that were expelled would say no ... the Freedom Charter reduced our struggle to a Civil Rights struggle ... The case of the so-called miracle constitution ... my foot! A constitution with no mention of land ... African people have been fighting for land for 400 years ... this constitution reduced land to a side issue ... how do you have food without land ... how do you have ... [real rights] without land? We have freedom for ... starvation ... Land is the major means of production.

In these words, Sobukwe is more than a historical figure; he is our contemporary. The political and ideological battles he waged are, in this context, more urgent than ever. To the long-standing historical issue of *Izwe Lethu* (Our Land), a new, distinctively post-apartheid political crisis has come to the forefront, one in which a democratically elected government seems to have turned on parts of its own population, as was the case in the Marikana Massacre:

> It is even worse than it was [in apartheid] ... [We have] the war of the state versus the people. When a state loses legitimacy and it is unable to deliver to its people, when a people petition and ask for what belongs to them, the state becomes more aggressive ... Marikana ... it must happen again. Another Marikana must come, because the state and the people are no longer on one side ... any time ... any time, I say let the fire come down. (Mokoape 2014)

We have noted how Sobukwe's name and legacy have been repressed. Yet in many of the commentaries cited above – certainly Mokoape's – we see the reversal of this process – repression coming undone. Sobukwe's name returns here with an energy proportionate to how it has been historically denied. Sobukwe here is a threatening personification of freedom, both for those who have benefited from the apartheid and post-apartheid era and for the ruling party and the state, who, in Mokoape's view, are waging a war against the people. Mokoape pulls together a wide cross-section of themes, both historical and contemporary – government grants, food scarcity, the 'miracle' constitution, the reduction of the fight against white supremacy into a civil rights struggle – into a single and fiery claim for the rights and humanity of those whom South Africa's post-apartheid consensus and national democratic transition have overlooked. The memory of Sobukwe thus lends both an identity and an impetus to a variety of political struggles that have, until recently, lacked a voice, an ideological programme, a moral political compass, a figural embodiment.

Sobukwe as signifier of decolonisation

At first glance, to draw a line from Sobukwe to the EFF as putative political heir seems an easy one. There are both historical and ideological or principled parallels. Both organisations were, after all, born of Youth League breakaways from the ANC. These breakaways were, moreover, inspired by many of the same reasons. Just as the PAC decried the ANC's adoption of the Freedom Charter in 1955, so – the parallel can be drawn – the EFF expressed its disdain for many aspects of the Constitution of the 'new' South Africa ratified in 1996. In both cases the ANC was charged with conceding far too much to the beneficiaries of white supremacy, including, as we have seen, the crucial issue of the land.[6] Moreover, the EFF's professed Pan-Africanism, like its prioritisation of land expropriation and its repeated references to the needs of the rural and dispossessed poor, calls to mind Sobukwe's legacy. So does the populism that both parties aspired to.

Things are, however, more complex than such easy parallels or appropriations permit. In fact, the relationship between Sobukwe and the EFF

6 It should be noted that there are aspects of the Freedom Charter from which the EFF takes inspiration, although clearly not the famous proclamation that 'the land belongs to all who live in it'.

is complex and deserves more sustained reflection than is possible here. Nevertheless, a few provisional comments are in order. Firstly, for all the parallels listed above (and several more we have not mentioned), it is curious that Sobukwe has, only fairly rarely, been cited in any explicit way by the EFF's leadership, at least publicly.[7] Truth be told, one is more likely to hear an inspirational appeal to Frantz Fanon than to Robert Mangaliso Sobukwe. There is perhaps an obvious reason for this – Sobukwe's name is intimately associated with the PAC, and invoking him thus runs the risk of losing votes to a rival political party. There is also a clear clash of values in the comparison between the autocratic leadership style of Julius Malema and Sobukwe's own repeated insistence on the transitory and strictly secondary role of political leaders relative to that of the people themselves. Indeed, it seems impossible to reconcile Sobukwe's forswearing of personal gains and his pronounced distaste for wealth, with the alleged corruption and the conspicuous displays of consumption that Julius Malema and associated EFF leaders have been so infamously associated with.

This comparison can be underscored by referring to Achille Mbembe's characterisation of Malema as embodying a South African form of lumpen radicalism, which Mbembe (2011, vi) defines as 'a political tradition of unruliness ... in which fantasies of male power, control and desire have always been deeply entangled with "war envy" and an ... insatiable appetite for money, luxuries and women'. While this may not, of course, be a fair reflection of the broader political culture of the EFF – one might be accused of conflating criticism of Malema with criticism of the EFF as a whole – it nevertheless suggests a stark contrast with Sobukwe's PAC, with its strict disciplinary codes, its emphasis on the necessary sacrifice of leaders, and its commitment in its disciplinary code that 'Members deport themselves with honour, dignity ... proper decorum ... and show a true respect for African womanhood' (Karis and Gerhart 2013, 495).

It is surely significant also that some of the most vocal advocates of a return to Sobukwe's political ideals – take the cases of writer and political

7 Floyd Shivambu, for example, cites Malema as saying: 'The EFF is a movement in a class struggle and appreciates its congress, black consciousness, pan-Africanist and ... socialist character ... in the struggle for economic freedom in a neo-colonial South Africa ... We are uniting Chris Hani, Robert Sobukwe, Steve Biko, and Che Guevara in the struggle for economic freedom' (Shivambu 2014).

commentator Malaika wa Azania and former EFF MP Andile Mngxitama – have become disillusioned with (or, in Mngxitama's case, expelled from) the EFF. This seems an indication that a different order of decolonising aspirations is perhaps to be found elsewhere, outside party politics generally and outside the political culture of the EFF more particularly.

Speaking about the student protests (particularly Rhodes Must Fall and Fees Must Fall) that swept across South Africa in 2015, Achille Mbembe (2016) notes the following:

> we have a generation of young people who are no longer willing to accept the national narrative as it has been constructed since 1994, meaning around key values of racial reconciliation, market economy, non-racialism and so forth. It's a generation of people who are more and more convinced that they have been sold a lie ... And they are determined to put on the table some of the questions we have put under the carpet for a long time – questions of property and ownership, questions of democratisation of access, questions of whiteness, and fairness. All those difficult issues we have not tackled enough, they are willing to bring them to the open, sharpen the antagonisms and get them resolved. And that shift, that cultural shift it seems to me is much more important than anything else, and it signals a new form of politics.

Ayabonga Cawe (2016) draws directly on PAC ideas – and thus, by extension, on Sobukwe – in his own analysis of the series of student protests sweeping across South Africa in 2015 under the banner of Rhodes Must Fall:

> the articulation of 'transformation' as a solution has found its most fervent critics among the youth, who are calling rather for 'decolonisation'. The project of decolonisation pursued by the youth is a project rooted in a particular understanding of racism and the colonial enterprise. It is an acknowledgement that the individual acts of racism occur in a world that affirms white supremacy ... as a norm ... Remedial action involves not only deterring people from being racist, but actually subverting the power relations that allow for such a situation in the first place. Such subversion requires, at a minimum, the resolution of the historic antagonism between blacks and whites in

> South Africa; *the land*. It is also an understanding that the resolution of the skewed property relations in South Africa including but not limited to land, without a political, cultural and pedagogic project centered on pan Africanism and black consciousness will not suffice.

Mbembe's mention of a 'new form of politics' is worth stressing here. This consideration, along with several other factors – the rejection of a constructed national narrative and 'questions of democratisation of access' – clearly overlaps with Cawe's analysis, particularly the latter's emphatic distinction between the agendas of decolonisation and transformation. Sobukwe operates here as a symbol for a counter-institutional decolonising impulse. This is not, of course, to confine the multiple aims and objectives of the various student protests to the signifier Sobukwe alone (although it is surely telling that one ambition voiced within Rhodes Must Fall was that of changing the name of Rhodes University to Robert Mangaliso Sobukwe University [Ndebele 2015]). It is, however, to assert that Sobukwe becomes one prospective name for a more encompassing project of decolonisation which extends beyond the given political and institutional structures of the post-apartheid condition. This fits with historical characterisations that underline a utopian dimension to Sobukwe's thought, and that identify him not as a pragmatic political organiser or figurehead but as a visionary, intellectual and moral leader, a practitioner of politics not – as Terblanche Delport (2016) puts it – as the art of the possible, but precisely as the art of the impossible. This, then, is a crucial part of what Sobukwe stands for today: decolonisation. And decolonisation understood not in a restricted or domesticated form (as the outcome of negotiated settlements, in the form of institutional concessions, and so on) but decolonisation as a mode of subjectivity and culture, decolonisation as a pervasive condition of political desire.

Sobukwe as personification of freedom

The name Sobukwe, we have suggested, stands today as a shorthand term for a series of repressed critiques of the post-apartheid order. More than just this, Sobukwe increasingly functions also as an ideal symbol for an alternative political future. It is in this sense that we can say that Sobukwe haunts our current historical situation; his unremitting critiques remain an uncomfortable reminder of those dimensions of political freedom that remain as yet unattained.

Before we draw to a close, we should note a prospective failing of our approach here. We have referred to Sobukwe both in a biographical, factual manner and also, even predominantly, as a symbol, as an image, a point of appeal and identification which gives voice to a cross-section of different struggles and political aspirations. In so doing, have we not risked losing sight of the 'real' Sobukwe? This is a particularly pressing question for us, tempted as we are to say that we now know better than most, that we have seen the 'real' Sobukwe, having visited him so intimately through his correspondence, his most private thoughts and confessions, interests and frustrations. We ask ourselves whether our discussion contributes both to the reinvigoration of Sobukwe as symbol and to the relative neglect of Sobukwe as an actual historical and biographical figure. Might it be the case, ironically, that Sobukwe, as person, ceases to feature within 'the personification of freedom' that he has here been taken to embody? Or, to take up the problem from a different standpoint: how might we present an impression of the man that has less to do with how his image has been used politically, and more to do with the sense that one has been graced with the presence of a 'good' man, an ethical man? This is a tension not easily resolved, for surely these are inseparable facets of what Sobukwe stands for.

The contrasting scarcity of literature on (and by) Sobukwe leaves the door open to his legacy being instrumentalised in a variety of strategic ways that might contrast with – or even starkly contradict – many of his own stated political agendas or social and cultural values. These are legitimate concerns. Pumla Dineo Gqola (2014) draws attention to Sobukwe's valuing of the imagination, to Sobukwe as a man 'who took great pleasure in the nonobvious, who relished works of the imagination … who understood the value of the imagination when unbounded'. These words apply not only to Sobukwe himself, but to how we should go about the explorative task of grappling with his life and its reinvigorated political significance for us today. To this sentiment, we can add another, returning once more to paraphrase Stuart Hall (1996, 14): 'Rather than trying to recapture the "true" [Sobukwe], we must try to engage the after-life of [Robert Mangaliso Sobukwe] … in ways that do not simply restore the past in a cycle of the eternal return, but which will bring the enigma of [Sobukwe] … flashing up before us in a moment of danger'.

References

Bunsee, Bennie. 2013. 'True Ideologies of Pan-Africanism Will Triumph'. *Sunday Independent*, 23 June. http://www.iol.co.za/sundayindependent/true-ideologies-of-pan-africanism-will-triumph-1536146.

Cawe, Ayabonga. 2016. 'Our Poisoned Inheritance.' *Daily Maverick*, 1 February. http://www.dailymaverick.co.za/opinionista/2016-02-01-our-poisoned-inheritance/?ref=yfp#.VsBv2Hn2bIU.

Daitz, Emma. 2022. 'Towards a Future Without White People: Robert Sobukwe and the Category of the African'. *South African Review of Sociology* 55: 112–130.

Delport, Terblanche. 2016. 'Asazi Ukuthi Iyozala Nkomoni: Robert Mangaliso Sobukwe's Historical Imagination of the Future', *Psychology in Society* 50: 35–52.

Dladla, Ndumiso. 2017. 'Contested Memory: Retrieving the Africanist (Liberatory) Conception of Non-racialism'. *Theoria: A Journal of Social and Political Theory* 64, no. 153: 101–127. https://www.jstor.org/stable/44862883.

Gerhart, Gail. 1978. *Black Power in South Africa: The Evolution of an Ideology*. Berkeley, CA: University of California Press.

Giliomee, Hermann. 2003. *The Afrikaners: Biography of a People*. Charlottesville, VA: University of Virginia Press.

Gqola, Pumla Dineo. 2014. 'Africa Is Still Waiting the Dawn'. *Mail & Guardian*, 30 May. http://mg.co.za/article/2014-05-29-africa-is-still-waiting-for-the-dawn/.

Hall, Stuart. 1996. 'The After-Life of Frantz Fanon: Why Fanon? Why Now? Why *Black Skin White Masks?*' In *The Fact of Blackness: Frantz Fanon and Visual Interpretation*, edited by Alan Read, 12–37. Seattle, WA: Bay Press.

Hook, Derek, ed. 2019. *Lie on Your Wounds: The Prison Correspondence of Robert Mangaliso Sobukwe*. Johannesburg: Wits University Press.

Karis, Thomas G. and Gail M. Gerhart, eds. 2013. *From Protest to Challenge: A Documentary History of African Politics in South Africa, 1882–1990*, vol. 3: *Challenge and Violence, 1953–1964*. Auckland Park: Jacana.

Kondlo, Kwandiwe. 2009. *In the Twilight of the Revolution: The Pan-Africanist Congress of Azania (South Africa) 1959–1994*. Windhoek: African Books Collective; Basel: Basler Afrika Bibliographien.

Kondlo, Kwandiwe. 2019. 'The "Political Spirituality" of Sobukwe's Leadership'. In *Robert Mangaliso Sobukwe: New Reflections*, edited by Benjamin Pogrund, 124–138. Johannesburg: Jonathan Ball.

Lebelo, Steve. 2014. 'Robert Sobukwe, African Nationalism and the Radicalisation of Resistance in the Era of Mass Mobilisation, 1952–1961'. Paper presented at Sobukwe Today Colloquium, University of Pretoria, 5 March.

Lodge, Tom. 1983. *Black Politics in South Africa*. London: Longman.

Lodge, Tom. 1991. 'A Liberal of a Different Colour'. *Transformation* 16: 76–87.

Lodge, Tom. 2011. *Sharpeville*. Oxford: Oxford University Press.

Malaika wa Azania. 2014. 'Why Robert Sobukwe Is Not Dead'. *Sunday Independent*, 23 February. http://www.iol.co.za/sundayindependent/why-robert-sobukwe-is-not-dead-1.1651306.

Mandela, Nelson. 1994. *Long Walk to Freedom: The Autobiography of Nelson Mandela*. Johannesburg: Macdonald Purnell.

Mandela, Nelson. 2011. *Conversations with Myself*. London: Macmillan.

Mangcu, Xolela. 2012. *Biko: A Biography*. Cape Town: Tafelberg.

Mbembe, Achille. 2011. 'Foreword'. In Fiona Forde, *An Inconvenient Youth: Julius Malema and the 'New' ANC*, vi–x. Johannesburg: Picador Africa.

Mbembe, Achille. 2016. 'You Can De-whiten a Language: Interview with Hans Pienaar'. *LitNet*, 27 January. http://www.litnet.co.za/interview-with-achille-mbembe/.

Methula, Dumisani. 2014. 'The Historical Legacy of Robert Mangaliso Sobukwe'. Paper presented at Sobukwe Today Colloquium, University of Pretoria, 5 March.

Mngxitama, Andile. 2016. 'Penny Sparrow: Racism's Sacrificial Lamb'. *Mail & Guardian*, 7 January. http://mg.co.za/article/2016-01-07-penny-sparrow-racisms-sacrificial-lamb.

Mokoape, Aubrey. 2014. Speech given at 90th birthday anniversary celebration of Robert Sobukwe, Graaff-Reinet, 5 December.

Ndebele, Linda K. 2015. 'Open Letter to Rhodes University Council: Rename University to R.M. Sobukwe University'. *Mayihlome News*, 3 April. http://mayihlomenews.co.za/open-letter-to-rhodes-university-council-rename-university-to-rm-sobukwe-university/.

Ndletyana, Mcebisi. 2013. 'Lest We Forget Our Struggle Heroes'. *Sunday Independent*, 24 March. http://www.iol.co.za/sundayindependent/lest-we-forget-our-struggle-heroes-1.1490711#.U618h31wbmI.

Ntloedibe, Elias L. 1995. *Here Is a Tree: Political Biography of Robert Mangaliso Sobukwe*. Mogoditshane: Century-Turn Publishers.

Pheko, Motsoko. 1994. *The Land Is Ours: The Political Legacy of Mangaliso Sobukwe*. New York: Tokoloho.

Pheko, Motsoko. 2014. 'A Leader Who Walked the Political Talk to the Finish'. Sobukwe Memorial Lecture, Methodist Black Consultation, Springs, 12 July.

Plaatjie, Thami ka. 2019. *Sobukwe: The Making of a Pan Africanist Leader*, vol. 1. Johannesburg: KMM Review Publishing.

Pogrund, Benjamin. 2015. *Robert Sobukwe: How Can Man Die Better*. Johannesburg: Jonathan Ball.

Seepe, Sipho. 2008. 'Sobukwe: Legacy Revisited'. *Sunday Independent*, 27 February. http://www.iol.co.za/news/politics/sobukwe-legacy-revisited-1.391095#.U615631wbmI.

Shivambu, Floyd. 2014. 'The EFF's First NPA an Inspiration of Hope: Siyaqhuba!' *Sunday Independent*, 21 December. http://floydn.blogspot.com/2015/01/eff-1st-npa-is-great-inspiration.html.

Soske, Jon. 2015. 'The Impossible Concept: Settler Liberalism, Pan-Africanism, and the Language of Non-Racialism'. *African Historical Review* 47, no. 2: 1–36. doi: 10.1080/17532523.2015.1130188.

Tabane, Rapule. 2012. 'Spare a Thought, and a Place Name, for Mangaliso Sobukwe'. *Mail & Guardian*, 9 March. http://mg.co.za/article/2012-03-09-spare-a-thought-and-place-name-for-mangaliso-sobukwe.

Teeger, Chana. 2015. '"Both Sides of the Story": History Education in Post-apartheid South Africa'. *American Sociological Review* 80, no. 6: 1175–1200.

Thompson, Leonard. 2014. *A History of South Africa*. New Haven, CT: Yale University Press.

Welsh, David. 2010. *The Rise and Fall of Apartheid: From Racial Domination to Majority Rule*. Cape Town: Jonathan Ball.

Worby, Eric and Shireen Ally. 2013. 'The Disappointment of Nostalgia: Conceptualising Cultures of Memory in Contemporary South Africa'. *Social Dynamics* 39, no. 3: 457–480.

Index

www.ingramcontent.com/pod-product-compliance
Lightning Source LLC
Chambersburg PA
CBHW021233190726
48289CB00005B/1309
* 9 7 8 1 7 7 6 1 4 8 5 6 1 *